WHITE COUNSELLORS – BLACK CLIENTS

To Pat, James and Ayesha

White Counsellors – Black Clients
Theory, research and practice

NICK BANKS
University of Birmingham

Ashgate

Aldershot • Brookfield USA • Singapore • Sydney

Published by
Ashgate Publishing Ltd
Gower House
Croft Road
Aldershot
Hants GU11 3HR
England

Ashgate Publishing Company
Old Post Road
Brookfield
Vermont 05036
USA

British Library Cataloguing in Publication Data
Banks, Nick
    White counsellors - black clients : theory, research and
    practice. - (Interdisciplinary research series in ethnic,
    gender and class relations)
    1. Cross-cultural counselling 2. Minorities - Counselling of
    I. Title
    361'.06'089

Library of Congress Catalog Card Number: 98-74440

ISBN 1 84014 146 8

Printed in Great Britain

Contents

List of Figures and Tables   vi
Preface   x
Series Editor's Preface   xii

1   An Introduction and Overview   1

2   Culture, 'Race' and Ethnicity: Their Significance to Counselling   20

3   The Cross-cultural Counselling Relationship   54

4   The Concept of Attitude and its Link to Transference   73

5   Counselling Theory and Practice   90

6   Research Methodology   127

7   The Questionnaire and Video Vignette Results   151

8   The Research Findings Related to the Research Objectives   214

9   Conclusions, Reflections and Recommendations   238

References   258
Author Index   287
Subject Index   294

List of Figures and Tables

Table 1   Ethnic group composition of England and Wales   21
Table 2   The distinction between emic and etic approaches   29
Figure 1 Bolton's (1979) continuum   64
Figure 2 Hypothesized extension of Bolton's (1979) continuum   64
Table 3   Comparative world view schematic   94
Table 4   A comparison of the facilitative conditions of counselling
          by theory   119
Table 5   Ethnic and gender backgrounds of pilot questionnaire
          survey subjects   133
Table 6   Age range of pilot questionnaire survey subjects   134
Table 7   Qualifications or training of the pilot questionnaire
          survey sample   134
Table 8   Length of counselling experience of the pilot questionnaire
          survey sample   134
Table 9   Number of those having experience of counselling Black
          client groups   135
Table 10 Counsellors' theoretical orientations   135
Table 11 Initial reliability analysis coefficient alpha scores for the
          three scales before item analysis deletion   138
Table 12 Correlation coefficients of the three scales   139
Table 13 Correlation coefficients of the two combined scales and
          the initial prejudice scale   139
Table 14 Ethnic group, gender and number of counsellors
          participating in video response   142
Table 15 Preferred counselling models   149
Table 16 Counsellor gender   153
Table 17 Counsellor ethnic background   153
Table 18 Counsellor age range   154
Table 19 Counsellor years of experience   154
Table 20 Experience of counselling Black clients   154
Table 21 The counselling model orientation of the white counsellors 155
Table 22 Highest level of counsellor academic qualifications   156
Table 23 Highest level of counselling qualification   156

Table 24 British Association for Counselling accreditation   156
Table 25 Counsellors pursuing British Association for Counselling
        accreditation   157
Table 26 Counselling service delivery focus   157
Table 27 Employment setting of counsellors   158
Table 28 Employment locality   158
Table 29 Residential locality   159
Table 30 Average number of clients seen in a week   159
Table 31 Use of family network in counselling   159
Table 32 Perceived value of family network use   160
Table 33 Openness to use of interpreter   160
Table 34 Actual use of interpreter   160
Table 35 Specific information for multi-cultural service delivery   161
Table 36 View of the need for different counselling approaches
        from white clients   161
Table 37 The existence of multi-cultural friendship networks with
        white counsellors   161
Table 38 Summary of results of stepwise multiple regression analysis   165
Table 39 Frequencies of counsellors who have read specific material
        on counselling ethnic minority groups   166
Table 40 Frequencies of counsellors with specific training for
        counselling ethnic minority groups   166
Table 41 Recorded frequencies of academic education variable   167
Table 42 Experience of counselling African-Caribbean clients   167
Table 43 Association between specific training in South Asian
        client need and length of counsellor experience   173
Table 44 Association between reading material on South Asian
        client counselling need and counsellor length of experience   174
Table 45 Association between reading specific material on the needs
        of African-Caribbean clients and length of counsellor
        experience   174
Table 46 Association with having specific training on the needs
        of African-Caribbean clients and length of experience   175
Table 47 Relative experience of participating in different types of
        training   176
Table 48 Association of participation in racism awareness training
        and belief in a different model for South Asian clients   177

Table 49 Association between participation in racism awareness training and belief in a different model for African-Caribbean clients 177

Table 50 Association between belief in a different model for African-Caribbeans and participating in cross-cultural counselling training 178

Table 51 Association between belief in a different model for South Asian clients and cross-cultural counselling training 178

Table 52 Association between combination training in African-Caribbean counselling needs and the belief in benefit of different counselling models 179

Table 53 Association between having had combination training on the counselling needs of South Asian clients and a belief in benefit of different counselling models than those used with white clients 179

Table 54 Association of reading material on the specific counselling needs of South Asian clients and the belief of benefit of a different model than that used with white clients 180

Table 55 Association of reading material on the belief of benefit of a different counselling model for African-Caribbean clients 180

Table 56 Association between counsellor orientation and gender 184

Table 57 Association between counsellor orientation and years of experience 185

Table 58 Association between counsellor orientation and actual use of family network 186

Table 59 Association between counsellor orientation and willingness to use an interpreter with African-Caribbean clients 186

Table 60 Association between counsellor orientation and willingness to use an interpreter with South Asian clients 186

Table 61 Association between counsellor orientation and actual use of an interpreter 188

Table 62 Association between a counsellor's orientation and having specific training for South Asian clients 189

Table 63 Association between a counsellor's orientation and reading specific material on South Asian clients 190

Table 64 Association between a counsellor's orientation and having specific training for African-Caribbean clients 190

Table 65 Association between counsellor orientation and reading specific material for African-Caribbean clients 191

Table 66 Association between the belief in the benefit of a different
counselling model for South Asian clients and counsellor
orientation   192

Table 67 Association between counsellor orientation and belief in the
benefit of a different model for African-Caribbean clients   192

Table 68 Association between length of experience and belief in
benefit of different counselling model for South Asian
clients than that used with white clients   194

Table 69 Association between length of experience and perceived
benefit of a different counselling model for African-Caribbean
clients than that used with white clients   194

Table 70 Association between actual experience of counselling South
Asian clients and a belief in the benefit of a different
counselling model than that used with white clients   194

Table 71 Association of actual experience of counselling African-
Caribbean clients with the belief in benefit of a different
model   197

Table 72 Association between length of experience and willingness
to use an interpreter with South Asian clients   198

Table 73 Association between length of experience and willingness
to use an interpreter with African-Caribbean clients   198

Table 74 Association between length of experience and actual use
of interpreter in counselling Black clients   200

Table 75 Association between length of experience and satisfaction
of use of an interpreter with Black clients   200

Table 76 Actual use of clients' family network (from Table 31)   201

Table 77 Association between training and use of family network   202

Table 78 Association between reading material on South Asian
clients and use of family network   202

Table 79 Association between training in the needs of African-
Caribbean clients and use of family network   202

Table 80 Association between reading material on African-Caribbean
clients and the use of family network   203

Table 81 Association between length of experience and use of client's
family network   205

Preface

Two aims were central to the present research: 1) to discuss and examine the existing attitudes and self-reported specific practice orientations of white psychotherapists/counsellors in their work with Black Clients; and 2) to identify what influenced the ability of psychotherapists/counsellors to work appropriately with the culturally different. Three main methods of data collection were used A postal questionnaire provided a national sample of members from the British Association for Counselling and obtained a usable sample of 360 respondents. The postal questionnaire comprised two parts. Firstly, that of a demographic data-gathering section and a five point Likert-type instrument, which formed the basis of a Cultural Awareness Inventory, to assess counsellors' attitudes towards Black clients. Secondly, a video vignette rating questionnaire was used. This was also a five point Likert-type instrument. With this latter inventory, 107 counsellors in training were asked to rate their feelings and reactions to either an African-Caribbean, White English, or South Asian female 'client', each of which was matched on a number of variables. All 'clients' had the same script: claiming to be distressed due to unplanned pregnancy. The third research instrument was a semi-structured interview schedule with which 20 counsellors were interviewed regarding their beliefs and practice orientations with Black client groups. This research did not directly observe practice but contains specific measures of counsellors' self-reported practice orientations and attitudes to practice mainly dealing with uses of interpreters and family.

The results suggest that with some self-reported practice orientations, and with some attitudes, counsellors do show measured levels of Eurocentrism and negative counter-transference. Significant gender differences were found ($p<.001$) in the emotional response of men compared to women towards the video vignette 'clients' but no gender differences were found in the Cultural Awareness Inventory. The results suggest that reading and training are effective change agents in preparing counsellors for cross-cultural work. Furthermore, the counsellors' ages and academic qualifications are statistically significant predictor variables of cultural awareness. The results also suggest that direct experience of working with African-Caribbean clients, but not South Asian clients, was a significant predictor variable of the score on the Cultural Awareness Inventory. Possible reasons are tentatively discussed in the context of Batson et al.'s personal distress theory and Festinger's cognitive dissonance theory. Recommendations are made for the training and supervision of counsellors which may suggest necessary curriculum changes to counsellor training courses.

Series Editor's Preface

This book addresses the Eurocentric attitudes and negative counter-transference practice orientations among white counsellors who deal with black clients. Using sophisticated quantitative research methods in triangulation with detailed qualitative analysis, the author identifies a number of factors that could be helpful in the training and practice of counsellors, especially those involved in cross-cultural work.

The book opens with a review of the inadequate theorisation of cross-cultural counselling compared to the theoretical saturation of the practice of white counsellors dealing with white clients. This makes the book a timely addition to the Fanonist and feminist critique of ethnocentric distortions in earlier research and publications on difference. Nick Banks concludes convincingly that: 'The effect of counter-transference in [multicultural counselling relationships] may be particularly destructive if counsellors were unwilling or unable to examine their cultural prejudice and racism.'

The book should be made compulsory reading for all counsellors, their clients and their trainers given that cross-cultural counselling is increasingly becoming the major context for all counselling due to the unstoppable growth of multiculturalism throughout the world. Students, researchers and teachers will also find the detailed quantitative and qualitative analyses useful in their own work even when the subject matter is different.

Biko Agozino
Liverpool

1   An Introduction and Overview

This chapter provides the reader with an overview of the area of cross-cultural counselling. The issues of counselling technique, practice and theory, empathy and rapport, the impact of racism and therapist attitude, transference and counter-transference are introduced, as well as the significance of language and cultural differences between white counsellor and Black client. The intention is to present the broad aims of the research and provide an introduction to the more frequent debates within the subject of cross-cultural counselling. A deeper analysis of the issues will take place in the thesis, as appropriate.

Verma (1985, p. 84) has noted that:

> traditionally, the whole focus in inter-cultural counselling is given to deficiencies of the recipients. It is rarely suggested that the greatest barrier to meaningful interaction in the counselling relationship may be the counsellor's lack of understanding of the socio-psychological and cultural background of the client.

If therapists or counsellors are to help those they encounter it is reasonable to suggest that they should have positive, or at least neutral or objective, attitudes towards those who seek their help.

This thesis will examine the attitudes white therapists have of African-Caribbean and South Asian (Indian, Pakistani, Bangladeshi) clients and how these may influence the therapeutic process . The 'racial' and cultural context in which Black and white people exist and its potential influence on counselling or psychotherapy will be explored in the literature review. The specific aims and objectives of this research will be provided at the end of this chapter.

It is worthwhile at this point to explain how the five ethnic groups which form the basis of this study will be referred to. Skellington et al. (1992, p. 13), after an extensive search, noted that:

> there is no one agreed set of terms in use among researchers in this field for different minority ethnic groups … a classification may be based on skin colour, or country of origin or descent. Terminology is also problematic because, over time, the terminology shifts: some terms fall into disuse and disrepute, while others change. Many terminological uses are controversial, and probably none is without its drawbacks.

1

Throughout this book the term 'Black' is used to refer to all people of African and South Asian descent where there is no need for specific identification. The use of a capital letter 'B' denotes the term as a noun, to identify a politically defined group, rather than the term implying an adjective based on skin colour alone. However, the use of the term 'Black' is not meant to imply an homogeneous group whose experiences are unified, but rather a heterogeneous group whose experiences and life styles are varied, and whose definition as Black in contemporary British society, where 'race' is a central concept, identifies and highlights a shared experience of personal and institutional racism (Cheetham, 1972; Ahmed et al., 1986; Miles, 1989; Mama, 1992). Where there is a need for specific identification the different ethnic groups will be referred to by country/area of descent, or in the case of people of white European descent, by the term 'white'.

Counselling or psychotherapy (the terms are used interchangeably throughout the book and a rationale for this will follow in chapter 5) and its application to individuals and specific groups has been enjoying a growth period for some years. The need to employ counsellors in a variety of settings – educational, health and most recently business – has been acknowledged (Allison et al., 1989). Differing perspectives on counselling in terms of its practice and nature are reflected in the many definitions of counselling and numerous theories, together with the application of theory to different areas of focus, e.g., family therapy, individual client based, HIV, etc. (Donnelly, 1981). In attempting to offer a practical, acceptable and broad perspective of counselling, its nature and practice, the British Association for Counselling (1985) defines counselling as follows:

> People become engaged in counselling when a person, occupying regularly or temporarily the role of counsellor offers or agrees explicitly to offer time, attention and respect for another person or persons temporarily in the role of client. The task of counselling is to give the client an opportunity to explore, discover and clarify ways of living more resourcefully and towards greater well being (BAC information Sheet No. 4).

Verma (1985, pp. 83–4) has defined counselling, perhaps more succinctly, as:

> … an interpersonal relationship in which one person (the 'counsellor') attempts to help another person (the 'client') to understand and deal with his/her problems in aspects of everyday life.

The process of counselling or psychotherapy, whatever definition one prefers, is a complex interaction between two people. This interaction becomes further complicated when the client and therapist are culturally and ethnically different. These differences constitute a major dimension of potential communication difficulty (Serpell, 1976; Littlewood and Lipsedge, 1989; Sue and Sue, 1990; Brislin, 1990; Locke, 1992). The goals of therapy are presumably to support clients, to enable them to review any negative assessments of themselves and facilitate the understanding of their uniqueness, worth, and to help them identify hidden strengths for challenging and coping with both internal and external pressure. Therapists will be unable adequately to help clients if they themselves are unable or unwilling to acknowledge, explore and change any negative stereotypical views of clients from different cultures that they may hold. Further exploration may need to take place about the questionable worth of over-applying Eurocentric counselling approaches with clients from different cultures (Burke, 1986; Littlewood and Lipsedge, 1989; Sue and Sue, 1990).

Although there is an abundance of theory (Fernando, 1989a; Jackson, 1995) to support the work of white counsellors with white clients, the focus of cross-cultural counselling where white counsellors are involved with Black clients is an area that is not well served by theory or substantial validated practice (Banks, 1991; Abramowitz and Murray, 1983; Sue and Sue, 1990). d'Ardenne and Mahtani (1989) have argued that cross-cultural counselling has its origins in practice rather than theory. As there is much less established methodology or well documented research to refer to compared to literature which exists for professional practice with white groups, the question of whether Black clients are receiving a second rate service based upon inappropriate theoretical and practice considerations may be asked. The appropriateness of Eurocentric counselling techniques will be specifically discussed later in this chapter.

Interest in the area of cross-cultural or inter-ethnic counselling in Britain has been relatively limited. The issues were first discussed by Cheetham (1972) focusing on the social work needs of culturally different groups. Later in 1982, British psychiatrists, Littlewood, Lipsedge, and Rack, addressed the impact of race and culture in the area of mental health. As well as limited interest, publications in the field of cross-cultural counselling and psychotherapy in Britain are sparse. The vast majority of literature to date addressing the area of cross-cultural counselling and psychotherapy originates from the United States and Canada where the adequacy of service delivery for culturally different (from the majority white culture) clients was challenged in the 1940s by Williams (Gardner, 1971; Sue, 1981; Jackson, 1995).

In Britain the few publications focusing specifically on cross-cultural counselling appeared in the late 1980s. Nafsiyat, an independent Black organization offering counselling and psychotherapeutic support in the community, published *Assessment and Treatment Across Cultures* in 1987 and then, in 1989, d'Ardenne and Mahtani's *Transcultural Counselling in Action* appeared. Lago and Thompson's chapter in *The Handbook of Counselling in Britain* was also published in 1980. Although a growth in interest can be demonstrated as a function of the (small) number of publications in Britain in the area of cross-cultural counselling and psychotherapy, there has, as yet, been no published material to suggest that this small amount of literature has had any effect on influencing service delivery to Black clients. This suggests that there should be some service delivery concern. However, as there are library shelves full of anthropological, sociological and psychological publications focusing on the culturally different and 'exotic' with little to suggest that these publications have been able positively to influence policy or practice in work with Black people, it should perhaps be of no great surprise that the few books available in the area of cross-cultural counselling have yet to demonstrate an influence on practice.

Parham (1989) has noted that much of the literature devoted to the participation of Black clients in the counselling and psychotherapy process has focused on the inappropriateness of many traditional approaches. It is fair to say that in the main, counselling theorists have been similar to equal opportunity employers in that they have viewed people without regard to gender or cultural background (White, 1972). Theories which have been formed from interaction with white, middle class people from Western Europe and the USA, have been applied to other groups without consideration for cross-cultural appropriateness or validation of technique (Hayes, 1972). It was seen as axiomatic that, in order to be effective, a counsellor and his/her approach should have regard for and understanding of the client's values, family structure, religious beliefs and sociocultural matrix in general (Rack, 1982; Sue and Sue, 1990). To quote a British anthropologist (Ballard, 1979, p. 164):

> For the practitioner, the question of whether the minorities ought or ought not to remain ethnically distinct should be irrelevant: The fact is that they are and insofar as his specialism, whatever it is, demands that he should take into account the social and cultural worlds in which his clients live, he needs to make a response to ethnic diversity. If he does not his practice is inadequate in purely professional terms.

Theories of counselling, psychotherapy and taught courses on counselling skills make attempts to outline approaches designed to make them effective. It has to be questioned whether these theories and skill based approaches developed in North America and Western Europe for white people are valid in their applications with African-Caribbean and South Asian (Indian, Pakistani and Bangladeshi) ethnic client groups, for reasons which will be briefly explored in this introductory chapter and in more detail throughout the book.

Theories of counselling were, and still are, composed of philosophical assumptions regarding the nature of 'man' (not women) and a theory of personality (London, 1964; Patterson, 1980; Corsini, 1984; Jewel, 1994). These characteristics are based on those observed with Western Europeans and as such are both ethnically and culturally bound. When not recognized by the counsellor, this may lead to a misapplication of theory and/or practice, with the result that service delivery becomes Eurocentric and hence inappropriate for the needs of Black client groups.

One extreme example of how the presentation of a particular ethnic group can be subject to ethnocentric distortion is provided by an early publication by Kardiner and Ovesey (1951). This study was based on the psychodiagnostic investigation of 25 Black clients. They described the following characteristics as being fairly prominent in the personality organization of Black people:

1　superficiality;
2　apathy and resignation;
3　repressed hostility;
4　the wish to be white;
5　identification with faeces;
6　intragroup aggression;
7　white ego-ideal;
8　inclined to gamble;
9　magical thinking;
10 inclined to alcoholism;
11 unconsciously resentful and antisocial;
12 weak superego development;
13 disorderly, unsystematic;
14 sexual freedom;
15 reject education;
16 poor discipline in childhood;
17 maternal neglect and rejection;
18 little respect for parents;
19 psychologically crippled;

20 distrustful;
21 live for the moment; and
22 hedonistic.

For Kardiner and Ovesey (1951) these formulations were meant to describe the typical personality of all Black people. It is easy to see from this example how stereotypical racist literature could influence the training and hence practice of therapists. Jackson (1980) has argued that such negative perceptions of Black people are largely due to the conceptual framework internalized by professional counsellors who 'unwittingly subscribe to the deficit hypothesis'. This meant that, rather than searching for environmental causal explanations of observed behaviours, it is believed that Black people have underlying deficiencies which are attributed to genetic and/or social pathology which limits the probability of achieving successful social adjustment. Since the onus of the difficulty is on the client, the counsellor's goal is that of 'encouraging' the client to adjust to an often oppressive status quo.

Frantz Fanon (1967) has argued that counselling theories commonly practised in Britain have their roots in the Western world, where they were devised, developed and formulated on the basis of a western philosophy of life which in many respects contradicts the traditional beliefs and ideology of those who have come from other parts of the world and have different religious and value systems. Fanon asserted that western counselling theory placed an unequivocal emphasis on individualism and self understanding and aimed towards the greater social independence of the individual. In contrast, in most Third World cultures, the individual identity was seldom recognized and there was less stress on the autonomy of the individual, with greater emphasis given to mutual interdependence within and between family groups. Here, again, lies the danger, if this cultural bias goes unrecognized, for Eurocentric practice with Black client groups.

Awatere (1982), speaking on her experience of counselling Maori clients, provided support for Fanon's view with claims that both humanistic and behaviourist counselling approaches placed undue emphasis on the needs of the individual and over-relied on notions of free will and autonomy as necessary preconditions essential for positive outcomes in the counselling process. Farrar and Sircar (1986), writing from a similar perspective, noted that with South Asian clients many of those seen have problems related to family; 'indeed most have problems related to family structure and process, and their relations with outside society' (p. 195). They asserted that with South Asian clients the importance of family dependence cannot be underestimated. They argued:

A Pakistani man sees himself as somebody's son, somebody's brother, but not primarily an individual in his own right. All decisions taken are referred to, and in some senses depend upon, other members of his family (p. 199).

Thus, even if a counsellor is counselling an individual client it would be necessary to recognize that she or he is dealing with part of a family and social system, rather than with just that one individual. Writing on the mental health needs of African-Caribbean clients, Burke (1980, 1986), a Black British psychiatrist, asserted that there was no doubt that family stress was the major aetiological factor in the disorders of African-Caribbean patients. Therefore, for this group, the limitations of individual therapy were apparent as there was a need to look at the person within a family system and then within a larger sociocultural matrix.

Looked at together, both Farrar and Sircar's (1986) and Burke's (1980, 1986) arguments suggested that family or group therapy may be a more appropriate form of intervention than the more common one-to-one counselling interactions with indigenous British clients, and indeed Burke (1986) found that with African-Caribbeans diagnosed as mentally ill, family-patient interaction was one of the most important factors in influencing a positive outcome.

Both Burke (1986), working with African-Caribbeans, and Farrar and Sircar (1986), commenting on South Asian families, stressed the importance of family acceptance in facilitating self disclosure with clients. Burke (1986) noted: 'It was my impression that only when I had established an adequate relationship could I learn of conflicts related to children, spouses or parents' (p. 187). Furthermore, Farrar and Sircar (1986, p. 201)) revealed that:

> The strictness of family roles and the strong hierarchy within the family also have to be recognized. The idea that a wife could openly show her negative feelings towards her husband with a stranger present is almost incomprehensible, and is very damaging. Expressions of difficulty have to be made through normal channels within the family. Allowing difficulties to be seen by other people is damaging to family status and great efforts are made not to let this happen.

It would seem that a counsellor would have to be accepted almost as a family member by the African-Caribbean or South Asian family, and the counsellor's ability to retain confidentiality be believed, before she could begin to work effectively with either of these ethnic groups.

Theories of counselling are also composed of a body of therapeutic techniques and strategies which are applied to clients with the hope of effecting change in either behaviour or attitudes. A counselling theory dictates what techniques should be used, when, why, and how. Sue (1981, p. 53) pointed out that:

> It does not take much training to see that client-centred counsellors behave differently from rational emotive ones. The fact that one school of counselling can be distinguished from another has implications; it suggests a certain degree of rigidity in working with culturally different clients who might find such techniques offensive or inappropriate.

There is a danger that counsellors will impose techniques according to the 'need' of theory rather than those based on culturally different client needs and values. The teachings and resultant practices based upon Freudian psycho-analytic therapy have often come under particular attack as to their lack of applicability to Black people. The general criticism was that Freud's original theory, which was based upon middle and upper class white, Jewish Austrian women of the late 1800s, has little to do with the sociocultural experiences of Black people. For example, many counsellors who adhere to this particular model believe the view advanced by Freud that a counsellor should be a 'blank screen' or a reflector of the client's difficulties. However, research has suggested (Scheffler, 1969; Sue, 1990) that such an approach was likely to be interpreted as indifference, remoteness and superiority to the culturally different or Black client. In opposition to the 'blank screen' approach was the finding that a willingness to reveal something personal is a necessary strategy for establishing an effective therapeutic alliance with the Black, culturally different client (Lefkowitz and Baker, 1971), and could build strong bonds of trust and rapport (Stikes, 1972).

It is true to say that, in general, theories of counselling have failed to agree about what can be considered desirable outcomes in counselling or how these outcomes should be evaluated. Within cross-cultural counselling parameters, the need for outcome evaluations that use objective measures is likely to be increased, as a sole focus on subjective accounts may simply confirm the power based dynamics of the relationship between different groups in an unequal society. For example, if a counsellor were to use a behaviourally based model it would be imperative for the counsellor to know what constituted 'reinforcement' in a cultural for a Black client and to understand the particular environmental conditions that effect a reward or punishment (Banks and Marten, 1973). This is as important as realizing that a sole focus on the client's 'dysfunctional' response repertoire for change or further development of skill may be inappropriate as positive outcome measures alone. To consider only these was implicitly to accept the notion that the problem was solely within the individual. This approach has been argued to encourage the counsellor not to take into account the sociocultural matrix of the Black client's environment. As Simpkins et al. (1973) have argued, there was a need to see Black people not as disadvantaged but as being placed in situations where they were at a disadvantage. The role of the counsellor holding the view of shifting the locus of the problems from individual to society was to attempt to influence changes at a structural or systems level which, when necessary or appropriate, could bring about a corresponding change in individuals (Gunnings and Simpkins, 1972).

There is evidence that counselling and psychotherapy may actually be damaging in terms of life expectations and self esteem to some clients under some circumstances. This is most likely to occur when theoretical approaches or practices are not demonstratively sensitive to the needs of the client. For example, a study by McCord (1978) traced 250 treated clients and 250 untreated clients from a matched control group after 30 years' termination from treatment. 80 per cent of the treated group thought they had benefited from the counselling (which was Rogerian supplemented by educational help and training in social skills, and lasted in most cases five years) but the employment, criminal and health records of both groups showed the group which received treatment to have done less well in all respects than the control group. The potential for damage to life expectations and self esteem may be much greater when counsellor and client are from different cultural and ethnic backgrounds. However, this can only be speculative as no direct evidence for the long term effect on Black clients receiving counselling from white therapists is available. Sue and Zane (1987) has raised the question of whether Black clients have poorer outcomes in therapy than white clients. Some researchers have found that a counsellor's ethnicity does not necessarily affect effectiveness (Pontoretto et al., 1986; Reed, 1988, 1986; Atkinson, 1985; Gordon and Grantham, 1979), while others argue that the 'race' of the counsellor does affect outcomes and that ethnic matching is the most effective pairing (Terrell and Terrell, 1984; Wade and Bernsein, 1991; Berman, 1979a; Flaskerud, 1986). In reviewing the available evidence, Atkinson and Lowe (1995) concluded that most (but not all) outcome studies have shown differential outcomes on the basis of the 'race' or ethnicity of counsellor and client. Therefore, we can only state, as Atkinson and Lowe (1995) and Abramowitz and Murray (1983) earlier noted, that the effects of 'race/ethnicity' on counselling outcome remain 'mixed' but with some clear preferences existing.

A significant problem in the provision in choice of counselling services, and by implication choice of counsellor, to Black people is the low number of Black counsellors available. The British Association of Counselling has some 7,000 individual and organizational members, whereas the Association of Black Counsellors has only 80 counsellors (personal communication by Joyce Thompson, Chair of the Association of Black Counsellors, 1990). Related professions are in a similar position. There are relatively few Black women or men working in psychology. The Association of Black Psychologists has approximately 25 members. The American Psychological Association only established a Society for the Psychological Study of Ethnic Minority Issues in 1987. The British Psychological Society has a Race and Culture Special Group part of the Division of Clinical Psychology with some 25 members and this is an ethnically mixed group, i.e., Black and white.

Challenges to Existing Counselling Models and Practice

In order to deal with the difficulties inherent in existing counselling theory and practice, Black therapists at Nafsiyat have begun to develop their own model of cross-cultural counselling. As part of this development, Acharyya (1987) has found it useful to inform Black clients that whenever they feel unable to explain their views or defend their beliefs adequately, they should bring an advocate with them. This supportive person could be either a friend, family member or a member of their community. This person was seen as a confidant who was assessed to have whatever necessary qualities the client felt would facilitate the counselling process. This innovation was quite a significant departure from the more traditional 'one-to-one', individual centred approach of contemporary counselling practice, and lent support to the findings and views of Burke (1986) and Farrar and Sircar (1986). The use of family members was seen as an effective means of developing rapport. As this went against accepted practice strategies it is possible that many traditionally trained counsellors may:

1 be threatened by this 'intrusion' into the sanctity of the counselling environment; or

2 feel personally devalued in not achieving the necessary rapport or facilitating disclosure with the culturally different client on a one-to-one basis; or

3 believe that others entering into the traditional counselling diad may essentially block the desired process and goals of the counselling relationship. Thus, resistance to this facilitating confidant may be great.

The role of language in counselling practice as it affects mutual understanding is another important consideration in achieving rapport. If people do not speak the same language then communication difficulties are obvious (Leff, 1981). Communication difficulties may be less obvious but not as serious when words and phrases are shared but not meanings. Here the possibility of mis-communication is great and its potential damage to the client-counsellor relationship significant. With South Asian clients, due regard must be given to the importance of English language difficulties and steps should be taken to overcome these. For example, there may be bilingual counsellors – a preferred option – or, less preferable, translators may be available. Unfortunately, interpreters may be prone to 'interpret' rather than 'translate' without sufficient awareness of the professional context in which the counsellor is working. Other problems include the client's having to relate to two people at once, with the possibility that the client will tend to respond to the interpreter and not to the counsellor. The effect of this shift of traditionally preferred counsellor dependence to 'counsellor support' dependence has not been adequately discussed or allowed for in counselling theory or technique (Leff, 1981).

The importance of the need for familiarity with the client's culture cannot be overemphasized, for this allows the therapist an appropriate point of entry for consideration of the client's difficulty (Ahmed et al., 1986). Farrar and Sircar (1986) have noted that hospitality towards a visitor is one of the cornerstones of South Asian culture. So knowing that it is likely one will be offered hospitality on visiting an Asian household, if counselling takes place there, and knowing the importance of this hospitality, helped establish a relationship. Farrar and Sircar asserted that by misunderstanding the custom of hospitality, professional workers have often felt they were being bribed, when this was not the case. From this example it should be recognized in a counselling context that the same behaviour or situation compared between cultures can have different meanings in different cultures. This view is connected to what can be termed a postmodernist position, which is characterized by the belief that there 'is no objective social world which exists outside of our pre-existing knowledge of or discourse about it' (Maynard, 1994, p. 15). To illustrate this further, a single young woman who becomes pregnant, whether they be white English, African-Caribbean or South Asian, may have a problem, but the problem may not be the same. Cultural familiarity helps to locate the client's problem within its cultural context and identify social and psychological landmarks necessary for the counsellor to begin to achieve empathy and rapport. This issue will be taken up in the research investigation. Pursuing a line of questioning or not may indicate to the client that no help can be obtained, as there is not enough detailed background understanding on the part of the counsellor. This could have the effect of creating a climate where the client feels alienated, frustrated and even further emotionally isolated from sharing a problem with others. The client may perceive the counsellor who was not in tune with cultural meanings and significance as detached, distant and at worst indifferent or unfeeling. Counselling theorists in the main all agree that this client perception and experience would severely hinder the counselling process (Rogers, 1951; Sue and Sue, 1990).

For those counsellors who believe that for the helping process to be facilitated it should be the duty of those from other cultures to be familiar with the majority culture (the counsellor's culture) and explain important differences to the counsellor, it should be recognized that this would change the nature of the counselling relationship, placing the client in a training or educational role as tutor to the counsellor. Again this would not facilitate the helping process. Another difficulty which may arise in cross-cultural counselling is counsellor and client having different cultural views, which shows itself as different value positions. The British Association for Counselling (1985a, p. 2) has stated that it is important:

> ... in a multi-cultural and multi-value society for the counsellors to respect the client's right to make value choices as he wants, although she may well feel responsible for ensuring that he has fully explored the consequences of his choices. The counsellor's prior membership of a particular group(s) may cause them to misconstrue a task/problem in a particular way. It is therefore important that in giving attention and respect to the client in order to allow him to make his own choices, she is able to avoid imposing her moral/cultural values on him and should offer him the choice of counselling elsewhere.

This assumes that the counsellor can make an objective self appraisal. Is the culturally encapsulated, Eurocentric counsellor able consciously to assess the degree to which his or her value (cultural) judgements affect the counselling relationship? A quotation by Ballard (1979, p. 165) may help to focus upon the difficulties of a cross-cultural counselling relationship:

> We cannot avoid making value judgements; and if we think they do not intrude on our professional work, we deceive ourselves. To all kinds of situations we

apply our own value systems, usually unconsciously. If we succeed in becoming conscious of them and question their applicability, we may find ourselves without any satisfactory response within our present contact.

I wish to take this argument further and draw here from feminist writings which argue that in attempting to understand 'difference', it is flawed to focus on this alone as: 'one risks the danger of masking the conditions that give some forms of "difference" value and power over others. In the context of "race" and ethnicity this can lead to the marginalisation of issues such as racism, racial domination and white supremacy' (Maynard, 1994, p. 10). Therefore, it is important to consider the ways that Black people's worlds are both differently organized and experienced from white people's, and that concerns about 'difference' should have at their centre a focus of questioning issues of hierarchy and power (Mackinnon, 1987). Maynard (1994) cites Rothenberg (1990) as arguing that: 'The force of racism is on the assigning of value to difference, which is then used to justify denigration and aggression, and not in difference per se' (p. 19).

Training Courses to Meet Diverse Cultural Needs

It should be asked whether a counsellor's training reflects the needs of diverse cultural groups. d'Ardenne and Mahtani (1989) argued that, rather than training's enhancing their meeting of Black client needs, their experience of formal and professional training as clinical psychologists limited their ability to work across cultures. They also noted that cultural issues in training were rarely given importance, and indeed were often minimized in the counselling relationship.

The difficulty that training may have in trying to influence (1) what counsellors do in terms of practice, and (2) how they perceive clients and their needs may be related to the psychological literature on attitude change, i.e., that it is difficult to bring about a long term change in attitudes with emotional topics (Oskamp, 1977; McGuire, 1985). That prejudice and racism are emotional topics for both Black and white people there can be little doubt. At an anecdotal level, having observed some 20 racism awareness training sessions where white participants were confronted with their prejudice and racism, it was rare that at least one trainee did not emerge crying, with many others visibly upset. Many writers (Burke, 1980, 1984; Ahmed et al., 1986; Dominelli, 1988; Dillard, 1988) have written on the destructive effect of prejudicial and racist attitudes in cross-cultural interactions.

The capacity for white counsellors to benefit from training and published cross-cultural counselling literature has to be questioned, as the wealth of literature on racism and its effects does not yet appear to have been taken on board. For example, white counsellors, although claiming to have skills in mutual understanding, empathy, rapport, etc. would seem to have difficulties with issues involving direct reference to race and ethnicity. Continuing at an anecdotal level (but nonetheless relevant and revealing), this has been my personal observation on occasions when I have been involved with the training of white counsellors and asked for their views on race and ethnicity in relation to counselling the culturally different. Even at training events with such explicit titles as 'Race and Culture in Counselling' – a conference held in March 1990 by the Association of Student Counsellors, a division of the British Association for Counselling – difficulties were demonstrated. For example, over 40 counsellors and psychotherapists attended two workshop sessions focusing on 'The Impact of Culture on the Therapeutic Process'. Counsellors were asked as a workshop exercise to 'generate words describing factors that stop people communicating with different cultures'. Out of the 51 words and phrases provided not one mentioned race, ethnicity, colour, prejudice or racism, although other predictable factors such as social class, sexual orientation and gender were mentioned. This omission was highly significant, given the theme of the conference. Was it that raising and discussing issues that revolve around or centre on colour, race and ethnicity creates an uncomfortable uneasiness in white counsellors? How does this influence their effectiveness and relationship in the cross-cultural counselling situation? How effective would the white counsellors be if they were to find themselves in a counselling encounter where they were brought face to face with client experience that would make it very difficult for them to deny the existence of racism and the importance and effect on the client's life of being culturally and ethnically different from the majority white culture in Britain?

Would the difficulty that the white counsellor experienced with considering issues of race and culture mean that the needs of the Black client would not be met? Would the Black client's experiences be negated by the white counsellor's inability to comprehend the Black client's position? In short, would the Black client's needs simply be neglected and ignored? What may need to be questioned here is the basis of social relations between different ethnic groups which allows for the fundamental knowledge or awareness base to meet differing needs to go unmet in a counsellor's basic training. Furthermore, it can be argued, there is a need to shift the focus of analysis from difference alone to social relations mediated through that of power and inequality, so that an analysis of that which converts this difference into oppression can be better understood (Bacchi, 1990).

Transference and Counter-transference

The concepts of 'transference' and 'counter-transference' as they relate to the cross-cultural counselling relationship are useful to explore briefly at this point as the process of transference may have a specific influence on what counsellor and client bring to the counselling relationship. These concepts will be explored in greater depth in chapters 3 and 4. Whether or not a counsellor chooses to work with these concepts as part of their theoretical orientation, all need to be aware of them and their potential impact. Theorists have viewed both the meaning and value of transference and counter-transference differently. It is a psychodynamic concept that describes a particular aspect of a therapeutic relationship. Jacobs (1988) saw transference as the replication in the therapeutic relationship by the client of historical, childlike patterns of relating to significant individuals, such as parents, but now acted out in relation to the counsellor. It was Jacobs' belief that aspects of transference existed in all human relationships and it was possible for counsellors to use this positively in the counselling relationship to influence the counselling process. Counter-transference, on the other hand, describes those feelings and ways of being in a counsellor shown when a counsellor related to a client as if the client were someone else from the counsellor's real or phantasized past.

Rogers (1951) viewed transference differently from Jacobs and other psychodynamically influenced therapists. He believed that counter-transference did not tend to develop in properly controlled client centred therapy with the counsellor. However, transference could exist with the client and it was the responsibility of the client to accept and own these attitudes rather than projecting them onto the counsellor. Here the responsibility rested solely with the client. Resistance to exploration of attitudes towards the counsellor's or client's 'race' by the counsellor, as a result of a belief that this was not important and was the client's preoccupation or personal transference, may result in confirmation for the client that difficulties of ethnic compatibility existed due to different experience. This could act as a disconfirming experience for the client, who may choose to terminate early. This was suggested in the view of d'Ardenne and Mahtani (1989) who defined transference as 'the attitudes and feelings placed by the client onto the counsellor in the therapeutic relationship' (p. 79). They believed that clients who have experienced a lifetime of racist practices will bring the scars of these experiences to the relationship. Since most counsellors in Britain will be from the majority culture, they will be identified with white racist society and could therefore be seen as both part of the problem and part of the solution.

Another definition of counter-transference was that posed by Truax and Carkhuff (1967), who saw the concept as meaning a lack of genuineness in the therapeutic relationship which came about through the effect of the counsellor's unconscious feeling, irrational fears and projections which the client unintentionally arouses. Here, training courses and adequate supervision of counselling practice have a definite role to play in supporting the development needs of the counsellor and the therapeutic needs of the Black client.

The effect of counter-transference in a counselling relationship when counsellor and client are from differing cultural backgrounds may be particularly destructive if counsellors were unwilling or unable to examine their cultural prejudice and racism. The effect of counter-transference in the cross-cultural counselling relationship would be that the client would not feel valued, positively regarded and the rapport and therapeutic relationship necessary for productive counselling to take place would not ensue. The effect would be further to compound the hostility of, and oppression by, white people (as counsellors) towards Black people (as clients).

Empathy and Rapport in the Context of Racism

For counsellors who wish to work with ethnically different clients, issues of racism will need to be addressed. Racism may affect the counselling relationship at both a conscious and unconscious level. Dominelli (1988, p. 6) has defined racism as:

> ... the construction of social relationships on the basis of the assumed inferiority of non-Anglo Saxon ethnic minority groups and following from this their exploitation and oppression.

It is important to consider the racism of the counsellor, institutional practice and racism embedded in counselling theory and practice. It is possible to distinguish between overt and covert racism, overt racism being a cluster of attitudes, values and often responses which may be partly submerged in the unconscious and thus require much more effort to overcome. Both views and responses may require a constant process of examination in order to overcome deeply rooted assumptions. Counsellors who do not do this may render counselling totally ineffective, as d'Ardenne and Mahtani (1989, p. 81) pointed out:

> ... unacknowledged prejudice is reflected back unconsciously in the therapeutic relationship. When this occurs, the client no longer experiences unconditional positive regard, genuineness and empathic understanding in the counselling relationship and may consequently withdraw. Worse than this, the unaware counsellor only perceives the client's withdrawal as non compliance or resistance.

This lack of self examination by white counsellors in their attitudes to minority cultures may in part explain some American findings by Sue et al. (1974) of a termination rate of more than 50 per cent after one contact with (white) psychotherapists among Black clients, as opposed to 30 per cent termination rate for white clients.

It has been argued that the acknowledgement of racism and racist attitudes and their psychological effects is a prerequisite for working effectively in helping relationships with ethnic minority clients (Parham, 1989; Helms, 1990). If a counsellor is expected to achieve empathy with a client, not only must they be aware of racism's undermining effects on the wellbeing of the client, but they must feel comfortable in discussing this with the client and realizing that they may have to identify, for the client, racism as the source of the client's difficulties. White counsellors who feel uncomfortable with the notion of racism are unlikely to be effective cross-cultural counsellors, as they will be unable to identify with a significant factor/influence in the experience of Black people in Britain (Ahmed et al., 1986; Miles, 1989; Skellington et al., 1992). The counsellor will need to be aware of the sociocultural matrix of Black individuals and the particular pressures that this exerts. Williams, in an early article in 1949, was of the view that while ethnic minority groups may have the same basic psychological needs as those of white people, frustrations, defeats and conflicts are intensified and faced more frequently because of their different culture and colour. This still appears true. For example, in looking at the reports of racially motivated attacks on Black people in Britain, the numbers during 1988, 1989 and 1990 were 4,383, 5,044 and 6,359 respectively (Runnymede Trust, 1991). Another indication of intensified need is the admission rates into psychiatric hospital for African-Caribbean born males and females, which were significantly higher than for white British people (Cochrane, 1979; Dean et al., 1981). Also, admission rates for Indian, African and Pakistani women tend to be higher than for other women (Dean et al., 1981; Hitch, 1981). Cochrane (1977) found that people of African-Caribbean origin were more likely to be diagnosed as schizophrenic, the rate being 290 per 10,000, compared to 87 per 10,000 for white people in England and Wales. Dean et al. (1981) found that, once age differences had been taken into account, Indian males were three times more likely to be diagnosed as schizophrenic and African-Caribbean males and females five times more likely than white British to be so diagnosed. The figures on racial attacks and mental health needs give some indication of the intensified therapy needs that colour and culture may bring to the therapeutic encounter.

It is acknowledged that in attempting to discover if existing theory and technique apply to counselling Black client groups, the practitioner and academic should resist the temptation to ignore individual differences. There is a need to recognize and acknowledge the individual experiences of Black people in Britain even if some common ground of social experience exists. Although racism is likely to be one of those common experiences that has left serious scars on Black people, the scars are likely to differ from one Black person to another. Counselling theory and technique should take account of the different experiences of African-Caribbean and South Asian ethnic groups if it is to be sensitive and appropriate for exploring the impact of those issues which are culturally different and distinct from the experiences of white people. Likewise, this book will not propose to stereotype all white counsellors as being ineffective with all Black clients. Again, individual differences will exist and some white counsellors, it is acknowledged, may be more effective with Black clients than some Black counsellors.

Research Objectives

To date no large scale attitude survey in Britain has been carried out to discover the attitudes that white counsellors hold towards Black client groups. Given the conflicting findings in the existing research about white counsellors' ethnocentric views and practices it seemed appropriate to launch an investigation into the attitudes therapists have of Black clients. The aims of this research were:

1 to examine the existing attitudes and self reported specific practice orientations of white therapists in their work with Black clients. (The specific practice orientations explored and the limitations of these are discussed and operationalized in chapter 6). A secondary aim was to:

2 identify what influenced the ability of counsellors to work knowledgeably and with cultural sensitivity with the Black client. More specifically, the objectives were to:

a) examine the existing views of counsellors on the significance of cultural and ethnic difference between counsellor and client in the counselling relationship (Nobles, 1976; Farrar and Sircar, 1986; Littlewood and Lipsedge, 1989; d'Ardenne and Mahtani, 1989; Lago and Thompson, 1989; Sue and Sue, 1990);

b) investigate the influences on the ability of counsellors to empathize with the position of Black clients in a social matrix (Cochrane, 1979; Littlewood and Lipsedge, 1989; Pinderhughes, 1989; Ridley, 1989);

c) examine the influences on counsellors' awareness of limitations in the use of Eurocentric models with Black client groups (Wilson, 1979; d'Ardene and Mahtani, 1989; Sue and Sue, 1990; Ivey et al., 1993);

d) explore the degree to which counsellors varied their usual attitude or strategic orientation to practice with white clients when counselling Black clients (Nobles, 1976; Atkinson, 1985; Casas, 1985; Lago and Thompson, 1989; Sue and Sue, 1990).

2 Culture, 'Race' and Ethnicity: Their Significance to Counselling

This chapter will attempt to show how a counsellor's understanding and use of the terms culture, 'race' and ethnicity may influence and affect the counselling process. The importance of the counsellor's acknowledgement of racism and its effects will also be discussed. As has been discussed in chapter 1, there is some danger in an over-focus on issues of difference without some acknowledgement of the conditions that 'give some forms of difference value and power over others' (Maynard, 1994). In considering the themes in this present chapter it must be emphasized that each must be seen in the context of inequality and power relationships, and that it is just as important to reach an understanding of difference through social and political hierarchy and issues of power that arise within these structures as it is through issues of culture, 'race' and ethnicity (MacKinnon, 1987).

It was seen as useful as an introduction to offer a brief history of postwar migration to Britain to set a social and political context as this lays a foundation to allow the reader better to understand the social-political matrix of Black peoples' lives in Britain. This is not meant to be a comprehensive analysis of postwar immigration but only a brief contextualizing discussion.

Postwar Migration

A shortage of labour in postwar Britain facilitated the migration of workers from the Caribbean and Indian subcontinent. The response of the indigenous population to this immigration is well documented (Husband, 1982; Allen, 1971; Mullard, 1973; Khan, 1979; Watson, 1979; Bagley and Verma, 1983) and will not be discussed in detail here. Until the 1991 Census there were no accurate figures available to indicate the ethnic variety of Britain's population. The previous population statistics were the 1981 population census in which the data collected focused only on place of birth. This focus excluded those Black individuals who were born in Britain and did not, therefore, give an accurate or reliable picture of the populations ethnic group composition. According to the 1991 Office of Population and Census Survey (OPCS, 1993) a total of 2,946,700 people identified themselves as being from what were termed 'ethnic minority groups'. This represented 5.9 per cent of the total British population (see Table 1).

Table 1   Ethnic group composition of England and Wales

	No.	**%**
White	46,936,500	94.1
Black Caribbean	499,000	1.0
Black African	205,400	0.4
Black – Other	176,400	0.4
Indian	830,600	1.7
Pakistani	454,500	0.9
Bangladeshi	159,500	0.4
Chinese	147,300	0.3
Other Asian	193,100	0.4
Other	280,900	0.6
Total persons	**49,890,273** *	**100.1**

Source: *Balarajan and Raleigh, 1992.*

* Column figures are rounded and do not exactly equal the total numbers

Table 1 provides some indication of the relative numbers of ethnic minority groups, although data are based on census returns and can be subject to some difficulties such as non return, particularly from those who do not speak fluent English or none at all – some 200,000 adults (Smith, 1977a; Brown, 1984) and those refuges who are fearful of their immigration status (Chambers, 1993).

Britain's Black ethnic groups are not spread throughout the country. Most tend to be concentrated in large urban conurbations such as London, Birmingham, Leicester and the large northern towns of Rochdale, Bolton, Manchester and Oldham as well as Bradford. Other areas of the country have few, if any, Black inhabitants. Many of the areas that Black people settled in during postwar immigration and continue to live in are those of the inner city where there is great social and economic disadvantage, such as poor housing conditions and unemployment, which are closely related to social class factors.

Britain had experienced previous immigration from Ireland and Eastern Europe but the new immigrants were significantly more distinctive in their colour and traditions. 'Coloured immigration' was seen as a 'problem' and was reported as such in the news media (Husband, 1982; Khan, 1987). Punetha et al. (1988, p. 253) have written that 'these people were considered 'outsiders' and their relationship with the British mainstream society was deemed marginal' . Racial discrimination denying employment, services and housing opportunities was widespread, necessitating the passing of the 1968 and 1976 Race Relations Acts. This has not stopped overt discrimination but has slowed it down, with the effect of changing its overt expression to covert (Miles, 1989; Skellington et al., 1992). For example, in 1971, the census showed that the unemployment rate of young African-Caribbean people in Britain was at least twice that of their white counterparts. Later, in 1978, Little et al. found that the number of young Black interviewees who were unsuccessful at interview was four times that of white teenagers with equivalent qualifications. Modood (1997) found that, as total unemployment increased, Black and other minority ethnic groups formed an increased proportion of the unemployment figures. A PEP study of nearly 300 company plants (mentioned by Smith, 1977) showed more than half practised some form of discrimination. A Labour Research Survey (1989, p. 14) noted that 'discrimination and racial harassment are unfortunately all too often part of the experience of working life for Black people'. These studies have indicated that decisions on whether to hire, offer development opportunities or promote may be taken on the grounds of 'race' alone and not individual merit.

In chapter 1 the incidence of racially motivated attacks (Runnymede Trust, 1991) was discussed, as was the greater mental health statistical over-representation of people of Black Caribbean and South Asian origin (Nazroo, 1997; Dean et al., 1981; Hitch, 1981). This gave some idea of the political, social and interpersonal context of many Black people's daily experience in Britain and how their life influences could be qualitatively different from their white counterparts. This is not a result of cultural inadequacy but the experience of prejudice and discrimination from the indigenous white community. The influences of this prejudice and discrimination will be further discussed later in this chapter.

Culture and its Influence on Behaviour

In attempting to define culture, Kraben and Kluckhohn discovered over 100 published definitions as early as 1952. The present writer will not add further to these but believes it necessary to offer some clarification as to what is meant by the term by exploring some commonly used definitions in the literature.

The term 'culture' has been identified (Segall et al., 1990) as a label for aspects of knowledge, status and attitudes that are learned and transmitted from generation to generation. Schweder (1977) saw culture as a tradition handed down that is basically anything produced by people. Culture was said to involve the total fabric of a person's life and provide security through structured ways of mastering the environment. The social and psychological significance of culture was seen as one's ability to interpret culturally specific symbols (White and Dillingham, 1973), i.e., the ability to originate, determine and bestow meaning upon things and events in the external world, and the ability to comprehend and act on such meaning. Thus, culture could be viewed as the heritage, traditions, values, attitudes, interpretations and behaviours of a social group or a social group's design for surviving and adapting to its environment. However, it is important to acknowledge that every person in a cultural group need not follow its cultural programme. In most societies, culture provides a broad range of options and there will always be those people who modify some of the 'accepted' and 'agreed' cultural programme and behave independently of cultural norms. For example, in some Muslim cultures it may be expected that the oldest son or daughter should marry first. However, educational pursuits of the oldest son or daughter may mean that marriage is delayed so that education and career opportunities can develop, thus encouraging the younger family members who are not following an educational path to marry first.

Torbiorn (1988) has argued that at a psychological level, if the individual is well adjusted to their own culture, that individual should have internalized many cultural norms into their frame of reference; that is, one conceives these norms as representing what is normal in the sense of being usual, appropriate and preferable. Thus, an individual will normally show a considerable degree of overlap between his or her values and norms of behaviour and those norms that are representative of their own culture. This does not mean that people are exclusively the products of their cultures, as culture will not provide cultural norms or a blueprint for behaviour for every situation an individual has faced or is likely to face. Also; culture evolves, and as individuals or groups become geographically mobile and interact with other cultural groups there may be a specific evolution of culture different from those non mobile individuals. For example, the cultural patterns of East African South Asians are distinct from those of Indian based groups of origin (Khan, 1979; Ahmed et al., 1986). The present research attempted to examine what happened when cultural background, through a therapist's frame of reference, interacted with counselling clients from a different culture. This present study was also an attempt to look at counsellors' opinions and self reported specific practice orientations to specified culturally different groups in terms of their willingness to consider the cultural needs of these people, as distinct from the cultural needs of white clients. There is evidence to suggest (Levine and Campbell, 1972; Ehrenhaus, 1983) that because aspects of a new or unfamiliar culture may appear as less normal, less known, less good and so on, reactions tending to the negative rather than the positive can be expected. This may not be due to aversion or hostility but may be, as Levine and Campbell (1972) have described it, the effect of a more general naive 'phenomenal absolutism' or a behavioural and attitudinal tendency to see things as either one or the other i.e., good or bad without consideration of a continuum of possibility. Further-more, the negative reaction to a cultural difference may grow in intensity if it touches on a fundamental or central aspect of an individual's own culture and of the individual as a member of that culture. This reaction within a counselling context may show itself at a counter-transference level, and if left at an unconscious or unchallenged position could seriously affect both the therapeutic alliance and counselling outcome. Left unacknowledged and unchallenged, it could block the establishment of several of the core conditions; unconditional positive regard, genuineness, and empathy (to be discussed in detail in chapter 3) necessary for successful counselling to take place.

The South Asian communities in Britain comprise a number of separate groups who differ in language, religion, history and areas of origin. Furthermore, there is no single, homogeneous group, e.g., although most people see Bangladeshis as Muslims, they may in fact be Christian, Hindu or Sikh and speak different languages or dialects. Thus, one needs to know more about an individual than area of origin alone to make a culturally sensitive or specific response. Furthermore, there can be a 'rural-conservative' or 'urban-progressive' divide (Henley, 1986) between the various groups and indeed some South Asians may have spent several generations in East Africa, which further influences their relative cultural behaviour. It should also be noted that, as about half of South Asians are now born in Britain (Berthoud and Beishon, 1997), many may maintain only certain features of 'traditional' culture and belief.

The extended family system in India and Pakistan has been described in detail by a number of writers (Khan, 1976,1979; Anwar, 1979) and will not be duplicated here as this is not the focus of the thesis. However, the main structure appears to be one of a defined hierarchy of authority with older male members heading this arrangement. This will be discussed within a theoretical context later in this section. Few family members are expected to become independent of the family. The duties and responsibilities towards the family members tend to be clearly defined and take priority over non-family members:

> He or she is not an individual agent acting on his or her own behalf .... The individualism and independence so valued in the west appears selfish and irresponsible to a Pakistani, who expects and values the elements of dependency and loyalty .... Family and kin take priority over individual preference (Khan, 1979: p. 43)

Marriages in the South Asian tradition tend to be arranged by the partners' parents, and the extent of choice of partner can vary considerably between individual families. Great emphasis is laid on the moral reputation of the family as a unit and its individual members, particularly the reputation of women. There are some areas where South Asian and white British cultural values may conflict, and these will be discussed in the context of Triandis' 'collective-individualistic' dimensions of cultural difference in this section and in chapter 5. Broadly speaking, the differences generally centre on a focus of independence and individualism for white British culture, and independence and mutuality for South Asians.

The African-Caribbean community is not homogeneous. Britain had 19 colonies in the West Indies. The largest group to emigrate to Britain were from the island of Jamaica. All Black Caribbeans are descendant from Africans who were forcibly removed from their country of origin and forced to work on plantations on the West Indian islands. As a consequence, much of the traditional language and elements of culture were forcibly removed. Aspects of European culture, religion, and language of the slave owners were imposed. The forced separation of families during slavery has resulted in many group behaviours which are not, strictly speaking, 'cultural' but have become internalized behaviours. For example, the family systems that exist in the West Indies are very different from those of West Africa (the part of Africa from where most African-Caribbeans originate). The extended family is an important support mechanism for individuals, as is the case in the South Asian community. However, the extended family may take a different form from that of the South Asian community, i.e., it consists of greater numbers of single women as mothers and as the main family linkage, particularly those in the grandmother role who traditionally cared for children left in the Caribbean during postwar immigration. Single parenthood is much more common. Mahay (1974) quotes figures as high as 70–74 per cent for Grenada. According to Rack (1982) this was not the outcome of 'indiscriminate promiscuity' but due to marriage's being deferred until enough money is available to set up home. Rack noted that for the African-Caribbean family, '[M]arriage is the seal set on a relationship, not the beginning of one' (p. 82). Furthermore, Rack noted that: 'this is not to say that family ties are weak or vague. A sense of family exists in Caribbean culture as it does in Asian culture (and much more than in English culture)' (p. 80). The degree to which single parenthood is tolerated depends on the social class and religious values of a particular family and it can not be taken for granted as being a 'culturally accepted norm'.

Brislin (1990, p. 22) has made the point that 'an awareness of culture and cultural differences was extremely important in interventions into people's lives'. Without this cultural awareness, ethnocentric, or more specifically Eurocentric, misinterpretations of clients needs could be made, leading to inappropriate service delivery. Triandis (1990) suggested that many people coming into contact with other cultures where differences conflict with their beliefs may react in an ethnocentric fashion by using their own ethnic group (in-group) as the assessment standard. A favourable assessment may be made if they reached in-group 'standards' or a less than favourable assessment if they did not. Triandis' view was that each culture provided a cognitive blueprint for construing and making sense of the world and that this was a ready-made *Weltanschauung*, or world view. For those who had limited exposure to another culture, no other world view was likely to exist. It would be a grave error when discussing 'cultural differences' to attempt to create a specific behaviour map that could be expected of individuals within a specific culture. As has been suggested, individuals may vary their behaviours according to the particular situation they encounter. There are dimensions of cultural difference or variation that have been proposed. Triandis (1984, 1990) has suggested that one of the most promising concepts is the 'individualism', 'collectivism' distinction that can account for much behaviour. He noted that the relative emphasis was toward collectivism in the eastern and southern hemisphere and individualism in the western hemisphere. In a factor analytic study, Triandis et al. (1986) found four factors which were related to individualism-collectivism. These were: family integrity, where the stability and continuation of the family were paramount; interdependence – living within a close knit social community which represented aspects of collectivism; and self-reliance with hedonism, which was related to a belief in the priority of the individual's needs and separation from in-groups representing the attachment of little importance to extended family members which both represented aspects of individualism. This allowed Triandis and his co-workers, when working with many different items within and across cultures, to refine measurements (Triandis et al., 1985 and 1988). They arrived at a number of what they termed 'defining attributes' of the construct. These can be summarized as:

1 Collectivist cultures pay more attention to the identifiable in-group and behave differently towards members of that group than towards out-group members. It is the unit of survival and the common fate of members that is of paramount importance. In-group fate and achievement are characterized by collectivists. Personal fate and achievement are emphasized by individualistic cultures.

2 Collectivist cultures place more emphasis on in-group goals than individual goals. Self reliance means 'I am not a burden on the group'. In individualist cultures, personal needs and goals take precedence over the needs of the group. Self reliance means 'I can do my own thing'.

3 In collectivist cultures, behaviour is mainly determined by in-group norms. The self is defined as an appendage of the in-group. In individualistic cultures behaviour is a product of individual likes and dislikes and the self is a distinct and separate entity.

4 Collectivists tend to emphasize hierarchy, which may be gender determined, and defer to this. A view that no internal disagreement should be known or shown to the out-groups prevails. In the individualistic cultures, confrontation can be displayed to the out-groups and can take place within the in-group to establish new values or norms.

5 Vertical relationships, such as parent-child, take priority over horizontal relationships, such as spouse-spouse in collectivist cultures and vice versa in individualistic cultures.

6 Certain values such as achievement, pleasure and competition tend to be more emphasized by individualist cultures whereas collectivist cultures tend to emphasize security, obedience and conformity for the sake of the whole.

The significance of this in counselling the culturally different client is that the collective-individualistic dimension of cultural difference, to name one dimension of possible difference, places a duty of awareness on the counsellor to challenge the models of 'normality' and social 'adequacy' that they may be working with in attempting to make sense of the culturally different client, without trying to stereotype and fit the client into a cultural 'pigeonhole' that allows no room or space for individual difference and development. As the reader will see in chapter 5, some counselling theories may place far too much of an emphasis on the individual client's needs without considering these within a social matrix of responsibility and external pressure over which the individual may have little control. Furthermore, Triandis makes the point that:

> There is also a tendency for collectivist cultures to rely on an ideological framework when they communicate. That is, they use a framework from a religious system ... or some other ideological framework as part of their communication. They assume the listener shares that framework. Of course, if the listener does not share that framework the communication will be very obscure. However, if the listener shares the framework, such use of the framework improves communication (p. 43).

This suggests that it is of paramount importance that the counsellor is knowledgeable about the culture of the individual and the significance that this has for communication and behaviour, if counselling is to be relevant and effective.

The Study of Cultural Distinction and Similarity

A pivotal or central concern for individuals interested in the study of culture is the relationship between the culturally unique and the humanly universal. Lonner (1979) refers to this relationship as the emic/etic distinction.

The distinction between these terms was first made by Pike in 1954 and later elaborated following a distinction in linguistics between *phonemics* and *phonetics* where Pike (1966) coined the terms *emic* and *etic*. The study of phonemics involves the examination of the sound used in a particular language, while phonetics attempts to generalize from phonemic studies in individual languages to a universal science covering all languages.

Higginbotham et al. (1988) have described the emic approach applied to cross-cultural counselling as related to behaviour change within one particular culture, while the etic approach applies a culture-free approach or uses universal dimensions to describe the behaviour changes operating in more than one culture (see Table 2) (Sturtevant, 1964; Brislin, 1976; and Berry, 1980). However, Higginbotham (1988) has noted that according to Sturtevant (1964), the 'etic approach uses a priori definitions and conceptual models of cultural content, imposed by an outside researcher, in order to compare human behaviour change among various societies' (p. 280).

Table 2   The distinction between emic and etic approaches

Emic approach	Etic approach
A Studies behaviour from within the system	Studies behaviour from a position outside the system
B Examines only one culture	Examines many cultures, comparing them
C Structure discovered by the analyst	Structure created by the analyst
D Criteria are relative to internal characteristics	Criteria are considered absolute or universal

Source: Pike, 1966.

Thus, an emic orientation focuses on the unique aspects of the culture under study. It is concerned with the personal world of individuals – their differences and beliefs, logic and methodology – while an etic orientation focuses on the universal and the general aspects of a culture based on the assumption that, in spite of obvious physical and socio-structural differences, human beings are basically similar in belief and motivation. The etically oriented investigator will study the culture with a focus on minimizing the distinctions between cultures in order to demonstrate the underlying similarity as being more important than the differences. This present study, when focusing on white counsellors' views and self reported attitudes to specific practices with Black client groups, assumes an emic focus.

There is an etic influenced tendency when researchers are exposed to another culture to compare and contrast it, often making judgments about the quality of the culture compared with the researcher's culture (Levine and Campbell, 1972; Ehrenhaus, 1983). Explanations of culture should seek to avoid value judgments based on politics, wish fulfilment, and aesthetic values. The erroneous interpretation and translation of the belief system of one culture by another has been defined as 'transubstantiation'. Von Lue (1975) originated the concept of 'transubstantive' errors, where the meanings, beliefs, values, and behaviours of one culture are erroneously compared, evaluated and interpreted by the values of another culture. Individuals who commit transubstantive errors assume that their own culturally bound experience is an adequate and appropriate guide to what is humanly universal and desirable, i.e., an ethnocentric view dominates.

Leff (1981) gave a useful example to illustrate this. He suggested that the content of people's beliefs, whatever their mental health status, stemmed directly from their life experience and was inevitably influenced by their culture. He noted that this was recognized in the generally accepted definition of the term 'delusion', 'namely a false belief which the person holds to firmly despite argument or proof to the contrary, and which is inconsistent with the information available to the individual and with the beliefs of his or her social group' (p. 8). He suggested that this underlying qualification was essential since in every culture people are brought up to believe things for which there was no direct evidence, e.g., 'Santa Claus' or 'Heaven ...' but which are held to with unshakeable conviction. To label these beliefs as delusions ... makes a nonsense of the term' (p. 8). Therefore, it is important to know in detail the cultural matrix in which people live their lives before deciding if beliefs are inconsistent with cultural group beliefs and meet the criteria of a delusion.

Thus, knowledge of other people's culture from an etically focused perspective is important in providing counselling and psychotherapy. It is generally accepted that culture does play an important role in one's personality, belief systems, and many other aspects of personality as well as behaviour (Jones, 1991; Draguns, 1981) and Western European counselling theories that claim to adopt a 'culture free' perspective may in fact be Eurocentric, denying the significance and value of other cultures and ways of being.

'Cultural Barriers' as an Emically Influenced Perspective

Punetha et al. (1988) have noted that South Asian immigrants in particular experienced marked problems in adaptation in Britain not only because of prejudice but also because of their own particular cultural attributes, motivations and aspirations. Ballard (1979) and James (1974) noted that in addition to large scale differences between the South Asian immigrants' home and the host country in terms of climate, culture, language and religion, many tried to maintain their religious and ethnic identities in Britain to the extent of keeping themselves separate from mainstream white society. This could be seen in light of Torbiorn's (1988) writings as a 'cultural barrier'. Torbiorn saw a cultural barrier as a bi-cultural and mono-directional reactional phenomenon, reflecting psychological limitations in the ability or willingness to understand, accept or adopt the norms of a foreign culture. The difficulty with accepting this definition would be in conceiving the separation or isolation of South Asians from mainstream white society, as argued by Ballard (1979) and James (1974), as a 'mono-directional reactional phenomenon'. Other writers (Skellington et al., 1992; Husband, 1987) have documented that although there may have been some wish on the part of these groups for separation there was also a very strong reaction from white society wanting to keep them at bay. Thus, the existence of a 'mutual' or 'dual reaction' must be considered if an accurate perception of the existence of cultural barriers as it relates to the experience of South Asian people in Britain is to be understood. Speaking less categorically, Torbiorn was willing to accept that a more general view of a cultural barrier could be that of 'individual reactions in situations of cross-cultural contact where cultural differences negatively affect an individual's ability, willingness to understand, accept and adhere to, or adopt the norms of a foreign culture' (p. 168). The relevance of this to counselling the culturally different was that difficulties in inter-cultural communications are often described as resulting from cultural barriers. However, difficulties may not be readily related solely to cultural differences, as communication interferences may be related to personal or situation specific factors that are not necessarily representative of the culture of those involved (Brislin, 1981; Pedersen and Pedersen, 1985). One such difficulty may be attitudes towards 'race' and 'racial' difference which tend to be heavily influenced by social and political factors and thus unequal power relationships.

Notions of 'Race'

Rex (1986) argued that the use of the terms 'race' and 'ethnicity' varied widely in popular, political and academic discourse so much that it was difficult to promote a reasonable discussion about what would be the best use of the terms.

Montague (1964) has written that the idea of 'race' was of relatively recent origin dating from about the 16th century. He suggested that when the members of a society acted out their emotions and beliefs in relation to members of other groups in discriminatory ways, based on a conception of the others which was socially determined by colour or physical difference we were clearly dealing with a racial group distinction. This distinction tends to be the social conception of 'race'. More specifically considered, the social idea of 'race' was the notion that there existed something called 'race'. This social idea of 'race' suggested that physical and behavioural traits were linked, and that different kinds of linkages of this nature characterized different peoples, thus accounting for both physical and behavioural differences. Furthermore, Montague argued, the social idea of 'race' implied that cultural achievement of individuals was determined by 'race'.

Montague has stated that although this kind of interpretation of the differences presented by different groups is appealing and comforting to those who indulge in it, it is in fact an inaccurate and false explanation as the social conception of 'race' goes beyond the facts and is in conflict with the evidence. He has argued strongly that the social idea of 'race' represents a collection of pseudo-logical realizations based on a confusion of emotions, prejudiced judgments and disordered values.

Montague has also asserted that the idea of 'race' was individually and socially destructive. Thus a counsellor having an unchallenged popular view of the existence of differences between people and groups based on the notion of 'race' would possibly not be acting in the client's best interests in considering the client's motivation to act or behave in certain ways, i.e., behaviour may be seen as biologically determined and driven (Fanon, 1967; Miles, 1989). Montague (1964) has observed there can be little doubt that the physical distinctions that are recognized to exist between different individuals of different populations were, and continue to be, associated with behavioural traits or peculiarities.

Later writers with similar observations of the terms usage noted that when discussing the idea of 'race' there was an unavoidable truth to face. For example, Miles (1989) wrote that as a way of categorizing groups of people, 'race' was based on a delusion, because popular ideas about racial classification lacked scientific validity and were moulded undeniably by political pressures and faulty thinking rather than by evidence from biology. From this arises a central tenet of postmodernist thinking: that theory is always historically and culturally specific and is therefore grounded in social reality; it is subjective and far from being objective and value free (Glaser and Strauss, 1967).

As for the attribution of characteristics of behaviour and personality to groups based on 'race', in 1965 UNESCO stated that current biological knowledge did not permit cultural achievements to be linked to differences in genetic potential and that any differences in the achievements of different peoples should be attributed solely to their cultural history (Bloom, 1971).

Rex (1970) has written that although the social and biological meanings of 'race' contain numerous falsehoods, what matters is the individual's point of view and how the individual recognizes the ways that subjective understandings of 'race' translate themselves into 'objective' consequences. As Thomas (1967) has argued, if people define a situation as real, it is real in its social consequences. Thus if people, both white and black, believe that 'race' determines possible psychological and social outcomes then it is likely to, as the term is invested with a social and causal reality. Attitudes about 'race' are not just interesting curiosities: they can form the medium of exchange in daily interaction between different groups. Thus, the complex social, political and personal manifestations of 'race' demand study in their own context and right rather than being dismissed in favour of biological reductionism, and determinism.

Ethnicity

The term 'ethnic' or 'ethnicity' has come into use relatively recently to bridge the gap between 'race' and 'culture'. Rack (1982) has argued that this may be because the term appears to have more neutral meanings. Just as the notion of 'race' has strong social underpinnings an examination of the literature suggests the same may be true for the term 'ethnicity'.

One definition of an ethnic group has been offered by Schermerhorn (1970) who saw it as 'a collectivity within a larger society, having real or putative ancestry, memories of a shared historical past, and a cultural focus on one or more symbolic elements defined as the epitome of their "peoplehood"' (Richardson and Lambert, 1986, p. 52). Similarly, Yinger (1981) has suggested that the term refers to a segment of 'a larger society whose members are thought, by themselves and/or by others to share a common origin and to share important segments of a common culture, and who, in addition, participate in shared activities in which the common origin and culture are significant ingredients' (Richardson and Lambert, 1986, p. 52).

Following a qualitatively different line of argument from the previous two writers, Watson (1984) argued that 'ethnicity' was not simply a euphemism for 'race' as physical appearance (presumably Watson's understanding of race) was only one of many possible criteria that could serve as the basis for ethnic divisions.

It is possible from the various notions and definitions of ethnicity to extract some key features of ethnic groups, such as:

1   shared culture;

2   regular social interaction in its widest sense, e.g., culturally focused celebrations; and

3   a sense of 'belonging' accompanied by a bond which has the function of securing the group in its identity.

However, the significance and influence of shared group physical characteristics is missing. Culture and belongingness may both bond individuals to a group and separate them from others, but they need to be actively signalled to others in order to be recognized. Physical characteristics such as colour, etc. cannot be hidden. There is no choice allowing the physically distinct individual or group to not disclose their origin or connections. The point that is being made is that colour and other unchangeable physical features go beyond the behavioural reactions that culture alone may evoke in others. Physical features or characteristics that are constantly displayed may initiate a response from others who do not share the same features, much as 'releasers' do in the animal kingdom. This ethological concept refers to the existence of a particular environmental stimulus which initiates a specific behaviour in the individual (or group) that comes into contact with the stimulus (Lorenz, 1981). The reader who is neither familiar nor comfortable with the notion of linking what is a concept normally used to describe an innate animal behaviour to that of individual human or group behaviour should note that evidence has been found in support of this theoretical comparison of human and animal behaviour (Lorenz, 1981; Eaves et al., 1989). Leaving aside for the moment the influence of physical features in marking one group as distinct from other, it is possible to consider that one key term in considering the notion of ethnicity is that of 'culture'. Lyon (1972) has attempted to distinguish between 'race' and 'ethnic' group analytically. Firstly, he believed that an ethnic group was defined culturally, whereas a 'racial' group was physically defined. Secondly, Lyon maintained that an ethnic group voluntarily erected barriers between itself and other groups, whereas a 'racial' group tended to be forcibly excluded and prevented from freely interacting with other groups. Thirdly, Lyon argued that ethnic groups enjoyed a sense of solidarity and demonstrated a capacity for mobilization of their collective interests, whereas 'racial' groups tended to be little more than residual categories which had limited prospects for collective efforts. Although Lyon's conceptualization represented a reasonable attempt to distinguish between terms whose meanings were often confused with one another, his efforts did not clearly establish a distinction. For example, he did not explain why a 'racial' group cannot be 'self defined', developing a positive sense of purpose and mutuality and display considerable organizational talents.

Banton (1988) maintained that in using the term 'ethnicity' for naming groups two tendencies have been recently apparent. Firstly, a tendency to regard ethnicity as an attribute of minorities, i.e., in Britain the English have not regarded themselves as an ethnic group because, being the largest and dominant group, there has been no pressure on them to ask what makes them distinctive. Secondly, there has been an assumption that whereas 'racial' groups are distinguished by appearance, ethnic groups are distinguished by cultural characteristics such as language, history, customs, shared attitudes, etc. Thus, ethnic groups may be seen as subdivisions of 'racial' groups.

Wallersteing (1960) has stated that the membership of an ethnic group is related to social definition and is an interplay of the self definition of members and the definition of other groups. Social ascription is a key characteristic that distinguishes ethnicity from voluntary affiliation of a group. For some groups there may be exceptions to this, but for people who also inherit distinct physical characteristics that signal them as being different in some way from the majority groups there is no choice. Furthermore, changes in an individual identity may evolve quickly but collective identities change much slower.

Morris (1968), in discussing some of the psychological criteria which distinguished ethnic group membership, noted that the group must 'feel themselves distinct' or must be thought to be similar to each other and distinct from others in certain ways to be considered an ethnic group. Morris returned to the internal characteristics of ethnic group membership by stating that it was important for members to identify themselves as a group and , furthermore, label themselves as a distinct group. Also, the feeling of being treated differently could lead to further and stronger group identification and affiliation for enhanced psychological security.

Members of ethnic groups may define themselves differently from the way in which they are defined by others. In many circumstances, it is necessary to start from a group's own self definition. However, Tajfel (1987) noted that being assigned and/or assigning one's self to a particular social category leads at the same time to certain negative consequences which include discriminatory treatment from others and negative perceptions, however vague. Tajfel (1978) argued that it was this social categorization that provides a form of social structuring or system of group orientation indicating the individual's and their group's status within a particular society. Tajfel (1978, p. 63) made the link between the self and social categorization in the concept of social identity, which was seen by Tajfel as 'that part of an individual's self concept which derives from their [sic] membership of a social group (or groups) together with the value of emotional significance attached to that membership'. Thus individuals defined their place and the place of their group within a particular social order. Oakes et al. (1994, p. 82) suggested that:

> The meaning and significance of their actions and attitudes in that context, depend upon social categorisation. Where the relevant categorisation divides individuals into social groups, action within that context will take on the distinct meaning and significance of inter-group relations.

For Tajfel, the group and its cultural traditions and values, how they were interpreted by the out-group, and how this interpretation was received by the in-group were of major influence in the process of stereotyping and group relations. This has particular relevance when considering the needs of those in a counselling or psychotherapeutic relationship. The imposition of a definition by another group may cause significant stresses as the individual struggles to disregard, or in some cases, introject this as part of their identity. A situation of internalized oppression may arise, where individuals act out the negative ascribed stereotypes of their group that are 'invented' by the oppressive group(s) as a means of rationalizing its oppressive behaviour. Bochner (1986) noted that Tajfel suggested that there was a generalized norm of hostility towards those of the out-group and that this was more than simply forming negative value judgments about a specific group and then behaving accordingly. Bochner argued that Tajfel's thesis was that individuals developed a subjective social order based on the classification of 'us' and 'them', and then learned or were socialized into the belief that it was acceptable to prefer and favour an in-group member and discriminate against an out-group member, even if there was nothing to be gained at a material or psychological level. Although both less powerful and more powerful groups are able to stereotype each other – i.e., the process is not just one way – it is the more powerful group who will have greater access to the resources of definition that will enable them to preserve their own image at the expense of the image of less powerful groups. This highlights the concept of power which will be further discussed in its counselling context in chapter 5.

Khan (1987) has noted that there was a popular notion in academic work on ethnic relations that it was minority cultural groups that have cultural beliefs and behaviours that were seen as problems for both themselves and the white indigenous group. An individual's meaning system was a constantly changing interpretation of the differences between his/her own perception of self and how he/she perceives others to see them. Khan (1987) argued that at the basis of cultural process and change there was a constant dynamic, often revolving around conflict and contradiction between ideas and action. For example, the links between meaning and action could be seen in the dysfunction which occurred in cases of sudden loss. This often produced an attempt to reconstruct meaning through personal relations and familiar, ritual actions. Here may lay the basic link with the significance of a culturally aware or culturally similar counsellor: emotional security and support through links with the past and the reconstruction of the old and familiar through new symbolic actions may provide psychological support by allowing the client, if necessary, to journey back through familiar territory in the form of reminiscence with a similarly experienced and travelled partner. It is possible that statistics which identify early termination of therapy among Black clients may be attributed to the lack of a culturally significant interchange related to the lack of culturally connected experience between a white counsellor and a Black client (Helms, 1985).

Political Awareness and Ethnic Group Affiliation

Although group social boundaries may tend to be actively guarded, for reasons of common purpose the boundaries may lessen. 'Blackness' used as a political term to indicate (as discussed in chapter 1) a common experience of oppression of African-Caribbeans and South Asians, is not seen as an ethnic or cultural group term, but denotes a political affiliation or coalition of oppressed ethnic and cultural groups pooling their resources for political struggle (Cheetham, 1972; Ahmed et al., 1986). An example of this can be seen in India where the caste system may separate people in terms of a social hierarchy. Immigration to Britain and a realization of sharing common obstacles to social and economic equality may ease this previous inherited social demarcation. For those with greater political awareness of the colonial 'divide and rule policy' cultural, religious and language difference may be subsumed in order to unite for a common purpose and cause of equality of opportunity and to advance a strategic collective position. Bailey (1963) has observed that unification has occurred within the caste system and that collective mobility was often a motive for a merger in the hope that a larger unit would stand a better chance of obtaining enhanced recognition and higher social status. This process can be seen as amalgamation, where two or more groups may unite to form a new group, larger than and different from any of the component parts. Thus, it has been argued that a collective consciousness or a political collective consciousness was one that was important to override historical or traditional group boundaries. As will be discussed under the headings of 'Racism and its effect on personality development' and 'Black identity development' in later sections of this chapter, the realization of common social and political needs between one's ethnic group and another in the context of racism can have important implications for one's mental health.

The Significance of Ethnicity and Culture to Therapy

Erikson (1950) studied the relationship between the positively functioning individual and ethnic identity. He concluded that a positive identity was essential to healthy psychological functioning. Erikson's conclusions were supported by research from empirical studies on Black people (Cobbs, 1972) and those of the Jewish faith (Klein, 1980), which found that individuals secure in their ethnic identity acted with greater autonomy, flexibility, and openness with people of their own background as well as those from different cultural backgrounds. Horney (1937), an eminent psychodynamic theorist, also recognized the relationship of culture and ethnic identity to healthy functioning and maintained that there was an overriding need for therapists to consider the cultural background of their clients. She said that: (a) human problems were incomprehensible out of their cultural context, and that it was essential for adequate treatment that the therapist understood the client's frame of reference; (b) it was difficult to interpret behaviour without knowing something about the value orientations of the culture or ethnic group the individual represents; and (c) the same behaviour may have very different meanings for individuals from different cultural or ethnic groups.

Some writers (Acosta, Yamamoto and Evans, 1980) have argued that Eurocentric therapists have not acknowledged Horney's criteria and therefore often lack the necessary knowledge to work effectively with Black groups. Horney's criteria are also related to the previously discussed work of Triandis on the dimension of individualism-collectivism, indicating the different world views that the culturally different counsellor and client may have. Acosta et al. discussed the problems that could occur as a result of conflict of values between the therapist and client and suggested that the counsellor's theoretical orientation must have a sense of the client's culture for therapy to be effective.

Pedersen, Draguns, Lonner and Trimble (1981) have also stressed the necessity of being knowledgeable about the client's culture and being flexible in therapy techniques. Draguns (1981) also highlighted the extent to which available descriptive information concerning the common factors of therapy (Garfield, 1971) and the necessary core conditions of therapy changed with the culturally different. Draguns also believed that one should expect complications in therapy when it was extended across 'racial', ethnic, subcultural, or cultural lines, and when the counselling orientation or perspective did not acknowledge cultural difference. As long ago as 1942 Rogers discussed the importance of blending Eurocentric models of psychotherapy with indigenous models in countries where psychotherapy was being imported. It was Rogers' belief that psychotherapy could not be isolated from its cultural context and that the usefulness of the therapy outside its cultural locale was limited unless that therapy was adapted to culturally identified needs. He stated that culture pervaded the conduct and experience of psychotherapy and a change in behaviour and wellbeing could only take place in relation to a cultural reference point. Thus, it would seem that a prerequisite for therapy was that therapists have, as part of their expertise, a knowledge of the culture in which they operate. This lack of acknowledgement, it seems, will disable or reduce the effectiveness of the counselling process. However, while stressing the necessity of attending to culture and ethnicity, Draguns' (1981) viewpoint was that it would be a great mistake to practice one specific psychotherapy with all people designated as African-Caribbean or South Asian. He believed, however, that possessing cultural-ideological knowledge about these groups provided the therapists with a point of entry into therapy. This ethnic or cultural-ideological information should serve as a source of hypothesis to be verified, discarded, and/or modified on the basis of information acquired during the therapy process.

Despite differences in culture between white therapists and Black clients, counselling theorists have tended to ignore the basic cultural differences underlying the psychological needs of Black people. They have elected to use the standards and values of the white majority culture to evaluate and treat Black clients (Sue and Sue, 1990). They have made the assumption that theories and techniques used with the majority culture should, and can be used with Black people (Wrenn, 1987; Draguns, 1981). The belief that everybody is to be regarded as the same in receiving therapy and that there are standards of normality and health that travel across cultural and ethnic boundaries has served as a barrier to culturally oriented approaches to therapy (Rack, 1982; Jackson, 1986; Fernando, 1989). The development of theories that can be equally applied to all clients regardless of ethnic or cultural background is seen as an idea worth pursuing from an etic standpoint. However, it seems impossible to separate theory and its perspectives from its historical and cultural context. The experience of racism may create significant differences in therapeutic need between ethnic groups and this will be discussed in the following section.

The Concepts of Racism and Prejudice and their Influence on Therapeutic Need

A number of writers have argued that the behaviour of the Black client must be interpreted in its appropriate social, cultural, political, and economic context (Pierce, 1969; Triandis, 1990; Jones, 1991; Lago and Thompson, 1989; Sue and Sue, 1990; Maynard, 1994; Mama, 1995). These writers have identified issues specific to the Black client that they view as important in the provision of therapy. Common to the writings of all these writers was the discussion of the effects of racism. Racism is not an easy concept to define, empirically measure or investigate. For this reason, perhaps, British law (1976 Race Relations Act) has confined itself to the behavioural outcome of racism in practice, that of 'discrimination'. Racism as an entity surfacing in counselling and psychotherapy has historically been referred to by a more clinically sanitized term: that of xenophobia, which has been defined by Reber (1985, p. 834) as a 'pathological fear of strangers or strange places'. People with this fear, rather than finding themselves involved in therapy may find like minded people to form structured organizations such as the National Front, a racist political party. Racism in psychology appears to be conceptualised mainly as a form of 'prejudice based on race and characterised by attitudes and beliefs about the inferior nature of persons of other races' (Reber, 1985, p. 607).

Jones (1972) has described three uses of the term 'racism' in the literature. Firstly, 'individual racism' which focused on the irrational beliefs and discriminatory behaviour of an individual. Secondly, there was 'institutional racism' which referred to the intentional or unintentional manipulation or toleration of institutional policies (e.g., housing allocations, admission criteria, occupational selection criteria) that unfairly restricted the opportunities of a defined group(s) of people. Thirdly, there was 'cultural racism' which could be defined as the individual and institutional expression of the superiority of one ethnic group's cultural heritage over another. As early as 1940 Benedict argued against too abstract or academic an analysis of racism. Her view appears just as appropriate now as it did then. The Benedict was of the opinion that the significance of racism must lie in its social consequences and that just as with any analysis of belief that goes beyond scientific knowledge, it can only be judged by its fruits and ulterior purposes. Pierce (1969) explored the concept of racism from a clinical, rather than academic, standpoint. He asserted that racism was a central, common experience having a profound impact on the daily lives of Black people. Mama (1995), following this theme of argument along gender lines, has suggested that 'for Black women, the dominant order is both racially oppressive in gendered ways and sexually oppressive in racialised ways' (p. 123). Pierce, moving from a sociopolitical view to a psychological perspective, viewed racism as a psychiatric problem, describing it as a 'primary mental illness'. He defined it as 'a delusion or false belief formed of morbidity, based on ethnocentric consciousness with a corresponding set of ethnocentric prejudices'.

In order to gain a deeper understanding of the significance of racism, it is useful to examine the cognitive and behavioural aspects of racism, those of prejudice and discrimination. This examination should allow for more understanding of the various mechanisms that undermine Black people's mental health. Allport (1954, p. 9), in his now classic analysis of prejudice, defined prejudice as 'an antipathy based on faulty and inflexible generalisation. It may be expressed or felt. It may be directed towards a group as a whole, or towards an individual because he is a member of that group'. Ashmore, in 1970, defined it as 'a negative attitude towards a socially defined group and toward any person perceived to be a member of that group' (p. 253). Prejudice was and is generally conceptualized as having a cognitive component, e.g., irrationally based beliefs about a group, an emotional or affective component, such as a strong dislike and a behavioural predisposition to avoid the group(s) in question (Harding, et al., 1969).

Whereas prejudice was seen as an attitude, discrimination was seen as a selectively unjustified negative behaviour towards members of a target group. According to Allport (1954) discrimination involved denying individuals or groups of people equality of treatment. Jones (1972, p. 4) defined discrimination 'as those actions designed to maintain own group characteristics and favoured position at the expense of the comparison group'. It should be noted that prejudice does not always lead to discrimination and that discrimination may have causes other than prejudice.

As argued, the two basic components of racism are prejudice and discrimination, prejudice being a disposition or state of mind, and discrimination being the action whereby members of one group single out members of another group for disparate treatment based on group characteristics. This disparate treatment victimizes and depresses individuals, preventing them from obtaining their needs and expressed goals. Pierce (1969), from his clinical standpoint, described racism as being comprised of macro- and micro-aggressions on every level of human functioning. The cumulative effect of these aggressions resulted in damage to the psychic structure of the individual, interfering with the capacity to think and behave rationally. Pierce stated that the racist system, through the use of these aggressions, distorted and undermined the ethnic specific characteristics of Black people. Pierce believed that these aggressions could be mediated through positive experiential intervention which will be discussed in the next section. However, before doing so it is worthwhile to consider the related concept of 'ethnocentrism'. Ethnocentrism has a meaning which is different to that of 'racism' or 'prejudice'. Its use in the literature tends to vary from that of being more closely akin to racism, e.g., the definition of Aboud (1987, p. 49) where '... ethnocentrism refers to an exaggerated preference for one's own group and concomitant dislike of other groups', to that of Wetherell and Potter (1992, p. 43) who suggest that: 'Broadly racism is seen as a problem of ethnocentrism, of explaining how preference for one's own ethnic and racial group is connected to a chain of discriminatory consequences.' The specific meaning that is attached to the use of this term in this work is that of the original founder of the term – Sumner (1906). Sumner first used the term in an analysis of people's links with their own groups and surrounding groups. He argued that:

> Ethnocentrism is the technical name for this view of things in which one's own group is the center of everything, and all others are scaled and rated with reference to it (pp. 12–3).

Sumner's view was that ethnocentrism was difficult to overcome as we had to become attached to our own ethnic groups. However, to avoid ecological catastrophes we had to learn to transcend our own cultures and develop, as a minimum, empathy with others (Segall et al., 1990). Research into ethnocentrism (Campbell and LeVine, 1968; Brewer and Campbell, 1976) has shown that all people have tendencies to:

1 define what happens in their own cultures as 'natural' and 'correct' and see what goes on in other cultures as 'unnatural' and 'incorrect';

2 perceive in-group customs as universally valid, i.e. to believe what is appropriate for their in-group to be good for all;

3 think that in-group norms, roles and values are, without question, universally correct and applicable;

4 act in ways that favour the in-group in terms of cooperation and support; and

5 feel pride towards the in-group and hostility, or at least contempt, towards the out-group (adapted from Triandis, 1990, p. 35).

Closely related to the concept of 'ethnocentrism' is that of the more specific concept of 'Eurocentrism' which implies that European and indeed, mainly northern European values, are at the centre or core of appropriate and acceptable behaviour or functioning. The use of the term also relates to the dominant cultural values of the white majority in the USA which is seen as heavily European influenced (Sue and Sue, 1990; Mama, 1995).

Ridley (1995) relates Eurocentric standpoints to the counsellor's role and suggests that counsellors see themselves as immune from an Eurocentric perspective, and assume they are able, by virtue of their training, to counsel clients from any background. This, he argues, is due to the Eurocentric nature of traditional counselling theory which asserts, in ignorance of its inherent Eurocentric view point, that its theories and techniques are appropriate to all regardless of gender, ethnicity or culture (d'Ardene and Mahatani, 1989; Sue and Sue, 1990) and that traditionally trained counsellors are able to adapt to client difference and meet differing cultural needs (Larson, 1982; Ridley, 1995). Littlewood (1992, p. 42) argued, within a cross-cultural psychotherapy context, that: 'While we can note similarities, we cannot 'translate' one set of understandings into another without a significant loss of meaning.'

Littlewood also argued that:

> The obvious 'liberal' approach is one which simply seeks to offer the European therapeutic model to others on the basis that this is the best we have ... any radical critique precisely this: that the provision of 'white' therapies for 'black' people presenting with problems that result from existing patterns of white-black dominance is problematic, to say the least. At its strongest, this argument would seem to implicate psychotherapy as only a more insidious variant of European middle-class authority, denying to others even the authenticity of their own expressions of distress: thus transforming and condensing down 'political' tensions into the less inconvenient form of 'individual' pathology (p. 41).

This non-recognition of the significance and influence of culture and ethnic difference, together with a non-recognition of the power relations between Black and white, form the basis for an Eurocentric approach to counselling. However, drawing upon Black feminist postmodernist positions allows us not to be over simplistic in framing issues purely in Black versus white terms. Oppression not only occurs between men and women but also between women and women as it does between men and men. Furthermore, it can, and does, occur between Black people in the Black communities (Maynard, 1994; Mama, 1995).

A Therapeutic Recognition of Racism's Effects

Pierce (1969) has described his approach to therapy with Black patients which involved teaching them to assume the responsibility for changing their environment. This change was accomplished by breaking through the pattern of micro-aggressions by not complying with the aggressor's expectations. Furthermore, Pierce's research suggested that discussions of racism and its effects on the client might be one of the practices that differentiate the effectiveness of white and Black therapists. However, it was possible that if Black therapists over-identified with Black clients on this issue that they may ignore or deny important issues and lose their objectivity and thus their ability to act as therapeutic agents of change. Conversely, white therapists who avoided or minimized the issue of racism and its effect on the daily lives of Black people in Britain would need to consider whether they were able to work effectively with Black clients (Boyd-Franklin, 1989). Lago and Thompson (1989) contended that the issue of racism needed to be addressed both in the training and practice of counsellors in any society that has pretensions of being a multi-ethnic/cultural society. Evidence exists to suggest that many counsellors see themselves as empathic, concerned and caring people who see clients as individuals regardless and independent of their cultural and ethnic backgrounds (Thomas and Sillen, 1972). Such a colour/culture blind approach is negating of the client, their experiences and their identity as well as the reality of the power dimension in Black-white or majority-minority group relations (Ridley, 1989). This issue will be discussed further in chapters 3 and 4, which are concerned with attitudes and transference issues.

Racism and its Effect on Personality Development

It is necessary to review the impact of racism on the personal world of Black people growing up in white dominated societies to show how the intrapsychic world of Black people differs from that of white people due to negative socialization forces. This is not meant to be an extensive review of children's ethnic identity development but a summary of some of the key issues that affect the developmental experiences of Black people in white societies. Social differences between ethnic and cultural groups, even when they take on fairly subtle forms can be reflected with significant sensitivity in the attitude of the people who are adversely affected (Clark and Clark, 1939, 1950; Milner, 1975; Burke, 1986; Tajfel, 1987). An extreme form of this internalization of negative self evaluation by members of Black ethnic groups has been described by a Black American psychologist, Kenneth Clark (1965). Clark has written that human beings who are forced to live under adverse conditions and whose daily experience is one of rejection and discrimination from white society will, as a matter of course, begin to doubt their own worth. Since individuals depend upon their cumulative experience with others for clues as to how they should view and value themselves (Erikson, 1965; Cross, 1971; Helms, 1987) children who are at the receiving end of rejection either directly or indirectly through the observation of the negative experience of family members in society, can begin to doubt whether they, their family, and their group deserve no more respect from the larger society than they receive. Clark has argued that these self doubts become the seeds of a pernicious self and group hatred, leading to a belief in one's own group inferiority. This process starts from early childhood, and the evidence comes from many countries where children of both African-Caribbean and South Asian origin are the minority within a white majority (Milner, 1971, 1975). Over 50 years ago Clark and Clark (1939) published the first of a long series of studies demonstrating that African-American children could be directly shown to have serious identity, identification and group preference problems starting at the age of three and sometimes extending into adulthood. Several writers have discussed the effect of oppression on the child rearing practice of Black Americans (Thomas, 1971; Willie, Kramer and Brown, 1973; Harrison, 1975; Kochman, 1981). In order to raise children who could cope and survive in a racist and discriminatory environment, black mothers were forced to teach their children: 1) to express aggression indirectly; 2) to be perceptive in recognizing the thoughts of others while disguising their own; and 3) to engage in ritualized accommodating-subordinating behaviours designed to lessen conflict and tension (Willie et al., 1973). This involved a 'mild dissociation' where both Black American children and adults may separate their true selves from their role as 'Black people'. A dual identity may often be used, where the true self was revealed to one's fellow ethnic group members, while the dissociated self was revealed to meet the expectations of prejudiced white people. This dual consciousness may cause significant psychological difficulties that need to be overcome in order to consolidate and express the true self.

In a large-scale study of 300 children aged 5–8 years, conducted in two cities in England, Milner (1975) was able to confirm and extend many of the previous findings from the United States with this 5–8 years age group sample concerning out-group preferences in children from African-Caribbean and South Asian ethnic groups. Milner (1975, p. 121) found that 'Black British children are showing essentially the same reaction to racism as their American counterparts, namely a strong preference for the dominant majority group and a tendency to devalue their own group'. In another study of British origin with children of South Asian background in Glasgow, Jahoda et al. (1972) found that this group had shifted their ethnic group preferences towards the majority white group by the age of 10. In considering the continued impact of racism and its outcome with adults, Burke (1986), an African-Caribbean psychiatrist living in Britain, has discussed how institutional racism creating social deprivation may lead to a pathological apathy and be one explanation of the high prevalence of frustration syndromes in both African-Caribbean and South Asian groups. Burke (1986) cited urban riots as being one extreme form of the expression of this frustration. The urban riot appeared, in Burke's view, to be a community phenomenon which seemed to result from a feeling of oppression and a reaction to poor social conditions in dilapidated ghetto areas (Moinat, Raine, Burbeck and Davison, 1972; Fields and Southgate, 1982). When high risk individuals of the subordinated group did not externalize their frustration they may internalize their feelings which could lead to an increase in psychosomatic disorders and depression among vulnerable populations who encounter racism (Burke, 1984).

Although it is difficult to establish hard evidence between the early rejection by children of their own group and its effects on their later development and behaviour, withdrawal from the wider community's systems of norms and values and the establishment of subgroups which have their own values has been seen as one possible effect of what is often called a 'search for identity'. This withdrawal may be rooted in the acceptance by Black groups in Britain of the image of themselves imposed by the dominant white group, and/or it may result in the rejection of this image through means which are ineffective in changing social situations and perhaps reinforce existing stereotypes and divisions. That identity difficulties as a result of discrimination, oppression and racism are a central influence on the lives of children of African, Caribbean and South Asian origin in Britain is clear (Milner, 1975; Stone, 1981; Verma and Bagley, 1982; Aboud, 1988; Troyna and Hatcher, 1992). This has been argued to have the effect of creating a distrust of the services on offer in what may be perceived through experience as a hostile society. A 'Third World consciousness' may develop in which the awareness and experiences of diverse cultural groups become similar as evidence for the significance of colour and its common link to the theme of oppression is made explicit. This of course does not suggest that all Black individuals will show identity 'pathology'. It may well be that certain individuals are more vulnerable than others in their development. Clearly much of the experience of oppression will not be an accurate picture of daily life for all Black people, although the significance of the effect of prejudice, discrimination and racism is one that few Black people living in Britain will be able to ignore. Brah makes a useful contribution to our understanding here when she distinguishes between 'the everyday lived experience and experience as a social relation' (1992, p. 141). Here 'experience' may refer to the single individual's biography and/or a 'collective experience' that refers to group histories and the way in which groups are located in the social structure and experience other groups relative to their own group position.

Other theorists have studied the effects of oppression and subjugation on the psychological functioning of Black people. As early as 1903 Du Bois identified the dual consciousness necessary for functioning in two cultures. Du Bois described the psychic conflict typically experienced by most Black people wanting to feel a part of white society while being constantly reminded that status boundaries based on skin colour existed. What Du Bois depicted was the confusion experienced by some Black people concerning self worth and their dependence on white society for self definition.

Black Identity Development

Much of the later research by Black therapists has centred on the establishment of a Black identity that was not totally dependent on approval of white society (Vontress, 1971; Cross, 1971; and Thomas, 1971). However, implicit in all of the models is some notion of bi-culturality, adaptation to one's culture of birth and white Anglo-culture.

One of the first Black theorists to propound a model of Black identification was Frantz Fanon (1967). In his role as psychiatrist he studied the psychology of both the Algerians and their French colonial oppressors. Fanon formulated a three stage theory of reactive identification demonstrated by Algerians but typical of other ethnically and culturally oppressed people, such as people of African-Caribbean and South Asian origin in Britain. The phases were:

1   the individual internalizes Western ideas, values, and norms by assimilating the culture of the occupying power;

2   the individual is disturbed and experiences an identity crisis, which leads to a quest for identity. This search often results in romanticization of the past and a repudiation of the culture of the oppressor; and

3   the individual severs ties to the oppressor and becomes active in changing the environment to one that is more conducive to growth and healthy functioning.

Fanon concluded that oppressed people must go through these three phases before they can move to cultural pluralism, through which cultures can confront and enrich each other. His view was that real universality resides in the decision to recognize and accept the reciprocal relativism of different cultures (Fanon, 1967).

In the United States, three psychologists working independently of each other (Thomas, 1971; Cross, 1971; Milliones, 1977) developed models depicting black cultural identification or the development of the Black identity. Their models describe the various stages that Black people traverse in becoming Black oriented. These models begin at a phase before the individual's cultural awakening, a period in which a Eurocentric view predominates. The individual moves on to an understanding and acceptance of Black cultures, ultimately leading to a pluralistic perspective at the final stage. These writers have taken a stage approach for the convenience of discussion and analysis rather than the belief that fixed exclusive categories exist. These models are not meant to be comprehensive theories of personalities but conceptual frameworks to aid understanding. Helms (1987) has provided an overview of the models. She summarized the basic features of these as being:

Stage 1 A time before the individual's cultural awakening in which the individual is enmeshed in viewing the world from a Eurocentric view. This stage was typically described as one in which the individual idealized white norms and culture and denigrated their own. The primary affective condition associated with this stage was poor self esteem and low group esteem. Erikson

(1965) has noted similar observations in the formation of non-white identities. He has written about the concept of 'identity foreclosure' where for the Black child and adolescent Eurocentric imposed images of Black ethnic groups created an active destruction of own group worth in the Black child's sphere of reference. The child attempted to separate itself from their own group or disinvest their belonging. This was necessary for psychological defence as so many negative images descended on the individual. The internal and personal conversation illustrating this process is 'They (Black groups) are like that. I am not like that, therefore, I am not like them because they are not like me'. From this the child emerged with a sense of group (and self) inadequacy and inferiority (Banks, 1990). This first stage was generally considered to be the least healthy, and counsellors are frequently warned against unwittingly reinforcing this form of identity confusion (Butler, 1975). For example, Brah and Minhas (1986) have written on the way in which the popular notions of culture clash, as experienced by young Asian girls, where an internalization of the implicitly 'superior' Western values which conflict with traditional (and by implication inferior) values and customs of their parents may affect the service that professionals provide by reinforcing feelings of ethnic group inferiority.

Stage 2 This was typically seen as a transitional stage where due to lack of acceptance by the white world and/or because of a personally meaningful life experience, there begins a period of conflict resolution. The specifics of this stage can be ambiguous. Thomas (1971) saw it as a period of withdrawal and cultural assessment, whereas Cross (1971) described it as a period of decision in which the person decided to become a member of their own cultural group.

Stage 3 This stage of identity resolution has been called immersion emersion by Cross (1971). Here the acknowledgement of racism appeared significant. The primary emotion tended to be anger resulting in 'militant' or acting out behaviour. Personal contacts and relationships tended to be exclusively limited to one's own cultural or politically affiliated members.

Stage 4 The final stage was one of positive internalization of one's own cultural identity and has been described as a transcendent stage. Here the person used his or her own experiences with white and Black groups to shape a perspective that best fitted their own life circumstances. No longer was it necessary to use cultural group membership to judge what was seen as valuable. In this stage self esteem as well as group esteem became positive.

The stage theories tend to be cognitive theories in that it is attitudes, perceptions and cognitions that are stressed. Helms (1987) has argued that as the stage theories had a strong cognitive orientation it was not possible, within the framework of such theories, to shift the client's identity confusion by a sole focus on personal construct exploration. Successful identity transformation appeared to involve a combination of personal readiness, prior cultural socialization experiences and educational experiences. The exposure of clients to situations demanding identity perception shifts would only accelerate identity transitions if the client was situationally ready and able to make conceptual sense of their new experience.

Semaj (1984) provided a thorough critique of all the transformation/ Black identity models. His criticisms rested on the view that: (a) they concentrated specifically on the development of Black political or oppression awareness; (b) they limited the range of experience in and validity of alternative identi-fication; (c) they did not take into account social class and its link to cultural imperialism; (d) they did not deal with regression from a higher to a lower stage of transformation; (e) they did not include a stage of autonomy and self determination in the final stage of transformation from the level of dependency and subjugation; and (f) they lacked adequate acknowledgement of ethnic group collective action to overcome oppression. Semaj also disagreed with the implication that identity for most Black people began with the phase of being anti-Black. It was his belief that the majority of Black people had never lost their cultural identity and that the transformation experience described by these models was only typical of the experience of the Black elite and intelligentsia. Whether all of Semaj's critical points are valid is a moot point. Further criticism centred around the inevitability of the link between reference-group orientation and personal identity. That is, it might be conceivable that a person dislikes the cultural group they are born into but likes themself nonetheless (Banks, 1976). The present writer has criticized the inadequacy of Banks' formulation in terms of the psychological defence mechanism of denial and reality avoidance (Banks, 1992). Mama (1995) has been critical of the samples used to conduct the Cross and Thomas models of Black identity development which were drawn from 'Ivy League' University based populations. She has suggested that an alternative approach to the study of what she terms 'racialised identities' using what she refers to as recent advances in post-structuralist theory. Mama uses the concept of 'subjectivity' instead of the terms 'identity' and 'self' to: 'indicate my rejection of the dualistic notion of psychological and social spheres as essentially separate territories; one internal and one external to the person' (p. 1).

Despite criticism, however, these models have been effective in pointing out aspects of developing a Black identity distinct from a white identity development, and have served a heuristic function. It may be possible that the value of these models lies within their client need identification or diagnostic value. Furthermore, Sue and Sue (1990) have quoted research, to be discussed later, that suggests that a Black client's individual reactions to the counselling relationship, the counselling process and to the counsellor are influenced by the cultural/ethnic identity of the client and not simply linked to ethnic group membership.

Furthermore, another contribution of the Black identity models that needs to be considered is their description of the influence of the social and political context in shaping Black people's identity in societies where they have experienced racism and discrimination as contributing forces on personality and behaviour. The ability to assist the Black client in developing an integrated Black identity which lessens conflict and confusion is a practice that might distinguish the culturally congruent counsellor from the culturally distant counsellor in practice.

White Identity Development

As well as there being a model of Black identity development, there is a model of white racial awareness development which was constructed by Helms (1990). The model was based on the view that white identity is '... closely intertwined with the development and progress of racism ...' (p. 49) As for the Black identity models, Helms was speaking within a North American context. However, there is no reason to suspect that parallels of white racial awareness development do not exist in Britain, as there is evidence for similar patterns of discrimination which has been previously discussed in this chapter. Helms empirically conceived of the five stage model which was a 'linear process of attitudinal development in which the white person potentially progresses though a series of stages differing in the extent to which they involve acknowledgement of racism and consciousness of whiteness' (p. 53). Unlike those of the majority of other theorists, Helms' model did not assume that the damaging effects of racism were only experienced by Black people. In her view the effects of racism were damaging also for the perpetrators, e.g., the absence of a positive white identity. In Helms' view this could be observed by asking a white person what they were 'racially'. Helms drew upon the work of Katz and Ivey (1977) and noted that you would typically get the answer, for example, of 'Italian' or 'English'. She quoted Katz and Ivey as saying 'White people do not see themselves as white' (p. 50). This was later elaborated as being a situation where, owing to white people's being in more powerful positions, there was little need to consider their 'racial' identity. The fact that Helms made use of the terms 'race' and 'racially' was not seen as a criticism of the model, as the terms were not seen as biological reductionism. Helms' usage appeared to be both a political identification as belonging to a powerful group and one of a psychological identification or acknowledgement that white people who originate from Europe did identify as an ethnic group even if they were culturally distinct. This could be observed from the institutionalized and cultural oppression of non-white groups. Helms' model could be summarized as the stages of:

1   *Contact* Here, white people became aware that Black people existed. The individual may approach Black people with feelings of interest and curiosity. Helms suggested that in the contact stage a white person may become aware of the negative reactions of whites towards Black people and white people in interracial unions.

2   *Disintegration* The white person's awareness which developed from the above forced them to realize both that they were white and what this whiteness meant in terms of privileges in a racist society. Helms suggested that this was a stage characterized by guilt and depression as the individual was forced to acknowledge their role and position in white society. Individuals tended to react in different ways. For example, compensating in taking on the 'Black struggle' or shying away from contact with Black people and reintegrating into (racist) white values and beliefs.

3   *Reintegration* Here the white individual became more positively biased towards their own culture and may have developed anti-Black sentiments. Depending on how the individual coped with their feelings – as discussed in the disintegration stage – by becoming personally active or uninterested in the challenge of racist values, the individual may enter the next stage.

4   *Pseudo independence* Helms saw this stage as one where white people started to possess an intellectual curiosity about Black and white relations. In this stage social contact became possible and interaction was not characterized by naivety or trepidation about Black people as existed in the 'contact' stage or the potential resentment or fear as in the 'reintegration' stage.

5 *Autonomy* In this final stage, the individual developed from having solely an intellectual curiosity about Black and white relations and ethnic difference to an understanding of differences both at a thinking and feelings level. White people in this stage could seek out and enter interracial contact because of being secure in their own racial identity and appreciative of cultural difference. Thus, as with Black identity development, the white person may either get stuck or move progressively through sequential stages with the possibility of unguarded, genuine social interaction with Black people.

In Helms' view, each of the above stages had its own unique effect on attitude, behaviours and feelings. From her work she suggested that racist attitudes may change faster than behaviours, that is to say that there may be a lag in time and that for those whose attitudes, emotions and behaviours were not congruent significant personal discomfort would exist. This may link to the theory of Personal Distress (Batson et al., 1987) and the observations of Pinderhughes (1989) which will be discussed in the next chapter and related to how counsellors, who may experience dissonance, may bring into play a variety of psychological defences to cope with incongruence.

3 The Cross-cultural Counselling Relationship

Introduction

The focus of this chapter is to enable the reader to make sense of the complexity of inter and intra-personal dynamics that can occur in the cross-cultural counselling encounter. It was suggested in chapters 1 and 2 that neither client nor counsellor enter the counselling dyad as 'blank slates'. Each comes with a previous ethnic group history, personal experience of encounter with the culturally distinct, and both will have developed attitudes towards each other's ethnic group through the usual social learning processes in the community, family, school and media. How this is acknowledged and dealt with is to a large degree dependent on the experience, knowledge, skills, and ultimately sensitivity of the white counsellor in understanding the memories, feelings and experiences that the Black client may need to explore in counselling. Feelings which arise between white counsellors and Black clients may reflect hierarchical relationships and attitudes existing in society which may be linked to social disadvantage, stereotyping and racism. These can be a potent source of therapeutic influence for both client and counsellor and need early acknowledgement for successful therapy to take place (d'Ardenne and Mahtani, 1989; Sue and Sue, 1990; Kareem and Littlewood, 1992; Ridley, 1995). Without such an awareness of the cross-cultural dynamic it is unlikely that counselling will be effective as the cultural specific needs of the Black client will not be recognized or addressed. To enable the reader to understand the complexity of the cross-cultural client-counsellor relationship the concepts of therapeutic alliance/working alliance, empathy, personal distress, cognitive dissonance and issues of transference will be explored in this section of the chapter. Later, the concept of attitude and its relation to transference will be further expanded.

Therapeutic Alliance/Working Alliance

Kanzer (1975) wrote that the concepts of the 'therapeutic alliance' and 'working alliance' could be traced to Freud's (1912) notion of the 'analytic pact'. The term therapeutic alliance or relationship attempted to stress the collaborative and facilitative aspects of the counsellor-client relationship during counselling. Fielder (1950, 1951) produced a series of studies that investigated the nature of the therapeutic relationship. He claimed to have found that therapists from different schools agreed upon the nature of the ideal therapeutic relationship. Fielder used a statistical approach called factor analysis which yielded one common factor of 'goodness' whose features were concerned with empathy or understanding. More recent studies by Mearns and Thorne (1988) and Book (1988) appeared to indicate that there was widespread if not universal agreement among theorists and therapists on the influence of the therapeutic relationship in therapy. It appeared that for some time after Freud's (1912) identification of the significance of the therapeutic relationship, therapists have regarded it as the 'central focus of the therapeutic process' (Menninger and Holzman, 1973). However, some writers in this early period (Lazarus, 1969) held the view that although relationship variables were extremely important and were necessary, they were insufficient in themselves and only functioned as a medium through which other factors could operate. This view was also echoed more recently by Trower, Casey and Dryden (1988) and Beutler et al. (1986). However, evidence has been accumulating for some time to show that a therapeutic relationship characterized by empathic understanding, respect and genuineness, without the use of particular theory focused methods, or techniques could, by itself, lead to client changes in behaviour. Truax and Carkhuff (1967, p. 116–7) summarized the results of this research some time ago:

> These findings suggest that the person (whether counsellor, therapist or teacher) who is better able to communicate warmth, genuineness and accurate empathy is more effective in interpersonal relationships no matter what the goal of interaction ... .

A later review by Truax and Mitchell (1971) discovered that the earlier findings had been replicated in the USA and cross-culturally. This review of the findings suggested that where warmth, genuineness and accurate empathy existed regardless of age, sex, degree of disturbance or even cultural and language contexts and, irrespective of counsellor training or theoretical orientation, there was a strong correlation with positive outcome. This suggested that interpersonal factors alone could lead to psychological change. Expanding on this idea, Paul (1967) put forth a frequently quoted statement in counselling research: 'The question to which all outcome research should ultimately be directed is the following: what treatment by whom, is most effective for this individual, with that specific problem, and under what set of circumstances?' (quoted in Patterson, 1980, p. 665). Krumboltz (1966) phrased a similar question pertinent to the focus of this research of counsellor's views and attitudes towards practice with Black client groups, which was:

> ... what we need to know is which procedures and techniques, when used to accomplish which kinds of behaviour change, are most effective with what kind of client when applied by what kind of counsellor? (cited in Patterson, 1980, p. 553)

These two statements with the evidence of Truax and Carkhuff (1967), Truax and Mitchell (1971) and Mearns and Thorne (1988) could lead us to question whether it was the therapeutic relationship or working alliance alone that may be the essence of counselling and psychotherapy, given that research has identified the personality characteristics or attributes that are necessary for effective therapy. These characteristics are repeated throughout the literature and were captured by Rogers as early as 1957 in a paper entitled 'The Necessary and Sufficient Conditions of Therapeutic Personality Change'. The focus of the present research in measuring counsellor views and attitudes towards practice with Black client groups attempted to discover to what degree the participating counsellors revealed those necessary and sufficient therapist factors. Patterson (1980) summarized the factors proposed by Rogers as:

1   All therapists need to manifest a real concern for their clients. They should be interested in their clients, care for them, and want to help them. Rogers (1957) used the term 'unconditional positive regard' to describe this. Other theorists have referred to warmth or non-possessive warmth, respect, praising, valuing, and accepting. While client-centred therapists would include a respect for the client's potential to take responsibility for himself or herself and to resolve his or her own problems, therapists from other orientations may not see this as important. The client-centred ways of being in having non-evaluative, non-judgmental attitudes towards clients also might not be shared by other orientations, for example, some may argue that Rational Emotive Therapy was judgmental and evaluative in its use of disputing 'irrational' client beliefs, where it was the therapist who defined

and decided what was a rational belief. This may of course be seen outwith an appropriate cultural context.

2 A second characteristic of all effective therapists was said to be honesty or a genuineness and openness. Rogers referred to this way of being as therapist congruence – a consistency between the thoughts and feelings of the therapist and the therapist's expressions to the client.

3 Empathic understanding was seen to be a necessary third aspect of a therapeutic relationship. In some form or other, though it varies in terminology, all of the major writers on counselling or psychotherapy have referred to this characteristic as being important. Although theorists have tended to vary in the degree of emphasis they have placed upon empathic understanding and therapists of varying persuasions may vary in the degree to which they are able to provide it, no one seems to deny its desirability, if not its importance.

4 The necessary attitudes or characteristics of the therapist as described may lead to a therapeutic relationship only if they were recognized, perceived, or felt by the client. Thus, the condition of mutual positive affirmation had to exist between the client and therapist for therapy to work. The therapist was said to exist for the purpose of the relationship only as he or she was perceived by the client.

We can see that in Rogers' view the client's perceptions, or how they understood the counsellor's interactions with them, were seen to be particularly important in ensuring positive counselling outcomes.

Bordin (1979) has shown the importance of bonds in the therapeutic alliance which could be argued to relate to mutual affirmation between the counsellor and client. His paper attempted to expand the concept of therapeutic alliance by focusing on specific components which need to be considered when viewing the significance of the bond between counsellor and client. These had to do with bonds, goals and tasks. The nature of the bond between counsellor and client deserved some attention in examining the nature of the Black client-white counsellor relationship as it related to the personal attitudes of the counsellor and their impact on the client. Mearns and Thorne (1988), writing from a client-centred or Rogerian perspective, have shown that: (1) when the counsellor demonstrated empathic understanding of the client's presented needs; (2) demonstrated genuineness during counselling; (3) showed unconditional positive regard of the client; and (4) when the client recognized and experienced these three important conditions, the client was helped to move to a position of greater psychological growth. A second necessary focus on the therapeutic alliance or bond in the counselling diad may lead one to focus on the client's feelings and views of the counsellor. This will be explored later in discussion of transference phenomena.

It could be argued that, given these findings, notions of 'race and culture' became irrelevant. However, later research by Goldstein and Michaels (1985) in extensively reviewing the topic concluded that early psychotherapy research made sweeping conclusions too readily in seeing high levels of therapist empathy as enhancing the therapeutic outcome irrespective of who the client and therapist were. A more moderate view that sees therapist empathy being facilitative in some instances and not others was necessary. For some clients what may be seen as culturally bound counsellor displays of empathy may be intrusive (Ivey, 1986). To understand this it was seen as worthwhile to explore empathy in some depth as it related to cross-cultural counselling.

Empathy and Cross-cultural Counselling

As has been indicated, early reviews of the literature (Truax and Mitchell, 1971; Anthony and Carkhuff, 1977; and Auerbach and Johnson, 1977) concluded that empathy was the foundation stone of effective counselling. Block (1986) reviewed literature which revealed aspects of good cross-cultural practice and noted that a constantly re-emerging factor was that of empathy. In a study of Hispanic clients, Levine and Padilla (1980) noted that clients from this ethnic group asked for counsellors who were sensitive to their feelings, who did not over-generalize and who were accepting and non-judgmental – all characteristics of empathy. For the purposes of this present research it was necessary to question whether, given the centrality of empathy, empathic qualities manifest themselves differently in different cultures, and could these differences, if they existed, be incorporated into what is presently Eurocentric counselling practice Ivey (1986) noted that touching (presumably with counsellors of the same gender) may be seen in many South American cultures as empathic but could represent intrusive and unwanted contact in North American cultures. In order to assess the precise role of empathy in the counselling process it was necessary to consider its meaning in some depth.

Eisenberg and Strayer (1987) noted that the role of empathy and related processes such as sympathy in social and moral development has been debated for centuries by both philosophers and psychologists (Hume, 1966; Allport, 1937; Blum, 1980). It was perhaps due to its wide ranging application that its precise definition has always been difficult. Eisenberg and Strayer suggested that some understand empathy to refer to a cognitive process similar to cognitive role taking or perspective taking (Deutsch and Madle, 1975). Others saw it as primarily an affective process with some cognitive aspects (Feshbach, 1978; Hoffman, 1984) and many practitioners saw empathy as a process that served a communication and/or information gathering function in therapy (Goldstein and Michaels, 1975).

Eisenberg and Strayer (1987) have attempted a synthesis of the very definitions and usages of the term and suggested that a useful definition was to see empathy as 'an emotional response that stems from another's emotional state or condition and that is congruent with the other's emotional state or situation' (p. 5). They argued that this implied that one could empathize with a broad range of effects. A simple way of conceiving empathy may be to say that one felt as though the counsellor were identifying and experiencing someone else's feelings as though they were his or her own.

In an early attempt to assess the facilitative components of empathy Reik (1948) described four aspects of the empathic process in counselling.

1   Identification – paying attention to another and allowing oneself to become absorbed in contemplation of that person.

2   Incorporation – making the other's experience one's own via internalizing the other.

3   Reverberation – experiencing the other's experience whilst simultaneously attending to one's own cognitive and affective associations to that experience.

4   Detachment – moving back from the merged interrelationship to a position of separate identity, which permitted a response to be made that reflected both understanding of others as well as separateness from them.

From this it could be argued that if Black clients produced material that was outside of a white counsellor's experience, reality, and thus understanding, the likelihood of empathic meeting will be diminished, if achieved at all. This appeared to be the essence of the argument against white counsellor's effectiveness with a Black client. For those client difficulties which were not personal in nature but which represented environmental or sociopolitical difficulties, the Eurocentric counsellor may encounter some significant blockages in understanding and relating to the Black client's social experience. An example would be the way that the concept 'ganga (cannabis) psychosis' has been used to explain the relatively high intake of African-Caribbean men in psychiatric admissions rather than looking at the personal or social pressures that may have led them to use the substance as a means of escaping these pressures (Littlewood and Lipsedge, 1989; Kareem and Littlewood 1992). Therefore, personal dysfunctions, rather than dysfunctions of sociopolitical systems, were inappropriately targeted in the assessment of needs of individuals from particular ethnic groups.

Continuing with Reik's view it could be suggested that the empathic listener was said to sense the feelings of the client but not be overcome or disabled by the pain or distress of the client. Book (1988) argued that notions of empathy such as those of Reik's tended to suggest a particular mode of gathering information about the internal world of another, but made no comment on how the information was used, whether for positive or negative intentions. He further noted that the best 'con men' in the world may be experts in the use of empathic information gathering, but this did nothing to support the feelings of those they interacted with.

Marcia (1987) made the point that the therapist's empathic processes were simultaneous with the client's ongoing production of information. As clients did not stop communicating while the therapists empathized, new spoken information and emotional or affective states were constantly being produced. The therapist, in order to be accurately empathic, could not just 'do' empathy but must be in an empathic state. Thus, empathy was argued not to be simply a technique of response but a way of being or 'merging' with the client for the purposes of emotional sharing and support. This distinction was seen as overcoming the earlier criticism of Book (1988).

For Rogerian orientated counsellors, empathy played a significant and central role in therapy. Rogerian theory postulated that individuals may devalue themselves due to restricting notions of 'self' revolving around internalized negative conditions of worth. In order to restore the 'organismic valuing tendency' the therapist must establish an atmosphere of positive regard, free of conditions. Thus, the therapist must attend to the client allowing the client's explicit and implicit feelings to enter into the therapeutic domain of awareness in order to gain understanding of the client's intra-personal world and then reflect this information back to the client with accuracy and sensitivity. This process was said to encourage the client in recognizing a feeling of positive regard from counselling and facilitate the counselling process.

Simply put, it could be argued that to some degree empathy was a process of strongly identifying oneself with another's emotional and cognitive state. For the counsellor who brought to the counselling relationship their own personal bias against other 'racial' groups empathy was unlikely to be possible as in-depth contact and identification with the client's emotional state would be blocked. A counsellor's prejudices and negative stereotypes would directly prevent him or her from entering into a meaningful relationship and using his or her professional skills in supporting Black clients. The overcoming of prejudices is not easy. At a conscious level they may be recognized and attempts made to guard against them, but at an unconscious level little recognition will be possible. The counsellor may act in a defensive manner, imposing their own reality on the client's communication in order to protect themselves at the expense of exploring their own feelings about personal vulnerability.

With classic psychoanalysis, Marcia (1987) has indicated that empathy was not emphasized as being useful other than for formulating accurate interpretations. Gedo (1981, p. 286) has argued that changing from the psychoanalytic ambience of 'cold and critical' to that of 'a warmly accepting atmosphere' was one that 'few clinicians can ... create without going out of their way'. He stated that while 'hovering attention' was acceptable relying on the 'healing' 'power of empathy' was not. Gedo saw the primary purpose of psychoanalysis as the acquisition of knowledge. It seemed that for Gedo any reliance or overemphasis on the use of empathy was tantamount to bad practice and needed to be avoided at all costs. Blum (1980), another psychoanalyst, agreed with Gedo from a less extreme standpoint in saying that 'analytic cure' was primarily affected through insight and not through empathy, acceptance, tolerance, etc. It was almost as though empathy was seen more as related to sympathy than in the client centred view and was being dismissed because of its perceived over-involvement in the client's emotional structure rather than being seen as in contact but separate from the client's emotional state. Sympathy, like empathy, has been defined in many ways. Wispé's (1986) definition suggested that the difference between the two terms was that sympathy was feeling for someone and referred to feelings of sorrow or feeling sorry for another. Wispé basically saw two aspects to sympathy:

1 increased sensitivity to the emotion of another which intensified the representation and internal reaction to the other person's predicament; and

2 the urge to take whatever mitigating actions were necessary as if sympathy for

the suffering of the other person is experienced as something to be alleviated.

Thus, sympathy may be seen as a mixture of pity and patronage and may deprive the client of autonomy. When counselling Black people we can speculate that the effects of racism and discrimination may move the caring counsellor from an empathic mode of being to a sympathetic mode of being, i.e., wanting to take actions and help the client take whatever actions are necessary to overcome the client's predicament (Pinderhughes, 1989; Batson and Coke, 1981). Therefore, counsellors could move from a passive empathic mode to an active doing mode. This may create a dissonance between training, theoretical orientation and personal feelings. Feelings of personal distress may arise in defence to an often quoted political saying: 'if you are not part of the solution you are part of the problem' (Katz, 1984). The white counsellor may come to recognize his- or herself as the oppressor in thought or (in-) action and may distance themself from the client's needs (Helms, 1990). There is some support for this speculation, and this is explored in the following section.

Counsellor Personal Distress as a Factor in Client Rejection

Batson and Coke (1981) discovered that when processing material related to another's distress some people may experience an aversive anxiety state not consistent or congruent with the other's state, leading the therapist to a self orientated egoistic reaction. In white counsellors this reaction may be one of psychological defence shifting away from an empathic mode when they have to consider the implications of their positions in a racist social structure (Katz, 1984; Pinderhughes, 1989). This response has been labelled 'Personal Distress' by Batson and Coke, who have suggested that its experience led those who encountered it to alleviate their own aversive state by distancing themselves from further personal involvement. Therefore, although both empathy and sympathy could be seen as other orientated, personal distress could be seen as a self orientated protective mechanism. As Batson et al. (1987, p. 179) stated:

> ... personal distress (feeling alarmed, upset, disturbed, distressed and the like)
> evokes egoistic motivation to have one's own emotional arousal reduced, whereas
> the emotional reactions that fall under the general heading of empathy (feeling
> sympathetic, compassionate, soft hearted, tender and the like) evoke altruistic

motivation to have the client's [sic] need reduced.

Batson et al. (1987) based their views on a series of investigations (Batson et al. 1981 and 1983; Toi and Batson, 1982) where it was consistently found that when helping had a low personal cost factor the sample participants who experienced significant increased feelings of distress as a result of witnessing another person suffer were much less likely to help that person if they believed they will not continue to see the person's suffering, even if they did not help. Thus, in the counselling situation one could postulate that if the counsellor had experiences of being overwhelmed by the Black client's experience of racism there may be a strong tendency to shift from empathic response to 'personal distress' as a personal coping mechanism of dealing with increased emotional arousal when they encountered feelings of helplessness and confusion in discovering issues of racism and discrimination which were outside of their experience. Batson et al. (1987, p. 180) noted that:

> The ease of escape from the other person's suffering suggested that people experiencing a relative predominance of stress were motivated by an egoistic desire to reduce their own distress. If they anticipated being freed from the stimulus causing their distress even if they did not help, then they were not likely to help. But if the only way they could escape from the stimulation was by helping, then they were likely to do so.

It seems that we could conclude that Batson's findings showed that people will take the 'easy way out' when this is available to them. Although Batson's sample was not a group of counsellors, Pinderhughes (1989) lent significant support to the possibility that counsellors may behave in the same way. She observed that the personal confusion and distress shown by white counsellors in dealing with issues of discrimination and personal racism was 'related not only to awareness of their entrapment in racism but also to a sense of mourning for the loss of innocence and perceived non-culpability that insight has forced them to give up' (p. 107). Therefore we could speculate using Batson's paradigm that racism, as discovered by white counsellors who were unprepared for its effects by way of experience and training, would function as an aversive stimulus. This would lead the white counsellor in their initial empathizing to experience the arousal of strong emotions raised by lack of cultural or sociopolitical awareness as an aversive reaction due to inability to cope. It was suggested that this would motivate inexperienced counsellors to withdraw from the Black client encountering racism to focus on their own emotional state. Thus, a white counsellor may become disabled in maintaining a facilitative environment within the cross-cultural encounter. This experience may, due to its emotional strength, continue with the white counsellor in the form of 'transference' material when meeting other Black clients whether or not racism was a factor in client counselling need. If this happened the therapeutic alliance, as an effective empathic bond between counsellor and client, would not be established. Therefore, the facilitative conditions of counselling, both the necessary and the sufficient, would not exist.

In helping us further to understand the relationship between empathy and personal distress it was seen as useful to consider Bolton's (1979) work. He placed empathy along a continuum that ranged from apathy to sympathy (see Figure 1).

Figure 1   Bolton's (1979) continuum

apathy   sympathy   empathy

Here, apathy was seen as a lack of feeling or concern so that to be apathetic was to be emotionally uninvolved or detached from the client's feelings. It may be that Batson's (1987) personal distress could also be located on this continuum to the left of empathy (see Figure 2).

Figure 2   Hypothesized extension of Bolton's (1979) continuum

apathy   sympathy   empathy   personal distress

The significance of the attempted linkage between apathy, sympathy, empathy and personal distress, was seen as the therapist's emotional responses taking on a greater repertoire of possibility in the counselling scenario. We may speculate that if the therapist's behaviour was perceived as 'flawed' when traumatic events were experienced by the therapist, this could cause an aversive emotional arousal, which may not be appropriately 'structured' to facilitate the positive and necessary conditions of therapy. This may be seen as an attack on the basic premise upon which therapy was built, i.e., that the therapist should be always warm, caring or at the very least an objective individual or emotionally distanced and controlled. Masson (1989) believed that we go to therapists expecting them to possess certain qualities, such as compassion, understanding, kindness, warmth, a sense of justice and integrity. The therapist who admitted not to possess these qualities would probably not be seen fit to engage in practice with a client. However, combining Batson's findings with existing notions of empathy and apathy such as Bolton's work of a continuum of responses opens the door of possibility that negative feelings could be experienced by the therapist. This will be explored further under the theme of 'counter-transference'. However , before this takes place it was seen as useful to consider a further cognitive process that may influence the client-counsellor relationship, that of cognitive dissonance (Festinger, 1957).

Cognitive Dissonance

Festinger's cognitive dissonance theory (1957) has been an influential account of how individuals seek to achieve consistency in their behaviour and beliefs. Festinger's theory, which has received wide empirical support, assumed that there was a drive towards cognitive consistency and that two cognitions which were incongruent or inconsistent would motivate the individual to reduce the resultant discomfort by harmonizing the inconsistency (Hewstone et al., 1988).

Hewstone et al. have argued that (p. 154):

> In general, dissonance theory predicts that people are motivated to expose themselves to (attitude) consonant information and to avoid attitude dissonant information in order to stabilise a decision (or existing attitude), and in such a manner to maintain cognitive consonance or avoid cognitive dissonance.

Further discussion of cognitive dissonance theory takes place in chapter 7, where it is discussed in the context of the cultural awareness inventory results.

Transference and Counter-transference

Transference, from the psychoanalytic standpoint, was a crucial mechanism in psychotherapy. Rogerian client-centred therapy, while acknowledging the phenomenon of transference as real, tended to see the process as unimportant to therapy. Among the various counselling theories the Rogerian and psychoanalytic views have tended to be the most directly opposed. A definition of transference (Jacobs, 1989) has been previously provided in chapter 1, i.e., where the client reacts to the counsellor as if they represented someone other than the counsellor. Jacobs (1989) wrote that although this was originally felt by Freud to be a barrier and defence to therapy, it became a way of seeing a past relationship reified in the therapeutic encounter. Therefore, it could prove to be important to insight and reworking what may have gone wrong in a past relationship. Basch (1980) has suggested that inability on the counsellor's side to appropriately cope with the transference reaction could create a web of problems and was a common reason for unsuccessful treatments. Basch (1980) has provided us with a more elaborated version of the definition than Jacobs (1989) for the purposes of considering the phenomenon in the cross-cultural counselling encounter. Basch suggested that transference could be viewed as a specific expectational set that predisposed the client to perceive, act and react towards situations and people in a somewhat decided way. Consequently the client could enter the counselling relationship with a fixed set of perceptions and feelings. For the Black client experiencing attempts of help by a white counsellor, historical experiences of racism in the form of present expectations may act at an unconscious or conscious level, intruding and interfering with a facilitative quality in the counselling relationship. Watkins (1989a) has argued that in seeing the transference pattern as an expectational set, difficulties that attach themselves to the pattern can be more easily discerned. The transference reaction was said to be an attempt to structure and define the present via the past or an attempt to maintain the status quo (Singer, 1970; Paolino, 1981). Here clients may involve themselves in self preserving interactions with the consequences of foregoing opportunities for self review and development. Thus, contrary to Freud's view presented by Jacobs (1989), transference could be seen as a defensive operation in terms of displacement which the client engages in 'in order to preserve self image and maintain predictability and control of the situation' (Laughlin, 1979). Singer (1970, p. 285) saw the transference process as 'a vehicle for self elimination'. For the focus of the cross-cultural counselling relationship Singer has provided further interesting views of the function of transference. He stated 'transference reactions reduce self awareness by helping maintain a world image in which all people are seen in essentially identical terms, thus eliminating differentiated experience' (p. 288). Therefore, it would seem that transference can serve to act as a levelling or 'homogenizing' process distorting the necessary facilitating factors in the counselling relationship. Watkins (1989a) argued that attention to the transference phenomenon was most important to all counsellors and it would seem necessary to add that this was likely to be of marked significance in the cross-cultural counselling encounter where the history and/or memory of contact for the client may be less than favourable, given the evidence of racism, discrimination and disadvantage in Britain.

No further discussion of these perceptions will be entered into at this point as the preliminary postal survey data collection suggested that this was best left for the 'Discussion of Results' section. It seems pertinent to say that for the client, feelings which were experienced during transference may indicate both past and present experiences of relationships with white people which, when related to racism, discrimination and disadvantage, may arouse a major source of distress for the client. The experienced therapist may be able to work through such difficulties with the client. However, there is some danger that the use of the strategy of emotional containment may actually facilitate the client to accept oppressive experiences or practices rather than act to overcome these.

Transference and Client-centred Therapy

As has been previously mentioned, Rogers' (1965) client-centred therapy view was that the phenomenon of transference in the therapeutic relationship was relatively unimportant to the process of therapy. Rogers recognized that for the psychoanalytic oriented therapist the concept of transference was close to the core of thinking and that this phenomenon developed into a relationship which was central to therapy. Rogers' view was that client-centred therapy differed in its way of dealing with transference phenomena. While Rogers' view was that transference phenomena existed in varying degrees in all clients this was not seen as a necessary part of the relationship in client-centred therapy for therapeutic exploration to take place. Rogers claimed that the client-centred therapist's reaction to transference should be the same as with any other attitude of the client, i.e., to understand and accept. This was due to the view that acceptance led to a realization in the client that those feelings existed within them, not within the therapist. This acceptance came about in Rogers' view at the point the client realized that the therapist was not attempting to evaluate, make moral judgments, or show approval or disapproval of past behaviours. Therefore, Rogers argued that the therapist's acceptance will eventually lead to insight in the client, and self acceptance. Rogers asserted that on the basis of clinical experience the experienced client-centred therapist rarely had difficulties in handling negative or positive transference in terms of hostility or affection. However, one of the attitudes that may cause difficulties was that which he termed 'aggressive dependence'. This was typically displayed by the client who believed that he or she was incapable of making their own decisions or managing themself, and insisted that the counsellor must take over and give more direction. Rogers further described the client with this type of difficulty as someone who may feel annoyed because he or she does not feel they are being understood, or receiving the guidance that they feel they need. Therefore, a feeling of antagonism may arise with the client towards the therapist. It is interesting to note that this description tended to fit one that was often given as an example of the dynamic of the cross-cultural counselling encounter with white therapist and Black client (Peterson et al., 1976; Alexander et al., 1976; Goldstein, 1981; Sue and Sue, 1990). We could speculate that Rogers may have identified this with Black clients more than with white. Whether this was so or not, he failed to address the possibility of this need in Black clients and what this could mean for client-centredness when applied across cultures. There is therefore the possibility that Rogers himself may have had some difficulty with the cross-cultural encounter but as a defence projected these difficulties onto the client as 'aggressive dependence'. Thus, it appears that client-centred therapy may not be client-centred when used to address client need across cultures by formulating a diagnostic category that allows counsellors to 'pigeonhole' a specific cultural need. Rogers (1965) provided us with more information that allows us to speculate further on the particular pressures that a client enduring racism may experience when he said 'transference attitudes are perhaps more likely to occur when the client is experiencing considerable threat to the organisation of self in the material which he is bringing into awareness' (p. 218), reminding the reader of the Cross (1971) model of Black identity previously discussed; this is precisely the type of difficulty the counsellor may encounter with the Black client who is at the 'encounter' stage of Black awareness where the effects of discrimination become so powerful for the client they can no longer deny they exist. Rogers (1965, p. 218) went on to say 'a true transference relationship is perhaps most likely to occur when the client experiences another as having a more effective understanding of his own self than he himself possesses'. Again, using the Cross model of Black identity, this was precisely what the experienced counsellor, familiar with the disabling effects of racism, may be argued to need in order to help lead the unaware client out of the denial stage into the awareness stage. For the counsellor who was truly nondirective, the intra-personal dynamics of distortion may be too great to expect the client to initially make sense of the disorganizing material or experience and cope on their own. Therefore, some dependency with clients experiencing racism may be inevitable and client-centred therapists, in order to be effective and therefore truly client-centred, may have to become at least initially directive in the sense of helping clients to organize and make sense of their painful experience. Directiveness may be necessary as the experienced pain of racism may disable the client in their attempts to construct meaning. The counsellor in the cross-cultural encounter needs to be cautious of Rogers' notion of 'aggressive dependency' and its potential lack of appropriateness in the cross-cultural counselling encounter.

Counter-transference

The corollary of transference is referred to as counter-transference. In counter-transference it was therapists who project the biases, prejudices and attitudes that are unresolved in their own personality onto the client (Giobacchini, 1972; Lorion and Parron, 1987; Watkins, 1989a). Counter-transference may interfere with or be destructive to the client's progress. Like transference, counter-transference was once viewed as a blockage to effective therapy (Jacobs, 1989). This was because a counsellor's feelings or views towards the client may have nothing to do with the client as an individual. The counsellor's views and actions towards the client may be a result of previous experiences with others of whom the client reminds the therapist. The client may, for some reason, trigger these feelings as a result of the counsellor's earlier unresolved experiences. MacCarthy (1988) made the point that counter-transference, based on explicit or unrecognized racist views, may significantly distort the therapeutic relationship. Griffith (1977), cited in MacCarthy's article, argued that attempts to assuage guilt by over-identification with the patient's culture, or avoidance of confrontation, as well as insistence on the universality of a patient's problems, thereby ignoring their culturally specific futures, have all been cited as manifestations of racially based counter-transference. Rack (1982) saw counter-transference as likely to be problematic whenever the counsellor and client were from different cultural backgrounds. In his view life experiences and value system differences inhibited the establishment of satisfactory connections so that empathy diminished in relation to cultural distance. If this is so, a rather bleak picture emerges for white counsellors working with Black client groups. For it suggests that cultural difference is an absolute blockage with which training will have little, if any, effect. It was seen as worthwhile to consider a feminist counselling perspective to reflect on a parallel argument existing with men working with female clients. Here the influence of gender may allow us an analogous perspective of the impact of cultural difference.

Kaplan (1985), writing from a feminist perspective, argued that an effective therapist should be more receptive to comprehending the experience of women living in a male dominated society and the associated effects. This required a capacity to be open to the communication of a woman with minimal interference from the (male) therapist's own projections, needs or conflicts that could have the effect of diminishing or negating the (female) client's experiences. She further suggested that male counsellors, were less likely to be able to confirm the validity of a female client's experience by direct reference to their own lives and that female clients were likely to raise feelings and events that challenged or disconfirmed a male therapist's own experience. This, she argued, could lead to difficulties with the male therapist drawing on areas of their emotional life as a basis for both personal reflection and intervention. Therefore, the emotional material of the client had a disorientating effect on the male therapist and could inhibit the process of therapy. We can speculate that if this was so for male therapists with women, then a direct parallel could exist with white therapists and Black clients.

Watkins (1989a) provided a helpful summary of the likely effects of counter-transference which could provide a framework to illustrate difficulties that could occur in a white counsellor's work with Black clients. Watkins questioned why counter-transference may arise in counselling and argued that to understand this the concept of identification needed to be examined. In his view, identification refers to the counsellor's ability to identify or share the client's experience, which in Watkins' view was crucial. When identification with client experience was optimal the therapist was better able to relate and understand the client and maintain an appropriate distance. When there was no optimal identification the counsellor/client relationship would be compromised as the counsellor would have difficulty in empathizing with the client. Watkins went on to discuss how, what he termed as 'identificatory pathways', and their existence or nonexistence, could facilitate or impede identification. He included the factors of : (1) similar or dissimilar values; (2) similar or dissimilar language; (3) similar or dissimilar demeanour and physical appearance; and (4) similar or dissimilar expectations which can exist to bond or separate client and counsellor. It seemed that similar identificatory pathways would facilitate counselling whereas dissimilar pathways would impede the counselling process. These pathways had both a conscious and unconscious focus which continued throughout therapeutic contact. Furthermore, Watkins saw counsellor identification as existing on a continuum. The midpoint of this continuum being optimal, the extreme right being over-identification and the extreme left being disidentification. With over-identification the counsellor could lose professional distance and become over-involved in the client's experience. Disidentification was the opposite, where the counsellor was not able adequately to relate to the client's experience, and included such behaviours as aloofness, coldness, antagonism and hostility. In Watkins' view over-identification or disidentification with a client were forms of counter-transference and interfered with the therapeutic process. This was understood to happen as a result of the client's transference reaction or non-transference reaction, which impacted on an unresolved area in the counsellor, causing conflictual and irrational reactions (Peabody and Gelso, 1982). This may happen in the event of a Black client's expressing criticism or anger towards a white person. Here, because of disidentification, the therapist could be in danger of responding defensively to the client, taking the anger or criticism as implying negative feelings about themself. Thus, a therapist could impose his or her own reality on their interchange, protecting self at the expense of confirming and exploring the client's emotions. The effect may be that the client experiences their feelings and emotions as harmful to others and enters into a cycle of self blame which inhibits the client's self expression and further damages their perceptions of self worth. Therefore, in this hypothesized interchange, the therapist embodies a persecutory encounter rather than a supportive and safe exploratory environment. Racker (1968) has suggested that therapists should attend to the possible danger of their not identifying with the client but more with the client's 'internal objects'. This can be further extended to include the danger that the therapist might identify with past or present external as well as internal objects in the client's life. It was postulated that if the therapist had more in common with others in the client's life than with the client, the likelihood of this 'other identification' would increase. Thus, counter-transference in the cross-cultural counselling situation could have an insidious effect. This may not be overcome as d'Ardenne and Mahtani (1989) suggested that counsellors were unlikely to examine their own racism and cultural prejudice and that a consequence of this was that unacknowledged feelings and thoughts could be reflected back into the therapeutic relationship. When this happens the client no longer experienced the necessary conditions for therapy to take place, i.e., those of: unconditional or positive regard, genuineness and empathic understanding. The relationship became persecutory rather than helpful and supportive, and the client was likely to terminate.

We can therefore see that in working with Black clients in the cross-cultural counselling encounter white therapists may have additional work to do in preparing themselves for the unconsidered effects of prejudice and racism within themselves. If therapy aims to help Black clients overcome negative stereotypical views of themselves and utilize their inner strengths for growth and development, therapists will need to recognize that they will be unable to accomplish this if they themselves are unwilling or unable to relinquish both seeing and reacting to a client in a disconfirming way (Greene, 1986).

4 The Concept of Attitude and its Link to Transference

This chapter attempts to relate two different concepts in psychology which have conceptual overlaps that are rarely discussed. This may be because the concepts of transference and attitude are traditionally seen as belonging to two different schools of psychology – 'transference' to that of counselling and therapy and 'attitude' mainly to that of social psychology. The concept of attitude and its relationship to the research and counselling dynamic will be explored. An attempt will be made to link the concept of attitude to the concept of transference initially through exploring possible conceptual overlaps and similarities and then, through the work of Ridley (1989), exploring some specific attitudes and transference phenomena that may be present in the cross-cultural counselling encounter.

The Concept of Attitude

This section will briefly explore the historical context of the attitude concept from its psychological development to its measurement and application in counselling the culturally different. An attempt will be made to show a link or a relationship towards the latter part of the section to the concept of cultural-transference. In reviewing the literature it became apparent that much of the material was 20 to 30 years old, and in some cases much older. Fox (1969, p. 117) has made the point that this should not cause concern to the researcher as 'research often runs in cycles, and thus there are periods of time in which a great deal of research is done in a problem area, then interests change, and then there is a hiatus of years in which little or nothing is done'.

No one discipline in the social sciences can lay sole claim to the concept of attitude. The concept belongs to many diverse areas ranging from industrial psychology and public opinion polling to social psychology. The meaning of the term 'attitude' has been the subject of extended debate in psychology. A key focus in this debate has been that of definition. The search for scientific accuracy and respectability for the attitude concept has resulted in a variation of definitions and characteristics, together with several techniques for its measurement. As definitions tend to be fine-tuned to accommodate advances in research, the attitude concept will probably continue to evolve. There are those who see attitude as purely a descriptive term implying the probability of behaviour towards or away from an object, those who see attitude as a latent mediating process which is said to be deep within an individual's personality which determines response, and there are those who see attitude as representing only the affective, cognitive or behavioural components. Indeed, definitions of the attitude concept are as plentiful as the academic areas that study it. Oskamp (1977) has cited Allport (1935) as having offered a long-standing and most widely adopted definition of attitude, this being:

> An attitude is a mental or neural state of readiness organised through experience exerting a directive or dynamic influence upon the individual's response to all objects and situations with which it is related (Allport, 1935).

There were several issues within this definition which need to be explored. 'Organised through experience' emphasized the point that attitudes are learned predispositions. The attitude a therapist adopts towards a Black client was seen as the product of experience during their maturation and development and influenced by the process of socialization e.g., their family, community, education and the media. The cultural influences they have been subjected to will determine the attitude they adopt. Experience was said to contribute to the attitude in three ways. First, from the information gained about Black people a system of beliefs were developed. This information could be misinformation creating racially prejudiced beliefs. Secondly, the consequences of previous experience or behaviour towards Black people influence the intention to act in the future, i.e., a general predisposition to act in a certain way depending on the circumstances. Lastly, the experience of Black people gained either directly or indirectly, through the experience of others, determines what they feel about Black people. This experience can be mediated through racially prejudiced views.

We can see that there is a diversity of definition, with researchers with a traditional psychometric approach agreeing (Oskamp, 1977) that the attitude concept has three sub-components:

1   a cognitive component, consisting of the ideas and beliefs which the attitude holder has about the attitude object, e.g., knowledge, opinions and beliefs;

2   an affective component – feelings and emotions. This referred to the feelings and emotions one had towards the object; and

3   a behavioural component, consisting of one's action tendencies toward the object.

Despite this widely held view of a tripartite distinction not all theorists are in agreement. Most notably, those who advocate situated discursive approaches argue that the tripartite distinction is flawed as it splits subject from object (Henriques et al., 1984; Maynard, 1995) and is therefore reductionist and of limited value. The value may be one of allowing conceptual exploration and in a recognition of the 'mundane reality' of attitude expression one should not allow conceptual distinctions to be come reified (Cherry, 1995). Oskamp (1977, p. 10) argued

> ... as honoured as this tripartite division is in tradition, and clear as it seems conceptually, there is still an important question about its empirical validity and usefulness. It is conceivable that one or more of the components are really unimportant and do not have any relationship to events in the real world. Or, it is also possible that the three components are so closely interrelated as to be indistinguishable when we attempt to measure them carefully.

The theoretical standpoint of attitudes having distinct and separate cognitive, affective and behavioural components has raised the question of consistency between the components (Oskamp, 1977). The view of separate components requires a relatively high degree of consistency between each component and if there is low consistency there should be no reason to see the three components as aspects of the same concept, i.e., they would need to be viewed as entirely independent entities. Oskamp (1977) also pointed out that if they were perfectly correlated on the other hand, they cannot be separate components, but would merely be different names for the same thing. In a review in 1969, McGuire concluded that the three components were so highly correlated that it was not worthwhile to maintain distinctions. An earlier opposing view was held by Krech et al. (1962) who found in their review only a moderately high correlation. Fishbein and Ajzen's (1972) viewpoint of beliefs, attitudes and behavioural intentions has tended to be the most favoured for purposes of conceptual utility (Oskamp, 1977) as it did not require a necessary connection between the three, i.e., the theoretical connection is looser. However, it does allow for a strong relationship under certain specified conditions. This will be discussed further in the next section of this chapter.

Kelvin (1970) offered a useful view. He made the point that the three components of attitude were best viewed as a balanced system, each dependent to a certain extent upon the others and in a state of dynamic equilibrium with the environment. As experience leads to an increase in knowledge and consequent change of belief about a topic behavioural intentions towards it and feelings about it may also alter. However, this did not allow for the mediation of experience through racially prejudiced views which may be resistant to change or continue with prejudicial consistency in negative perceptions.

Cook and Selltiz (1964) emphasized the affective component as a latent disposition, along with many other inferences, that determined a variety of behaviours toward an attitude object or class of objects. They included in the attitude concept statements of belief and feelings about the object and approach-avoidance actions. Favourable or unfavourable evaluations of the object or the class of objects could be inferred from behaviours and intentions. However, Shaw and Wright (1967) restricted the attitude concept to evaluative reactions based on cognitive processes. They claimed that this limiting of definition to evaluative reactions was an advantage in that attitude theory more closely corresponded with operational procedures and practices in the measurement of attitudes using attitude scales.

Theoretical Distinctions between Beliefs, Attitudes and Behavioural Intentions

Fishbein and Ajzen (1972) posed a theoretical approach which maintained a somewhat different distinction between the three components. They suggested that the term 'attitude' be exclusively reserved for the affective dimension, indicating a positive evaluation or favourability towards an object. The cognitive dimension they labelled as 'beliefs', which they defined as indicating a person's subjective probability that an object has a particular characteristic. The behavioural dimension they referred to as 'behavioural intentions', defined as indicating a person's subjective probability that he or she would perform a particular behaviour towards an object. Fishbein and Ajzen (1972) pointed out that a person may have various beliefs about the same objects and that these beliefs are not necessarily always related. The same situation also held true for behavioural intentions. By contrast, these authors say, all measures of a person's affect towards a particular object should be highly correlated and such responses should be quite consistent with the same person's answers to an attitude scale evaluating the particular object. A final point to note about

Fishbein and Ajzen's view of attitudes is that there was no necessary congruence between beliefs, attitude and behavioural intentions, though some writers would consider them components of the same attitude. Thus, these distinctions provide a justification for treating the three concepts as entirely separate entities. Oskamp (1977) argues that this viewpoint seemed to have both theoretical and empirical advantages over the older tripartite view of attitude components. Allport (1954) has argued that the central feature of all definitions of attitude was the idea of readiness for response. That is, an attitude was not behaviour, not something that a person does, rather it was a preparation for behaviour, a predisposition to respond in a particular way to the attitude object (Oskamp, 1977). Bochner (1982, p. 21) has stated:

> That there is a great deal of evidence … that knowingly enacting the role of a subject in a scientific enquiry markedly affect how individuals will respond to an experimental treatment, it has also been established that statements of attitude often do not accurately predict behaviour - people do not always do what they had intended doing, nor are their actions always consistent with their stated values and beliefs.

This would suggest that a cautious note must be given when trying to correlate any study of attitudes to actual behaviour of subjects under study (Bochner, 1980; Cherry, 1995). A classic experiment in the area of attitudes and their behavioural linkage was that of La Piere (1934) who travelled extensively throughout the USA visiting hotels and restaurants with a Chinese couple. It appears that there was widespread anti-South East Asian prejudice at the time. Service was actually refused once in over 200 restaurants. Six months later, La Piere wrote to these hotels and restaurants asking if they would accept Chinese people. 92 per cent of the responding hotels answered no. This suggests that there may not always be a correlation between attitudes and actual behaviour. However, rather than asking *if* attitudes and behaviour are correlated, it may be more worthwhile to ask *when* they are correlated or *which* attitudes correlate with *what* behaviour (Zanna and Fazio, 1982). Ajzen and Fishbein (1977), following a review of the literature, concluded that a close correlation can only be found when both measures – i.e., behaviour and attitude – correspond in their degree of specificity. For this study it can only be a tentative speculation that the measured attitudes and behavioural intentions will correlate, as there was no actual observation of direct behaviour. However, the aim of this study was not to make causal links with attitudes and behaviour but to examine the existing views and self reported attitudes to specific practices of white therapists in their work with Black clients.

Although attitudes influence and affect behaviour, Shrigley (1983) noted that the prediction of behaviours from attitudes was a probabilistic one and not one of a predictive relationship. This limits the degree of accurately predicting behaviours from measured attitudes until better measuring instruments, which are not available at present, are developed. Finally, Ward (1995, pp. 62–3), in a recent summary of the area indicated that:

> Despite the powerful data arising from social psychological studies on attitudes, there has been scant evidence that attitudes predict actual behaviour. This has long been a controversial issue in social psychology, and empirical research has traditionally demonstrated only modest correlations between the two ... Behaviours are affected by multiple factors including personality , motivation and situational variables.

Although there exists no literature which addresses the links between the concept of attitude and the concept of transference, Allport's view provides us with a direct link to the concept of transference. This link can be made clearer by reiterating Basch's view (1980) that transference was a specific expectational set that predisposed the client to perceive, act and react towards situations and people in a somewhat decided way. A further link to the concept of transference was the view that attitudes have a motivating or driving force. Oskamp (1977) noted that attitudes were not just a passive result of past experience: 'instead they impel behaviour and guide its form and manner'. Allport (1954) suggested this motivating force by describing an attitude as 'exerting a directive or dynamic influence'. Another important feature of the concept of attitudes to note was their relatively enduring nature. Newcomb et al. (1965) provided evidence for the relative stability of attitudes over a period of 25 years. For example, they showed that North American students' political and economic attitudes, measured when they were in college in the early 1930s, were significantly related to their voting patterns in the 1960 presidential election between Kennedy and Nixon (Newcomb et al., 1965). Also, the evaluative aspect of attitudes is commonly stressed. That is, an attitude was generally seen as a disposition to respond in a favourable or unfavourable manner to given objects. From this, Oskamp (1977) suggested that a comprehensive definition of the concept of attitude was that offered by Fishbein and Ajzen (1975, p. 6): 'a learned predisposition to respond in a consistently favourable or unfavourable manner with respect to a given object'. This definition and view of attitudes links conceptually to that of the concept of transference, as transference is a behavioural outcome of an attitude towards the client. It is behavioural in that it affects the process, content and outcome of therapy. Transference has within it a notion of set, readiness to act, a physiological basis and a degree of permanence if not self, supervisor, or client identified. Furthermore, it is learned and is evaluative in nature. The reader can then see that the concept of transference as it exists in counselling therapy relates to the concept of attitude as it exists within the psychological literature. There appears to be a definite conceptual link with transference's being a tendency to react towards the client as though they represented someone other than the client. It is attitudinal in its nature, and indeed, from reviewing the literature, appears to be a specific label for an attitude within the counselling encounter. 'Transference', like 'attitude', has separate but interrelated beliefs, affective and behavioural components.

The Measurement of Attitudes

Thurstone, a psychologist teaching psychological measurement at the University of Chicago in 1924, gave scientific acceptance and respectability to the attitude concept by quantifying and measuring it objectively. Here, what may appear as an uncritical acceptance of what counts for scientific knowledge needs to be understood within a postmodernist framework. Cherry (1995, p. 93) has argued that '[O]ne could argue that if quantification provided greater precision, it may have done so by leaving out much important detail in its unnecessarily rigid categorisation of respondents' agreements and disagreements to various statements'. This needs to be borne in mind before the methods of quantification are seen as being obviously preferable over those of qualitative approaches.

Following the psychometric tradition, Bogardus (1925), a sociologist from Chicago, had a similar idea to that of Thurstone by measuring attitudes in the form of his 'social distance scale'. This scale was a graded spectrum of questions about 40 different 'ethnic/cultural groups or nationalities'. Subjects were asked to rate these questions according to degrees of possible social affiliation, from casual visitor to marriage partner. Although Bogardus developed the first attitude scale, Thurstone has generally been given the credit, being the first to measure objectively and quantifiably the concept of attitude in the tradition of psychometrics that prevailed at that time (Fleming, 1967).

In 1932, Likert, a statistician for the Department of Agriculture, developed the first direct method of measuring the intensity of attitude. Likert took Thurstone's method of equal appearing intervals and did away with the jurying process. This process was long and laborious, where up to 300 judges could be used to rank the position that different scale items should appear. Thurstone had assumed that the jurying process had made his 11 point scaling continuum one of interval measurement instead of ordinal measurement. With Likert's scaling procedures, respondents themselves judged the favourableness or unfavourableness of items according to their own attitudes. Likert also introduced item analysis techniques to increase the scale's validity and reliability. The Likert model of scale construction was, according to Crano and Brewer (1973, p. 239) '… the most popular approach to the generation of reliable attitude measurement devices'. This section will finish with another word of caution related to that made earlier in this section. Cherry (1995, p. 93) cites Potter and Wetherell (1987) as arguing:

> The aim is futile because the variability of accounts is obscured in attitude measurement studies. One can argue that there is tremendous precision in variability – that is, the collection of details eventually adds up to a clearer picture of the phenomenon of interest in all its complexity. Whatever the case, what falls out of the discussion is a questioning of the assumption that the quantification of what people think and feel is somehow a better form of knowledge than any other possibility.

The present writer acknowledges the view that Lott (1985) has argued: i.e., that scientific truths regarding the acceptability of theory and methods are not independent of time and place and what gains acceptance and credibility today may be debated and critically challenged tomorrow. As Mama (1995, p. 9) argues, from a postmodernist perspective:

> More theoretically inclined feminist thinkers have opted not to through the baby out with the bath water … arguing that knowledge production can be enhanced and greater objectivity can be achieved if we recognise that knowledge cannot be absolute and universal.

Discursive Approaches

Following from the cautionary note of the last section, it is worthwhile discussing alternative approaches to the traditional psychometric approach. The traditional psychometric view as previously outlined is in contrast with discursive approaches to the study of attitudes. Whereas the psychometric view was that attitudes can be discerned by a quantified 'snapshot' picture in time, discursive approaches do not see attitudes as having a static or fixed position. Rather, attitudes are seen as a 'dynamic process which individuals take up and change positions in discourses' (Mama, 1995, p. 89). Thus, 'individuals have many discourses and discursive positions available to them, and the positions they take up are momentary, changing with the different social contexts and relations they find themselves in' (Mama, 1995, p. 99). Furthermore, the view is that people may have multiple subjectivities, as various positions are available to them at any given time and individuals may exist in or adopt different positions simultaneously, sometimes contradicting previously expressed positions. This is not to say that an individual's changing their views as they subjectively explore a subject shows a lack of understanding or a clear position. Discursive approaches recognize that understanding is continually being produced out of exploration and a process of movement through various discursive positions coming from social and historical knowledge and experience (Maynard, 1994; Bhavnani, 1994; Mama, 1995). Different options are available at any one time to any one individual, although not all may be available at the same time to all individuals (Mama, 1995). Ward (1995) notes that a range of alternative methods of attitude measurements are available and that no one is preferential to another, as each has its limitations and use. The main approach taken in this survey-based research is a quantitative analysis which fits the survey questionnaire-type design.

The Concept of Attitude Related to Counselling the Culturally/ Ethnically Different Client

Sundberg (1981) has stated that the attitudes a counsellor held, especially prejudice, are related to effectiveness in counselling.

Prejudice was seen as a weak competitor of the attitude concept. Prejudice was, as Fleming (1967, p. 362) put it: 'hopelessly prejudicial'. However, prejudice was useful in helping to explain the attitude concept. Attitudes could involve cognitive content, i.e., beliefs that were inaccurate and incomprehensible. In other words, all prejudices were attitudes, but not all attitudes were prejudice. Prejudice could be seen as a readiness to respond and this readiness to respond was seen as forming part of the attitude concept (Allport, 1954). Readiness to respond is also related to the concept of transference where 'attitude' was the readiness to respond and 'transference' could be seen as the actual response or outcome. As Sherif (1976, p. 230) said:

... my preferences or antagonisms (attitudes) have little consequence apart from my ties with others, apart from my reference persons and groups, apart from 'our' relationships to the other parts of society.

In other words, attitude objects could not be separated from their social situations. For Shaw and Wright (1967), attitudes were the end products of the socialization process, a process which included people, cultural products and objects, events and behaviours. Relationships existed between a person and these specific aspects of reference of the environment. Shaw and Wright believed that an attitude entailed having an existing predisposition to respond in some way to social objects which in interaction with situational and other dispositional variables tended to guide and direct the individual's overt behaviour. A further link of the attitude concept to the concept of transference was the view that attitudes were social. An attitude was said to have a specific social referent or a specific class of reference. These references could be either concrete or abstract, and take on a social significance because they had been learned in a social context. Learning may be personal, through direct experience with the referent, or it could be impersonal and indirect via learning implicit societal norms, learning from others who have had direct contact with the referent, and learning selectively transmitted information. They cited several studies (Bloombaum et al., 1968; Harrison, 1975; Kelly et al., 1977; Sandler et al., 1978) which demonstrated the negative effect of counsellors' prejudicial attitudes on the counselling process and outcome with culturally/ethnically different client groups. For example, Merluzzi and Merluzzi (1978), in a study which asked white graduate counselling students to rate case studies labelled as 'Black client', found that they rated these more positively than 'white client' labelled case studies, and therefore seemed to overcompensate with Black clients. Some of the studies looking at counsellor attitudes (Bloombaum et al., 1968) have shown that the racial and cultural attitudes were similar to those found in the general population, i.e., that prejudice and racism existed despite training to the contrary. It is useful at this point to examine what some of these attitudes found in the general population as a means of considering the attitudes that counsellors may hold. Skellington (1992) has described the attitudes of British society in discussing the 1984 British Social Attitudes Survey, the first large scale survey of its kind, and shown a society that was seen by more than 90 per cent of the adult population to be racially prejudiced against its African-Caribbean and South Asian members (Jowell et al., 1984). It appears that more than one third of white British society classified themselves as racially prejudiced, and 42 per cent thought racial prejudice would be worse in five years time. In 1986, two years later, the British Social Attitudes Report suggested an equally pessimistic picture of the perceived extent of racial prejudice for the 1990s. In July 1991 the Runnymede Trust and National Opinion Poll produced the findings of the largest national study of attitudes to racism conducted in Britain. This indicated that 66 per cent of white people thought Britain was a very or fairly racist society compared to 80 per cent of African-Caribbeans and 56 per cent of Asians. 20 per cent of white British people did not want a neighbour of a different 'race'. The survey found that racial prejudice amongst white people correlated highly with social class and age, i.e., the higher the social class and the greater the age of an individual the more likely the person was to be racially prejudiced. There were also indicators that racial prejudice against Asian people was stronger than against African-Caribbean groups. The finding that racial prejudice amongst white people showed a positive correlation with increasing levels of social class contradicted much of what the literature on attitudes has consistently indicated. For example, Shuman et al. (1967) suggested that higher social class and greater education tended to be related strongly with increased literacy levels, so that when social change occurs 'the more literate man will be quicker to perceive the change and will find it easier to redefine his beliefs' (p. 11). Whereas previously it had been established that the strongest predictor of non-prejudicial attitudes was higher education or literacy (Weissbach, 1977), the 1991 Runnymede Trust and National Opinion Poll did not support this view of an openness to social change where it related to issues of cultural and ethnic difference. Despite earlier research in the USA showing that counsellors held similar attitudes to those that one would find in wider society, the assertion that this would be true in Britain in the 1990s can only be speculative at this point, as no confirming or disconfirming evidence exists.

Ridley (1989) argued that both racism and prejudice were significant sources of adverse attitudes in counselling. Although the concepts of 'race' and racism have been discussed in previous chapters, the process variables outlined by Ridley will be discussed here as they relate directly to the attitude concept and allow the reader to see the impact of attitudes that a counsellor may not recognize or regard as adversive to counselling the culturally/ ethnically different client. Ridley argued that the seven counselling process variables he identified fell into the category of 'individual, unintentional, covert racism'. According to Sedlacek and Brookes (1976) most racism was unknowing or unintentional with most people being unaware of the damaging effects of this behaviour upon ethnic minority groups, 'it is because of this unawareness that unintentional, covert forms of racism are the most insidious' (Ridley, 1989, p. 61). Ridley identified seven prominent adverse attitudes which could arise in cross-cultural counselling and these will now be discussed in turn.

Colour-blindness

Ridley argued that colour-blindness was an illusion based on an erroneous assumption that clients who were culturally/ethnically different were simply another client (Bernard, 1953; Thomas and Sillen, 1972; Griffith, 1977; Block, 1981). Comments from the therapist such as 'culture and ethnicity do not enter into and affect the counselling relationship', and 'if I counselled Black clients I believe that I would begin to know them so well that I would not see them as Black' signalled that the therapist had a colour-blind attitude. Ridley stated that there were several causes of colour-blindness. For example, the counsellor may need to feel impartial. This may be due to a feeling of discomfort in discussing issues related to ethnicity, culture and colour, or the counsellor may feel insecure about their own views on culture and ethnicity or may have unresolved feelings around these issues. Furthermore, the counsellor may fear hurting the client by discussing issues of colour, ethnicity or culture and/or fail to understand the significance of the client's cultural background.

Colour-blind counsellors removed the Black client from the specific conditions of their history and experience. The counsellor's denial of colour disregarded the central importance of colour and ethnicity in the psychological experience of the client. This removal from the specific conditions of history and experience also simultaneously disregarded the undeniable influence of the counsellor's whiteness upon the client (Sager et al., 1972). The negative consequence or effect of colour-blindness may be the automatic labelling of deviations from white, middle class standards and norms as evidence of pathology. Ridley (1989) argued that counsellors who fail to understand the culture of the Black client tended to regard the client's values and cultural idioms as inherently inferior to their own values. Colour-blindness was one of the dominant contributing factors to the disproportionate representation of ethnic minorities in pathological mental health diagnostic categories where no mental health need existed (Edwards, 1982; Ridley, 1984).

Colour-consciousness

Colour-consciousness was seen as an illusion based upon the erroneous assumption that all of the client's problems came from being culturally/

ethnically different (Adams, 1950; Bernard, 1953, Block, 1981; Griffith, 1971; Thomas and Sillen, 1972). This was the opposite illusion of colour-blindness. A therapist who saw the difficulty Black people face solely in terms of colour, culture or ethnicity was probably showing a high degree of colour-consciousness. Ridley (1989) argued that the illusion stemmed from the correct view that many Black minority groups have been subjected to a lifelong history of oppression and control. Ridley further argues the incorrect conclusion was that these groups, and thus all individuals within them, have developed an irreversible mark of oppression that showed itself essentially as a permanently disabled personality. Often a major cause of colour-consciousness was the therapist's guilt about the discrimination Black people receive in society. In some colour-consciousness counsellors the burden of guilt for the total majority group was carried whether or not they themselves have been overtly racist, 'neurotic guilt often underlies their attempt to atone for racism for which they are not directly responsible' (Ridley, 1989, p. 63).

The primary negative affect or adverse consequence of colour-consciousness was the overlooking of what may be real counselling need or psychopathology. A secondary consequence was that minority clients may be given special privileges and relaxed standards of treatment. This resulted in an unintentional failure to offer counselling or treatment for significant mental health needs.

Cultural-transference

The general concept of transference has been discussed previously and will not be dealt with in detail here. Cultural-transference, as discussed by Ridley (1989), was a specific form of transference which referred to the emotional reactions of a client of one ethnic group transferred to the therapist of a different ethnic group. This was likely to happen where the client had previous significant experiences with members of the therapist's ethnic group outside of the therapeutic encounter. In some cases the client's feelings towards the therapist may have little to do with how the therapist actually treats the client. However, negative, or in some cases positive, feelings could be evoked in the client simply because the therapist was a member of a particular ethnic group. Ridley noted that although not the original source of the client's frustration, the counsellor may show incompetence by not responding appropriately to or handling the transference. The unskilled or uninsightful therapist may fail to recognize the transference or minimize its significance, if and when it is recognized. A further difficulty may be the therapist's inability to employ constructive interventions to resolve the conflicts underlying the transference. The skilled counsellor should correctly ascertain what difficulty that interaction with white people is causing in transference situations. Cultural-transference could reveal a client's racial motivations. Counsellors engaged in cross-cultural situations needed to be especially alert to these cultural-transference client reactions as they could be of major importance in therapy. As clients re-enact their emotions and experiences, the skilled counsellor could have a unique opportunity to work with emotional material that might otherwise be inaccessible to therapy.

Cultural-counter-transference

Cultural-counter-transference referred to the emotional reactions of the therapist from one ethnic group projected onto the client of another ethnic group. Therefore, as the concept of counter-transference, which has previously been discussed in chapters 1 and 3, counter-transference referred to the emotional reactions and projections of the therapist towards the client. The reaction could be caused by the therapist's anxiety towards the client. Ridley (1989) noted that the mere presence of the client could evoke intense emotions in the therapist similar to those experienced in past interactions with other members of the client's ethnic group. Also, unfamiliar cultural mannerisms, idioms, expressions and values could elicit intense feelings in the therapist. Ridley believed that these projections may also be reinforced because they are shared by members of the therapist's own group. Because of this shared experience, therapists were hindered in their ability to do objective reality testing. Therefore, such therapists were more likely to accept these feelings as rational responses rather than as irrational responses, or to own their own personal idiosyncrasies. This suggested that, where therapists had a supervisor who was of the same ethnic group as themselves, the opportunity for reality testing within the supervision session may be limited. Essentially, the therapist may not have an objective basis from which these irrational reactions could be judged. The negative consequence of cultural-counter-transference was that the difficulties that the therapist had could be attributed to the client. Thus, the emphasis of therapy could become oriented towards treating the therapist's projections and emotional difficulties rather than actual problems within the client. This could introduce the danger that some clients may accept the therapist's projections as a valid assessment, and those others who rejected the assessment could be seen as uncooperative and difficult, the outcome being that the client's real presenting problems remained untreated.

Cultural-ambivalence

Ridley's (1989) experience suggested that white counsellors often had ambivalent motives in treating Black clients. On the one hand, they might exhibit a high need for power and dominance (Jones and Seagull, 1977). Such counsellors had a need to maintain absolute control over Black clients. It was suggested that their need for power was motivated by insecurity, intimidation and perhaps the perception that the client may seek reprisal for injustice. In viewing this issue, Pinderhughes (1973, p. 104) stated:

> ... one problem area for many patients lies in the unconscious needs of many psychotherapists to be in helping, knowledgeable or controlling roles. Unwittingly they wish to be in control and have patients accommodate to them or their style or approach. More Black patients than white perceive in this kind of relationship the basic ingredients of a master-slave pattern.

Vontress (1981) has called the high power or control need of white counsellors the 'great white father syndrome'. This syndrome led counsellors to act in a condescending, paternalistic, and ultimately disempowering manner. Ridley argued that the danger here was that the counsellor reinforced learned helplessness and passivity in the client. On the other hand, white counsellors may simultaneously exhibit a high dependency need. In this case, counsellors may expend considerable energy in seeking security through gaining acceptance in their relationship with the Black client. The counsellor's motives may be a wish to be absolved of any guilt, real or imagined, for being racist. Jones and Seagull (1977) have suggested that some white professionals, in fact, were motivated to counsel Black clients almost completely as a result of their guilt about racism.

Pseudo-transference

Black clients respond defensively to racist attitudes and behaviours shown by the white therapist. The client's behaviour was then misinterpreted and seen by the therapist as some form of inherent pathology (Thomas, 1962; Thomas and Sillen, 1972). What the therapist did not see was the possibility that the client's reactions had a basis in reality. Thomas (1962, p. 899) stated:

> ... disturbed, unhealthy responses of the patient in the therapeutic situation cannot, however, be assumed to be necessarily transference phenomena. They may be 'pseudo-transference' responses to unhealthy attitudes or behaviour of

the therapist, and therefore not an accurate reflection of the patient's neurosis. The well known countertransference phenomena caused by an unhealthy pattern of individual origin in the therapist can produce such pseudo-transference reactions.

Thomas (1962) has suggested that clients may be especially sensitive to stereotypical attitudes shown by the counsellor as they were repetitions of their exact same experiences of everyday life. Ridley (1985) has argued that the client's susceptibility to pseudo-transference can be increased due to the greater power of the therapist and the vulnerability or dependence of the client.

Misinterpreting Client Nondisclosure

Client self-disclosure was seen as an important and necessary goal for successful therapy to take place. Despite this acknowledged therapeutic need, considerable research has indicated the difficulty that Black client groups may have in self-disclosure (Ridley, 1984, 1985; Sue and Sue, 1990; Sue, 1981). The socialization of Black client groups often conditioned them to be cautious of white group therapists. The expectation and thrust of the white therapist for client self-disclosure may create a paradoxical and threatening situation for the client. As Ridley (1989) said, on the one hand, the client can remain non-vulnerable through nondisclosure but forfeit the potential benefits of the therapy. On the other hand, the client can choose to self-disclose but risk being misunderstood through cross-cultural mis-communication. This paradox could create a 'no win' situation that was contraindicated for successful therapy to take place (Ridley and Tan, 1986). Misinterpretation of client nondisclosure results from the therapist's incompetence and inability to differentiate cultural needs from mental health needs. Whether this incompetence resides in a skill or personality base remains uncertain and controversial. As long ago as 1953 Benedek suggested that successful therapy was:

> The unfolding of an interpersonal relationship in which transference and countertransference are utilised to achieve the therapeutic aim. This definition indicates that the therapist's personality is the most important agent of the therapeutic process (p. 208).

Within the concept of countertransference there is an increasing emphasis on the mutual, interpersonal character of the therapist-client relationship, how analyst and patient influence each other at both a conscious and unconscious level, and as objects of both reality and fantasy. The therapist must acknowledge the part that they play in the counselling encounter.

It is seen as worthwhile to consider four myths that Briggs (1979) has argued many therapists bring with them to their work which can contribute to countertransference. These myths are:

1 therapists love their clients;
2 therapists are endowed with magical powers of understanding;
3 a good therapist's clients are grateful; and
4 therapists are eternally forgiving (pp. 136–7).

The significance of these myths is that counsellors cannot take the working alliance for granted, and, particularly when there are cross-cultural factors in play, issues of attitude and countertransference must be heeded.

5 Counselling Theory and Practice

This chapter will briefly consider the theoretical perspectives of the three counselling orientations identified as being the most commonly used in the survey sample questionnaire responses. The application of these in a cross-cultural setting will be discussed. In the final section, issues of power in the counselling relationship will be explored, as this was a frequently emerging theme in the survey questionnaire written response section and it seemed appropriate at this point to make comment on the significance of this in counselling, as it is an often forgotten dynamic in the literature.

In previous chapters the terms 'counselling' and 'psychotherapy' or 'therapy' have been used interchangeably. It should be questioned whether a valid distinction can be made, and if so what this might be. The term 'therapy' is commonly used in the literature as a shorthand form of the term 'psychotherapy'. However, the distinction between 'counselling' and 'psycho-therapy' is one which is often debated in the literature. No detailed attempt to review this debate will be attempted here as this was not a research objective. The reader is referred to Patterson (1986), George and Cristiani (1990), and Belkin (1988) for a good review of the literature, if desired. Attempts robustly to distinguish between counselling and psychotherapy have not met with consensus. Some practitioners think that a distinction need not be made and have used the terms interchangeably (Hahn, 1953; Patterson, 1986). Others tended to believe there was little equation between the two (George and Cristiani, 1990). George and Cristiani (1990) quoted Hahn (1953) as saying that the most generally agreed view was that counselling and psychotherapy could not be clearly distinguished as there existed differences as well as significant overlaps. Patterson (1986) was quoted by Belkin (1988, Introduction, p. 16) as holding the majority view.

> It is concluded that there are no essential differences between counselling and psychotherapy in the nature of the relationship, in the process, in the methods or techniques, in goals or outcomes (broadly conceived) or even the kinds of client involved.

This thesis, in agreement with the views of Patterson (1986), made no distinction between the theories or practice on this basis, and saw counselling and psychotherapy as having broadly similar techniques, strategies, objectives, activities and processes.

Although there has been a growing literature to suggest that there was a need to consider how appropriate contemporary counselling theory and practice was in a cross-cultural relationship, there still appeared a long way to go before new approaches could be identified and incorporated into the training programmes of counsellors. For those from a Western European focused culture, counselling theories appeared to be spiralling.

Corsini and Wedding (1989) reported that in 1984, 250 counselling approaches were documented. Two years later in 1986, Karasu documented over 400 approaches. It would be a difficult, if not impossible task to do justice to an evaluation of all these models in terms of what they can contribute to counselling competence in a cross-cultural setting. It is therefore proposed that three of the more well known and widely practised forms or orientations of counselling and therapy, as discovered in preliminary analysis of the survey sample, will be discussed in this chapter. These will be psychoanalytic, client-centred or Rogerian therapy, and eclectic practice.

Before discussion of these theoretical perspectives takes place it was seen as useful to note that scholarly interest with counselling Black clients could be traced to the 1940s, when counsellors confessed to uncertainty and confusion about their role and the applicability of counselling Black people (Williams, 1940). Since then contemporary theorists and practitioners who were aware of cross-cultural differences affecting the counselling relationship and outcome have queried whether it was better to pair the counsellor and client in respect to ethnicity or whether culture and the barriers it could present in achieving empathy and rapport could be overcome by counsellors of a different ethnicity to that of Black clients (Draguns, 1981; Lago and Thompson, 1989; Sue and Sue, 1990). Before looking at the relevance of the specified counselling theories to Black client groups, an examination of the difficulties a culturally bound Eurocentric counsellor may encounter will be undertaken, as one needs not only to examine the 'tool' but the value base of the worker which will effect competency. Theoretical orientation per se has been argued to indicate little of what may actually happen in the therapeutic encounter and does not seem to have a determining or significant outcome effect (Luborsky, Singer and Luborsky, 1975; Bergin and Lampert, 1978). Embracing one theoretical orientation in preference to another could lead us to assume that this, to a large extent, indicated the extent to which a therapist was committed to and influenced by the theory as it related to the views of the nature of person-kind, the implicit or explicit models of mental health and to the techniques of practice supported in their counselling orientations. For example, have theories of therapy promoted an image of Black ethnic groups as equal to white European ethnic groups? Have they offered advice and guidance to the therapist in dealing with issues that may be specific to Black ethnic groups in relation to culture and the pressures of living in predominantly white societies? Have the methods and goals of therapy acted to develop or restrict, validate or invalidate the self-knowledge or experience of individuals from Black ethnic groups? These influences were likely to impact on both the content and process of therapy and as such the nature of the client therapist relationship. This, in turn, was likely to have some effect on how the client saw and experienced the value of therapy, their commitment to continue in therapy, improvement in the client's personal development and evidence of psychological and/or behavioural change at the end of therapy.

It was in 1965 that Wrenn (see Wrenn, 1987), a white male therapist, wrote a paper entitled 'The Culturally Encapsulated Counsellor', stating that 'certainly the values that one holds – convictions of the worth of things and of people – are culture bound ... My values are for now and me – not for all time or for all people' (p. 392). This statement is as true now as it was then. Mama (1995), more recently, writing from a Black feminist perspective has taken the epistemological position that:

> All knowledge is socially situated. Therefore there is no such thing as value-free social theory, and the goal of intellectual rigour can best be served not by claiming objectivity and ignoring the values underpinning one's intellectual work but rather by acknowledging the commitments, motivations and conditions that are likely to have played a part in its production (p. 2).

Many contemporary writers have suggested that an important and necessary starting point by white counsellors for work with Black clients was to address their own perspectives and role in contributing to racist practice. Sager et al. (1972) have argued that too often white therapists unconsciously viewed Black clients as possessing primitive feelings and drives that contrasted with the allegedly more complex emotional experiences exhibited by white clients. A substantial amount of research coming from the United States has examined the judgements of white therapists in working with Black clients and demonstrated significant bias (Watkins, Cowan, and Davis, 1975; Schneider, Schneider, Hardesty, and Burdock, 1978; Comas-Diaz and

Jacobsen, 1991; Fernando, 1991; Rack, 1982; Ponterotto and Pedersen, 1993). The data examining the attitudes of white therapists' judgments of Black clients have found equivocal outcomes in analogue studies (Merluzzi and Merluzzi, 1978; Bamgose, Edwards and Johnson, 1980; Bloch, Weitz and Abramowitz, 1980; Stevens, 1981). Stronger evidence of racial bias on the part of white therapists came from archival and epidemiological data (Yamamoto, et al.; 1968; Mayo, 1974; Cole and Pilisuk, 1976). In general it has been noted that Black people receive less favourable treatment strategies in comparison to their white client counterparts (Atkinson, 1987; Casas, 1984; Atkinson and Schein, 1986; Kareem and Littlewood, 1992; Locke, 1992).

Counsellors in both Britain and the United States are likely to have been influenced by a huge number of theories advanced during what can be termed the deficit model era. These therapeutic models have guided clinical conceptualizations of normality, abnormality and ultimately client treatment (Wilson, 1979; Sue and Sue, 1990). Most theoretical approaches in counselling and therapy grew out of work with narrowly defined ethnic and cultural groups, almost exclusively white European or white North American, with some tendency to include Jewish groups (Franklin, 1971). These approaches have been marked in their tendency to exclude or disregard the experience of diverse cultural groups. Thus, these models have tended to be Eurocentric in their approach and in conceptualizations of 'explaining' human behaviour. Thus, psychotherapy models and their resulting psychological realities tended to reflect a European and (white) North American reality. These models of reality have often denied or dismissed the significance of other cultures ideologies and the recognition of differences, not deficits, in the behaviour, concerns and psychological reality of other ethnic groups. For example, Nobles (1976) offered a model (see Table 3) that attempted to distinguish between a Western European and African view of the world. In his argument, an ethnic group's world view illustrated its philosophy of humanity and governed its everyday relations with others.

In this model, it was argued that European values have tended to place greater emphasis on, among other things, individualism, competition, domination over nature, rigid adherence to time, value of the Protestant work ethic, a future time orientation and a striving for status and power (Shostrom, 1967; White, 1984; Katz, 1985). Nobles (1972), Mbiti (1970) and White (1984), speaking on the African ethos, and Khan (1990), on the South Asian ethos, argued that a holistic humanistic philosophy is the principle feature with these cultural groups. Here there was a focus on interdependence, collective survival, harmonious blending and a strong role for the elderly.

Table 3   Comparative world view schematic

European world view	psycho-behavioural modalities	African world view
Individuality	– psycho-behavioural –	Groupness
Uniqueness	modalities	Sameness
Difference		Commonality
Competition	– Values and customs –	Cooperation
Individual rights		Collective responsibility
		Cooperativeness and
		interdependence
Separateness and	– Ethos –	Survival of the tribe
independence		One with nature
Survival of the fittest		Experiential community
Control over nature		
Experiential community		

Source: *Nobles, 1976, p. 24.*

White (1984, p. 5), writing on the difference between African and European values said:

> The African world view begins with a holistic conception of the human condition. There is no mind-body or affective-cognitive dualism ... Emotions are not labelled as bad; therefore there is no need to repress feelings of compassion, love, joy or sensuality.

White (1984, p. 11) contrasted this with the European world view:

> At the heart of the European [sic] world view is the problem of the mind body dualism inherited from Descartes. This dualistic thinking has generated a number of dichotomies along the lines of rational-irrational, ego-id, good-bad, affective-cognitive, human-animal, primitive-civilised and master-slave.

White argued that these dichotomies have led to and encouraged debate as to which side of the dualism should control behaviour. He noted that in the Protestant ethic the feeling processes were considered the bad, destructive element in the human condition, an element that needed to be controlled by the mind. The display of emotion and feelings was seen as sinful and destructive and so needed to be resolved before one could gain self control. We shall see shortly that this notion was central to Freudian psychoanalytic theory.

Psychoanalytic Perspectives

For Freud (1856–1939) it was necessary to create the notion of the unconscious as a mechanism for the storage of 'bad' instincts, sensual drives and aggressive urges, and to have these bad instincts controlled by the good forces represented by the ego and superego. Freud developed his observations of his client group into an extensive theory of human behaviour, referred to as psychoanalytic theory. This encompassed both a therapeutic technique known as psychoanalysis and a theoretical model of personality. Other models, referred to as psychodynamic models – e.g., Klein, Jung and Adler – have emerged from Freud's original theory with modifications. Freudian personality theory was so complex that it would be impossible to present it in total here. Although an overview will be offered, it is not the concern or intention of this book to present a detailed picture of the personality structure represented by the concepts of id, ego, and superego. Nor will the intricacies of the theories of the stages of psychosexual development and their relation to psychopathology be discussed. The purpose of this book is to focus on the position of psychoanalysis as it pertains to the conception of Black people and therapeutic practice. Essentially, with psychoanalysis (the therapeutic approach of psychoanalytic theory), behaviour was evaluated within the context of early traumatic childhood experiences, the unconscious and basic biological instincts. Treatment was concerned with the interpretation of repressed feelings and motives through techniques such as free association, dream analysis, analysis of resistance and transference, confrontation and clarification, and the use of projective techniques (Pietrofesa, Hoffman and Splete, 1984; Maroda, 1991).

Psychoanalytic Personality Structures

The therapeutic aims of psychoanalysis have been reformulated over the years in the light of clinical experience of therapists and clients. In the early days, Freud (1949) was able to state the aim of psychoanalysis simply as that of making what was unconscious conscious. This was in keeping with the model he had devised dividing the mind into two regions, unconscious and conscious, between which there was a filter or sensor whose function was to block unacceptable wishes moving from the unconscious to the conscious. As Freud further developed his model through increasing clinical experience he appeared to lessen the significance in the distinction between the unconscious and the conscious, and reformulated his model in terms of the relationship between the three mental structures, the 'id', 'ego', and the 'superego'. These three mental structures or systems are interrelated and behaviour is a function of the interaction between them. A brief overview of the systems is useful to aid conceptualization.

The Id Freud saw the id as the original system of personality, composed of all that exists at birth including basic instincts. The id was the reservoir or container of all psychic energy which fuelled or drove the other two systems, the ego and superego. Freud believed that the id could not tolerate tension which it discharged immediately in order to return the individual to a homeostatic state. The principle of tension reduction was called the 'pleasure principle'. The role of the id was to satisfy the needs of the individual by decreasing psychic pain and increasing pleasure with no concern for external realities, morality or social/moral concern.

The Ego According to Freud, the ego existed to negotiate and mediate between the driving force of the id functioning at an unconscious level and the objective world of reality. It was the role of the ego to take decisions about which needs or instincts to satisfy and to 'negotiate' a socially and personally acceptable outcome between the conflicting demands of the id, superego and objective reality of the outside world. The ego was seen by Freud to be in control of the healthy functioning individual. The ego used intellect and reason to satisfy the individual's needs. The ego employed the 'reality principle', i.e., it negotiated the realistically acceptable course of action between the demands of the id and superego.

The Superego This structure represented the moral and traditional values of parents, family, community and society which were absorbed or internalized by the child. A simple mechanism for this transmission was that of praising and encouraging children for good or socially approved behaviour, and punishing or even rejecting them for bad or socially inappropriate or unacceptable behaviour. The superego had two subsystems, 'conscience' and 'ego ideal'. The behaviour which was socially unacceptable became part of our controlling conscience, which stopped further unacceptable behaviour by punishing us with guilt, shame and unease. Acceptable behaviour and feelings of pride and contentment resided in the ego ideal.

The role of the superego included inhibiting the instinctual unrestrained impulses of the id, convincing the ego to work towards moralistic goals as opposed simply to functional, workable ones and striving for perfection. The superego formed out of the ego during childhood as a result of a complex interplay between parents and children. The function of the superego was to incorporate into the psychic apparatus a source of moral guidance which is passed on from generation to generation. In Freud's (1933) view, the past, the tradition of the 'race' and of the people, lived on in the ideologies of the superego. According to Freud (1933), it was through this historically repeated transmission of authority from parent to child that a consistent morality existed to form cultural traditions. The superego, therefore, was the psychic source of authority which guided the ego along a path of cultural development which, over centuries, produces a specific culture or civilization.

Thus, according to Freud, personality was a highly complex energy system which involved a constant interaction or battle between the instinctual pleasure-seeking drives of the id, mediating forces of the ego and the inhibiting forces of the superego. Freud's view of personality and, by implication, human nature, was highly deterministic. Individuals were motivated by their instinctual or biological drives, which had to be controlled and overcome. This notion has been criticized early in this chapter by White (1984). Freud continued to speak in terms of the id as being the unconscious and the superego having links with the unconscious, but the primary concern became the nature of the interaction between them. In this revised model the ego was cast as an 'entity' serving three functions with role conflict as to which function to prioritize: the demands of the id for immediate instinctual gratification, the demands of the superego for obedience and renunciation, and the limitations or inhibitions as a result of external reality.

Difficulties in healthy functioning were seen as a result of an imbalance between the id, ego and superego arising from an imbalance of influence by one of these structures or unresolved inner conflict.

Therapeutic Goals

The goal of therapy from the Freudian view was one where the individual gave up his or her efforts to keep their impulses from awareness and began to react to situations, chiefly people, in terms of their present demands rather than as though they were repeating demands made on them in infancy. Freud (1933) argued that the intention of psychoanalysis was to strengthen the ego so as to make it more independent of the superego and to widen its field of perception so that it can appropriate fresh portions of the id as a means of achieving greater control. This was a particularly interesting view, given that the superego was composed of 'pieces' of information passed to the individual from family, community and society as a whole. In cross-cultural terms the lessening of the influence of the superego and strengthening of the ego would mean an increase in the importance of individuality and a lessening of the influence of the individual's community and family networks. This would be in contradiction to the work of Burke (1980, 1984 , 1986) and Farrar and Sircar (1986) who all argued for the increased recognition of family and societal importance for African-Caribbean and South Asian client groups. Furthermore, the work of Nobles (1976) and his concept of the European and African view as illustrated in Table 3 suggested that one of the important differences between people of African origin and those of European origin which needed to be addressed in considering appropriate practice was that people of African origin are group, more than individual, oriented. Functioning as a group tends make people more interested in the survival of the group than of the fittest individual. Thus, collective responsibility becomes seen as a more appropriate concern than that of independence and selfhood. The attempted facilitation of individuality and separation of the group or family may, within both the African-Caribbean and South Asian client groups, lead to an increase in tension and anxiety as it works against group norms and traditions. Thus, use of Freud's notion without consideration of cultural differences would mean that 'psychological health' would be interpreted as that which most conforms to the culture and values of the dominant (white) group. The effect of this may be a pathologizing of Black culture's values, and lead to a persecutory therapy which reflected in the therapy sessions those oppressions which occurred in wider society.

Psychoanalytic theory has tended to assume that the unconscious could not be made conscious except through the medium of transference. By transference, which was discussed in chapters 1 and 3, Freud meant the way in which the client would react to the therapist at some point as if he or she represented some important figure in the client's early life, but not in terms of the individual therapist's own characteristics. The psychoanalytic therapist used transference as a technique of support which enabled the client to proceed with full expression, to face feelings that have been avoided and to become aware of these feelings as they are being expressed towards the therapist. Thus, the therapist was seen as acting as a medium or catalyst for the client's expression of neurotic views.

Critics have noted that psychoanalytic theory tended to be quite limited in its view of environmental factors and cultural experiences other than those expressed by Freud's narrow middle class, female, Viennese and mainly Jewish client group (Katz, 1985). Suinn (1985, p. 675) suggested that the psychoanalytic approach, along with behaviourism, attached 'universal meanings to words, actions and events'. Thus, feelings and behaviours were interpreted using the same criteria regardless of an individual's cultural background. For example, negative transference reactions may be initiated in some clients as a result of the passive therapist's stance required by psychoanalytic relationships. This was particularly true for African-Caribbeans, who may equate the feelings of loss of control in therapy with what Maultsby (1982, p. 50) referred to as '... the old hatred, white master, and black slave relationship'. This reaction could come about as a result of perceptions of being observed and evaluated rather than supported and comforted.

Evidence for the initial psychological impact of cultural differences in interaction and communication which may endure in individuals for some time comes largely from anthropology and psychiatry. Oberg (1960) has been credited by Furnham (1988) with first using the term 'culture shock'. This involved six aspects:

1 strain as a result of the effort required to make necessary psychological adaptation;
2 a sense of loss and feelings of deprivation with regard to friends, status, profession and possessions;
3 rejection by and/or rejection of members of the new culture;
4 confusion in role expectations, values feelings and self-identity;
5 surprise, anxiety, even disgust and indignation after becoming aware of culture differences; and
6 feelings of impotence as a result of not being able to cope with the new environment.

From these criteria it may be speculated that Black clients who may be experiencing a sociopolitical need as a result of difficulties with entering white social structures may continue to experience anxiety and feel unsupported with the psychodynamic counselling focus. Although Oberg's article was brief and anecdotal, other writers have attempted to improve on the concept mainly, as Furnham (1988) noted, by placing the emphasis on different problems, e.g., Guthrie (1975) with 'culture fatigue', Smalley (1963) with 'language shock', Byrnes (1966) with 'role-shock' and Ball-Rokeach (1973) with 'pervasive ambiguity'. Furnham noted that no one has attempted to specify how, why or when different people did or did not experience different aspects of culture shock, or to specify the relationships among the various facets of culture shock, to order their importance or to suggest in which order they are most likely to occur. Boch (1970) suggested that culture shock was primarily an emotional reaction that was consequent upon people's not being able to understand, control and predict behaviour, which appeared to be a basic need. Others have attempted to understand the psychological impact of cultural distance in terms of individuals' lacking points of reference, social norms and rules to guide their behaviour. Seeman (1959) discussed the concepts of alienation, anomie and ideas of powerlessness, meaninglessness and self and social estrangement. The point being made here is that rather than experiencing a comforting counselling experience in the 'blank screen' psychodynamic encounter, Black clients may continue to feel cautious and defensive as their negative and anxiety-evoking social experience is repeated in the counselling interchange.

In looking at the mental health needs of foreign students studying in Britain, Still (1961) discovered that although 14 per cent of British students showed evidence of psychological problems, the percentage of foreign students showing psychological disturbance was higher. For example: Nigerian students – 28.1 per cent; Indian students – 17.6 per cent; and Pakistani students – 18.7 per cent. This allows us to speculate that cultural difference could generate particular difficulties for those who experience living day to day in a foreign culture. For those individuals from ethnic minorities who are long term residents in Britain the effect may be no less. Psychologically disturbed behaviour has been shown by some surveys to be exhibited by higher numbers of people from Black communities than white British communities (Nazroo, 1997; Rwgellera, 1980; Littlewood and Lipsedge, 1981, 1989). We can speculate that difficulties of meaning and interaction that occur with an individual in a foreign culture could exist not only at a societal level but also at the interpersonal level between client and counsellor where expectations of understanding and personal meaningfulness by the client are not achieved by the counsellor.

Psychoanalysis and Racism

At a global level, criticisms of Freud's theory in respect to its application to Black client groups have been related to the subordinate and inferior status between the ethnic groups that was explicit in his theory and were presented as natural and grounded in biology.

In considering relationships between different ethnic groups, Littlewood and Lipsedge (1989) argued that psychoanalysis had a strong tendency to ignore the historical relations between societies, e.g., slavery, indentured labour and colonization. Freud's view that the superego guided the ego along a path of cultural development which produced over time a specific culture of civilization lacked awareness of the influence that colonialization, enslavement or oppression could exert. With Freud's notion it was thought that culture or civilization developed independent of each other with no attempt by the economically powerful to control and dominate less powerful groups. Power has been seen as a central dynamic in cross-cultural encounters (Katz, 1984; Pinderhughes, 1989). Taking a developmental perspective such as Freud embodied in his theory, some writers have posited that power was a systemic phenomenon, a key factor in functioning, from the level of the individual where 'submission to power is … the earliest and most formative experience in human life' (Wrong, 1980, p. 3, quoted in Pinderhughes, 1989, p. 110). The power relationships that existed between individuals and groups determined whether their interactions were characterized by features of dominance or subordination or equality and mutual respect. The theme of power will be developed further at the end of this chapter. In Freud's consideration of Black and other ethnic minority groups, conflict between societies was reduced to conflicts between different childbearing practices or, as Littlewood and Lipsedge (1989) state, the Black 'problem' in Britain has been conceived as the 'fault' of Black parents. Furthermore, psychoanalysis tended to see relations between Black and white as related to Black pathology with Black cultures being static, frozen, and awaiting white European psychoanalytic analysis. The power relationship between client and therapist was not acknowledged in therapy. There was an identified need in work with Black client groups to see power as a critical and pivotal concept. Recognition of the importance of power relationships between individuals and groups could help the therapist to bring into operation strategies for achieving change in the lives of socially powerless groups. As Bertrand Russell (1938) noted: the concept of power is fundamental in those theories that were people focused in the same way that energy was of fundamental concern in the physical sciences.

It is not suggested that psychoanalysis has nothing whatsoever to offer one in considering Black and white relations. Psychoanalytic interpretations rest on a belief in the formative role of early childhood. Racism and its development has been seen as related to the development of value control, during the child's 'anal period'. This period or phase had an emphasis, in the

Freudian view, in developing a balance between input and output, a boundary between oneself and excrement, together with a preoccupation with dirt. It has been argued by Littlewood and Lipsedge (1989, p. 53) that:

> ... an accident of skin pigmentation allowed the European to use this early anal experience as a metaphor for later political realities: that black is equated with faeces, with the dirty part of ourselves.

This clean/dirty parallels white/black, us/them, in Littlewood and Lipsedge's (1989) view.

Projection, a Freudian psychological defence mechanism which allowed for feared or disliked aspects of one's self to be projected onto others, has been argued by Kovel (1970) to be a defence to which modern white society was particularly prone in dealing with its own intolerable self truths. A reductionist or fragmentary empirical line of thought allowed a split or separation between idea and feeling or thought and emotions which have been carried into social behaviour resulting in Auschwitz or the slave trade. Thus, the unacceptable bits of one's own self or culture could be projected onto another as a way of distancing one's self from personal or social review.

Emphasis on the hidden fantasies of a racist society, and Eurocentric psychology, involves every white person in a responsibility for racism and a responsibility for self examination. Littlewood and Lipsedge (1989), in their review of psychoanalysis and its relationship to racism, argued that there were certain limitations in the psychoanalytic approach.

1 It was assumed that psychological mechanisms, derived from universal childhood experience, actually generated racism rather than perpetuating it in each generation. Race riots have been attributed to 'father hatred' (Sterba, 1947) and minority groups were seen as victims of displaced aggression (Alexander, 1977).

2 We were still left with the need for economic and political understanding to explain why in a particular society racism existed and functioned.

3 Emphasis on latent racism and the unconscious guilt associated with it led to a situation where aggressive racism may be seen as healthy and even preferable to the strategies of liberal adversive racism (Kovel, 1970).

Psychoanalysis with Black Ethnic Groups

Griffith (1977), a psychoanalytically influenced psychotherapist, has argued that psychotherapy with Black clients in the USA has tended not to be successful as there was a tendency in clients to demonstrate hostility by missing appointments and by being silent during sessions. It was argued that the primitive 'character structure' of Black groups made psychoanalysis unsuitable. Psychoanalysis stressed the importance of the therapeutic relationship between client and therapist, independent of the social context in which it occurred. Initially psychoanalysis was able to ignore cultural differences between client and therapist, as in its early development both client and therapist tended to originate from the same cultural groups. As client and therapist later became culturally distinct, attempts by clients to raise issues of cultural difference were interpreted within psychoanalytic theory as 'resistance' or attempts to distance and keep the therapist at bay as well as avoid insight. Given the theorized avoidance of the culturally distinct client wishing to raise culturally focused questions, it was not too difficult to see how a Black client and/or their cultural group could become to be seen as childlike or immature in the therapeutic context as the nature of the relationship between colonialist (influenced) therapist and colonized client was already cast in adult-child terms. Littlewood and Lipsedge (1989) have pointed out that some psychoanalytic theorists such as Muensterberger (1969) have conceived Black people as childlike and thus unrepressed. The theorists have held inconsistent and contradictory simultaneous views that non-European cultures were neurotic (too repressed) or psychotic (repressed). Littlewood and Lipsedge (1989, p. 167) have further argued that in much psychoanalytic literature: 'The central theme is the same: the pinnacle of evolution is the 'optimally adjusted personality' of the white European.'

Furthermore, as women, according to Freud (1933), had weaker superegos than men, it followed that the elite rulers of the world must be men. In examining another aspect of Freud's thought, it can be seen that not only should the elite rulers consist of men, but of white, Anglo-European men. Mama (1995, p. 126) has noted that feminists in the postmodernist tradition 'have viewed psychoanalytic practice as normative: aimed at persuading women with legitimate grievances to remain in their allotted place in society'. As though it were too obvious to need argument, Freud (1933, p. 246) asserted that 'the leadership of the human species' has fallen upon the 'great ruling powers among the white nations' (cited in Hodge and Struckman, 1975, p. 182).

Reinforcing his notion that white European nations represented the higher form of civilization was Freud's acceptance of the notion of 'primitive' cultures: 'primitive men, on the other hand, are uninhibited: thought passes directly into action' (Freud, 1950). Since the advance of civilization depends on instinctual renunciation and the inhibition of instinctual satisfaction, it followed that these 'primitive' cultures were lower forms. Among the 'primitive' peoples Freud included 'the Negro races of Africa', 'the Melanesian', 'Polynesian' and 'Malayan' peoples, the 'native peoples of Australia', and the 'native North and South Americans' ('Indians').

One early psychoanalytic therapist (Lind, 1914), in examining the dreams of Black Americans, argued that 84 per cent of the dreams were 'simple wish fulfilment dreams' while Thomas and Sillen (1972) in quoting Jung, a notable analyst strongly influenced by Freud and his psychoanalytic tradition, in a discussion of his theorized cultural strata in the mind, asserted that American Black ethnic groups 'have probably a whole historical layer less' and warned white Americans that 'living with barbaric races exerts a suggestive effect on the laboriously tamed instinct of the white race and tends to pull it down'. The racist ideology was explicit. There clearly was no intention to make psychoanalytic theory or its derivatives applicable to non-European clients. Nevertheless, some attempts have been made to mesh psychoanalytic theory and practice with non-European groups.

Grindrashekhar Bose, mentioned in Kakar (1990), founded the Indian Psychoanalytic Society in 1922. Bose wrote to Freud and pointed out the difficulties of theory universality.

> During my analysis of Indian patients I have never come across a case of castration complex in the form in which it has been described by European observers ... the difference in social environment of Indians and Europeans is responsible for the difference in modes of expression in the two cases (p. 436).

Bose pointed out that the difference in Indian reactions was possibly due to the fact that children growing up naked until the ages of nine or 10 (girls until seven years of age) was culturally influential as differences between the sexes never came as a surprise. It appeared that Freud chose to ignore this observation as he did not respond to it in his letter of reply to Bose.

Kakar (1990), an Indian psychoanalyst, noted that a preoccupation of sceptics about the practice of psychoanalysis in India had to do with the question of how such an esoteric art had relevance with a cultural group whose metaphysical assumptions concerning the nature of man, society and the world were strikingly different from those societies in which psychoanalysis was traditionally developed and practised. He noted the difficulties of pursuing culturally idealized goals in a country where individualism stirs only faintly and where there is a subordination of the individual to the super-ordinate family interest. Kakar (1990) also raised the difficulty of the practice of psychoanalysis in a culture that considered societal boundaries to be obstacles and autonomy a curse. Karkar further argued that there was a danger in trying to fit the theory and practice of psychoanalysis to South Asian clients and culture, even with a culturally knowledgeable practitioner, in that in order to achieve 'relevance' and 'meaning' clients may come to be led to the point where they are providing more what the therapist wishes to hear and thus distort the clinical data beyond salvation. This is to say that the therapist, in order to generate material, may be over-reliant on leading questions. This may have the influence of going down the preferred road of the therapist rather than exploring the self identified concerns of the client.

Vontress (1981), in considering the psychoanalytic approach with clients of African origin and European analysts, drew upon the work of Fromm (1973), who pointed out that an individual's nature, passions and anxieties were cultural products. As such it seemed tenable that problems of adaptation varied from one culture to another. The techniques that analysts use to initiate the expression of material in the conscious often require therapists to draw upon their own cultural experience and theoretical knowledge to arrive at an understanding of a client's difficulties. Vontress argued that this was the major difficulty in cross-cultural therapy seen from a psychoanalytic standpoint, i.e., as 'the human psyche is culturally loaded, can healers who are not recipients of the same conscious and unconscious cultural loadings of their clients understand the revelations of the latter?' (p. 26).

Jacobs (1989), in considering the limitations of psychoanalysis, stated that psychoanalysis required considerable time and experienced therapists whose training was long and costly. Thus, one could argue that the use of psychoanalysis in developing countries may be questionable as a resource consideration alone. Furthermore, limitations in terms of client characteristics were also noted. For example, some clients may have more concern with getting rid of symptoms than achieving deeper understanding or insight. Jacobs also noted that the type of client who will find psychoanalysis questionable was the one who tended to want the therapist to take away the symptoms by 'magical words', advice or prescription, and this may relate to the difficulties Kakar (1990) noted previously in distorting clinical data. Jacobs (1989) formed the impression that a client who presented with only one symptom and felt there was nothing else in life worth talking about would not be suitable for psychoanalysis. The cultural significance of these limitations to the individual who was unfamiliar or uninitiated to Western insight therapy would appear to present a massive block to psychoanalytic efficacy. The 'limitations' of individuals may in fact be more related to cultural characteristics, not allowed for or considered in psychoanalysis, and Karkar argued that it was this cultural relativism which tended to limit psychoanalysis. Furthermore, Jacobs, in further considering the limiting factors in the psychoanalytic approach, argued that if the client was unable to relate to the therapist, both in the sense of finding difficulty in relating his or her thoughts and feelings and also in the sense of making a relationship, then it was likely that the usefulness of the approach would be questionable in terms of each holding such different assumptions that the working alliance between the therapist and client would not occur.

From this discussion we could conclude that although psychoanalysis may offer some insight into the nature of racism the theory itself incorporates racist ideology and thus its philosophical appropriateness and cultural relevance to Black client groups tended to be at best limited, and at its worst damaging and destructive. It is possible to argue from the previously presented evidence that Freud's psychoanalytic theory was thoroughly compatible with and supportive of Western imperialism and colonialism, as well as of Western racism and sexism. In Freud's view, as discussed, the world should be run by the strongest superegos, who happen to be men not women, and who happen to be from the 'higher' forms of civilization, which happen to be white European societies. 'Civilization' he defined in terms of traditional Western dualism: instinctual renunciation, control of nature, affirmation of reason and intellectuality over sensuous experience. In short, as Hodge and Struckmann (1975) have argued, Freud's basic fallacy was that of provincialism: he assumed the superiority of his own environment, and the inferiority of anything which differed from it.

Client-centred Therapy

Carl Rogers, the originator of what is now called client-centred therapy, trained as a clinical psychologist in the USA. He evolved a theory of therapy and then a theory of personality, during the years of 1930–61. Some writers have argued that although Rogers was exposed to the work of Freud in his training, he was only marginally influenced by it (Merry, 1988), in that he rejected psychoanalytic ideas about 'human nature' and its diagnostic analytical methods. Others have argued that initially Rogers saw himself essentially as a diagnostician and as an interpretative therapist, whose goal, very much in the psychoanalytic tradition, was to help clients gain insight (Schenbaum and Kirs, 1979). Counselling, as it then existed in the 1930s, was divided into two main schools, one of behaviourism and one of psychoanalytic counselling, neither of which was able to address concepts such as self, creativity, personal growth and personal meaning. Freud's view of human nature as driven by unconscious motives did not fit in with Rogers' experience of working directly with people in the process of change.

Rogers was interested in finding out what counsellors did that seemed to contribute to their clients' personal growth, and what they might do that interfered with it. He recorded and analysed hundreds of hours of client/counsellor meetings, and from the outcome of this analysis began to develop the approach to counselling that he first called 'non-directive therapy'. By the late 1940s 'non-directive therapy' became known as 'client-centred therapy' (Merry, 1988). This change of name was meant to emphasize that it was the client who was at the centre of the process, not the therapist or the therapeutic technique. Later, Rogers used the term 'person-centred' to allow for the extension of his work into education and management fields outside the therapy arena (Mearns and Thorne, 1988). Merry argued that although the client-centred approach has been taught as a simple set of techniques, this reflected a fundamental misunderstanding of the approach. Rogers saw the foundation of successful therapy as a real, authentic meeting between equals in which the client was understood, cared for and respected as a person capable of positive change and growth.

Rogers' central hypothesis was that 'individuals have within themselves vast resources for self understanding and for altering their self-concepts, basic attitudes, and self directed behaviour; these resources can be tapped if a definable climate of facilitative psychological attitudes can be provided' (1980, p. 115).

Thus, this counselling approach stressed the ability of clients to determine issues important to them and to solve their problems. Rogers (1957) published a focal paper in the development of client-centred therapy which stimulated much debate and research. He argued that three main conditions needed to be present for constructive therapeutic change to happen. These were that:

1 the therapist was congruent, i.e., authentic or genuine in his/her relationships with clients. In other words, the therapist was not just an anonymous 'expert' but was present as a person;

2   the therapist experienced and communicated unconditional positive regard for the client. In other words the therapist should have a warm, caring and non-judgmental attitude; and

3   the therapist experienced an empathic understanding of the clients inner world and manages to communicate this understanding to the client.

As discussed in chapter 3, research continues to identify therapist empathy, positive regard and congruence as being crucial in facilitating change and growth in clients. However, there were also a number of other considerations affecting the success or failure of the therapeutic process, such as the client's belief in therapy, the amount of time spent in therapy, and the client's capacity to utilize the relationship effectively, as well as the gender and ethnicity make-up of the client/counsellor dyad (Kaplan and Yasinski, 1980; d'Ardenne and Mahtani, 1989).

Rogers' view differed from the psychoanalytic and tradition in that his theory shifted from diagnosis and interpretation to listening and reflecting back to the client allowing them to take the lead. In marked contrast to Freud's irrational and unsocialized human, Rogers' (1961, p. 91) view of humankind was basically 'socialised, forward moving, rational and realistic'. Rogers' view was that deep down in the core of their beings people have no desire to strike back or hurt but rather wanted to rid themselves of such feelings. The goal of counselling was to help facilitate the release of the potential and capacities of the individual. Counselling offered a relationship in which incongruous experiences could be recognized, expressed, differentiated and integrated into the self. The idea was that the individual became more congruent, less defensive, more realistic and objective in his/her perceptions, more effective in problem solving, more accepting of others with the individual's growth, development and adjustment moving closer to the optimum. For Rogers, a client's behaviour could only be understood from the client's observational vantage point. Thus, the focus of therapy was on the client's subjective observable responses. The therapist was seen as having two primary tasks in working with the client on these responses. The first was to create the conditions in which such responses would be verbalized and explored, so that the client could essentially change her- or himself. Essentially the three therapist factors of genuineness, unconditioned positive regard and empathy, combined with the client's recognition of these factors, were seen as both necessary and sufficient for producing constructive personality change in the client (Rogers, 1957, 1975).

The therapist's second task, in Rogers' view, was to facilitate changes in the way that clients perceive and evaluate themselves. In this way the client could be freed of inaccurate perceptions and begin to become what they inherently wish to be. The therapist should not work directly to change perceptions by interpretation or exploration, but attempt to direct the client's attention to them. It was assumed that once the client learned to think in an undistorted way, behavioural change would follow. As the direction of change was within the client's control, the client did not need to develop a dependency on the therapist and neither should she or he see the therapist as wiser or more knowing. The therapeutic task was to influence the direction of the work but not to influence the content. Using this approach it was assumed that the therapist's values, biases and counter-transference would not interfere with therapy.

Client-centred therapy assumed that there was a rational course of human development that would result in a healthy, well adjusted person, as long as that course was not blocked, distorted, or interfered with by faulty learnings. It was the dynamics of this process rather than a sequence of stages which was the focus of Rogers' theory. The driving force behind individual development was said to be the 'actualising tendency' which was the need to 'actualise, maintain and enhance the experiencing organism' (Rogers, 1951, p. 487). Rogers assumed that the healthy person was aware of their behaviour and would consciously choose behaviour which was most beneficial to achieving their goal. However, as incongruities developed between those behaviours motivated by the actualizing tendency and those responded to positively by others a state of anxiety or tension could result. This could cause perceptions of reality to become distorted or denied. This was seen as impeding the normal developmental process (Rogers, 1957).

In asking what implications or applications this approach may have for Black groups it would seem that Rogers' theory has attractions for all ethnic groups. It should be noted that Rogers was one of the first theorists to begin to consider the needs and position of non-European groups. This consideration was only in terms of the effect of contact with white culture and its effect on them. In 1957 Rogers wrote (p. 437):

> ... it seems desirable that the student should have a broad experiential knowledge of the human being in his cultural setting. This may be given, to some extent, by reading or course work through anthropology or sociology. Such knowledge needs to be supplemented by experiences of living with or dealing with individuals who have been the product of cultural influences very different from those which have moulded the student.

Exploring cultural difference in 'Becoming Partners: Marriage and its Alternatives' (1971), Rogers described the experiences of a Black man married to a white woman. Rogers also wrote about the experiences of multi-ethnic encounter groups, and in the 1980s he brought together racist whites and angry Black people in South Africa. The lasting effect of this, in terms of producing the desired effect, needs to be questioned and probably suggests that if there is no motivation for change then change will not take place.

It was apparent that Rogers attempted to readjust the balance of power in the counsellor-client relationship. However, assessing his writings suggested that he over-focused on subjective evaluations. He failed to identify sociopolitical or interpersonal forces which affected white and Black people and restricted Black people's available options. By taking a phenomenological or subjectivistic point of view, Rogers did not identify the objectively observable aspects of the environment and their potential impact on the development of an individual or an individual from a distinct oppressed ethnic group. It can be said that Rogers' theory did not appear distorted in its application to Black people but neither did it elucidate developmental or therapeutic processes specific to Black groups living in white societies.

Masson (1989), in an examination of Rogers' three essential conditions for successful therapy, also gave reasons for concern. Looking at therapist congruence or genuineness, unconditional positive regard and empathy, he argued that these conditions only appeared genuine because the circumstances of therapy are artificial. Since the client was only seen for relatively short periods of time the therapist was, in theory, able to suspend judgment. If the therapist was a real person with the client (as Rogers insists should/needs to happen) then it was likely, unless the therapist was superhuman, that they would have the same reactions as to other people in real life. We do not unconditionally accept everyone we meet, Masson (1989) argued. If the therapist managed to do so it was artificial, not reality, and therefore this was play acting, or the very opposite of what Rogers claimed to be the central element in therapy i.e., 'genuineness'. There does seem to be some significant denial of reality about this issue. For example, Thorne (1989, p. 118) argued that in a client-centred therapist 'genuine acceptance is totally unaffected by differences of background or belief system between client and therapist for it is in no way dependant on moral, ethical, or social criteria. This statement, even within the counselling situation, seemed a mammoth ideal for the mortal counsellor to have to live up to and was an example of the over-optimistic, sanguine and unrealistic view of the world in which the client-centred therapist could indulge. Masson (1989) discussed the difficulties that a therapist may have with a client in that it may be difficult to experience unconditional positive regard for some instances which might include a rape or murder. Masson questions how a client should register the lack of any perceived positive regard and argues that in Rogers' scheme, because it does not encompass such negative possibilities, the client could not.

Masson continued, in a further attack on Rogers' position, by claiming that a great attraction of the Rogerian method was its simplicity: 'The ideas in Rogers' work are simple, straightforward and very few. One can learn them in a few hours' (1989, p. 240). Masson (1989, p. 241) went on to quote Harper's comments on how appealing Rogers' therapy was to therapists with little training.

> The client-centred way appeals to the young, the insecure, inexperienced prospective therapist as, at least superficially, the easy way. It is unnecessary for the therapist to have any great knowledge of personality diagnosis or dynamics, and he takes no real responsibility for guidance of the disturbed client … Any permissive, warmly loving person can readily become a therapist via the client-centred system.

One of the most insurmountable difficulties for counselling African, Caribbean and Asian clients living in white society would seem to be the lack of sociopolitical or structural context of client-centred therapy. It would seem that Rogers was not keen to address structural inequalities. For example, in a study of therapy with schizophrenics, Rogers (1962) uncovered some oppressive practices within the hospital regime. Masson (1989, p. 69), in examining this, quoted a passage from Rogers:

> … it was inconsistent with our view of psychotherapy and a part of our agreement with the hospital that the therapist had no administrative authority or function in the hospital … Any course of action seems unsatisfactory. To stand up for the patient or to fight for what are perceived as his rights is to intrude on the hospital administration in a way that will surely and naturally be resented.

It seemed that Rogers was willing to compromise his theory and ethics by coming to terms with coercion and violence for the purposes of publication. From this example one could generalize the lack of support that client-centred therapy could be expected to provide Black groups on understanding and overcoming racist oppression. This was further reinforced by Rogers' view of 'troubles' coming from within and not from the real world. Thus, the difficulties with which clients came to the therapist were not seen as initiated by society or socially caused but as self created, with the clients being at least partially responsible for the experienced tension and conflict. This appeared to reflect a position of 'blaming the victim'. Awatere (1982), speaking about Maori counselling, made a strong statement on her views when she said that she had found herself remaining cynical of both humanistic and behaviourist traditions in counselling, as both were individualistic and ultimately blamed the victim for being a victim. Awatere asserted that both traditions assume that individuals could determine their future by the mere fact of changing their behaviour. When one considered the forces of structural oppression this theoretical view was considerably weakened. Awatere further argued that humanistic traditions such as in the client-centred approach offered people an escapist route by dwelling on the self, self-awareness, self-actualization. When a person felt oppressed, it may be difficult to understand why or how to initiate change, or what change to initiate. By dwelling on the self there was no action to change the roots of the oppression, politically or socially. Awatere argued that oppressed people should, as well as looking at self, consider other strategies for change; the understanding, confronting and changing of structures or systems. With Rogerian theory the knowledge base necessary to consider and cope effectively with problems that are systemic in origin or those that have been influenced by systemic factors has not been developed. There was an overemphasis on the client as being able to conquer and master their universe and a 'victim-blame' bias whose principal theme was a tendency to hold individuals responsible and to blame them for their difficulties, regardless of other evidence. Banks (1992a) has commented on how, despite equal qualifications and work experience, Black people in Britain were still disadvantaged and discriminated against in gaining employment, and how ineffective existing counselling techniques may be in helping Black people to understand the sociopolitical nature of their difficulties. Thus, therapy becomes a way of adjusting people to meet the needs of the status quo, rather than challenging and confronting the status quo,to produce the necessary changes to produce the desired outcome. It would seem that Rogers' theory was useful for those difficulties which reside in the client's internal world, but much less useful when the client's difficulties are those of external sociopolitical pressures.

The Eclectic Practice of Therapy

As there was a dearth of British research on eclectic practice there was a need to draw heavily on North American findings to illustrate how this method of service delivery may operate in practice.

Garfield and Kurtz (1977), in an American study, noted that a growing number of therapists described themselves as eclectic. What this meant was that they claimed to select techniques and methods from a range of therapeutic orientations. In apparent agreement with Garfield and Kurtz, Dryden (1989) saw eclecticism as selecting what appeared to be best from a number of therapeutic sources, systems and styles. At face value this would seem to be a wise and useful way of practice. If this was what these therapists were doing then it may be seen as difficult to be critical of their actions, as it could be argued that this suggested a flexibility of approach which may be tailored to meet individual client needs. However, whether this way of proceeding actually meets client need may be questionable. As early as 1949, Snygg and Combs wrote that an eclectic approach led to inconsistency and contradiction, as techniques derived from conflicting frames of reference were bound to continue to be conflicting. It would appear clear that for some writers eclecticism has been considered undesirable. Brammer (1969) noted that eclecticism in counselling has referred to selecting out, or choosing from various systems or theories. Presumably the best tended to be selected by counsellors, but often no criteria of what was best could be stated with any degree of agreement. The choice, as Patterson (1980) noted, tended to be always an individual one without a theoretical framework to rely on. Also, the choices made changed with different clients as was judged expedient in working with individual clients. Therefore, prediction as to what an eclectic counsellor would do would range from difficult to impossible, as it would all depend on the individual circumstances of the client and presumably the whims of the counsellor. Patterson (1980) argued that often choices were not well integrated or systematized into any framework or generalized into any principles. Therefore, every eclectic counsellor was different from every other one. This suggested that this term to describe a particular way of working had, in practice and principle, little definitive meaning or use.

Indeed, Garfield and Kurtz (1977), in a study of 154 eclectic counsellors, discovered that 145 respondents used as many as 32 individual combinations from a diverse range of therapeutic orientations. The difficulty with this was that most combinations were ad hoc and used in an idiosyncratic way. What was discovered was that when therapists described themselves as eclectic they may not be fully or adequately communicating to clients what actually takes place in the counselling situation. Rogers (1951, p. 8) referred to the attempt to reconcile or integrate diverse schools of thought as 'a superficial eclecticism which does not increase objectivity and which leads nowhere'. Elsewhere, (1956, p. 24) he referred to a 'confused eclecticism' which 'has blocked scientific progress in the field' of counselling.

When the therapists in the Garfield and Kurtz (1977) study were asked to choose two theoretical orientations that were most characteristic of their eclectic approach the following emerged. The top five of the integrated models were:

1   psychoanalytic and learning theory;
2   neo-Freudian and learning theory;
3   neo-Freudian and Rogerian;
4   learning theory and humanistic; and
5   Rogerian and learning theory.

Furthermore, Garfield and Kurtz discovered that while about 40 per cent of the eclectic respondents had not previously adhered to any one theoretical perspective, the other 50–60 per cent had. It appeared that for those with previous theoretical allegiances the largest movement occurred in the shift from psychodynamic approaches to eclectic approaches. This may represent a dissatisfaction with the rigidity of psychodynamic approaches in meeting diverse client needs.

In another American study, Prochaska and Norcross (1983), with a sample of 410 psychologists, found that 30.2 per cent chose 'eclectic' as most descriptive of their therapeutic orientation. Asking the subjects to select one out of the list of counselling orientations underpinning their eclectic approach showed that 45 per cent practised psychodynamic, 24.6 per cent humanistic and existential, 17.5 per cent behavioural and 12.8 per cent an unlisted or 'other' orientation. It appeared that psychodynamic and psychoanalytic approaches are an influential and dominant feature in the mix of eclectic practice.

In asking eclectic therapists to 'define or explain your eclectic theoretical view', Garfield and Kurtz (1977) found that 72 out of their sample of 154 replied that they used 'whatever theory or method seemed best for the client'. The researchers suggested that the sample believed that pragmatic approaches were selected to meet the individual needs of the client. However, it had been previously suggested in the writings of Patterson (1980) that this may mean choices were haphazard and not part of a systematic framework of principles.

Nineteen respondents in the Garfield and Kurtz study replied that they used and integrated two or three orientations in therapeutic practice. Twenty-two respondents claimed an amalgamation of orientations or aspects of these. The research of Garfield and Kurtz (1977) and Norcross and Prochaska (1982), while interesting in its descriptive account, did not provide the necessary detail of what eclectic therapists actually do in the counselling situation in terms of responding to clients to be able confidently to criticize the value of eclectic approaches.

Carkhuff and Berenson (1967), Thorne (1967) and Brammer (1969) attempted to bring some meaning to the term eclecticism and labelled their approach as 'eclectic stance', claiming it to be systematic but open, although they did not explicitly define eclecticism. The eclectic stance was a 'recognition that no one theoretical orientation or series of techniques is adequate to deal with the complexities of multiple persons' (p. 6). Eclecticism was, or should be, a systematic, integrative theoretical position, whereas the atheoretical, unsystematic approach to which the term eclecticism has been applied is 'syncretism', and not a true eclecticism (English and English, 1958). Patterson (1986) saw eclecticism as differing from the mono-theoretical positions of schools in that it was more comprehensive, attempting to integrate or synthesize the valid or demonstrated elements of narrow or restricted theories. However, Patterson did not recognize a sharp line between eclecticism and any other theoretical approach to counselling, as many practitioners would argue that they are not rigid or dogmatic but recognize the tentativeness of their approach. Eclecticism was seen as a more comprehensive, loosely organized set of techniques or approaches than a formal model, and attempted to be all inclusive. It should be noted that the development of an eclectic position requires the availability of a number of theoretical positions which, while lacking in comprehensiveness and inclusiveness, have a demonstrated validity in terms of experience and of research. Although some, such as Dryden (1989a), would doubt that such systems exist, it could be argued that practitioners should not wait for complete validation of schools of therapy to go beyond what is known in order to integrate different models. Thorne (1967) argued that a true eclectic position was not a hotchpotch of disconnected facts, torn from context, unrelated to any unifying structure, lacking in global perspective, unsupported by valid theoretical models, and barren as to a research stimulating hypothesis. Thorne argued that true eclecticism was the opposite of this since it utilized theoretical unifying principles from various schools to interrelate and integrate pertinent facts from all sources. It was seen as inductive rather than deductive. He said:

> Instead of starting with theoretical preconceptions and then checking the fit of the facts to the model, the eclectic practitioner usually proceeds inductively gathering and analysing the data and only later attempting to construct

explanatory theories ... their main problem in all clinical work is to discover the organisational dynamics of the person under study rather than to invent one out of the possible theories. (p. 43)

Dryden (1989a) has noted that to refer to the eclectic approach to therapy fell prey to a notion of a 'uniformity myth'. In reality, eclecticism may be approached from a variety or multitude of different avenues. Bernard et al. (1989) noted that existing research had not been able to distinguish any consistency differences between those therapists who identified themselves as non-eclectic except for the variable of clinical experience. They cited research (Walton, 1978; Norcross and Wogan, 1983; Norcross and Prochaska, 1982) which indicated that therapists who showed a preference for eclecticism tended to be older and more experienced than those who adhered to one theoretical orientation. Thus, it was possible that, with greater experience, diversity and flexibility may evolve.

Dryden (1989a) attempted to describe a number of different types of eclecticism, some of which are described here for the purposes of this thesis.

Theoretical Eclecticism

Therapists using this approach were argued by Dryden to follow a particular therapeutic orientation but did use particular techniques developed in other orientations that were consistent with their own orientation. In doing so, Dryden argued they were acknowledging the technical limitations of their own orientation and believed that the effectiveness of their approach to counselling could be enhanced by use of techniques from other schools.

Combination Eclecticism

Dryden argued that combination eclectics attempted to integrate two or more approaches in therapy at a 'high order level'. However, as Garfield and Kurtz (1977) have shown, the most popular of the combined approaches were those of psychoanalytic and learning theory. One needed to be both cautious and sceptical of this 'high order' attempt at integration. Yates (1983) considered this impossible as the two orientations had fundamentally different assumptions on the 'nature of man' and epidemiology. However, Wachtel (1977) argued that such an integration of models was both possible and useful as it provided the therapist with a wide range of practice options. The difficulties that may be involved in attempting to integrate these two approaches as they related to different theoretical assumptions could be considered in the structure of the unconscious. With psychoanalytic or psychodynamic schools there was a focus on the underlying conflicts and needs which the client was said to have little awareness of. With a behavioural approach there was more commonly a focus on the development of alternative behaviour patterns and ways of changing interfering environmental concerns. Bernard et al. (1989) argued that although the concept of the unconscious seems to suggest incompatibility between the two schools of thought, this was only the case if one compared classical psychoanalysis and radical behaviour therapy, i.e., if one compared the two extremes. Contemporary psychodynamic therapists (e.g., Wachtel, 1977; Garfield, 1980; Mahoney, 1980) began to recognize the importance of conscious thoughts, action and environmental factors just as behavioural therapists have recognized the importance of cognitive factors and the importance of 'implicit thoughts'. Meichenbaum and Gilmore (1984) have indicated that all therapies deal either directly or indirectly with the clients hypothesized cognitive structures. They have argued that the psychodynamic goal of making the unconscious conscious parallels the cognitive-behavioural therapists' attempts to have clients identify automatic assumptions about themselves and others. Thus, there was some tentative evidence for a convergence with seemingly differing schools of thought.

Technical Eclecticism

Dryden quoted Lazarus (1981) as describing technical eclecticism as an approach that 'implies using many techniques drawn from different sources without also adhering to the theories or disciplines that spawned them'. Such practitioners were argued to be more concerned with pragmatic clinical issues than theoretical ones and focused on what technique worked for whom, and under what particular conditions.

Lazarus (1981) has developed an approach described by Dryden (1989a) as an example of technical eclecticism – it is called 'multi model therapy'. One of the criticisms levelled at the behaviour therapies was that they addressed themselves specifically to the symptom or pathology rather than to the more complex interactive and psychological difficulties in the client. Lazarus (1981), recognized that most problems were interactive throughout different areas of a person's functioning, attempted to identify specific areas where treatment interventions should take place and to develop effective strategies for implementing these interventions. While this was a behavioural approach, it went beyond the limits of most behavioural approaches and focused on the total person in all areas of functioning (Belkin, 1988). However, Dryden (1989a) argued that this model rested on a set of basic theoretical assumptions which were not closely related to Lazarus' pragmatic clinical approach.

Integrationism

The therapeutic integrationist approach was described by Garfield (1982) as one where the therapist attempted to delineate and operationalize some of the common variables which seemed to play a role in most psychotherapies (see Table 4) and to use this as a basis for a clearer delineation of therapeutic principles and procedures. Dryden (1989b) pointed out that apart from behavioural procedures being shown by some studies to be more effective than non-behavioural procedures for selected disorders, there was no clear cut superiority of any therapeutic orientation over others. Therefore, in Dryden's view, the search for therapeutic variables needed to be shifted to the level of looking for therapeutic factors which counselling orientations have in common. Table 4 shows how Hansen et al. (1977) saw the commonality of therapeutic factors in therapy among several major theories and research investigations.

Garfield (1980, 1982), was a leading writer in this area, and has indicated the following therapeutic variables as being common to different therapeutic approaches:

1   the therapist/client relationship;
2   interpretation;
3   insight and understanding;
4   catharsis;
5   emotional expression and release;
6   reinforcement in psychotherapy;
7   desensitization;
8   relation;
9   information in cognitive-therapy;
10 reassurance and support;
11 modelling;
12 confronting one's problems;
13 clarifying and modifying client expectations;
14 providing a credible therapy framework; and
15 credible rationale for treatment.

Table 4   **A comparison of the facilitative conditions of counselling by theory**

	Rogers	Adler	Horney	Sullivan	Alexander
1	Congruence implicated	–	–	Personally	–
2	Empathy	Understanding	Understanding	Awareness	Understanding
3	Positive regard	Friendly way	Friendly interest	–	–
4	Unconditional regard	–	–	–	–
5	–	Intuitive guessing	–	–	–

	Dollard and Miller	Wolpe	Shoben
1	–	–	–
2	Empathy	Empathy	Understanding
3	Acceptance Positive outlook	Respectful seriousness	Warmth
4	–	–	–
5	Mental freedom Restraint	Communicate desire to serve	Nonretaliatory Permissiveness Honesty of communication

	Van Kaam	Dreyfus	May
1	Sincerity	Openness	Encounter
2	Acceptance	Understanding	Empathy
3	Gentleness	–	–
4	Nonjudgemental	Letting-be	Nonthreatening atmosphere
5	Creativity	–	–

	Fiedler's study	Truax's study	Carkhuff
1	–	Genuineness	Genuineness
2	Understanding	Accurate empathy	Empathy
3	Warm interest	–	Positive regard
4	–	Nonpossessive warmth	–
5	–	–	Concreteness
		Immediacy Confrontation	

Source: Hansen et al., 1977.

There would seem to have been some overlap with those variables identified by Hansen et al. (1977) and Garfield's view. Garfield saw the effectiveness of therapeutic procedures and techniques as being derived from the potency of one or more of the common factors in the list above. Dryden (1989a) argued that the approach of looking for commonalities in therapeutic practice gave therapists a broader perspective for viewing the therapeutic value of widely different techniques and provided them with the possibility of using alternatives.

Haphazard Eclecticism

Dryden has discussed those whom he describes as 'haphazard in their therapeutic approach' and suggested that there were those who deserved this label, although he offered no evidence in support of his statement. He described those under this label as people who attended weekend workshops and 'try out techniques on the next few unfortunate clients whether or not their clients' problems warrant such methods' (1989a, p. 351). He claimed that such 'therapists' wander around in a daze of 'professional nihilism', experimenting with new fad methods indiscriminately. Dryden continued to condemn this type of practitioner with the statement:

> Haphazard eclectics have a very restricted view of psychotherapy, tend to overvalue the therapeutic potency of techniques, underplay the value of developing and maintaining a therapeutic alliance and do not have a thorough understanding of common therapeutic variables and their importance (p. 351).

Clearly this type of practice would be worrying for any client group. The significance of eclecticism as a way of working with Black client groups becomes apparent when one considers the view of Dryden that eclectic therapists tended to be guided by theoretical concepts which are determined by a set of personal factors. What Dryden appeared to be implying was that eclectic therapists choose methods according to personal preference and personal 'philosophy of life'. Whether this included a Eurocentric, philosophical model is worthwhile considering.

Standal and Corsini (1959) have shown how a number of therapists described how they handled what they termed 'critical' incidents in counselling. The conclusion they drew from this data was that critical incidents were often handled in a spontaneous or intuitive fashion which therapists did not fully comprehend at that time, or indeed later, after some reflection. Their attempts to understand their actions may be described as post hoc rationalization (Dryden, 1989a). Thus, it would seem fair to comment that therapists steeped in both white European cultural experience and theory could draw upon this as a 'instinctual frame of reference' when considering critical incidents with Black client groups, particularly when one considers that, as has been argued by Standal and Corsini (1959) and Dryden (1989a) some eclectic therapists adopt a theoretical perspective that suits them personally. One has to question whether this has any therapeutic utility or validity in general, and specifically in working with cross-cultural encounters. Therapeutic alliance implications appear to suggest that it is valuable for therapists to discuss openly with their clients different methods and approaches that could be used to enhance therapy (Dryden, 1989a). Allowing the client to involve themselves in the selection of the most appropriate method would seem beneficial to outcome and there is evidence to suggest that clients who were involved in selecting techniques, and presumably therefore therapists, did better in therapy than those who received a randomly assigned or non-preferred treatment (Devine and Fernald, 1973). This may be due in some part to the findings of Bordin (1979) in looking at therapeutic alliance, that the probability of effective therapy was enhanced if therapist and client had a shared understanding of the nature of the client's problems. This appears an obvious assumption and was seen as particularly pertinent to the consideration of the needs of the culturally different client encountering the Eurocentric counsellor.

Thorne (1989) and Book (1988) have argued that from the variables previously indicated by Garfield (1980, 1982), one of the most important was that of the counsellor-client relationship. If clients did not believe that a therapist truly understood their problem or were uncertain about the therapist's interest in them, the chances for a successful therapy were much reduced. This was seen as true even if the therapist objectively did understand the problem quite well and was interested in the client. Thus, client belief about a therapist, independent of therapist understanding, was important. This was likely to be a significant consideration in cross-cultural therapy as it was related to client perceptions of empathic connectedness which were discussed in chapter 3.

Culturally Connected Approaches

If Western models are claimed to be Eurocentric and thus invalid in their approaches to Black client groups, this begs the question of what alternatives exist and how they differ from current Western models. One such alternative was the transcultural counselling approach suggested by d'Ardenne and Mahtani (1989). They stressed that their approach 'offers a perspective on counselling rather than a particular school of thought' (p. 5). They provided criteria of the essential components of transcultural counselling which were:

1   a counsellor's sensitivity to cultural variations and the cultural bias of their own approach;
2   a counsellor's grasp of cultural knowledge of their clients; and
3   a counsellor's ability to face increased complexity in working across cultures.

They stressed in (3) above that this did not suggest more problems to face in counselling the culturally different but more a shifting of possible prejudice and work in an area which may be new with little prior experience to consider appropriate direction. d'Ardenne and Mahtani then moved on to highlight other components that they argued needed to be emphasized, such as the role of transference and counter-transference (which was discussed in chapter 3) the establishment of professional boundaries and the realization that those seeking counselling were in personal transition, perhaps within 'an alienating and often hostile environment' (p. 7). These components, except for the recognition of environmental factors, did not differ markedly from the previous counselling models and would seem, as discussed in chapter 2, to follow an emic perspective (Pike, 1966) which acknowledges the particular needs of individuals within their own cultural framework, rather than starting with an assumption of needs from a position of no knowledge of the culture of the individual with which the counsellor aims to work. However, a further significant component of the model suggested by d'Ardenne and Mahtani was the need for transcultural counsellors to be able to examine 'their own cultural assumptions and face the fears they themselves might have of being separated and alienated' (p. 7). d'Ardenne and Mahtani were of the view that the term 'transcultural' as opposed to 'cross-cultural' 'emphasises the common experiences and tasks facing clients and counsellors, who are aware that their values, assumptions and practices are not absolute' (p. 7). d'Ardenne and Mahtani readily admitted that they did not consider their stance on culture to be neutral owing to their observations of many ethnocentric counsellors. The writers adopted a moral position on the importance of positive regard of a client's culture which they argued provided them with an underlying framework for practice. One of the central tenets of their view in adopting a moral stance of positive regard for a client's culture was that they assumed 'that at present, the majority culture is hostile to people from other cultures' (p. 12). This view would seem to be consistent with Tajfel's (1978, 1987) out-group, in-group postulations. d'Ardenne and Mahtani argued that this showed itself in counselling, ranging from 'counsellors blaming their client's cultures for the problem, to being ignorant and patronising towards clients' (p. 12). d'Ardenne and Mahtani assumed that once counsellors became culturally sensitive and aware they would provide a more effective transcultural service for their clients. They did not, however, provide a definition of what they meant by 'aware'. This awareness might be one of cognitive knowledge as opposed to the more meaningful experience, suggested by Rogers (1951), of living with or dealing with people who were culturally different, or Pinderhughes' view (1989), which stressed the importance of making emotional connections with a client and their cultural difference. Awareness of the cognitive knowledge variety may not be sufficient on its own. The emphasis of this model, unlike traditional models, would appear to be the recognition that individuals could not be removed and worked with independent of the social and political context in which they developed. In transcultural therapy the client's difficulties were recognized as inextricably linked with the wider social context and therapists were encouraged to broaden their focus to include an examination of the individual's political and social environment (Skodia, 1989). As with other therapies, it was based on the relationship between client and therapist but there was an emphasis on acknowledging and working with difference.

Another alternative model is the Afri-centric model based on Afri-centrism which has been defined as 'the belief in the viability of people, customs, beliefs and behaviours emanating from African lands' (Jackson, 1986, p. 132). Related to this view was the consideration of 'the survival of the community and harmony with nature, resulting in values and customs built on co-operation, collective responsibility and interdependence' (Semaj, 1984, p. 162). Afri-centric models, unlike traditional European models, acknowledged the estrangement of all people of African origin from the inherited cultural roots while holistically examining the consequences of such alienation (Baldwin, 1980). A growing focus of counselling was the growing realization of the need to work with cultural factors in the therapeutic process (Jones, 1984; Kareem and Littlewood, 1992). This was beginning to shape the 'culturally different model'. Unlike the deficit model predecessors, the rationale of this model was the recognition that, rather than assuming a universality of behaviours, cultural minority groups were often bi-cultural and needed to be worked with in relation to these particular 'interlinked' cultural frameworks (Katz, 1985). At present there is no South Asian equivalent to the Afri-centric model. This may be due to the fact that most people of South Asian background have not been separated from their countries of origin by force, i.e., slavery, and as such have not been involuntarily separated from their language, religion and cultural roots. These, for the most part, remain intact, so that cultural patterns are explicitly bound up in religious practices and routes of family transmission in daily interaction. At this point the need for a politicized exploring and regaining of lost cultural history is perhaps much less than with those of African origin, particularly those who were forcibly separated from their cultural roots, i.e., African-Americans and African-Caribbeans. Also, most South Asians are able to identify their family place of origin, often with the actual detail of village, town or city known, which culturally roots them in a geographical context. This is not so for most African-Caribbean people. Therefore, for South Asian clients, as an ethnic group, loss of cultural roots may be less of a problem than with people of African-Caribbean origin and the need for a politicized specific movement of recognition of the need to *regain* the lost culture appears much less. There are, of course, organized movements to *maintain* the cultural background of South Asian groups, for example, Islamic schools.

The Relationship of Power, Client and Therapist Interaction

The concept of power as it influenced the interaction between the client, therapist and the sociopolitical environment in which they live their daily lives was first raised in this chapter. The view taken was that power was a central dynamic in cross-cultural encounters. d'Ardenne and Mahtani (1989) have argued that not only do all counsellors enjoy a position of power, but that in a cross-cultural setting this position is compounded by the discrepancy of status that existed between cultures. Pinderhughes (1989) has argued that in the main the issue of power and lack of power inherent in the roles of the therapist and client, their cultural group status and how this affects process and outcome has been largely ignored in the counselling literature. An attempt has been made to illustrate to the reader how the concept of power in counselling theory and technique has not been considered as one of central significance in the role of counselling. In helping us to understand the complexities of power and the various levels at which it exists, it was necessary to consider some possible definitions. Heller (1985, p. 30) has defined power as 'the capacity to produce the desired effect on others; it can be perceived in terms of mastery over self as well as mastery over nature and other people'. Wrong (1980, p. 2) has argued that 'power involves the capacity to influence for one's own benefit the forces that affect one's life'. Power can be seen in the role of the therapist who is seen as the expert who 'treats' whereas the client seeks guidance with their difficulty. d'Ardenne and Mahtani's (1989) view was that in the cross-cultural counselling encounter where the counsellor was from the dominant culture, the counsellor was likely to be seen as having both the professional, cultural and presumably personal power. Freud was quite explicit about his view of the power inherent in the role of the therapist. He wrote that 'analysis is a situation in which there is a superior and a subordinate' (quoted in Masson, 1989, p. 41). Thus, it could be argued, as did Masson (1989), that if any disagreement between the client and therapist took place it was assumed that the therapist was more likely to be right as the therapist was 'more objective, more disinterested, more knowledgeable and more experienced in interpreting human behaviour' (Masson, 1989, p. 41) than was the client. Here we may speculate that therapists, as Bell (1989) has suggested, may make use of their power to support and boost their own needs. Thus, therapy for the powerless could be an essentially oppressive experience. Earlier writers such as Ferenczi (1932), writing from a psychodynamic perspective, argued that therapy infantilized clients and that, far from helping them to overcome difficulties, therapy resubmerged them in an infantile relationship in which the therapist emerged as the powerful individual (quoted in Masson, 1989). Thus, as Pinderhughes (1989, p. 111) has asserted 'they [therapists] may use their helping role to reinforce their own sense of competence by keeping subordinates in a one-down position as patients, incompetents and persons needing help'. To some extent it could be argued that Rogers attempted to address the power imbalance in the client-therapist dyad. He altered the traditionally preferred 'patient' to client and called his approach 'client-' or 'person-centred' or 'non-directive', which could be seen as attempting to relocate the traditional balance of power and control in the therapist's activity. He actively avoided the use of jargon or professionalistic labelling and criticized the 'medical model of illness', and the medical hierarchy that was so prevalent in his time. However, he did not address the sociopolitical factors or external forces which both helped to create and maintain people's distress. It was as though, despite Rogers' emphasis on empathy and being with the client, he believed that the difficulties that people encountered in therapy were not socially caused but self created and maintained, focusing on distress as simply internal, with no external forces at work. Black clients need to experience themselves as competent and valuable and not imprisoned in the status quo of a subordinate cultural group hierarchy that blocks them achieving their goals. As Pinderhughes (1989, p. 111) has so well put it:

> ... when they [therapists] fail to help clients change negative cultural identity; do not help them change perceptions of being powerless and victims; do not help them learn to behave in ways that do not collude in their own victimisation, in the victimisation of their group or in the aggrandisement of helpers and their cultural groups, they reinforce powerlessness in their clients. These behaviours signify that helpers are meeting their own needs for a sense of power by exploiting their client's failure to have acquired it .

When one considers the basics of racism, as Katz (1984) has written, where its development and perpetuation rests with white people who have created policies and practices that serve their advantage and benefit and continue to oppress minorities one can see that Eurocentric counselling theory and practice is inextricably linked to what is a philosophy and technique that attempts to alter people to fit in with oppressive regimes, rather than offer a basis for personal and political challenge. Bell (1989) has argued that it must be understood that those people with the least power in British society are the most vulnerable to mental health problems and also the least likely to be offered non-invasive methods of help which could address the external sources of their distress. Women, Black ethnic groups and unemployed people are all over-represented in the mental health system (Cochrane, 1979; Littlewood and Lipsedge, 1989).

6   Research Methodology

Previous chapters have considered the contextual and theoretical underpinning of the research as a whole. As previously discussed in the first chapter, the aims of this research were to examine the existing attitudes and self reported specific practice orientations of white therapists in their work with Black clients. A secondary aim was to identify what influenced the ability of counsellors to work appropriately with the culturally different. This chapter will describe the research methodology, and discuss the design and conduct of the collection of data for the survey and fieldwork element of the study. The intention is to provide the reader with insight into the data collection techniques and support the integrity of the measures used and thus the research findings.

Theoretical Considerations

As early as 1970 Webb and Salancik argued that knowledge of attitudes tends to be:

> ... anchored in information collected from a single method in restricted settings – verbal reports in the laboratory ... Interviews and questionnaires may intrude as a foreign element into the social setting they would describe; they may create as well as measure attitudes; they may elicit atypical roles and responses; and they are limited to those respondents who are accessible and who will co-operate (p. 317).

While this may be true, it is one of the accepted constraints of employing the 'scientific method' where there is a need for the situational control of independent variables to observe measurable changes in manipulation of dependent variables. Webb and Salancik expanded their critique to argue that although the definition of a social attitude solely by responses to a list of questions is 'eminently legitimate' it may be naive to believe that Likert response categories can assess an attitude in its entirety adequately, as there are inherent risks in self report information. Every data gathering method has its own specific bias (Webb et al., 1966). Reference has been made throughout the preceding chapters to the feminist postmodernist school of thought which has argued that the notion of disembodied or value-free truth is problematic (Maynard, 1994; Bhavnani, 1994; Mama, 1995). Such writers have argued rightly, in the present writer's view, that: 'knowledge production can be enhanced and greater objectivity can be achieved if we recognise that knowledge cannot be absolute and universal' (p. 9). This is to say that all knowledge is socially situated and 'the goal of intellectual rigour can best be served not by claiming objectivity' (Maynard, 1994, p. 2), but by an acknowledgement of the values and motivations that have contributed to the production of the knowledge. The present writer takes the view held by Bacchi (1990) that in any analysis of 'race' and culture there is a need to shift the analysis from one of cultural issues alone to the social relations which convert this difference into oppression (Maynard, 1994) and that the processes of racism and racial oppression might be better understood by some focus on issues of white privilege and power (Maynard, 1994; Bhavnani, 1994).

Although a considerable amount of research on attitudes is done with the subject's being aware of the content focus of the study, this need not present methodological concerns as long as the researcher is aware of this and takes steps to correct explicit bias. One way of overcoming the bias of any single approach is to 'converge on knowledge by simultaneously considering information from multiple variants within multiple data classes' (Webb and Salancik, 1970, p. 318). Thus, some issues of subjectivity may creep into any method as a single approach. When a more holistic view is required a single method may not be adequate to generate the data required. Control over possible error or bias stemming from a simple method of attitude data collection can be minimized by the use of additional data collection methods or multiple approaches. The use of multiple methods increases the objectivity of data collection. This approach is also suggested by Burgess (1984), who has encouraged researchers to pursue a range of methods when dealing with complex questions. Cohen and Manion (1985) have argued that this multiple technique or triangulated approach, particularly where it combines qualitative and quantitative methods, leads to greater flexibility which increases the validity and generalization of the gathered data. The investigator can therefore be more sure that the collected data and consequent outcome is not simply an artefact of one specific method. Furthermore, as Hitchcock and Hughes (1989) note, the combined use of several methods may help in gathering additional and supplementary information.

The Research Methods Employed

A questionnaire supported by a semi-structured interview using a sub-sample of 20 counsellors who responded to the questionnaire was used. In addition, the responses of counsellors in professional training were collected by giving a video response rating scale after observation of one of three video trigger scenes to ascertain the strategic orientation or self reported specific practices of counsellors towards a South Asian, African-Caribbean or white European female client. The methodological detail of this will be expanded later. Due to copyright restrictions the video response rating scale cannot be reproduced and the reader is referred to the original text of Brody (1990).

All interviews were tape recorded to prevent the interviewer's time and attention having to be given over to note-taking during the interview and, where appropriate, individual interviewees were asked to clarify their answers and provide further information. To take the discursive position as discussed in chapter 4 into account, interviewees were encouraged to explore their subjectivities and were never guided away from such exploration. There was a recognition that valuable material could come from the individually preferred 'verbal paths' of the interviewed counsellors and as such the interview proforma acted as a framework for subject entry rather than a 'straitjacket' to restrict individual response.

The questions for the semi-structured interview were composed from issues raised by the 'comments sheet' of the questionnaire. Commonalities of themes from the counsellors' comments were collated into questions to allow counsellors to explore issues that were indicated, as both useful and necessary for exploration. Creswell (1994) has stated that flexibility exists in the reduction of interview data into meaningful categories. He has suggested the use of Tesch's (1990) eight steps in doing this. These were seen as useful guidelines. The steps were:

1   get a sense of the whole. Read through all of the transcriptions carefully. Perhaps jot down some ideas as they come to mind;

2   pick one document (one interview) – the most interesting, the shortest, the one on the top of the pile. Go through it, asking yourself: What is this about? Do not think about the 'substance' of the information, but rather its underlying meaning. Write thoughts in the margin;

3   when you have completed this task for several informants, make a list of

all topics. Cluster together similar topics. Form these topics into columns that might be arrayed as major topics, unique topics, and leftovers;

4   now take this list and go back to your data. Abbreviate the topics as codes and write the codes next to the appropriate segments of the text. Try out this preliminary organizing scheme to see whether new categories and codes emerge;

5   find the most descriptive wording for your topics and turn them into categories. Look for reducing your total list of categories by grouping topics that relate to each other. Perhaps draw lines between your categories to show interrelationships;

6   make a final decision on the abbreviation for each category and alphabetize these codes;

7   assemble the data material belonging to each category in one place and perform a preliminary analysis; and

8   if necessary, recode your existing data (from Tesch, 1990, p. 142).

Development of the Research Questionnaire

Wiersma (1986), Bell (1987), Keeves (1988), and DeVellis (1991) have all offered general guidelines for the design of questionnaires in order to make them easier to complete and analyse. These writers have argued that the task of designing the questionnaire is both laborious and difficult; it demands patience to construct every item with precision in order to eliminate ambiguity and prejudicial overtones. However, there may still exist to some degree a vagueness of wording which might confuse respondents and could give rise to erroneous data. In addition to avoiding ambiguities through the use of simple non-jargon words and simple grammatical construction or syntax , it must also be borne in mind that the interest and motivation on the part of respondents are important factors in the design of questionnaires. DeVellis (1991) in particular has provided useful guidelines for questionnaire development and it is within these particular guidelines that the development of the questionnaire was undertaken. After reading the large amount of literature on attitude scaling (Fishbein, 1967; Reiser, 1981; Summers, 1970; Hoinville et al., 1978; Oskamp,

1977; Shaw and Abdel-Gaid, 1984; DeVellis, 1991) a Likert-type scale technique was decided upon as the most relevant and effective method of data gathering. DeVellis (1991) has written that Likert scales and derivatives of this approach are widely used in instruments measuring opinions, beliefs and attitudes and have remained the most commonly used method, as there have been few major recent advances or breakthroughs in techniques of scale construction since this method was developed. Although there is some resistance to the use of quantitative methods alone to measure and elicit attitudes in the context of quantitative scale comparison, there was little argument in the literature about the usefulness of Likert-type scales in relation to other existing scales.

The Initial Questionnaire

After compiling the questionnaire items into a structured instrument there were two parts to the total 147 item pool in the pilot questionnaire. Part 1 consisted of 47 items using nominal dichotomous scaling to ascertain demographic and personal data regarding age, gender, ethnicity, level of training, length of counselling experience, experience with counselling black client groups and counselling theoretical orientation. Part 2 of the survey questionnaire consisted of a five-point Likert-type attitude scale ranging from strongly agree (1) to strongly disagree (5), which was devised by using Sue and Sue's (1981, 1990) work on ethnocentric or specifically Eurocentric assumptions that have been identified as being held by white North American counsellors in work with culturally different client groups. This item pool consisted of 100 statements measuring attitudes associated with:

1   assimilationist views which related to a need for Black clients to accept the status quo, blend into white British culture and reject or adapt their culture, and the use of colour blind notions. These items were seen as a measure of 'racial prejudice' (40 items);

2   items that elicited awareness of the influence and affect of racist and discriminatory practice in counselling and society in general. These items were seen as an awareness of the oppressive sociocultural matrix of Black clients or a measure of 'racism awareness' (27 items); and

3   ethnocentric or Eurocentric counselling practice items that measured attitudes about the respondents' views on counselling service delivery and

the adaptation of practice for the particular needs of culturally different ethnic groups. These were seen as a measure of orientation towards counselling 'practice issues' (33 items). Inferences about counselling practice, as there are no direct assessments or observations of practice in this study, can only be tentative. However, awareness of the relevant issues regarding intentions should be seen as helpful to considering the potential counselling process.

The pool of six experts allocated each of the items to one of these constructs which it was envisaged, according to construct validity notions, would be validated with statistical analysis.

It was realized that not all of Sue and Sue's North American findings might be true of white British counsellors in work with African-Caribbean and South Asian client groups. However, as both British and North American counsellors are trained in the same counselling orientations and use similar methods, given the influence of this training, together with being of a similar dominant ethnic group position, it was considered reasonable to explore for the existence of a broadly similar constellation of views, and to test this assertion was the broad aim of the research. The available empirical evidence mainly from the USA (Dillard, 1987; Patterson, 1986; Cox, 1986; Marsella and Pederson, 1986; Sue and Sue, 1990) and the evidence from the UK (Rack, 1982; Burke, 1980, 1984, 1986; Littlewood and Lipsedge, 1989) mainly of an anecdotal and case study nature, suggested that similar attitudes with British and American counsellors could be expected.

The Pilot Survey

The pilot survey was the next step in devising a Likert-type questionnaire. The aim of the pilot survey was to allow for item pool meaningfulness or face validity to be tested with both a group of white counsellors and a group of Black counsellors, all having some interest in work with counselling Black clients. Furthermore, it was hoped that they would be able to offer critical comment on the item pool as a further means of determining construct face validity. A pilot sample of 73 counsellors and social workers with counselling training and experience who were as representative as believed necessary for the purposes of questionnaire validation was used. This was a convenience sampling technique of individuals drawn from those who attended four one day post-qualification courses on counselling. Questionnaires were sent to all 80 individuals who had signed up for these four independent courses and participants were asked to complete the questionnaire and bring this along to the counselling course. Thus, completion of the questionnaire was obtained before counselling course attendance, ensuring that any course training bias did not enter into the subjects' responses. The non-return from seven course participants was due to illness. All subjects were given the same information and instructions, i.e.:

> This research questionnaire is a pilot measure to discover counsellor views on the needs of Black client groups. Please complete the questionnaire and write any critical comments you have about the sequence of items, wording, grammar, or understandability of items on the sheet at the back of the questionnaire. You are also invited to provide any additional statements for inclusion at the end of this sheet, and to say why some items, if any, should not be included, or should be reworded. Thank you for participating.

The specific research aims were not presented to the sample group to avoid response bias. Subjects were informed that after they had completed the questionnaires, they should place them on an indicated table in the corner of the room, which was not directly observable by myself. Thus, a degree of anonymity was observed.

Questionnaire Pilot Study Results

Table 5 indicates the pilot study subjects' ethnic and gender backgrounds.

Table 5   Ethnic and gender backgrounds of pilot questionnaire survey subjects

Gender and ethnicity	Sample number
White British females	40
White British males	23
African-Caribbean females	5
African-Caribbean males	1
South Asian females	4
South Asian males	0
Total	**73**

Observation of the results (Table 6) shows that the sample ranged in age categories of 20–59 years.

Table 6   Age range of pilot questionnaire survey subjects

Age range	Sample number
20–24	4
25–29	10
30–34	25
35–39	18
40–44	11
45–49	8
50–54	4
55–59	3
Total	73

Table 7   Qualifications or training of the pilot questionnaire survey sample

Qualifications	Sample number
First degree	12
Certificate in Counselling	7
Diploma in Counselling	4
Counselling skills training	7
Counselling supervision	6

A large proportion of the sample is seen to be adequately qualified (Table 7).

Table 8   Length of counselling experience of the pilot questionnaire survey sample

Counselling experience	Sample number
2 years or less	7
2–4 years	31
5–7 years	15
8–10 years	12
10–12 years	4
13 or more years	4

A large proportion of the sample is seen to have extensive years of counselling experience (Table 8).

Table 9   Number of those having experience of counselling Black client groups

Yes	40
No	27
Not indicated	6

It would appear that the majority of the pilot sample had experience of counselling Black client groups and could be thought to make appropriate comments for the alteration of the questionnaire (Table 9).

Table 10   Counsellors' theoretical orientations

Counselling orientation	Sample number
Rogerian	33
Psychodyamic	15
Cognitive-behavioural	5
Egan	1
Eclectic	18
Other	1

There appeared a wide range of counselling orientations with a high proportion favouring a Rogerian client-centred model (Table 10).

Pilot Questionnaire Revision

The final questionnaire was revised, taking into consideration the pilot sample's comments. This reduced the item pool from 100 Likert-type scale items to 83 Likert -type scale items. Furthermore, some changes were made to the wording of the retained item pool.

Sentences were deleted as a result of the comments of the pilot group and judges regarding: 1) item irrelevancy to overall research theme; 2) unlikelihood of difference among counsellor response; 3) item covered elsewhere in Likert-type scale; 4) ambiguous meaning or for the final eight items; 5) too extreme in their statements. The Likert-type scale items were amended because of either: 1) wording confusion; or 2) an attempt to depersonalize the statement, i.e., indirectly probing counsellor attitudes/practice.

Another amendment was the inclusion of a 'comments sheet' at the back of the questionnaire to allow counsellors to provide: 1) qualitative comments as they saw appropriate; and 2) names and addresses for interview contact. The questionnaire, in its initial distribution form, consisted of 83 Likert-type scale items and 47 biographical items. The Likert-type items were assigned as follows:

1   33 items to the proposed scale of practice issues;

2   19 items to the proposed scale of racial awareness;

3   31 items to the proposed scale of racial prejudice.

The validity analysis results of these scales will be presented in a later section of this chapter.

Specialist computing staff were consulted to ensure the format was suitable for data input and analysis of results. As stated previously, the function of the pilot survey was to determine common-sense face validity and meaningfulness of the item pool, with the intention of using participants' comments to revise the final form of the questionnaire. No analysis to determine the relationship or interaction between the variables was carried out at this stage as this was not the aim of piloting the questionnaire.

Final Questionnaire Distribution

The final version of the questionnaire was sent to the British Association for Counselling's Research Committee and its Race and Culture Committee before agreement to allow use of their membership postal list. Both committees reviewed and agreed the questionnaires content and gave permission for use of their membership list postal service, but not direct use of their postal list, i.e., it was agreed that the questionnaires could be sent directly through the postal service to preserve and ensure anonymity. A systematic sampling method of selecting every 11th postal packet to place the questionnaire in was employed for this cross-sectional survey.

This two committee review of the questionnaire created an additional step in its validation, as another pool of experts was able to (but did not) suggest amendments. A covering letter explaining the origins of the research project was attached to the questionnaire, since this technique, according to Creswell (1994) and Scott's (1961) findings, creates a favourable impression and encourages a higher response rate. The cost of the questionnaire return was met by use of a business reply service envelope. It was expected that this facility, at no cost to the respondent, would also increase the chance of questionnaire return (Creswell, 1994; Sudman and Bradburn, 1974).

The intended treatment for questionnaire instrument analysis was factor analysis, and the rationale for this will be discussed later. According to Comrey's (1988) criteria, a minimum number of 200 returns for questionnaire validity was indicated. Therefore, a minimum target return of 200 questionnaires was set. In support of this, Fowler (1993) has argued that as a general rule of thumb, sample sizes above 150–200 increase measuring precision but 'after that point there is a much more modest gain to increasing sample size' (p. 35). However, DeVellis (1991) cited Nunnally (1978) as seeing a sample size of 300 as being an adequate number, sufficiently large to eliminate subject variance. DeVellis, however, was of the view that in his practical experience even fewer subjects may suffice. A review of the evidence suggested that a 200 sample size was fair and 300 was good (Comrey, 1973). More recently, Comrey (1988) has argued that a sample size of 200 was adequate, and indeed DeVellis (1991) noted that it was not uncommon to see factor analysis used in attitude scale development on much more modest samples, i.e., 150 subjects. The issue to be noted was that the use of larger sample sizes increases the generalization of the conclusions. As considerable survey research suggests that postal returns on sensitive issues may be as low as 30 per cent, 600 questionnaires were sent through the British Association of Counselling's journal. A return of 411 questionnaires provided a response rate of 68.5 per cent. However, 51 of these questionnaires were returned uncompleted. 45 of these were voluntary agencies who took the journal for reading material but employed no counsellors and did not offer counselling services. Six were returned with a note of refusal to participate with the research because of its alleged objectionable focus, e.g., one returned questionnaire had written on the covering letter 'counsellors are sensitive to all groups of people regardless of colour and there is no use in pushing a political point'. 22 questionnaires were from people of either South Asian, Chinese or African-Caribbean ethnic groups which, due to small sample size and wide ethnic group variation, were excluded from the analysis.

Since the sample size exceeded the initial 200 respondent target and the upper criterion of 300 set by Nunnally (1978) it was considered that the sample size was more than adequate for attitude measurement. The sample size of

338 usable questionnaires also avoided another pitfall in survey techniques – that of sample non-representativeness where the respondents are qualitatively different from the target population as a whole (DeVellis, 1991; Creswell, 1994).

It must be stressed at this point that no intention to construct a standardized attitude test scale was intended. However, it was recognized that some statistical validation of the research questionnaire was necessary. The statistical validation technique chosen was that of factor analysis and Cronbach's alpha coefficient.

Final Questionnaire Revision

Factor analysis using an oblique rotation produced 25 factors. Kim (1970) has suggested that after three factors have been extracted, the rest may have statistical importance but loose their common-sense meaning as they become difficult to interpret. A scree test (Cattell, 1966; DeVellis, 1991) was used to help decide which factors to retain and focus upon. This confirmed that the initial three factors should be concentrated upon. These factors accounted for a total of 37.3 per cent of the variance.

McKennel (1970) has described what she referred to as a rapid and reliable method to total scale construction by the use of factor analysis and Cronbach's alpha. The use of the reliability coefficient, alpha, was an improvement of Likert's (1932) original item analysis (McKennel, 1970; DeVellis, 1991). The aim of item analysis techniques was to 'purify' the scale by keeping only the most valid items from the item pool.

Table 11   Initial reliability analysis coefficient alpha scores for the three scales before item analysis deletion

Scale	Cronbach's alpha	Coefficient
Racism awareness	.81	19 items
Racial prejudice	.88	31 items
Practice issues	.76	33 items

As alpha coefficients above .7 are considered as very acceptable measures (Cronbach, 1951; DeVellis, 1991), it was considered that the three initial scales met the necessary criteria of instrument validation (Table 11). Those individual items which produced low alpha scores and inter-item correlations were deleted from the scales and only the most valid items were retained. However, although Cronbach's alpha provides a robust test of validity and reliability for scale development requirements it does not allow, in itself, a comparison of the interrelation of scales or their discriminant characteristics. In order to be sure that the scales were in fact measuring different aspects of the survey samples attitudes a correlation test was performed to assess the inter-scale correlation and thus the extent to which the three scales were discriminating between the postulated scale measures. The results of the Pearson correlation test are presented in Table 12.

Table 12   Correlation coefficients of the three scales

	Practice	Racism awareness	Prejudice
Practice	1.0	.81	.69
Racism awareness	.81	1.0	.68
Prejudice	.69	.69	1.0

As can be seen, the scale correlations are high, suggesting that they may not be measuring distinct attitudes. The scales appeared to be a duplication in measurement. Additional inspection of the individual items and discussion with four experienced counsellors and an experienced statistical analyst suggested that, because of conceptual overlap and relatedness, two scales could be collapsed or combined to form one scale. The combined scales were those of 'Practice issues' and 'Racism awareness' as both the judges' opinions and the high correlation suggested that these scales were the most related. A further correlation test was performed to assess the discriminant character of the resultant scales, and the results, which are presented in Table 13, indicated that again, there was little discriminant utility between the two new scales as they were still highly correlated.

Table 13   Correlation coefficients of the two combined scales and the initial prejudice scale

	Scale 1	Scale 2
Combined scale	1.00	.72
Initial prejudice scale	.72	1.00

Further discussion with the four experienced therapists and the statistical analyst suggested that there was an argument for retaining the combined scale and rejecting the initial prejudice scale as:

1   there was a marked preference for many of the individual items contained in the combined scale because of their specific wording; and

2   there was a statistical reliability argument (Fowler, 1993) that favoured the greater length of the combined scale as, 'retaining ... items provides a bit of additional insurance that the reliability will not drop below acceptable levels on a new sample ...' (DeVellis, 1991, p. 105).

Given the subjective preferences of the experienced counsellor and the empirical arguments of correlation and validity, it was proposed that the initial prejudice scale be withdrawn from the statistical analysis. This would not affect the original research aims and objectives because of the variation and number of data gathering techniques employed.

The combined scale obtained a Cronbach's alpha of .91 and was seen by the four evaluating therapists as a more focused and wide ranging test of counsellor cultural awareness. With this in mind it was entitled the Cultural Awareness Inventory. Reber (1984), in defining the term 'inventory', has indicated that 'the term applies broadly; any check list, instrument, test or questionnaire that assesses, traits, opinions, beliefs, aptitudes, behaviours, etc. may be so labelled' (p. 374).

A high score indicated a relatively favourable attitude, i.e., high cultural awareness, whereas a low score indicated a relatively unfavourable attitude i.e., low cultural awareness. The Cultural Awareness Inventory is not printed in this book due to potential further research and marketing considerations.

Video Vignette Response Measures

According to Bochner (1980), the apparent discrepancy between attitudes and behaviour is one of the major unresolved issues in social psychology. This has been discussed in chapter 4. This unresolved issue has attracted a great deal of theoretical and empirical attention (Fishbein, 1967; Calder and Ross, 1973; Liska, 1974; Kiesler and Munson, 1975). The conclusion that Bochner drew was that, as a result of the complex relationship between attitudes and behaviour, some research questions are best served by an experimental design which attempts to measure the intentional, behavioural or affective aspect of attitude. Several writers (Sherman, 1980; Kelman, 1974; Bochner et al., 1975; Bochner, 1980) have suggested that specific behavioural or affective orientated attitude research designs are particularly appropriate where issues of strong societal and institutional norms are present. The issue of 'race' and attitudes towards the culturally different, as is the focus of this research, is clearly one of these issues. As Bochner (1980, p. 331) argued: 'whenever a topic is enveloped by a powerful cultural 'ought', conventional studies of behavioural intentions are particularly susceptible, and hence more likely to reveal ideal rather than actual behaviour patterns'.

To overcome this difficulty of social desirability response set, a third method of data collection to supplement the survey questionnaire and interview methods was used. The vignette study derives from methods used in experimental social psychology. Typically, ratings or other responses are made by the focal group of such vignette material as video or audio tapes, or written case study material. The method attempts to create an analogy of an actual situation such as the counselling encounter. The method permits control of factors not controllable in naturalistic circumstances. The vignette study using video tape has been used successfully in the study of gender stereotyping and bias (Thomas and Stewart, 1971; Magnus, 1975; Johnson, 1978), and the study of Black and white counselling students' skills (Berman, 1979a, 1979b). Pearce (1997), using video scenes to discover cultural biases in British trainee counsellors, found that trainees did not display biases in attributing positive comments to the white counselling subjects nor negative judgments to ethnic minority counselling subjects. In general, the video vignette studies provide a method that is not counselling client invasive since actors can be used. Also, the same video tape scene can be shown to different audiences over time allowing for the presentation to be tightly controlled and greater ease of data collection as the video is portable to different settings.

Sherman (1980) noted that the intention of vignette studies was often to look for evidence of bias and that given the popularity of the method, this assumption is increasingly questionable. Although this method may be popular in the USA, it appears relatively novel in Britain and one can assume that respondents will be less suspicious than in the USA of a vignette study's intended use. The video vignette responses were collected over a period of two years. This involved obtaining video vignette responses from counsellors who had a minimum of two years experience and had qualifications in psychiatric nursing, counselling certificates or diplomas and/or social science degrees and were undergoing certificated one and two year postgraduate training courses in individual and family counselling. Table 14 shows the experimental group composition.

Table 14   Ethnic group, gender and number of counsellors participating in video response

Ethnic group	No.
White males	21
White females	86
Total	**107**

The video vignette scenes were modelled on Scene 8, a 30 second trigger scene from Clark and Lagos' *Multi-racial Video Scenes*, Leicester Polytechnic. The client here was a young South Asian woman, who presents as a counselling client at an initial or first counselling session. She appears distressed and desperate. The woman says:

> I've come to see you because I think I'm pregnant and I don't know what to do. I mean me being an Indian girl and pregnant my mom's gonna kill me and my dad will murder me. Oh, I'm in such a situation. If I only had something I could do about it. I don't want an abortion because I don't believe in them. I don't think they are right. Oh, but maybe that's the only way I could get out of it.

Two similar video scenes were made of an African-Caribbean woman, and a white English woman. Variables such as age, physique, accent, style of dress, attractiveness (a highly subjective variable) and setting were controlled so as to make the emphasis of the video scene one of colour, ethnicity and the common concern of unplanned pregnancy.

Respondents only rated one video scene and therefore each rating scale response for each 'client' was an independent subject's design. The respondents were all given the same instructions, i.e., 'you are going to be shown a video tape of a woman who is requesting your counselling services. I would like you to watch the video tape and then complete the video vignette rating scale.' The items for the video response rating scale were composed by Brody (1990) and named the 'Vignette Rating Scale'. Brody created the initial scale by reviewing several case study approach texts and extracting common feelings and responses reported by counsellors and identified by supervisors as being experienced in counter-transference reactions. She argued in attempting to form a scale that:

> It should be emphasised that the ambiguity and complexity that characterise the concept of countertransference necessarily complicates the process of forming an instrument to measure it. Countertransference is a highly personal, subjective and often sensitive issue that does not lend itself well to empirical research. The more precisely one attempts to measure countertransference, the more the richness that characterises the concept may be diminished (p. 61).

This was in keeping with the views of other more recent writers (Watkins, 1989b; Maroda, 1991). The advantages of using video response measures as an indication of likely counsellor behaviour were that all counsellors could be compared in their appraisal and response to the same or similar stimulus. Responses can be collected on paper. Furthermore, group discussions, which can be initiated after response collection, could contribute to the collection of cultural responsiveness data and the identification of culturally orientated values that may be brought into the counselling situation. Brody stated that the scale was designed to investigate therapists' countertransference reactions to clients using actual clinical case material, and was also designed to simulate an actual treatment situation. However, she used written case study material which was posted out to therapists rather than the video scenes shown to counsellors in this research study. The material she used was adapted from the work of Spitzer et al. (1983) who had compiled a book of case study material.

Brody did not claim or report any attempts at statistical standardization or validation of this instrument, which she referred to as the 'Vignette Rating Scale', as she claimed the instruments were 'created for use in this research and are exploratory in nature, no construct or predictive measures of validity are available at this time' (pp. 70–1). However, she claimed that the strongest evidence 'lies in the results themselves' (p. 71). She also claimed that '[c]ontent validity is indicated by the fact that the items included in this scale are representative of what is considered to be theoretically linked to countertransference' (p. 71).

The present researcher decided to subject the Vignette Rating Scale to the rigours of statistical testing. As with the Cultural Awareness Inventory, a Cronbach's alpha coefficient test was performed and, after some inspection of results and recoding of the items, produced an acceptable coefficient alpha of .74. This showed the instrument to be both a reliable and acceptably valid measure of the construct of countertransference. As a further test of face validity the Vignette Rating Scale was also shown to three experienced counsellors who commented favourably on its composition. The scoring of the Vignette Rating Scale was different from that of the Cultural Awareness Inventory as there was no intended degree of 'favourability' or 'unfavourability'. The Vignette Rating Scale was seen as a measure of the degree of variation in emotional response of the counsellors to the different ethnic group 'clients'. For some items of this scale low scores indicated less emotional response than usual and high scores indicated more emotional response than usual. For other items the scoring as previously indicated was reversed. The distinctions are made clear for the reader, when they became necessary, in chapter 7. The overall function of this scale was to measure the degree to which counsellor's emotional response to the 'video client' was affected by the 'client's' ethnic group. The reader is informed that not all of the items on the proforma formed part of the standardized Vignette Rating Scale: some were intended as questionnaire type items and were discussed independent of the scale, and this is made clear at the appropriate point of discussion in chapter 7.

Statistical Treatment of Results

For the purposes of statistical analysis four statistical procedures were used. These were a multiple regression analysis, the 'F' test for analysis of variance (ANOVA), and, in conjunction with this test, a Scheffe test, and a chi squared (x^2) test. A non-statistical discussion of the use of these tests follows. As this research was not a statistical investigation no detailed statistical discussion of the statistical functioning and components of these tests will be entered into.

Multiple Regression Analysis

Kim and Kohout (1975) described multiple regression as a general statistical technique in which one can analyse the relationship between a dependent variable and a set of independent or predictor variables.

The uses of the technique are:

1   to find the best linear prediction equation and evaluate its prediction accuracy; and

2   to control for confounding factors in order to evaluate the contribution of a specific variable or set of variables; and

3   to find structural relations and provide explanations for seemingly complex multi-variate relationships.

This writer was interested in describing the strength and direction of the relationship between the dependent variable of the Cultural Awareness Inventory and a number of independent variables, from the survey questionnaire.

The independent variables (V) were:

V2	=	Gender
V4	=	Age of counsellor
V15	=	Years of counselling experience
V22	=	Experience of counselling African-Caribbean clients
V5, V6	=	Academic educational qualifications
V7, V8, V9	=	Applied counselling qualifications
V19, V20, V21	=	Experience of counselling South Asian clients
V33, V35	=	Specific training
V34, V36	=	Specific reading.

Thus, nine independent variables were entered into a stepwise regression analysis to determine which provided the best predictors of influence on the Cultural Awareness Inventory. The nine independent variables entered into the stepwise analysis were drawn from Part 1 of the demographic section of the postal questionnaire. These variables were those which could be expected to have some face validity causal effect on, or linkage with, the Cultural Awareness Inventory. Variables that may have had a spurious connection such as whether the counsellor worked part or full time, or the employer of the counsellor, were not entered, as these were not seen as specific determinants on effect of counsellor attitude.

One Way Analysis of Variance (ANOVA)

Bryman and Cramer (1994) noted that although some writers have argued that parametric tests should only be used on interval/ratio data (Stevens, 1946), others (Bryman and Cramer, 1994) argued that this restriction was unnecessary. The analysis of variance test used in this investigation was the 'F' test, which is an estimate of the between groups' variance or mean square, as it is referred to in the analysis of variance, which is compared with an estimate of the within groups variance by dividing the former by the latter. The basic reasoning behind the 'F' test is that if the group or sample come from the same population, then the between group's estimate of the population's variance should be similar to the within group's estimated variance. The 'F' test only indicates whether there is a significant difference between one or more of the groups. It does not indicate where this difference exists. As there was no prior expectation of where differences may exist, a post hoc test was carried out. The test used was the Scheffe test, which Bryman and Cramer (1994) describe as a 'conservative' test in that it is least likely to find a significant difference between groups where no such difference exists.

Cross-tabulated Data

The chi square test (x^2) was used for cross-tabulation comparison of data to investigate whether the relationship between given variables arose by chance or whether there was a statistically significant relationship unrelated to chance probability. The x^2 test allows the investigator to compare the observed frequencies in each cell in a contingency table with those that would occur if there were no relationship between the two variables. Thus, the x^2 test allowed a comparison of actual frequencies with those which would be expected to occur on the basis of chance alone. The greater the difference between the observed and expected frequencies, the larger the resulting x^2 value; and taking into account the degrees of freedom, the greater the significance value. Bryman and Cramer (1994, p. 153) have stated that 'cross-tabulation is one of the simplest and most frequently used ways of demonstrating the presence or absence of a relationship'. Also, Bryman and Cramer (1994) have noted that x^2 does not provide confirmatory information about the strength of a relationship, e.g., a $p<.001$ does not indicate a closer relationship between two variables than a $p<.05$ level of significance. x^2 only tells the investigator how confident they can be that the relationship is not due to chance alone.

The Reduction of Information to Meaningful Themes

To make the discussion of the results conceptually meaningful the survey results and video vignette statistical analysis will be discussed, as appropriate, under the theme headings of 'Practice Issues', 'Counsellor Qualifications' and 'Counsellor Orientation'. The interview data will be presented in chapter 8 to illustrate the discussion and support the research findings. Where data is gathered from more than one source the process of data analysis is often an eclectic process (Creswell, 1994) and there is no single 'right way' (Tesch, 1990). The objective was to reduce the volume of data into a meaningful context that could usefully be interpreted as a meaningful whole. Tesch (1990) referred to this process as 'de-contextualisation' and 're-contextualisation' and argued that this process resulted in a 'high level analysis', while much work in the analysis process consisted of 'taking apart [the volume of collected data] ... the final goal is the emergence of a larger, consolidated picture' (p. 7).

Tesch (1990) has provided the researcher with eight steps to enable a systematic process of analysing textual data which, in the case of interview data, even when a structured interview method is employed, may result in unstructured data. The steps that Tesch suggested were outlined earlier in this chapter.

These guidelines helped to form the process of integrating the interview narrative into the discussion of the outcomes of the statistical analysis of the survey questionnaire and the video vignette case study for chapter 8. The objective was to search for meaningful and useful patterns that would allow the development and use of themes for textual discussion. To a large degree the survey questionnaire items, together with the video vignette case study, dominated the generation of the themes as the function of these instruments was to measure issues of counsellor qualification, orientation and practice issues in the context of cultural awareness. From these themes the narrative data of the interviews were woven into the summarized quantitative data in chapter 8 to provide a qualitative contextualization of the attitudes of the 20 interviewed counsellors.

The Operationalization of the Theme of Counsellor Qualifications

Counsellor qualifications were seen as: (1) the number of years a therapist had been practising; (2) whether the therapist had direct experience of delivering therapy services to Black clients; (3) the certificated or 'academic' qualifications a counsellor had; and (4) the specific training or reading that the therapist had undertaken on the needs of Black client groups. The questionnaire items that measured the certificated or academic qualifications a counsellor had were:

V5   holding a first degree
V6   having a postgraduate qualification other than counselling
V7   having a certificate in counselling

V8   having a diploma in counselling
V9   having a Masters degree in counselling
V10   having undertaken skills training in counselling.

From the above variables applied counselling and academic study distinctions were obtained by taking account of responses that were mutually exclusive and/or combined through the use of the SPSS (Statistical Package for the Social Sciences). Thus, discrete variables of 'Counselling Qualifications' and 'Academic Qualifications' were created. The individual variables that were merged to form these new discrete variables were:

Counselling qualifications   skills only
                               certificate only
                               diploma only
                               Masters degree

Academic qualification   degree
                           postgraduate qualification other than
                            counselling.

Counselling Experience

The questionnaire items related to the direct experience of counselling South Asian clients, i.e., V1 – having counselled Indian clients, V20 – having counselled Pakistani clients, V21 – having counselled Bangladeshi clients were combined to form a new independent of 'experience of counselling South Asian clients'. There was also the single variable of V22 – experience of counselling African-Caribbean clients.

The Operationalization of the Theme of Counsellor Orientation

Counsellor theoretical orientation was measured by the self categorization of counsellors as given in variable 45, where counsellors were asked to indicate their preferred counselling model. For the purposes of this investigation only three models were used in the comparative analysis, i.e., those with the largest numbers of respondents. The total picture of the range of preferred counselling models was given in Table 10. Those used in the analysis are shown in Table 15.

The choice of the eclectic orientation in favour of the Egan model (9.8

Table 15   Preferred counselling models

Counselling model	Number	Percentage
Rogerian	91	27
Psychodynamic	76	23
Eclectic	26	8

per cent of respondents) was due to the visual examination of the category of 'other' (18.6 per cent of respondents) showing the majority to be using an 'eclectic' model of some form, i.e., 33 out of the 49 who self categorized as other or 9.8 per cent of the total sample respondents giving a more accurate eclectic sample of 59 or 16.5 per cent of the total sample. In addition to V45, the self categorization of the therapists, the variables of V41, the belief in the benefit of a different counselling model for South Asian clients and V42, the belief in the benefit of a different counselling model for African-Caribbean clients was seen as a specific indicator of counsellor model orientation.

The Operationalization of Counsellor Practice Issues

The theme of counsellor practice issues was operationalized as those variables or factors which were connected to what a counsellor self reported as doing, had done or was willing/not willing to do with clients. Thus, this theme was one which employed the concept of self reported counsellor action with clients, where self reported action was something that had been carried out in actuality or a willingness or non-willingness to consider certain action with a client. Thus the theme was limited to self reported specific behaviour and intentions. As mentioned previously, it is acknowledged that only tentative inferences about counselling practice can be made as there was no direct assessment or observation of actual counsellor practice. However, the measures that are obtained do relate to counsellors' attitudes to practice, and provide self reported practice strategies as they relate to the limited and specific range of variables investigated. The specific variables connected with this theme were those of:

1   V27 – use of clients' family networks to affect the counselling relationship and the related outcome of V28;

2   V29 and V30 – the willingness to use an interpreter when counselling Black client groups;

3   V31 – the actual use of interpreter services and the related outcome variable of V32;

4   V41 and V42 – the belief that Asian and African-Caribbean clients may benefit from the use of different counselling models or approaches.

Included under the theme of 'Practice Issues' was the Vignette Rating Scale used with the video case studies. The countertransference ratings were seen as an element of practice, as Maroda (1991) states in her use of countertransference that prior to acknowledging these feelings and using them in therapy to affect change that:

> I was plagued by feelings of restraint and artificiality. I felt as though my analyst was trying too hard to contain my emotional experience and that I, too, was restraining my patients expression of their emotions ... [In not engaging with the transference] .... What presented the greatest difficulty for me was that I found myself being moved by many of my patients' pleas to respond more emotionally to them ... I felt that the strong emotional pull that certain patients elicited in me was the very siren song that I was duty bound to resist ... I began these experiments with countertransference committed to the idea that my immediate emotional reaction to the patient was the most important thing to reveal ...' (pp. 1–3).

From Maroda's quotations we can see that there is a link between countertransference and therapist practice, and influence on the client-therapist relationship.

7 The Questionnaire and Video Vignette Results

In chapter 1 the specific objectives of the research were stated. They are restated in this chapter to make the questionnaire and video vignette data analysis, which is the aim of this chapter, contextually meaningful. Furthermore, there are a number of theoretical postulates which follow from the reviewed theory and research which guided the empirical study that will be associated with the research objectives. The objectives and theoretical postulates were:

1 the first research objective was to examine the existing views of counsellors on the significance of cultural and ethnic differences between counsellor and client in the counselling relationship. One theoretical postulate of relevance here is that without an awareness of client culture and cultural differences, attitudes towards Black clients will be informed by Eurocentric counselling notions (Nobles, 1976; Farrar and Sircar, 1986; Littlewood and Lipsedge, 1989; d'Ardenne and Mahatani, 1989; Lago and Thompson, 1989; Sue and Sue, 1990);

2 the second research objective was to investigate the influences on the ability of counsellors to empathize with the position of Black clients in a social matrix. Another theoretical postulate which arises from the reviewed literature and is related to this objective is: counsellors with no training, reading, or direct experience related to Black clients will be less culturally aware than those who do have the relevant training, reading and direct experience (Pinderhughes, 1989; Ridley, 1989; Sue and Sue, 1990; Ivey et al., 1993);

3 the third objective was to examine the influences on counsellors' awareness of limitations in the use of Eurocentric models with Black client groups. The theoretical postulate offered in 2) above is of relevance here, i.e., counsellors with no training, reading, or direct experience related to Black clients will be less culturally aware than those who do have the relevant

training, reading and direct experience (Pinderhughes, 1989; Ridley, 1989; Sue and Sue, 1990; Ivey et al., 1993); and

4   the fourth objective was to explore the degree to which counsellors vary their usual attitude or strategic orientation towards practice with white clients when counselling Black clients. A theoretical postulate related to this research objective is: counsellor empathy towards client will diminish in relation to cultural distance (Littlewood and Lipsedge, 1989; Ridley, 1989; Ivey et al., 1993; Banks, 1995).

The reader is reminded that these objectives and theoretical postulates were investigated using three main methods: a postal questionnaire survey of counsellors; a video vignette case study of experienced counsellors in professional training; and interviews with selected counsellors. A descriptive account of the demographic and practical survey questionnaire data results follows in the next section, with a later section to provide the cross-tabulated and multi-variate analysis results through which the theoretical postulates and the objectives will be explored in an 'embedded' context. This embedded context discussion approach is taken from the school of postmodernist thought discussed throughout the preceding chapters. The postmodernist position is one that is in contrast with the modernist viewpoint which argues for a search for grand theories and objectivity and 'the assumption of a rational and unified subject. In contrast, postmodernism emphasises fragmentation, deconstruction and the idea of multiple selves' (Maynard, 1994, pp. 15–6). Furthermore, it is not about the splitting of subject and object (Bhavnani, 1994). What follows here is an analysis of situational location in history, culture, time, and content. There is no intent to formulate a grand theory of the 'white counsellor'.

The Demographic and Practice Questionnaire Data Results

The following descriptive cross-sectional demographic and practice survey data was collected from the questionnaire sent through the British Association for Counsellor's postal service. The attitudinal results are presented in the next section, where the analyses of the counsellors' attitudes and practices are outlined.

Table 16 indicates that a much higher percentage of respondents were female. This did not come as a surprise and reflected general observations at counsellor training courses and conferences.

Table 16   Counsellor gender

Gender	No.	%
Female	263	77.8
Male	75	22.2
Total	n = 338	

Table 17   Counsellor ethnic background

Ethnicity	No.	%
White European	338	93.9
Black African-Caribbean	10	2.8
Black African	3	0.8
South Asian	3	0.8
Chinese	5	1.4
Other	1	0.3
Total	n = 360	

Observation of Table 17 indicated that the vast majority of counsellors were white European and that a small minority were from the various ethnic minority communities. The higher proportion of Chinese respondents came as a surprise, given their numbers in the general population. This may indicate social class differences between the Chinese and the white-Anglo population. For the purposes of this research it was only the responses of the 338 white European counsellors that were considered, as the ethnic minority group questionnaire respondents were too diverse and small in number to justify comparative analysis.

Table 18 shows that the majority of the white counsellors was in the age range of 35–49 years, with a lower percentage under 34 years and over 65 years of age.

The largest band of experience was that of 2–7 years and then 8–12 years (Table 19). The significant numbers of years of experience in the bands above 'Less than two years' indicates that the responding counsellors were those with significant experience. The 'missing category' reflected those counsellors who qualified their different lengths of experience for both different client groups and service delivery focus.

Table 18   Counsellor age range

Age band	No.	%
20–34	63	18.6
35–49	193	57.1
50–64	76	22.5
65+	6	1.8

Table 19   Counsellor years of experience

Years	No.	%
Fewer than two	43	12.7
2–7	163	48.2
8–12	72	21.3
13 or more	56	16.5
Missing	4	1.2

Table 20   Experience of counselling Black clients

Ethnicity	Yes	%	No	%
Indian	156	46.2	128	52.2
Pakistani	136	37.8	224	62.2
Bangladeshi	67	18.6	293	81.4
Afro-Caribbean	208	57.8	152	42.2

Table 20 suggested that a fair percentage of counsellors did have some experience of counselling clients of Indian, African-Caribbean and Pakistani origin with the sample of counsellors showing much less experience with the Bangladeshi community.

Observation of Table 21 allows the reader to see the preferred counselling orientation of the respondents. The orientation of the person-centred, psychodynamic and eclectic approaches were those which were most favoured. These approaches have been discussed previously in the chapter 5 to provide insight into their practice implications with Black client groups. The category of 'other' initially appeared to indicate a significant proportion of different models that were not accounted for in the pre-coded questionnaire categories.

However, further inspection of all of the questionnaires revealed that only two counselling models were of numerical importance, these being: transactional analysis – 10 counsellors or approximately three per cent of the total, and existential therapy – four counsellors or approximately one per cent of the total. Some of the other 49 responses (i.e., two) were mainly what could be described as 'fringe' counselling approaches, e.g., 're-evaluation'.

Table 21   The counselling model orientation of the white counsellors

	No.	%
Rogerian	91	26.9
Psychodynamic	76	22.5
Egan	33	9.8
Eclectic	26	7.7
Gestalt	11	3.3
Cognitive	8	2.4
Behavioural	7	2.1
Systems/family	4	1.2
Rational-emotive	4	1.2
Other	63	18.6
Missing cases	15	4.4

A number of responses, a total of 33 or 9.8 per cent, to the 'other' category were in fact indicative of an 'eclectic' model with two or more of the questionnaire response categories indicated. However, the lack of use of the 'eclectic' questionnaire category may have indicated that a non-integrative form of eclecticism was being identified, i.e., where the multi-model approach was distinct and separate according to the perceived client/therapist need. Adding this 9.8 per cent to the 7.7 per cent of counsellors who overtly identified themselves as 'eclectic' gave an overall eclectic counselling orientation count of 59 counsellors, or 17.5 per cent of the total.

The 4.4 per cent of missing cases may not simply represent a missed response but may indicate a response by counsellors who are either undecided in their preferred model due to lack of experience or converting to another model due to changed experience, e.g., further training, and remained, at the point of questionnaire response, undecided.

Table 22 shows the range of academic qualifications obtained by the sample group.

Table 22   Highest level of counsellor academic qualifications

Qualification	No.	%
First degree	77	22.8
Postgraduate non-counselling qualification	129	38.2
No academic qualifications	132	39.1

Table 23   Highest level of counselling qualification

Qualification	No.	%
Skills training	65	19.2
Certificate	100	29.6
Diploma	121	35.8
Masters degree in Counselling	20	6.2
No counselling qualification	31	9.2
Receiving counselling supervision	205	60.7

Table 23 shows the range of counselling qualifications obtained and the number receiving supervision.

Table 24   British Association for Counselling accreditation

Accreditation	No.	%
Yes	30	8.9
No	304	91.0
Missing	4	1.2

Table 24 shows that the vast majority of counsellors were not British Association for Counselling accredited. Table 25 shows the proportion of counsellors pursuing accreditation with the British Association for Counselling. Those in the missing category of 9.8 per cent were assumed to be considering the possibility of pursuing accreditation and not able to provide a definite/absolute 'yes' or 'no' response.

Inspection of Table 26 indicated that a high proportion of the responding counsellors worked in the delivery of counselling to students, marriage guidance agencies, family and occupational/staff care counselling. Inspection

Table 25   Counsellors pursuing British Association for Counselling accreditation

Accreditation	No.	%
Yes	142	42.0
No	163	48.2
Missing	33	9.8

Table 26   Counselling service delivery focus

Area	No.	%
Student	52	15.4
Marriage guidance	29	8.6
Family	25	7.4
Occupational/staff care	24	7.1
Bereavement	22	6.5
Alcohol/drug	17	5.0
Disability	14	4.1
HIV/AIDs	12	3.6
Sexual abuse/rape crisis	8	2.4
Other	134	39.6
Not specified	1	0.3

of all the questionnaires to determine the high number of responses to the 'other' category showed that the majority of counsellors responding to this worked across several of the categories, including a non-provided category of 'private practice', which may have tended to focus on relationship and personal issues. A counsellor not employed in an agency specializing in a particular or specialized client group need may not neatly fit any one category. This view was confirmed to some degree by comparing the total number of 134 counsellors in Table 26 to the high response of the 'private practice' category in the Table 27 to show the employment setting of counsellors.

Table 27 showed the setting in which counsellors were employed, the largest employment/work category being that of 'private practice'. The high response to the 'other' category was explained by counsellors who worked across a number of settings, e.g., private practice and voluntary or health authority employment.

Table 27   Employment setting of counsellors

Employment	No.	%
Private practice	115	34.2
Voluntary agency (e.g., marriage guidance)	65	19.2
Health authority	55	16.3
Education authority	36	10.7
Social services	16	4.7
Polytechnic	10	3.0
Probation	2	0.6
University	2	0.6
Other	30	8.9
Not specified	7	2.1

Table 28   Employment locality

Employment locality	No.	%
Mainly white and suburban	71	21.0
Ethnically mixed and suburban	46	13.6
Mainly white and rural	42	12.4
Mainly white and urban	56	16.6
Ethnically mixed and rural	3	0.9
Ethnically mixed and urban	117	34.6
Missing cases	3	0.9

Table 28 indicates that the majority of counsellors worked in diverse areas, with a larger percentage working in areas that were 'ethnically mixed and urban' than those which were 'mainly white and suburban'.

Table 29, showing residential locality, contrasted with that of the employment locality in that a higher proportion of counsellors lived in 'mainly white and suburban' areas than in 'ethnically mixed and urban'. Therefore, counsellor residence and area of work were reversed in terms of frequency of occurrence. That was to say that there was a trend to live in 'mainly white suburban areas' but work in 'ethnically mixed and urban' areas.

Table 30 shows the range of average numbers of clients worked with in a week, with approximately 60 per cent of counsellors seeing fewer than 10 clients on average a week.

Table 29   Residential locality

Residential locality	No.	%
Mainly white and suburban	125	37.0
Ethnically mixed and suburban	38	11.2
Mainly white and rural	66	19.5
Mainly white and urban	40	11.8
Ethnically mixed and rural	3	0.9
Ethnically mixed and urban	63	18.6
Missing cases	3	0.9

Table 30   Average number of clients seen in a week

	No.	%
Fewer than four	112	33
5–9	101	29
10–14	55	16
15–19	32	6
20–24	14	9
24 or more	18	5
Not specified	6	1

Table 31 shows that the majority of counsellors have not used the family network in counselling. Those who did not respond were assumed to be either only offering a 'no' response or be perceiving the question as inappropriate/ irrelevant due to counselling model orientation and preferred/experienced ways of working.

Table 31   Use of family network in counselling

	No.	%
Yes	121	35.8
No	191	56.5
Not specified	26	7.2

Table 32 shows that of those counsellors who did use the family network, the vast majority found it helpful.

Table 32   Perceived value of family network use

	No.	%
Helpful	110	92.4
Not helpful	9	7.6

Table 33   Openness to use of interpreter

	Yes	%	No	%
African-Caribbean clients	111	32.8	142	42.0
South Asian clients	159	47.0	104	30.8

Table 33 shows that a fair number of counsellors were open to the use of interpreters with both South Asian and African-Caribbean client groups.

Table 34   Actual use of interpreter

	No.	%
Have used interpreter	42	12.4
Have not used interpreter	125	37.0
Missing	171	50.6

Table 34 indicates that although there may have been an openness to using interpreters, the vast majority of counsellors had not used such a service. This large number in the 'missing' category were assumed to be in the 'have not used interpreter' category.

Table 35 shows that a high proportion of the sample group of counsellors had not undertaken specific training in counselling African-Caribbean, or South Asian client groups, although a higher number had read specific information, than had trained, on the needs of South Asian and African-Caribbean clients.

From the collected responses (Table 36) the reader is able to see that almost two thirds of the responding sample of counsellors did see a need for different counselling approaches for South Asian, p<.001 (2 tailed) and African-Caribbean, p<.001 (2 tailed) client groups. Those in the missing category may have been those who were undecided or unsure through lack of experience of the need for different counselling approaches for South Asian and African-Caribbean clients.

Table 37 show that roughly one third of the sample had Asian or African-Caribbean friends who they saw on a regular basis outside of work.

Table 35   Specific information for multi-cultural service delivery

	Yes	%	No	%
South Asian clients				
Training	78	23.1	260	77.0
Reading	139	41.1	199	58.9
African-Caribbean clients				
Training	86	25.4	252	74.6
Reading	140	41.4	198	58.6

Table 36   View of the need for different counselling approaches from white clients

	Yes	%	No	%	Missing	%
South Asian clients	150	63	89	37	99	29
African-Caribbean clients	142	60	88	38	108	32

Table 37   The existence of multi-cultural friendship networks with white counsellors

	Yes	%	No	%
Asian friends	116	34.3	222	65.5
African-Caribbean	128	37.9	210	62.2

Implications for Counselling Black Clients

There are a number of observations which can be made with respect to the training and experience of this cross section of counsellors with Black client groups. The majority of counsellors were found to have no specific training and to have read about the particular counselling needs of Black client groups. With South Asian and African-Caribbean clients, 77 per cent and 74.6 per cent respectively, of the sample group, had not received specific training in working with these client groups. This lack of training exposure was revealing of what is not happening on training courses. However, higher percentages, i.e., approximately 60 per cent of counsellors claimed to have read specific material about the needs of South Asian and African-Caribbean clients. Quality training should be seen as the cornerstone of good practice. It has been argued (Pinderhughes, 1989; Sue and Sue, 1990) that good counselling practice is likely to hinge on the understanding and attitudes that the counsellor brings prior to the onset of counselling. Pinderhughes (1989) and d'Ardenne and Mahatani (1989) have argued that, for an appropriate delivery of counselling service to Black clients, the counsellor should have an awareness of how racism informs and affects themselves as individuals, the society they live in and the social and emotional impact of 'race' and racism on Black people. More specifically, Ridley (1995) identified in his North American research that many counsellors assume that they are able to counsel clients regardless of the client's background. This arose, according to Ridley, from the inherent philosophy of counselling theory; that its techniques were appropriate for all people, regardless of their ethnicity, gender or culture. As Ridley argued: 'Traditionally trained counsellors tend to believe they are competent enough to adapt to any differences among clients and serve their best interests' (p. 11). The assumption of universality of need, and thus approach, has, to a significant degree, been assumed without critical analysis.

Counselling Course Curriculum Issues

As so few counsellors had received specific training (23 per cent for South Asian and 25 per cent for African-Caribbean client groups) or had read specific material (41 per cent on both the needs of South Asian and African-Caribbean clients) there is a need to question the applicability of counselling course curriculum content for meeting the needs of Britain's multi-cultural population. However, what the present research did not record was whether the numbers of counsellors who had undertaken training or reading with the ethnic groups in question were those who had more recently been on counselling courses. It may be that counsellors with more recent counselling training experience were those who were more likely to have read or received training in cross-cultural counselling issues.

Furthermore, it may be questioned why a higher percentage of counsellors than have received training with African Caribbean and South Asian groups saw these groups as having a need for different counselling approaches from white clients? This difference in perception of need may reflect the number of counsellors with direct experience of the groups in question. There remains a concern here: without having received an adequate foundation of training to assess Black client need how can this assumption of differing need be qualified in any direction?

Implications for General Counselling Practice

Counselling supervision is a requirement of the BAC's Code of Practice. The results of this research however, indicate that only 61 per cent of counsellors received the necessary supervision. In their draft document on supervision, the BAC (1987, p. 2) stated that supervision was for the supervisor's self awareness and for the benefit of the client: 'The primary purpose is to protect the best interests of the client.' The supervisory element can be seen as a process of checks and balances on counsellor interaction with clients which helps counsellors to review and explore whether their delivery of service is appropriate. It would seem that since few counsellors had received training in cross-cultural issues, adequate supervision to ensure appropriate service delivery with Black clients would be essential. Furthermore, there is a need to ask whether the supervision resource that counsellors have available would be knowledgeable of cross-cultural issues? Who trains and supervises the supervisors in aspects of offering a cross-cultural service?

Counselling Orientation

Although there have been no prior surveys to indicate the orientation range of BAC counsellors, Dryden (1989a) has cited surveys from the USA exploring the eclectic combinations of psychologists belonging to the Psychotherapy Division of the American Psychological Association (Garfield and Kurtz, 1977). The five main combinations in their sample of 154 respondents were: 1) psychoanalytic and learning theory; 2) neo-Freudian and learning theory; 3) neo-Freudian and learning theory; 4) learning theory and humanistic; and 5) Rogerian and learning theory. A study of psychotherapists by Prochaska and Norcross (1983) found that 30 per cent of the sample described themselves as 'eclectic' and that the four most common theoretical perspectives underlying their approaches were psychodynamic (45 per cent), humanistic and existential (25 per cent), behavioural (18 per cent) and other (13 per cent). These findings are different from those of the present survey, which found only 7.7 per cent defining themselves as eclectic. The specified combinations were, in the main, those orientations of Rogerian/psychodynamic (45 per cent) or Rogerian/cognitive-behavioural (35 per cent). Upon inspection of the 'other category', it was noted that 33 of the respondents out of the 49 who self categorized themselves as being in this category, or 9.8 per cent of the total sample of respondents, were in fact indicating a dual or combination approach which could be seen as an 'eclectic' model. Therefore, a more accurate representation of the percentage of those using an eclectic model of some form was 59 respondents or 16.5 per cent of the survey sample. This percentage is, even allowing for some re-coding of responses, much lower than has been found with North American survey samples. It would appear, given that the survey respondents could self categorize as using a combination of models under the 'eclectic' response, that British counsellors, more than their North American counterparts, show more of a leaning towards a single orientation in their self reported practice.

Professional Development Issues

A further revealing statistic is the low number of counsellors, 8.9 per cent, who had obtained BAC accreditation. With a further 42 per cent pursuing accreditation, this would appear to represent a relatively low percentage of counsellors, if this survey is representative of the membership, who have taken accreditation on board. Although the BAC does not set a minimum requirement for a counsellor's qualification, in light of general proliferation of counselling courses at various levels (and perhaps, more contentiously, of dubious worth) it may be now time to do so, given the 9.2 per cent of counsellors in this survey who had no counselling qualifications, the 19.2 per cent of counsellors with only counselling skills training and the high proportion of counsellors not receiving obligatory supervision of their work.

The BAC may, as the British Psychological Society has done with the term psychologist, wish to register and 'protect' or limit the use of term 'counsellor'. This would help to ensure that issues of quality control and service delivery are assured by those who use the term to describe themselves and their professional activities. A further action to reassure Black clients may be to ensure that counselling courses seeking BAC accreditation include relevant training to meet the needs of Britain's diverse cultural communities.

The Multiple Regression and Chi Squared Analysis

This section presents the results from the multiple regression analysis and the chi square (x^2) cross-tabulations. The results will be discussed under the theme headings of 'Counsellor Qualification', 'Counsellor Orientation' and 'Practice Issues' as previously introduced and operationalized in chapter 6.

Multiple Regression Analysis

The rationale for this analysis was given previously in chapter 6, where nine independent or predictor variables were selected as possibly having a causal influence on scores on the Cultural Awareness Inventory.

There are several ways in which multiple regression can be used. Where a clear causal model exists, path analysis is appropriate (Blalock, 1971; Atkin, 1979). As there is little previously published material in the area of this book on which to base such a model, a more exploratory approach seemed indicated, and stepwise multiple regression was selected (Draper and Smith, 1966; Kim and Kohout, 1975). Table 38 summarizes the results.

Table 38   Summary of results of stepwise multiple regression analysis

Independent variable	R^2 change	Total R^2	Raw correlation	Final beta value
Specific reading	0.14 **	0.14	0.38	0.23
Specific training	0.05 **	0.19	0.38	0.19
Academic qualifications	0.03 **	0.22	0.24	0.15
Age of counsellor	0.02 **	0.24	-0.20	-0.16
Experience of counselling African-Caribbean clients	0.01 *	0.26	0.28	0.13

** $p < 0.01$ * $p < 0.05$

Five of the nine variables were sufficient to explain 26 per cent of the variance of the dependent variable, Cultural Awareness Inventory score. The remaining four variables did not yield significant increase in R^2 (at the five per cent level). The nonsignificant variables were 'Applied counselling qualification', 'Gender', 'Experience of counselling South Asian clients' and 'Years of counselling experience'. The five variables yielding significant increases in R^2 in the stepwise regression will now be discussed in turn in order of their relative contribution to the model.

Specific reading

Table 39 gives the relative percentages of counsellors who have, and have not, read specific material.

The variable of specific reading accounted for 14 per cent of the total variance explained. The direction of the relationship between specific reading and the Cultural Awareness Inventory was positive (Beta = .23). This is to say that reading specific material on the needs of ethnic minority clients suggests

Table 39   Frequencies of counsellors who have read specific material on counselling ethnic minority groups

		Read specific material	
Yes	**%**	**No**	**%**
160	47	178	53

that a higher or more favourable score will be obtained on the Cultural Awareness Inventory, meaning the counsellor is more likely to be culturally aware. However, it may be argued that this is to some degree confounded with aspects of personal motivation and that reading is not a causal factor as such. Those counsellors who begin with a higher level of awareness may be more inclined to read specific material on the needs of ethnic minority client groups.

Specific training

Table 40   Frequencies of counsellors with specific training for counselling ethnic minority groups

Specific training	%	Specific training	%
Yes		**No**	
94	28	244	72

Table 40 gives the relative percentages of counsellors who had, and had not, received training in the needs of Black client groups.

The variable of specific training had a positive relationship (Beta = .19) with the Cultural Awareness Inventory. Specific training in the needs of ethnic minority groups included racism awareness training and cross-cultural counselling training. Again, the direction of any causality is unclear since those who seek out and undertake this training (it is not a compulsory part of many counselling courses) may, in fact, already be personally disposed towards or have high levels of cultural awareness.

Academic Qualifications

Table 41 gives the percentages of counsellors who had a first degree or postgraduate academic qualification.

Table 41   Recorded frequencies of academic education variable

First degree or postgraduate academic qualification

Yes	%	No	%
206	61	132	39

Having a first degree or postgraduate academic qualification was the next most effective predictor of scores on the Cultural Awareness Inventory, the relationship being positive (Beta = .15), suggesting that graduates had more favourable scores.

Age of Counsellor

The variable of age of counsellor had a negative relationship with the Cultural Awareness Inventory (Beta = -.16). This is to say that as age of counsellor increased, the score on the Cultural Awareness Inventory decreased. This suggested that counsellors who were older tended to be less aware than counsellors who were younger, or that as age increased so did Eurocentrism. Table 18 gave the counsellors' age ranges. It is interesting to note that, although it did not add significantly to the variance explained, 'Years of counselling experience' on its own had a small positive correlation with scores on the Cultural Awareness Inventory (r = 0.09). There is clearly some interaction here: according to the stepwise regression, age per se appears to produce *less* favourable scores, whereas experience may produce *more* favourable scores.

Experience of Counselling African-Caribbean Clients

Table 42   Experience of counselling African-Caribbean clients

Counselled African-Caribbean clients

Yes	%	No	%
208	58	152	42

Table 42 gives the percentages of counsellors with experience of counselling African-Caribbean clients.

The experience of counselling African-Caribbean clients was the final predictor variable in the model. The effect on the Cultural Awareness Inventory was relatively small (Beta = 0.13). The result suggested that for those counsellors who did not have experience of counselling African-Caribbean clients, there was a small but statistically significant tendency to obtain lower or less favourable scores on the Cultural Awareness Inventory. This suggested that those counsellors with no experience of counselling this client group would show much less awareness of the importance of cultural issues. But again the causal direction is not clear: for example, the reputation of counsellors who are not culturally aware may be known to clients, who avoid them, preferring those whose reputations are more positive in the context of cultural awareness.

Summary of the Multiple Regression Analysis

There were five predictor variables which resulted from the stepwise multiple regression analysis. Of these five 'specific reading' and 'specific training' accounted for 19 per cent of the 26 per cent of the total variance explained. This indicated that of the five predictor variables 'specific reading' and 'specific training' accounted for the largest effect on the Cultural Awareness Inventory. It can be seen from Table 39 that a higher proportion of the sample had read specific material (n = 160, 47 per cent) than had received training in the needs of Black clients (n = 94, 28 per cent). Therefore, the greater number of those who had read specific material than those who have trained may tentatively explain this particular relative order of the independent variables which may be more related to the relative experience of the sample than actual effect on the model.

The relationship of the predictor variables with other variables will be investigated throughout this chapter under the relevant subheadings of either 'counsellor qualification', 'counsellor orientation', or 'practice issues'.

The Subject Variable of Gender

Although gender was not identified as a predictor variable, i.e., there was no significant relationship between gender and the Cultural Awareness Inventory, sometimes variables which are not statistically significant demand analysis and discussion in their own right but do not, after this, command an integrated discussion in the text narrative (Babbie, 1990; Creswell, 1994). In the context of this investigation this was true of the subject variable of 'gender'. As gender tends to be a key subject difference in many counselling research investigations, the non-statistically significant result, was in fact, socially and psychologically significant. In view of other research findings, the nonsignificant statistical relationship of gender with the Cultural Awareness Inventory may come as a surprise to some. For example, Mogul (1982, p. 3) has argued that 'many consider women to have intrinsic qualities that make them better suited than men to be psychotherapists, or more useful for certain patients'. This view that women are better suited to be psychotherapists may in part be explained by the model of Gilligan (1982) who has suggested that male and female beliefs about the nature of reality differ significantly. She used a 'linear' model to illustrate the process of 'typical' male thinking versus a 'relational' model to illustrate the pattern of women's thinking. There is perhaps a risk here of being perceived as oversimplifying what are two complex models of gender cognition difference. However, simply put, Gilligan (1982) has suggested that 'linear' or 'typical male thinking' focuses on specified objectives and results and is goal orientated. Women on the other hand tend to be 'relational' in cognition and consider the possibilities and relationship of outcome on others before taking action. Gilligan's (1982) model suggested that in many cases the direct straightforward approach of 'linear' thinking may be much less sensitive to the emotional needs of others compared to the 'relational' model. Basically the argument was that women, as a group, tended to be more sensitive to the needs of others. Thus, gender, it has been argued, was a subject variable that affected communication style and consequently empathy and rapport which were seen as the relationship building blocks of counselling. What evidence for this enhanced sensitivity exists?

Previous research comparing white counsellors with white clients and the effect of gender variation has not found a proven relationship between gender and outcome (Grantham, 1973; Pardes et al., 1974; Geer and Hurst, 1976; Garfield and Bergin, 1978; Parloff et al., 1978). Indeed, two studies found that women seeing women had a poorer outcome (Meyer and Freeman, 1976; Mintz et al., 1976), while one earlier study showed the opposite outcome (Hill, 1975). It would seem that there was little empirical support for the view that gender affected outcome although it may indeed affect the process of therapy (Chaplin, 1988; Walker, 1990). Within this study gender alone has been shown not to be a predictor variable as to the degree of counsellor cultural awareness. However, in view of the relatively low number of men in the sample compared to women, another investigation may well wish to test this proposition further.

The Relationship Between Counsellor Qualifications and Cultural Awareness

The reader is reminded that 'counsellor qualification' was operationalized as the number of years a therapist had been practising, whether the therapist had delivered direct therapy services to Black clients, the certificated qualifications a counsellor possessed and the specific training or reading a therapist had undertaken on the counselling needs of Black client groups. These variables and their relationship with other variables were discussed throughout the next section

Levels of Counsellor Qualification

The reader is reminded that years of experience was not a significant predictor variable resulting from the multiple regression analysis. Many would perhaps argue that experience would be an expected influential factor due to the effects of consolidation of knowledge and practice. Sue (1981a, p. 142) argued that although '[i]t is a generally accepted idea that experience increases the ability of the therapist to treat patients, it seems likely that this rather gross variable is tapping numerous qualities that may be assumed to increase with age and experience, e.g. confidence, security, integration, flexibility and knowledge'. In a review of the literature, Luborsky et al. (1975) noted that experience was one of the few therapist factors having a reliable relationship to outcome. Sue (1981) referred to the research of Bergin and Lampert (1978) and Meltzoff and Kornreich (1970), which also supported the value of experience on positive outcome measures. However Auerbach and Johnson (1977), in a more recent review than those previously cited by Sue, were not as supportive of the finding that experience was highly related to outcome, although the more experienced therapists were more likely to have positive therapy outcomes than the least experienced. It should be noted that these studies were not those with a cross-cultural influence; they were studies of white therapists with white clients. Furthermore, the criteria of experience, i.e., length, breadth and quality, may have differed between the studies so that they may not have been measuring the same criterion as in this particular investigation. Another factor may be the interaction between age and experience as discussed earlier. Older counsellors appear to have less favourable scores on the Cultural Awareness Inventory and these may mask the effects of experience.

The Relationship of Direct Experience of Counselling Black Clients with the Cultural Awareness Inventory

The reader is reminded that the relationship of the Cultural Awareness Inventory with experience of counselling South Asian clients was found to be nonsignificant, whereas the relationship of the Cultural Awareness Inventory with experience of counselling African-Caribbean clients was statistically significant ($p<.05$). Table 20 gave the relative percentages of counsellors who had, and who had not, counselled South Asian and African-Caribbean clients. Those counsellors who had direct experience of counselling African-Caribbean clients tended to be more culturally aware in their view than those counsellors who had no direct experience of counselling African-Caribbean clients. Why this was not so for South Asian clients may be because counsellors experienced both a degree of 'personal distress' (Batson et al., 1987) and 'cognitive dissonance' (Festinger, 1957). The theory of cognitive dissonance was first mentioned in chapter 3 and will be discussed further later in this chapter.

The statistical significance of the direct experience result may also be an artefact of the multiple regression analysis when variance of the independent variable is small, i.e., the number in one cell (those with experience) is relatively small. On the other hand, it may suggest that there was something specific to encounters with the South Asian group which did not enable cultural awareness in counsellors. It may be that direct experience with a culturally distinct community who may display less opportunity or motivation for adoption of European cultural norms due to their distinct culturally influenced social and psychological set does not facilitate the counsellor's openness to change through direct experience (Sue and Sue, 1977a). It may be, in line with Tajfel et al. (1969, 1978), that the greater the perception of cultural difference or out-group difference, the less an adequate level of 'cultural openness' or cultural awareness is facilitated in counsellors. However, this can only be speculative as the available data do not allow further conclusions on the exact mechanism in operation in promoting cultural awareness. The particular position of the South Asian communities and counsellor attitude will be further explored in the section which investigates the influence of counsellor theoretical orientation.

The empirical outcome of the relationship between the Cultural Awareness Inventory and having direct experience of counselling African-Caribbean clients was seen as a further construct and content validation of the Cultural Awareness Inventory, as the inventory was able to measure distinctions between attitudes related to distinct cultural groups. Furthermore, the outcome showing more awareness through direct experience or 'activity based' contact with certain culturally different groups was consistent with the findings of other investigations (Sherif et al., 1961; Miller and Brewer, 1986). It should be noted that it may well be that those counsellors who are informally assessed by clients to be less culturally aware are avoided before counselling begins. However, this informal assessment by clients prior to counselling may be impractical (unless clients are knowledgeable of the counsellors' reputation), but does provide some insight into why early termination may be shown with some counsellors by some clients (Sue, 1981a; Sue, 1981b; Sue and Sue, 1990). As Sue (1981b, p. 102) argued:

> A basic assumption underlying counselling and psychotherapy is that the relationship which the counsellor/therapist establishes with a client can either enhance or negate the process. When the emotional climate is negative, and when misunderstanding or little trust exists between the counsellor and client, counselling can be both ineffective and destructive.

Lack of success with Black clients owing to a non-recognition of the external forces which influence their life may bring about negative feelings towards these groups because of feelings of powerlessness being initiated in unsuccessful counselling encounters. Counsellors, as a way of coping with the client's difficulties, may react by blaming the individual client for their position and inability to change. As discussed in chapter 3, the findings of Batson et al. (1987) in considering the concept of 'personal distress' and the observations of Pinderhughes (1989) supported this proposition, i.e., initial feelings of empathy with clients who later overwhelm the counsellor with significant cultural difference may be translated into 'empathic distance' which may become aversive stimuli and cause counsellors to withdraw emotionally from clients who they perceive themselves as unable to help. Therefore, these client circumstances, the impact of social forces on client life chances, and opportunities for this particular group may be threatening to a counsellor's own emotional needs. This has links with other research studies. For example, a study by Robbins and Jolkovski (1987) operationalized counter-transference as 'withdrawal of involvement'. This operationalized definition may not be sufficient, as it only acknowledged one end of the continuum and did not take into account the emotional 'over-involvement' part of the counter-transference continuum. However, it is possible that feelings of intense emotion may cause the counsellor to withdraw their involvement, and this would fit with the findings of Batson et al. (1987). Also, using Robbins and Jolkovski's operational definition as a means for considering why direct experience of counselling South Asian clients did not show a statistically significant effect with the stepwise multiple regression analysis may allow us to speculate that counsellors were experiencing greater counter-transference difficulties with South Asian clients. Other influences on cultural awareness will now be explored.

Cross-tabulated Variables Related to Counsellor Experience

Further analysis was undertaken to ascertain whether having received specific training in Black client needs was a function of years of counsellor experience.

Table 43   Association between specific training in South Asian client need and length of counsellor experience

	Length of experience			
Specific training	**0–2 years** %	**2–7 years** %	**8–12 years** %	**13+ years** %
Yes	23	27	29	37
No	78	73	71	63
	n = 40	135	55	43

$x^2 = 2.54$, d.f. = 3, p>.05

The results (Table 43) showed that there was no association between having had specific training in South Asian client need and length of experience. Therefore, length of experience did not suggest the likelihood of having received training. There was, however, a detectable trend for counsellors with longer experience to involve themselves more in training, but this was not statistically significant across the years of experience bands and may have been an artefact of more opportunity due to longer years of experience to involve themselves in such training.

The possible association between reading material on South Asian client need and length of counsellor experience was considered next.

The results (Table 44) showed a statistically significant association between length of counselling experience and having read material on the counselling need of South Asian clients, p<.01. Observation of the percentages in the table suggested that with longer experience there was likely to be a greater

**Table 44   Association between reading material on South Asian
client counselling need and counsellor length of experience**

Reading material	Length of experience			
	0–2 years	2–7 years	8–12 years	13+ years
	%	%	%	%
Yes	24	48	53	61
No	76	52	48	39
	n = 38	141	59	49

$x^2 = 12.92$, d.f. = 1, p>.01

chance that reading had taken place. Further statistical analysis was done to
explore for an association between reading specific material in the needs of
African-Caribbean clients and the length of counsellor experience.

**Table 45   Association between reading specific material on the needs
of African-Caribbean clients and length of counsellor
experience**

Reading material	Length of experience			
	0–2 years	2–7 years	8–12 years	13+ years
	%	%	%	%
Yes	28	47	54	63
No	72	53	46	38
	n = 39	137	61	48

$x^2 = 11.01$, d.f. = 3, p>.01

Again, as with South Asian clients, the results (Table 45) showed that
there was a statistically significant association, p<.01, between reading specific
material on the needs of African-Caribbean clients and counsellor length of
experience. Observation of the cell percentages suggested that the longer the
length of experience the greater the chance that the counsellor would have
read specific material. This may simply be a result of time's affording greater
opportunity rather than increased motivation alone. The effect of years of
experience was explored further with the variable of having participated in
specific training on African-Caribbean client needs (Table 46).

As with the result with South Asian clients, there was no statistically

Table 46   Association with having specific training on the needs of African-Caribbean clients and length of experience

Specific training	Length of experience			
	0–2 years %	2–7 years %	8–12 years %	13+ years %
Yes	23	29	36	38
No	78	71	64	62
	n = 40	136	55	42

$x^2 = 2.23$, d.f. = 3, p>.05

significant association between specific training in the needs of African-Caribbean clients and length of counsellor experience. Therefore, only reading material on Black clients had a significant association with counsellor length of experience. These results suggested that more experienced counsellors were more likely to have read about the needs of the culturally different than to have received training. The lack of a statistically significant difference between counsellors of different lengths of experience participating in training may be a negative indicator of the curriculum input of professional counselling training courses in cross-cultural counselling. However, there are other ways of gaining knowledge about client need, and these were explored in the next section.

'Classroom Based' Learning

Pinderhughes (1989) made the point that classroom based learning, e.g., lectures, seminars, reading and discussion could affect cultural self understanding but that 'the emphasis may be primarily conceptual rather than experiential' (p. 240). Therefore, Pinderhughes suggested that the necessary emotional and thus deeper levels of learning might not take place sufficiently to affect what the counsellor did in the counselling exchange. This may also be so with reading, even though counsellors can engage and order their thoughts and feelings in private. The relationship between the Cultural Awareness Inventory and reading on the needs of Black clients was shown to be statistically significant at the p>.01 level. The result suggested that reading on Black client need had a positive effect on reducing counsellor Eurocentrism. However, the more critical individual may comment that those who were less Eurocentric may have been more open to reading, and therefore the only conclusion that could be made was that those who had taken the time to read were less inclined to Eurocentric beliefs. Therefore, reading may not be a causal factor in the promotion of cultural awareness. Even if reading did help to promote cultural awareness, this result would not allow us to explore Pinderhughes' (1989) assertion that any increase in cultural awareness or the reduction of Eurocentrism occurred only at a conceptual or cognitive level and not at a experiential or emotional level. However, the point stood that some aspect of Eurocentrism was less in those 47 per cent of counsellors who had read specific information on the service delivery needs of Black clients.

As well as the multiple regression analysis of independent variables by the dependent variable of the Cultural Awareness Inventory, chi squared cross-tabulations were carried out. These additional analyses were necessary to assess the possible further relationships between counsellor qualification and other related variables which could have explanatory utility. In the following sections the rationales for, and results of these additional analyses were provided.

The Effects of Particular Types of Training

Pinderhughes (1989) has extolled the virtues of experiential training. The multiple regression analysis indicated that those counsellors who had training scored more favourably on the Cultural Awareness Inventory than those counsellors who had no training. Further analyses to ascertain if there were measurable differences in effect between the different types of training experiences was performed.

Cross-cultural counselling workshops tend to work less with the emotional content of cultural difference than does racism awareness training (Katz, 1984; d'Ardenne and Mahtani, 1988; Sue and Sue, 1990). Observation of the cross-tabulation between counsellors who had undertaken a racism awareness training course and a cross-cultural counselling training workshop (see Table 47) suggested that more counsellors had experienced racism awareness training than cross-cultural counselling training, p<.001.

Table 47   Relative experience of participating in different types of training

	Yes %	No %
Experience of racism awareness workshop	77	23
Experience of cross-cultural counselling training	12	88
	n = 338	

$x^2 = 11.54$, d.f. = 1, p<.001

To investigate the specific effect of certain forms of training, a cross-tabulation was performed on those having participated in racism awareness training and belief in the benefit of a different model for South Asian clients.

Table 48   Association of participation in racism awareness training and belief in a different model for South Asian clients

	Yes %	No %
Participation in racism awareness training	70	30
No participation in racism awareness training	83	17
	n = 64	25

$x^2 = .90$, d.f. = 1, NS, p>.05

Observation of the statistical result (Table 48) indicated that there was no statistical association between participation in racism awareness training and a belief in a different model for South Asian clients. The possibility of an association between belief in a different model and participation in racism awareness training was further explored with African-Caribbean clients.

Analysis of the affect of racism awareness training on counsellors' belief in a different model for African-Caribbean clients produced a nonsignificant result (Table 49), as with South Asian clients, suggesting that there was no association between participating in racism awareness training and belief in a different model for African-Caribbean clients. The affect of cross-cultural counselling training and its potential influence on counsellor views was explored in the next statistical analysis.

Table 49   Association between participation in racism awareness training and belief in a different model for African-Caribbean clients

Belief in different model for African-Caribbean clients	Yes %	No %
Participation in racism awareness training	69	31
No participation in racism awareness training	82	18
	n = 60	25

$x^2 = .77$, d.f. = 1, NS, p>.05

Again, as with racism awareness training there was no statistically significant association between the participation in cross-cultural counselling training and the belief in a different model for African-Caribbean clients (Table 50). The possible influence of cross-cultural counselling training on the belief in a different model for South Asian clients was then considered.

Table 50   Association between belief in a different model for African-Caribbeans and participating in cross-cultural counselling training

Belief in different model for African-Caribbean clients	Yes %	No %
Participation in cross-cultural counselling training	80	20
No participation in cross-cultural counselling training	67	33
n = 51	16

$x^2 = 1.21$, d.f. = 1, NS, p>.05

Table 51   Association between belief in a different model for South Asian clients and cross-cultural counselling training

Belief in benefit of a different model for African-Caribbean clients	Yes %	No %
Participation in cross-cultural counselling training	79	21
No participation in cross-cultural counselling training	68	32
n = 51	16

$x^2 = .86$, d.f. = 1, NS, p>.05

As with African-Caribbean clients there was no statistically significant association between participation in cross-cultural counselling training on the belief in the benefit of a different model for South Asian clients (Table 51). It may be that cross-cultural counselling training and racism awareness training were not specific enough in their subject matter or not effective enough as independent strategies to influence counsellors' views on the benefit of a different model for the Black ethnic groups in question. It appears that, with those variables investigated for an association, neither form of training is more effective than the other on its own.

Belief in a different model was perhaps less likely to be influenced by emotional exploration than a cognitive appreciation of the reasons a different model may be necessary. Therefore, it may be that neither racism awareness training nor cross-cultural counselling training was sufficiently tapping the aspects that convince counsellors of the reasons for and value of a different model. A different form of training may have had a different influence on counsellors' understanding and viewpoint. To test this further, statistical analyses were performed to explore for a relationship between having received what was termed 'combination training' in the counselling needs of African-Caribbeans and South Asians. Combination training was defined as participating in courses related to a combination of issues of cultural knowledge, sociopolitical factors relevant to the four particular ethnic groups and self exploration of the counsellors' understanding of their own culture and ethnic group membership.

Table 52   **Association between combination training in African-Caribbean counselling needs and the belief in benefit of different counselling models**

Belief in benefit of a different model	Yes %	No %
Combination training in African-	45	25
Caribbean counselling need	55	75
	n =120	79

$x^2 = 7.9$, d.f. = 1, NS, p<.01

This cross-tabulation was statistically significant, p<.01, and observation of Table 52 allowed us to say that there was a greater chance with those who had received a 'combination' form of training in the particular needs of African-Caribbean clients having a belief that different models than those used with white clients could be necessary for this client group. This relationship was explored in a cross-tabulated analysis with South Asian clients.

Table 53   **Association between having had combination training on the counselling needs of South Asian clients and a belief in benefit of different counselling models than those used with white clients**

Belief in benefit of a different model	Yes %	No %
Combination training in South	40.3	19
Asian counselling need	59.7	81
	n =120	79

$x^2 = 10.2$, d.f. = 1, NS, p<.001

This cross-tabulation was statistically significant, p<.001, and observation of the results in Table 53 suggested that there was a strong association between having had a 'combined' form of training in the needs of South Asian clients and a belief in the benefit of the use of different models than those used with white clients. It may be that this 'combined' form of training more closely resembles that of 'academic training' which was shown to be significant in its effect with the Cultural Awareness Inventory. Therefore, the previous two statistical results may be confirming of the greater effect of 'academic training' rather than indicating any new issues of influence.

The possible association with reading material and the belief in the benefit of a different model was explored with both South Asian and African-Caribbean clients.

Table 54   Association of reading material on the specific counselling needs of South Asian clients and the belief of benefit of a different model than that used with white clients

Belief in benefit of a different model	Yes %	No %
Reading material on South	59.9	43.2
Asian counselling need	40.1	56.8
	n =137	81

$x^2 = 5.68$, d.f. = 1, NS, p<.01

The results (Table 54) suggested that there was a statistically significant association, p<.01, between having read specific material on the counselling needs of South Asian clients and a belief in the benefit of a different counselling model than that used with white clients. This statistical association was further explored with African-Caribbean clients.

Table 55   Association of reading material on the belief of benefit of a different counselling model for African-Caribbean clients

Belief in benefit of a different model	Yes %	No %
Reading material on African-	62.2	47
Caribbean counselling need	37.8	53
	n =127	83

$x^2 = 4.72$, d.f. = 1, NS, p<.05

As with South Asian clients, this cross-tabulation (Table 55) was statistically significant, and observation of the cells allowed us to say that there was a greater chance of those who had read material on the particular needs of African-Caribbean clients having a belief that there was a need for different models of counselling than those used with white clients. The previously discussed proposition that a cognitive influence was necessary to convince counsellors of the need for a different model was supported. There may be further influences on the belief in a different model for Black clients and these will be explored in the Counsellor Orientation section.

Summary Discussion

Gender, Age of Counsellor and Length of Experience

Gender of counsellor was found not to have a significant effect with the Cultural Awareness Inventory. The independent variable 'age of counsellor' showed a statistically significant effect with the Cultural Awareness Inventory. Younger counsellors were found to obtain more favourable scores on the Cultural Awareness Inventory than were older counsellors.

Having a greater number of years' experience in itself was not a statistically significant predictor of the cultural awareness a counsellor may have of Black client groups. This result contradicted the findings of studies that had compared the influence of length of experience of white therapists and experiencing negative attitudes when working with white clients (Cohen, 1952; Little, 1957; Klagsbrun, 1967; Searless, 1987). For example, Blum (1986) asserted that the more experience a therapist had, the easier it was to analyse and resolve any negative attitudes the therapist may have unconsciously held. In investigating the influence of experience, Hill (1975), in a review of the literature, suggested that inexperienced counsellors were more affected by clients they liked or disliked and tended to give more direct advice, whereas experienced counsellors were more open and flexible, focusing more on the client's need than technique. Several studies have identified the ability of experienced therapists to be relatively more accepting of their clients and create a more favourable therapeutic environment (Strupp, 1958; Blum, 1986; Tracey et al., 1988). Blum (1986), in particular, noted that having negative attitudes towards the client was only one of the difficulties that therapists with relatively little experience were likely to face, the others being 'inexperience, lack of knowledge and uncertainty in the face of the bewildering complexity of the patient's associations' (p. 362). With this research experience was not a significant predictor of cultural awareness. However, the interaction of age and experience is clearly complex, and further research is desirable.

The Effect of Training and Reading

There was no significant relationship between length of experience and having had training in the counselling needs of Black clients, although there was a trend with the more experienced counsellors to have had this specific training. Given the possibility that the less experienced counsellors were more likely to have received more recent counsellor training, the trend for more experienced counsellors to have been more involved with specific training for service delivery to Black clients gave rise for concern related to counselling course curriculum.

Both the independent variables of reading and training had a significant relationship with the Cultural Awareness Inventory in that those who had read tended to have more cultural awareness towards Black clients. A note of caution must be sounded with regard to the effect of reading. As previously suggested, those who have read may have been predisposed to have a more open or a less Eurocentric attitude, and therefore much less culturally aware to begin, with than those who had not sought out specific reading material.

'Combination' training, which may be related to academic forms of training, was statistically significant in its association, with a belief in a different model for both African-Caribbean and South Asian clients.

Direct Experience

Having direct experience of counselling African-Caribbean clients appeared to have the effect of enabling counsellors to score more favourably on the Cultural Awareness Inventory than those counsellors who had no experience. This was not a statistically significant finding for counsellors with experience of South Asian clients. This distinction was somewhat puzzling, and it has been speculated in the section discussing this result that it may be that the greater perceived cultural distance between white counsellors and South Asian clients may act as negative indicator of positive outcome which creates feelings of 'personal distress' (Batson et al., 1987) in counsellors who experienced aversive reactions or negative attitudes towards clients from South Asian ethnic client groups.

Training and Cultural Awareness

As previously shown, the level of academic qualification, but not the level of counselling qualification, was significant in its effect with the Cultural Awareness Inventory. Why applied counselling training did not have an effect was puzzling and deserved some discussion. It was speculated that academic forms of training engaged counsellors at primarily a cognitive level and did not tap the emotional experience of counsellors. Academic training therefore, may lay a necessary foundation to be able to conceptualize the distinct needs of the culturally different and training that has as its basis, a focus on emotional issues, may not be enough in itself. Also, training of a form other than that related to academic based training (e.g., 'combination training'), that takes place without a foundation of academic training in place may not allow the counsellor to adequately conceptualize the issues related to counselling the culturally different and may therefore be ineffective.

This section has presented the data analysis and interpretation of the results relating to the theme of counsellor qualification, which was operationally defined as the number of years of counsellor experience, experience of direct therapy service delivery to Black clients, the certificated counselling or academic qualifications held by the counsellor, and the specific training or reading of material which focused on Black clients' counselling needs. The next section discusses the theme of counsellor orientation and how this related to counsellor attitudes and practices.

The Counsellor's Theoretical Orientations

To explore the relationship between counsellors' personal characteristics, attitudes and practice in the context of counsellors' orientation, a number of items from the questionnaire were statistically investigated. These were gender, use of family network, use of interpreter, specific training and reading, years of experience, and belief in the benefit of a different model. As previously discussed, to make the results conceptually meaningful only those theoretical orientations that formed the three most popular or frequent preferences of counsellors were compared, these being the 'psychodynamic', 'Rogerian' or 'client-centred' and 'eclectic' models.

Counsellor Orientation and Gender

Table 56   Association between counsellor orientation and gender

	Counsellor gender	
Counsellor orientation	**Female %**	**Male %**
Rogerian	68	32
Psychodynamic	83	17
Eclectic	87	13
n = 180		50

$x^2 = 9.5$, d.f. = 2, p<.01

The association between counsellor gender and counsellor theoretical orientation was statistically significant at the p<.01 level (Table 56). Observation of the cell percentages suggested that there was a greater chance that male counsellors would be of the Rogerian or client-centred theoretical orientation than of the psychodynamic or eclectic orientation, and for women to follow an eclectic or psychodynamic model rather than Rogerian model. The reasons for this were not clear and will not be further explored as this was not within the research objectives. However, this difference may relate to the relative satisfaction that the different models offer men and women in interpreting the world. If so, then the personal attractions of the psychodynamic model to women therapists may outweigh the negative gender attributions of some of the psychodynamic schools of thought. This is an interesting proposition that could not be explored here as it was not within the research objectives.

Counsellor Orientation and Length of Experience

In chapter 5 it was noted that Masson (1989) had argued that the Rogerian model tended to be preferred by those with little experience, as it could be learned relatively quickly. To test this assertion a cross-tabulation between years of experience and counsellor orientation was performed.

The results of this analysis (Table 57) show that there was no statistically significant association between counsellor orientation and years of experience. It appeared from this that experience was not a variable affecting a counsellor's preferred model. Therefore, Masson's assertion appeared unfounded in

Table 57 Association between counsellor orientation and years of experience

Counsellor's orientation	Years of experience			
	0–2 years	2–7 years	8–12 years	13+ years
Rogerian	10	54	2	15
Psychodynamic	13	45	33	9
Eclectic	8	49	18	25
	n = 24	113	55	36

$x^2 = 11.33$, d.f. = 6, NS, p>.05

its claim that the Rogerian model was more attractive to those with little experience. The next section investigated the possible relationship between counsellor orientation and the Cultural Awareness Inventory.

Counsellor Orientation and Use of Family Network

The relationship of the counsellor's orientation on the use of the family network was investigated to see whether a counsellor's orientation influenced the use of the family network, as different models have been argued by some to have more of an individual emphasis and play down systemic or family/community/ personal support network influences (Boyd-Franklin, 1989; Sue and Sue, 1990).

The statistical analysis (Table 58) showed that there was no statistically significant association between a counsellor's theoretical orientation and actual use of family network. This indicated that no one particular orientation was likely to make more or less use of the family network than another orientation. The effect of a counsellor's orientation on use of interpreters was then investigated, as some writers have suggested that some orientations are much less willing than others to alter traditional, standard practices (Pinderhughes, 1989; Maroda, 1991).

Counsellor Orientation and Use of Interpreters

The statistical analysis (Table 59) indicated that there was no statistically significant association between a counsellor's theoretical orientation and willingness to make use of an interpreter with African-Caribbean clients. However, there was a trend for counsellors following an eclectic or Rogerian

Table 58   Association between counsellor orientation and actual use of family network

Counsellor orientation	Use of family network %	No use of family network %
Rogerian	29	71
Psychodynamic	38	63
Eclectic	42	58
n =	76	138

$x^2 = 2.51$, d.f. = 2, NS, p>.05

Table 59   Association between counsellor orientation and willingness to use an interpreter with African-Caribbean clients

Counsellor orientation	Willingness to use an interpreter %	No willingness to use an interpreter %
Rogerian	40	60
Psychodynamic	35	65
Eclectic	44	56
n =	68	56

$x^2 = .85$, d.f. = 2, NS, p>.05

Table 60   Association between counsellor orientation and willingness to use an interpreter with South Asian clients

Counsellor orientation	Willingness to use an interpreter %	No willingness to use an interpreter %
Rogerian	52	48
Psychodynamic	50	50
Eclectic	71	29
n =	102	78

$x^2 = 5.67$, d.f. = 2, NS, p<.05

family network. With this in mind an analysis to ascertain if an association between a counsellor's orientation and willingness to use an interpreter with South Asian clients was performed.

Observation of the results in this analysis (Table 60) showed that there was a statistically significant association between counsellor orientation and willingness to use an interpreter. Those counsellors who were eclectic were more willing to make use of an interpreter than those counsellors who were of Rogerian or psychodynamic orientations. It may be that working within an eclectic framework with South Asian clients allowed counsellors to consider more fully the particular needs of clients within the multi-model and multidimensional framework of Ivey et al. (1993).

Considering the meaning of the previous two analyses the reader is reminded of the result in Table 33, which suggested more willingness by counsellors to use an interpreter with South Asian than African-Caribbean clients. Why willingness to use an interpreter should be less with African-Caribbean clients was perhaps, at face value, obvious, but may have neglected the particular needs of those not born in Britain, as will be highlighted in the transcribed interviews in a later section. The largest single African-Caribbean group in Britain is of Jamaican origin and perceived as English language speaking (Nanton, 1992). As such it may be that counsellors did not perceive this group as having distinct second language needs. Counsellors would seem to hold the view that, as South Asians speak a demonstrably different language to English, there was a greater need to consider an interpreter than with African-Caribbean clients, who may not be perceived as having a significant language difference. The available research suggested that this was an erroneous assumption (Dominelli, 1988; d'Ardenne and Mahtani, 1989). There are distinct subtleties of language usage and meaning within 'Black Caribbean English', and thus the assumptions of lack of interpreter need with African-Caribbeans among counsellors could be interpreted as dismissive of client need.

To investigate for the further influence of counsellor orientation it was seen as useful to consider the relationship of counsellor orientation and actual use of interpreters as there may have been a difference between willingness to make use of an interpreter and actual use of interpreter services. Table 61 shows the outcome of this investigation.

The statistical analysis indicated a statistically significant association between a counsellor's theoretical orientation and actual use of an interpreter, $p < .01$. Inspection of the cell percentages suggested that psychodynamic and eclectic counsellors were more likely to have used interpreters than were Rogerian counsellors. This result contradicted the general assertion in the literature, as many writers have suggested that it was psychodynamic counsellors who would tend to be more 'stuck' in inappropriate forms of counselling delivery than other theoretical orientations (Sue and Sue, 1990;

Table 61   Association between counsellor orientation and actual use of an interpreter

Counsellor orientation	Use of an interpreter %	No use of an interpreter %
Rogerian	8	92
Psychodynamic	36	64
Eclectic	22	78
n =	23	85

$x^2 = 8.8$, d.f. = 2, p<.01

Kareem and Littlewood, 1992; Ivey et al., 1993). Because of the result obtained in this comparative analysis it was suggested that this perception may need to be reviewed. There may be a number of reasons associated with counsellors' lack of openness to use interpreters. Among these, one may be that it showed an attitude in counsellors that those clients who had language interpretation needs were best served by those counsellors who spoke the necessary language (or dialect); another may be that interpretation services were of little use and interfered with the process of counselling.

Sue and Sue (1990, p. 46) have made the point that 'use of standard English to communicate with one another [in the counselling situation] may unfairly discriminate against those from a bi-lingual or lower class background'. Sue and Sue made a further related point in that having a bilingual background may lead to much misunderstanding even 'if the Third World person cannot speak his or her own native tongue' (p. 46). It appeared that some studies (Smith, 1957; Smith and Kasdon, 1961) have shown that a background where one or both parents have spoken their mother tongue can culturally influence the acquisition, understanding, and use of English.

De Shazer (1991) used Hintikka and Hintikka's (1986) description of Wittgenstein's understanding of language and its meaning which was:

> … one can use language to talk about something only if one can rely on a given definite interpretation, a given network of meaning relations obtaining between language and the world (p. 59–60).

Marcos (1979) suggested that bilingual clients who did not use their mother tongue may not be able to access significant aspects of their emotional experience as they may not have the complexity of language to explain themselves without a loss of emotional complexity and experience.

Furthermore, lack of attention to bilingual clients' language needs may impede rapport building and thus negate an essential aspect of the therapeutic alliance.

To discover whether there was an association between counsellor theoretical orientation and participating in specific training or reading material related to South Asian clients' needs, as this may have informed the identification and selection of appropriate services, further statistical analysis was carried out in the next section. This initially examined this possibility with the South Asian client group as this was the particular ethnic group that counsellors showed a willingness to make use of an interpreter. The use of interpreters is further discussed in the 'Practice Issues' section of this chapter, as this presented as a logical connection and extension of this particular theme. The next section will explore the possible relationships between a counsellor's orientation and the participation in training and reading specific material on the needs of Black client groups.

Counsellor Orientation and the Influence of Training and Reading

Observation of the statistical analysis (Table 62) indicated that there was no statistically significant association between counsellor orientation and having specific training in the needs of South Asian clients. The association between reading specific material on the needs of South Asian clients and counsellor orientation was examined next, as this may also have influenced the identification and selection of appropriate interpreting services and thus have contributed to satisfaction of use.

Table 62   Association between a counsellor's orientation and having specific training for South Asian clients

Counsellor orientation	Specific training	No specific training
	%	%
Rogerian	24	76
Psychodynamic	28	72
Eclectic	37	63
n =	55	136

$x^2 = 2.76$, d.f. $= 2$, p>.05

The statistical analysis (Table 63) indicated that there was no statistically significant association between reading material on South Asian clients' needs

Table 63   Association between a counsellor's orientation and reading specific material on South Asian clients

Counsellor orientation	Reading material	No reading material
	%	%
Rogerian	47	53
Psychodynamic	44	56
Eclectic	59	41
n =	99	102

$x^2 = 3.10$, d.f. = 2, p>.05

and counsellor theoretical orientation. Therefore, there remained an unidentified influence on greater use of interpreting services by psychodynamic therapists. Given the previous two statistical analyses on the influence of reading and training with South Asian clients, it was considered appropriate to contribute to the available knowledge, to calculate cross-tabulations on the association between counsellor orientation and having had specific training or reading material on the needs of African-Caribbean clients.

The statistical analysis in Table 64 showed there was no statistically significant association between having training on the needs of African-Caribbean clients and counsellor theoretical orientation as with the results with the relationship between training on the needs of South Asian clients and counsellor orientation. The relationship of reading material on African-Caribbean client needs and counsellor orientation was explored (Table 65).

Table 64   Association between a counsellor's orientation and having specific training for African-Caribbean clients

Counsellor orientation	Specific training	No specific training
	%	%
Rogerian	27	73
Psychodynamic	31	69
Eclectic	43	57
n =	63	130

$x^2 = 3.55$, d.f. = 2, NS, p>.05

Again, the statistical analysis outcome showed there was no statistically significant association between reading specific material on the needs of African-Caribbean clients and counsellor theoretical orientation as with the

Table 65   Association between counsellor orientation and reading specific material for African-Caribbean clients

Counsellor orientation	Reading material	No reading material
	%	%
Rogerian	48	52
Psychodynamic	48	52
Eclectic	59	41
	n = 104	91

$x^2 = 1.77$, d.f. = 2, NS, p>.05

lack of a statistically significant association between reading material on the needs of South Asian clients and counsellor orientation.

The results of the four previous analyses indicated that there were no statistically significant associations between training or reading on the needs of South Asian or African-Caribbean client groups and counsellor orientation which allowed the conclusion that counsellor orientation did not appear to be of predictive value in suggesting whether a counsellor was likely to be specifically informed about African-Caribbean or South Asian clients' needs. Regardless of this, there was a detectable trend in the interviews with counsellors with a Rogerian theoretical orientation to assert the 'value free' foundation of this model, and this is illustrated in the next chapter. The results of the statistical analyses presented in the section on use of interpreters did not support the views expressed in the interviews, as in the main, counsellors with an eclectic or psychodynamic approach appeared from the survey results to be more in tune with Black client needs as regards to the use of an interpreter and use of the family network to influence the counselling outcome. The next section explores the relationship between the belief in the benefit of a different model for Black clients with counsellor orientation.

The Belief in the Benefit of Different Counselling Models

The belief in a different model for South Asian clients, although not influenced – as previously discussed in the 'Counsellor Qualification' section – by racism awareness training, or cross-cultural counselling training, but mainly by focused or specific training, may also be influenced by counsellor theoretical orientation, as some writers have suggested that certain counselling models are more rigid and less open to change than others (Sue, 1981a; Ivey et al.,

1993). To test this proposition, further statistical analyses were carried out. The association between the belief in the benefit of different counselling models than used with white clients for African-Caribbean clients with the counsellor's theoretical model, was tested.

Table 66   **Association between the belief in the benefit of a different counselling model for South Asian clients and counsellor orientation**

Counsellor orientation	Yes %	No %
Rogerian	59	41
Psychodynamic	60	40
Eclectic	69	31
n = 102		62

$x^2 = 1.18$, d.f. $= 2$, NS, p>.05

The results of the statistical analysis (Table 66) showed that there was no statistically significant association between the belief in the benefit of a different model than used with white clients for South Asian clients and counsellor orientation. This was further explored with African-Caribbean clients.

Table 67   **Association between counsellor orientation and belief in the benefit of a different model for African-Caribbean clients**

Counsellor orientation	Belief in different model %	No belief in different model %
Rogerian	56	44
Psychodynamic	61	39
Eclectic	69	31
n = 99		63

$x^2 = 1.93$, d.f. $= 2$, NS, p>.05

Observation of the statistical analysis outcome (Table 67) showed that there was no statistically significant association between the belief in the benefit of a different counselling model for African-Caribbean clients and a counsellor's theoretical orientation. The results of the two previous statistical analyses suggested that the belief in the benefit of a different model, for both South Asian clients and African-Caribbean clients, was independent of a counsellor's theoretical orientation.

The possible need for a different counselling model when working with the culturally different has been reflected in the writings of several researchers. Just as culture, ethnicity, gender, age and sexuality are likely to affect social interaction, Sue (1977a, 1981) has argued that a counsellor's theoretical orientation was likely to influence their communication approach and thus the relationship that was established with a client. Sue and Sue (1990, p. 69) argued that 'different cultural groups may be more receptive to certain counselling/communication styles because of cultural and socio-political factors'. He went further, to suggest that often this was likely to mean a preference for a more 'active-directive' form of helping than a nondirective one (Pederson et al., 1981; Trimble, 1981; Ruiz, 1983). Boyd-Franklin (1989) argued that therapists must be willing and able to be flexible and draw upon the work of many different schools of therapy. In support of this view, Ho (1992) argued that to be effective, the delivery of counselling should be multidimensional, i.e., directed at the various components of the client's environment, multi-disciplinary, involving diverse professional groups when necessary, and multi-model offering a combination of individual, family and group treatments (Gibbs et al., 1989; Ho, 1992).

Although years of counsellor experience was shown not to be a predictor variable with the Cultural Awareness Inventory, it was seen as reasonable to test the association of this variable with other variables. To test the possibility that years of counsellor experience may influence counsellors' openness to the benefit of a different model, the following statistical analyses were carried out. The results (Table 68) showed that there was no statistically significant association between length of experience and perceived benefit of a different model for South Asian clients than used with white clients. This was further explored with African-Caribbean clients.

Again the results (Table 69) indicated that there was no statistically significant association between length of experience and perceived benefit of a different counselling model for African-Caribbean clients than used with white clients. It appeared from the results of the two previous statistical tests that experience alone was not an indicator of belief in the benefit of a different counselling model for South Asian or African-Caribbean clients.

To test further for the association between counsellor influences on belief of the benefit of a different model and specific experience, a further statistical

Table 68   **Association between length of experience and belief in benefit of different counselling model for South Asian clients than that used with white clients**

Length of experience	0–2 years %	2–7 years %	8–12 years %	13+ years %
Belief in benefit of a different model – yes	58	58	72	67
Belief in benefit of a different model – no	42	42	28	33
n =	26	117	53	42

$x^2 = 3.44$, d.f. = 3, NS, p>.05

Table 69   **Association between length of experience and perceived benefit of a different counselling model for African-Caribbean clients than that used with white clients**

Length of experience	0–2 years %	2–7 years %	8–12 years %	13+ years %
Different model – yes	52	58	70	68
Different model – no	48	42	30	33
n =	25	111	53	40

$x^2 = 38$, d.f. = 3, NS, p>.05

Table 70   **Association between actual experience of counselling South Asian clients and a belief in the benefit of a different counselling model than that used with white clients**

Belief in benefit of different model	Yes %	No %
Experience of counselling South Asian clients	63	38
No experience of counselling South Asian clients	63	37
n =	150	89

$x^2 = .008$, d.f. = 1, NS, p>.05

test was performed. As with the variable of years of experience, although the variable of experience of counselling South Asian clients was not found to be a predictor variable with the multiple regression analysis, it was seen as valid to test its relationship with other variables.

Observation of the results in Table 70 indicated that there was no statistically significant association between the direct experience of counselling clients of a South Asian background and a belief in the benefit of a different model.

The survey sample's practice with South Asian ethnic groups will be examined later to see if counsellors were connecting the use of family network to use of a different model as the use of the family network did, in principle and practice, constitute a different model from the individual emphasis of most of the counsellors' work settings and theoretical orientations.

The reader is reminded that the multiple regression analysis showed direct experience of counselling South Asian clients not to be a significant predictor variable with the Cultural Awareness Inventory. Given this finding, the result of the chi square analysis showing a non-statistically significant outcome for the influence of direct experience with South Asian clients and its relationship with belief of the benefit of a different model was, in the context of Batson's personal distress theory, surprising. This was because it could be argued that having the view that South Asian clients could benefit from a different model would release counsellors from any 'personal distress' that may exist about the appropriateness of their skills and the adequacy of their preferred model (Batson et al., 1987). An explanation of this lack of belief in the benefit of a different model may lay in Festinger's cognitive dissonance theory (1957) as discussed in chapter 3. Some further discussion of cognitive dissonance theory at this point is seen as necessary to contextualize the debate that will follow. Cognitive dissonance theory stated that when an emotional state was established between two simultaneously held attitudes or cognitions which were inconsistent with each other because of the individual's belief and overt behaviour, the reduction or resolution of the conflict was proposed to function as a motivation for attitude change in that inconsistent beliefs were changed to become consistent with behaviour. This proposition suggested that there may be an element of defence or denial operating, whereby counsellors saw greater cultural difference in terms of individual pathology and not individual difficulty related to different culturally influenced and driven options. Counsellors may have felt more confident with people of African-Caribbean background than South Asian background, and indeed the findings of Banks (1995) that white people see people of African-Caribbean background as closer to their own background than people of South Asian origin have supported this view. The process that may be at work in counsellors' not seeing the benefit of a different model for South Asian clients was that counsellors were dealing with their cognitive discomfort with greater cultural difference by attributing difference in cultural need, and thus difficulties in counselling, to individual client pathology and not their preferred model.

If counsellors did attribute difficulties to clients rather than review the use of their preferred model, it is an aspect of concern that needs to be addressed in supervision. However, this may not be a realistic expectation, as a review of two studies (Harrison 1975) found no significant relation of prejudice and dogmatism with white supervisors' ratings of white counsellors' effectiveness. It appeared that white supervisors who may be blind or insensitive to prejudice and dogmatism were not seeing this as an issue to be dealt with in counselling supervision. This suggests an area of need in both supervisor selection and training, as well as counsellor training and supervision. The belief in the benefit of a different model for African-Caribbean clients was investigated to see how counsellors saw the needs of this group.

Observation of Table 71 suggested that there was a statistically significant association between having had experience of counselling African-Caribbean clients and a belief in the benefit of a different counselling model than that used with white clients. This finding, in the context of cognitive dissonance theory, presented as a conceptual fit, as recent evidence (Banks, 1995) has suggested that white British people believe African-Caribbeans to be more similar to their own cultural group than the South Asian ethnic groups and therefore, as suggested previously, more able to see potential counselling process difficulty in terms of individual pathology and not difficulty related to counsellors' own preferred model, cultural differences, or the oppressive social and economic conditions that the client experiences in day-to-day living. Having to take the latter into account may not fit conceptually with the usual theoretical and practice emphasis on individual responsibility for self. The previous pieces of data analysis related to counsellors' perception of the need for different counselling models gave some support to the view that counsellors were more comfortable with identifying a culturally 'closer' group as needing a different model than a culturally 'distant' group (Banks, 1995). This also fits with the multiple regression analysis showing direct experience of African-Caribbean, but not South Asian clients, to be a significant predictor variable. Therefore, with a culturally distant group, counsellors are less culturally aware, as would be expected. The South Asian client's needs may have been seen as related to individual pathology.

Ivey et al. (1993) have argued that effectiveness in counselling meant an ability to be receptive to developmental client need and shift one's counselling style as appropriate, and that rigidly adhering to the requirements of one theoretical orientation may be unhelpful, inappropriate or even antagonistic

Table 71   **Association of actual experience of counselling African-Caribbean clients with the belief in benefit of a different model**

Belief in benefit of different model	Yes %	No %
Experience of counselling African-Caribbean clients	68	31
No experience of counselling African-Caribbean clients	51	49
n = 142	88

$x^2 = 7.09$, d.f. $= 1$, p<.05

to the counselling needs of culturally different clients. A case study example of this will be provided in the 'Practice Issues' section, where a white female counsellor inappropriately challenged a Pakistani woman on the need to consult her brother, and accused her of overdependence on members of the extended family (Thomas and Althen, 1989). In attempting to point the way forward with respect to the appropriateness or otherwise of Eurocentric models, Bavington (1992) has made the salient point that there was little use in attempting to invalidate the value of all therapies constructed in the West for white European people. His view was that a more useful start was to use a synthesis of methods, the content of which was likely to be universal, while also using the basic concepts from other cultures of perceiving or construing the world. He noted that this was an area of work which had still to be explored.

In this section the influence on the preferred counselling model of therapists was investigated. It has been shown that a counsellor's orientation alone was not of predictive utility in suggesting the service that a client would receive or the degree of cultural awareness that a counsellor would have. The next section addresses practice issues related to counsellor attitudes.

Practice Issues

This section addresses issues of the counsellors' practices and the relationship of these to attitude items on the postal questionnaire. Links with this data will be made with the Vignette Rating Scale that counsellors completed with the three video vignette case studies. The reader is reminded that 'practice issues' were operationally defined as those variables which were connected with what a counsellor has done, or was willing/not willing to do with clients. Thus, the theme of counsellor action or more precisely, in some cases, intent, with clients was employed. There were several variables connected with this theme. The use of interpreters was identified in the previous section as an important service offering in meeting the needs of both South Asian and African-Caribbean clients. This is explored next in the context of the counsellors' practices.

Counsellors' Openness to use of Language Interpreters

Table 72   Association between length of experience and willingness to use an interpreter with South Asian clients

Length of experience		0–2 years	2–7 years	8–12 years	13+ years
		%	%	%	%
Willingness to use	yes	59	60	60	62
an interpreter	no	41	40	40	38
	n =	32	130	53	47

$x^2 = .05$, d.f. = 3, NS, p>.05

The results showed (Table 72) that there was no statistically significant relationship between willingness to use an interpreter with South Asian clients and length of experience. The willingness to use an interpreter with African-Caribbean clients was investigated.

Table 73   Association between length of experience and willingness to use an interpreter with African-Caribbean clients

Length of experience		0–2 years	2–7 years	8–12 years	13+ years
		%	%	%	%
Willingness to use	yes	42	47	43	36
an interpreter	no	58	53	57	64
	n =	31	128	49	44

$x^2 = 1.54$, d.f. = 3, NS, p>.05

The results (Table 73) showed that, as with South Asian clients, there was no statistically significant association between willingness to use an interpreter with African-Caribbean clients and length of counsellor experience.

The percentages in Tables 72 and 73 indicated a lack of willingness to use an interpreter with both South Asian and African-Caribbean clients based on years of experience alone. However, as previously shown, there was a significant relationship between counsellor orientation and willingness to use an interpreter with South Asian clients. This result was subjectively confirming of the Cultural Awareness Inventory multiple regression analysis indicating the variable of years of experience not to be a significant predictor variable of cultural awareness. So far the willingness or lack of willingness to use interpreters has been discussed. The next section looks at the actual use of interpreters in the counselling situation.

The Actual use of Interpreters with Black Clients

To explore whether there was a relationship between length of counsellor experience and counsellor use of interpreter services a cross-tabulation was carried out. It could be expected that simply having a greater number of years of experience would provide a counsellor with increased opportunity to make use of interpreter services.

The results showed (Table 74) that there was no statistically significant relationship between actual use of interpreter with Black clients and length of experience. However, observation of the cell percentages showed a nonsignificant trend for those with longer experience to have made more use of interpreters than those with fewer years of experience. Although not indicated as a significant predictor of cultural awareness, it may be the larger, but non-statistically significant, trend of use of interpreters by those counsellors with more years of experience suggested a greater recognition of a need to work with non-English speaking or nonstandard English speaking clients. However, it is important to be cautious in making generalizations from the relatively low number of counsellors who have made actual use of interpreter services. The use of interpreters may reflect specialist counselling roles in specialist agencies. The data to distinguish the background and need of client interpreter services was not a focus of this investigation and was not available to discern the type and variety of use. Neither were data available to distinguish the quality of interpreter service available to the counsellors.

Ho (1992) has made the valid point that for interpreter services to be effective 'the interpreter must be carefully selected and oriented' (p. 142). He further noted that part of this selection includes the matching of clients not only on language but also cultural issues. Furthermore, it was important for interpreters to understand their specialist role in the counselling process, which Ho saw as serving as a link between therapist and client. It was important that the interpreter saw themselves in a neutral role which did not contribute their own 'interpretation' to the client's words and feelings. Furthermore, the same interpreter should always be used with the same client to allow for 'relationship'

Table 74   Association between length of experience and actual use of interpreter in counselling Black clients

Use of an interpreter	Years of experience			
	0–2 years	2–7 years	8–12 years	13+ years
	%	%	%	%
Yes	10	22	38	30
No	90	78	62	70
n =	21	78	62	70

$x^2 = 6.72$, d.f. = 3, NS, p>.05

building and continuity. Confidentiality should always be maintained, as work with interpreters from the same culture may entail community links outside the counselling context. A relatively weak measure of the quality of interpreter service may actually be the satisfaction of outcome. This is explored in the next statistical analysis.

Table 75   Association between length of experience and satisfaction of use of an interpreter with Black clients

Satisfaction in use of an interpreter	Years of experience			
	0–2 years	2–7 years	8–12 years	13+ years
	%	%	%	%
Yes	100	44	54	38
No	0	56	46	63
n =	2	18	13	8

$x^2 = 2.77$, d.f. = 3, NS, p>.05

The results (Table 75) showed there was no statistically significant association between length of counsellor experience and satisfaction of use of an interpreter with Black clients.

The assessment of client need as it related to their position in a social and cultural matrix was explored next in the use of a client's family network.

Use of Family Network

There may sometimes be a link between use of an interpreter and the use of a client's family network, i.e., family members may be (inappropriately) used for this service. Table 76 gives the frequencies of actual use of the client's family network to effect the counselling process.

Table 76   Actual use of clients' family network (from Table 31)

	No.	%
Use of family network	121	36
No use of family network	191	57
(Not specified)	(26)	(7)

p<.001 (2 tailed)

Ho (1992) has made the point that it was essential that interpreters not connected with the family be used. The point has been made previously that this was necessary to ensure confidentially and therefore facilitate the building of trust and rapport in the counselling exchange. The present writer was aware of several examples of the inappropriate use of children or younger family members as interpreters by counsellors with the effect of client reluctance to proceed and early termination. Visual comparison of the frequencies in Table 34, the table showing the actual use of interpreter services, and Table 76 (31) showing the actual use of the family network, suggested that there was likely to be little confusion between the two uses, i.e., the difference in numbers suggested that family networks were being used for more than interpretation services alone. Furthermore, as could be seen from comparison of Table 77 showing satisfaction of the use of interpreter services and Table 32 showing the perceived value of family network use, there was a much greater satisfaction of use of the family network. The recognition of the value of the family network is, from a cross-cultural standpoint, encouraging (Burke, 1980; Farrar and Sircar, 1986). These results showed a positive use of the family within the counselling context relating client needs to their social matrix.

The relationship between training and reading material on the use of the client's family network was explored next as a further measure of variables influencing counsellor practice. The statistical analysis (Table 77) revealed that there was no statistically significant association between having used a client's family network and having received specific training on South Asian client need. The effect of reading material on the use of the client's family network was then explored.

The statistical analysis (Table 78) indicated a statistically significant association between use of the client's family network and reading material

Table 77   Association between training and use of family network

Use of client's family network		Yes %	Yes %
	Yes	48	52
Specific training for South Asian clients			
	No	38	62
	n =	107	156

$x^2 = 2.33$, d.f. $= 1$, NS, $p > .05$

Table 78   Association between reading material on South Asian clients and use of family network

Use of client's family network		Yes %	Yes %
	Yes	46	54
Reading material on South Asian clients			
	No	33	67
	n =	108	166

$x^2 = 4.5$, d.f. $= 1$, NS, $p < .05$

on Asian clients' counselling need. This suggested that reading enhanced awareness in counsellors which showed itself in a practical way. The association between the needs of African-Caribbean clients and use of the family network was explored next.

Table 79   Association between training in the needs of African-Caribbean clients and use of family network

Use of client's family network		Yes %	Yes %
	Yes	48	52
Training in the needs of African-Caribbean clients			
	No	37	63
	n =	106	156

$x^2 = 2.50$, d.f. $= 1$, NS, $p > .05$

Statistical analysis (Table 79) revealed that there was no statistically significant association between use of the client's family network and having received training in the needs of African-Caribbean clients. This result was the same as that for the South Asian client group. The effect of reading material was explored next.

Table 80   Association between reading material on African-Caribbean clients and the use of family network

Use of client's family network		Yes %	Yes %
	Yes	44	56
Reading material on African-Caribbean clients			
	No	35	65
	n =	107	164

$x^2 = 2.60$, d.f. = 1, NS, p>.05

The statistical analysis (Table 80) indicated that there was no statistically significant association between use of the client's family network in counselling and reading material about African-Caribbean clients' needs. This result contrasted with the statistically significant association of reading material on South Asian clients and use of the client's family network. It appeared that for African-Caribbean clients neither training nor reading had influenced counsellors in their use of the family network to affect the counselling process or outcome.

It was seen as useful to illustrate the significance of family involvement with a case study to show how counsellors may be ill-equipped to consider the social context of client need and the adverse effect this might have.

Thomas and Althen (1989) cited a case study in their experience where a Pakistani female student in the USA told a female counsellor that she was unable to make decisions about leaving her abusing husband until she had discussed the issue with her brother. From this response the counsellor assessed the woman as lacking in assertion skills and unable to take responsibility for self. The counsellor challenged the woman on this point, and the woman, feeling further persecuted by the counsellor's lack of appreciation of her cultural position, did not return. It appeared that the female counsellor had been unable to make cultural links with the significance of the family network in a different culture. In support of this possibility Maynard (1994, p. 14), writing from a postmodernist feminist perspective, has argued that:

The impact of 'race' may mean that the chief sites of oppression are not the same for black and white women. Black feminists have shown, for example, that for some women the family can be an arena for resistance and solidarity against racism [and presumably, oppression in general] and does not necessarily hold such a central place in accounting for women's subordination as it may do for white women.

Ivey et al. (1993) have assessed most Western approaches to psychotherapy as having their foundations in an over-focus on the individual, despite the individual's living in a family context and the availability of research to show the importance of therapy in a family context. For example, both Bateson et al. (1956) and Burke (1980) have discovered that people who received therapy and treatment within a family environment both had fewer relapses and made quicker recoveries than clients treated individually. The idea of systemics, i.e., the impact of family systems and support networks, is not a new idea to therapy (Minuchin, 1974; Haley, 1976) and indeed some writers have gone so far as to consider the network not only as immediate family members, but also the extended family and friends (Speck and Attneave, 1973), and indeed Cottone (1991) argued that the 'cultural' influence of family therapy was greatly influencing the more traditionalist, individualistic models of counselling. The data presented in Table 31 supported this view. Further support for the increased use of family networks in individual counselling was provided in Table 21 with the finding that those counsellors who, normally worked within a systems/family framework constituted only 1.2 per cent of the sample compared to 36 per cent of counsellors who had actually used the family network (see Table 31) and 16 per cent who could be said to be expected to usually work with the family owing to counselling service delivery focus, i.e., marriage guidance and family therapy work (see Table 26). Still more evidence for the openness of counsellors to consider use of the client's family network came from observation of Table 81.

The results showed a statistically significant association between length of counselling experience and use of the client's family network to effect change. Observation of the cell percentages suggested that those with longer experience had made a greater use of this than those with fewer years of counselling. This may be simply due to a greater opportunity to make use of the family network which longer experience provides rather than greater cultural awareness as confirmed by the multiple regression analysis results.

This section looked at the influence of the counsellors' practice and its relation to a number of variables and their influence on counselling service delivery to the culturally different. Differences in counsellor practice with the

Table 81 **Association between length of experience and use of client's family network**

Years of experience		0–2 years %	2–7 years %	8–12 years %	13+ years %
	Yes	18	41	37	50
Use of family					
	No	82	59	63	50
	n =	39	151	67	54

$x^2 = 10.37$, d.f. = 3, p<.01

different ethnic groups were revealed and possible explanations offered. The next section presents the outcome of the Vignette Rating Scale video studies.

The Vignette Rating Scale

This section investigates counsellors' attitudes towards the three video vignette case studies where female, South Asian, African Caribbean or white 'clients', who believed themselves to be pregnant, were presented to counsellors in training. All the 'clients' had the same script as a means of holding the personal message of each constant. These counsellors were asked to rate their feelings and reactions to a list of 26 different variables on a five point Likert-type scale (the Vignette Rating Scale). The reader is reminded that Vignette Rating Scale was seen as measuring counter-transference, which was seen as a measure of the degree of variation in emotional response between the different ethnic group 'clients'. For the Vignette Rating Scale, for some variables (those of anxiety, frustration and hopelessness) the scoring pattern was reversed so that low scores indicated more emotional response than usual and high scores indicated less emotional response than usual. For the other significant variables the scoring pattern remained that of a low score indicating less emotional response and a high score indicating more emotional response than usual. The reader is reassured that the discussion of each individual analysis of variance result will make the direction of counsellor response clear. The Vignette Rating Scale, therefore, measured the counsellors' self assessed attitudes towards their emotional responses and the degree to which their emotional responses to the video 'client' was influenced by the 'client's' ethnic group.

Analysis of individual items from the Vignette Rating Scale and their relationship to the variables of counsellor gender, counsellor length of experience and client ethnicity are discussed next. Not all were statistically significant but as a nonsignificant result can contribute to knowledge, appropriate discussion will take place, as this information was considered to be of major importance in contributing to the knowledge base in this area, which is almost nonexistent.

ANOVA of the Vignette Rating Scale by Counsellor Gender

There was a statistically significant relationship between the Vignette Rating Scale and gender of counsellor, F (1, 105) ='17.31, p<.001. Observation of the mean scores suggested that men rated themselves as feeling more of an emotional response (M = 67) than did women (M = 61). This would suggest that men were experiencing a greater degree of emotionality than women in working with the presented pregnant female 'client'(s). As the video 'client(s)' were presenting with a concern that some feminists may argue had a female focused need (Chaplin 1988), it may not be surprising that men experienced a greater degree of emotion, and therefore 'transference reaction', in objectively dealing with the client's need. The next ANOVA investigated the relationship between the Vignette Rating Scale and counsellor length of experience.

ANOVA of Vignette Rating Scale by Counsellor Length of Experience

As in the multiple regression analysis with the dependent variable of the Cultural Awareness Inventory, there was no statistically significant relationship (ANOVA) between the Vignette Rating Scale and years of counselling experience, F (4, 98) = .59, p>.05. Therefore, from this analysis it was possible to conclude that counsellor length of experience did not influence the self assessed degree of emotional response to the 'clients'. This result was not consistent with some of the previous published findings in the literature. For example, Strupp (1960) summarized the available findings at that time as being that less experienced counsellors tended to be more insecure and more affected by the personal characteristics of the clients, whereas more experienced counsellors tended to be more open, sure of themselves and focused on the client's needs. More recent findings (Tracey et al., 1988) have been in agreement with those of Strupp and have suggested that inexperience may pose a particular form of difficulty for therapists which included recognizing and working effectively with counter-transference (Heimann,

1950; Blum, 1986). However, as in the present empirical study, other empirical studies involving trainees have found less confusion about counter-transference feelings and therefore no effect of experience on counter-transference. It was possible that the demonstration of counter-transference in the studies was linked to the difficulties of the client groups under study rather than experience alone. The existing research was also exclusively composed of white client groups. To shed more light on the possible effect of ethnicity the relationship between the Vignette Rating Scale and 'client' ethnic background was investigated next.

ANOVA of Vignette Rating Scale 'Client' Ethnicity

It was found that there was no statistically significant relationship between the Vignette Rating Scale and the ethnic group of the 'client', $F(2, 104) = .70$, p>.05. It would appear from this that the counsellors were not having an overall different emotional reaction to 'clients' due to the 'client's' ethnic background. This would be a positive finding in one sense as it suggested that counsellors may, as a group, be responding to clients related more to the difficulty they bring rather than over-responding with high emotion to the 'client's' culture. However, another perspective may be that each pregnant video 'client' has a difficulty, but the problem, and thus the potential solution, was different for each. The white and African-Caribbean 'client' may have a difficulty with parental aspirations but because of cultural issues the stigma was likely to be much more with the South Asian 'client'. The question may be asked whether the counsellors were aware of this significant cultural difference and therefore aware of the additional difficulties that culture might bring to unmarried pregnancy? Another perspective may be that it was the individual message of the client that was important and this should override the membership of the cultural group to which they belong, as the message they gave to the counsellor about their situation was their interpretation of their personal predicament. One way of investigating what counsellors may be feeling was to explore the individual statistically significant responses to the Vignette Rating Scale, and this is presented next. However, the analyses which follow will not allow us to always determine the reason or motivation for any differences in responses should they exist.

Individual variable analyses In this section the statistically significant ANOVA results investigating the relationship of ethnicity of the client to the individual Vignette Rating Scale items are discussed. Although the Vignette Rating Scale was formed as an 'integrated' or 'consolidated' measure of emotional response, the individual emotions of counsellor response were seen as important to explore as these were seen as potentially providing greater insight and offering a more detailed and in depth understanding as to what specific feelings counsellors may be experiencing in their dealings with the 'clients'. This was seen as a recognition that therapist's emotional reactions are subtle and complex and that any investigation into emotions required careful attention to specific emotions. Although Pearce (1997), in a relatively small subject sample, did not find significant differences in counselling trainee's emotional responses in general to video material, she did not specifically test for different emotions.

The reader is informed that although at first it may have appeared necessary to do two-way ANOVAs with the following analyses to take into account the statistically significant effect of gender, when one took into account the relatively low numbers of men compared to women, a difficulty of subdividing these men across the various categories became apparent, which may have produced spurious results. Therefore, only one-way ANOVAs were computed. The statistically significant results will be discussed in turn.

ANOVA of Ethnicity of 'Client' by Anxiety

The relationship of the 'client's' ethnicity and the degree of anxiety experienced by counsellors was significant, $F (2,104) =10.29$, $p<.001$ level. Observation of the group means indicated that the degree of anxiety was higher for the South Asian 'client'($M = 2.29$) and the white 'client' ($M = 2.86$) than the African-Caribbean 'client' (3.00). A Scheffe test confirmed a statistically significant difference at the $p<.05$ level for the African-Caribbean 'client' and the South Asian 'client'. This suggested that if counsellors were acknowledging cultural difference, as the overall analysis suggested, then they appeared to be withdrawing from emotional involvement with the African-Caribbean 'client'. If so, this would lend some support to the earlier discussed operationalized definition, in the 'Counsellor Qualification' section, of Robbins and Jolkovski (1987). It may be that where 'clients' were seen as not having a difficulty as a result of their perceived cultural group norms, there could be a reduction of emotional involvement. If this was happening, it would have serious implications for service delivery to an African-Caribbean client, particularly since the vignette 'clients' were all giving the same message of desperation in need. It may be that the counsellors were showing cultural-counter-transference (Ridley 1989) as discussed in chapter 3, or culturally 'pigeonholing' individuals regardless of expressed personal need. The next statistically significant result was that of the relationship between the ethnicity of 'client' and the 'sense of challenge' felt by the counsellors.

ANOVA of Ethnicity of 'Client' by Sense of Challenge

The result was significant, $F (2,103) = 7.51$, $p<.001$. Inspection of the group means indicated that a greater degree of challenge was being experienced in 'work' with the South Asian 'client' ($M = 3.90$) than with the white ($M = 3.33$) or African-Caribbean 'client' ($M = 3.27$). A Scheffe test confirmed this difference to be statistically significant at the $p<.05$ level. The direction of the challenge was that more was experienced with the white 'client' than the African-Caribbean 'client'. The greater sense of challenge felt with the South Asian 'client' may be an acknowledgement of greater cultural difference and the 'client's' therefore having a greater difficulty with unplanned pregnancy than the other 'clients'. The smaller degree of challenge felt with the African-Caribbean 'client' may be related to the view, as expressed in the group discussions after the video exercise, that unmarried pregnancy within this cultural group was seen as a common occurrence and therefore less of a challenge. If so, this view would have appeared to ignore what this particular 'client' was saying about her individual position and could therefore be, once again, as with the result of less anxiety in Table 85 above, an indication of negative cultural-counter-transference (Ridley, 1989).

ANOVA of Level of Frustration by Ethnicity of 'Client'

The results of the relationship between the degree of frustration experienced in 'working' with the 'clients' were significant, $F (2,102) = 4.36$, $p<.02$. Observation of the group means suggested that the counsellors experienced a greater degree of frustration with the South Asian 'client' ($M = 2.66$) than with the white 'client' ($M = 2.88$), with the least degree of frustration being experienced with the African-Caribbean client ($M = 3.24$). This was significant at the $p<.05$ level, as indicated by a Scheffe test. Why this may be so was puzzling. Group discussion after the video exercise revealed that many counsellors did not comprehend exactly why a single African-Caribbean woman should experience unplanned pregnancy as a problem and were therefore uncertain as to how to approach or comprehend her needs. Again, this seemed to ignore the 'client's' own assessment of her difficulty and allowed the researcher to identify a process of cultural-counter-transference in operation.

ANOVA of Level of Hopelessness by Ethnicity of 'Client'

There was a statistically significant result of F (2.103) = 4.71, p<.01. This suggested that counsellors were having difficulty with comprehending the particular circumstances of the individual 'clients'. The hopelessness felt with the African-Caribbean 'client' (M = 3.30) was significantly less than with the other two 'clients', as indicated by a Scheffe test result at the level of p<.05. Observation of the ANOVA result group means indicated that there was a greater degree of felt hopelessness for the South Asian 'client' (M = 2.81) than the white 'client' (M = 3.22). Again, this may be related to Robbins and Jolkovski's (1987) definition of counter-transference as withdrawal of emotional involvement from a 'client' with little need for support from a cultural stereotype perspective. Once again counsellors may have been ignoring the personal message of the African-Caribbean 'client', indicating a personal need independent of the cultural stereotype employed by the counsellors.

ANOVA of Ethnicity of the 'Client' by Wanting to Know More about Family Circumstances

The next piece of statistical analysis was concerned with the relationship between the ethnicity of the 'client' and counsellors wanting to know more about her family circumstances. The ANOVA result was statistically significant at the level of p<.001. A Scheffe test indicated that the counsellors' need to know more about the family circumstances of the 'clients' was significantly greater for the South Asian 'client' than the other two 'clients', at the level of p<.01. This would suggest that there was a recognition of the need for more family involvement with the South Asian 'client's' culture but a tendency to perhaps dismiss the importance of this involvement for the other two 'clients'. Once again, there was the possibility that counsellors were ignoring the personal individual messages of all the 'clients', irrespective of their cultural group. This was suggested as all the 'clients' had the same script and stated that the reactions of family were most important to them in considering their personal positions and options. The feelings of counsellor competence to support the 'clients' were next assessed.

ANOVA of Perceived Level of Counsellor Competence by Ethnicity of 'Client'

The results from this statistical analysis indicated that there was a statistically significant difference, F (2,103) =16.56, p<.001. Observation of the group means suggested that counsellors felt themselves to be significantly less competent in their ability to support the South Asian 'client' (M = 2.39) than the white client ((M = 3.02) and the Africa-Caribbean 'client' (M = 3.24), and this was confirmed by a Scheffe Test result at the level of p<.05. This perceived lack of competence was confirmed in the next ANOVA result with an item which did not form part of the Vignette Rating Scale.

ANOVA of Counsellors Wishing to Refer Elsewhere by 'Client' Ethnicity

The result, F (2, 102) = 3.61, p<.03, indicated that counsellors were much more likely to refer the South Asian 'client' (M = 3.29) elsewhere for counselling support than the white client (M = 3.08), and much less likely to refer the African-Caribbean client elsewhere (M = 2.72). This was seen as a strong indicator of the degree of difficulty the counsellors would have in working with someone perceived as culturally different within the predictions of personal distress theory (Batson et al., 1987) and to some degree confirmed the previously discussed counsellors' ratings of the degree of anxiety they would feel in working with the South Asian 'client', as it could be argued that referring a 'client' elsewhere because of cultural difference was a sensitive measure of experienced anxiety. However, the counsellors were much less likely to refer the African-Caribbean client elsewhere for counselling support than the white client. The reasons for this are unclear. Is it the case that counsellors perceive her, within a rigid cultural stereotype, to need less support for her difficulty?

Throughout this book the term 'cultural difference' has been used to imply the degree of difference white counsellors were likely to feel in comparing their culture to the culture of the African-Caribbean and South Asian 'client'. This assumption was validated by the counsellors' ratings, as can be seen in the next ANOVA result. The questionnaire item of 'cultural difference' did not form part of the Vignette Rating Scale.

ANOVA of Ethnicity of 'Client' by Perceived Importance of Cultural Difference from Counsellor

Observations of the group means suggested that the white counsellors felt the South Asian 'client' (M = 4.33) to be furthest from their cultural group. This was confirmed by a Scheffe test result at the p<.05 level. The importance of the African-Caribbean 'client's' cultural difference (M = 3.38) was seen as less important than that of the white client (M = 3.80). This result may be seen as particularly concerning as it suggests that African-Caribbean client's cultural differences may be ignored and the individual client's needs remain unmet when counsellors engage with them in a stereotyped way.

ANOVA of Ethnicity of 'Client' by a Need in Counsellor to Know the 'Client' Felt Valued and Liked

A significant result, F (2,103) = 3.18, p<.05, was obtained. This was particularly revealing, as there was a greater need in counsellors to know that the white 'client' (M = 3.72) knew that they valued and liked them. For the reader's information, this item did form part of the Vignette Rating Scale. A Scheffe test confirmed this difference between the two other 'clients' to be at the p<.05 level of significance. The need for the South Asian 'client' (M = 3.55) to know they were liked was the next highest with the African-Caribbean client last (M = 3.32). This result could be interpreted in light of the findings of McClure and Hodge (1987, p. 35) in a study of counter-transference which found that:

> If strong feelings of liking are present, clients are viewed as having personalities closer to the therapist's personality ... When strong feelings of disliking are operative, the therapist's distortion of the client's measured personality runs in the opposite direction and is viewed as more dissimilar from the therapists personality than it is measured to be.

The researchers suggested that the therapist's distortion was evidence of counter-transference arising from the therapists unconscious attitude of liking or disliking the client. The differential response found in the present study may be identifying that there was a degree of 'favouritism' or counsellor need for approval from a particular ethnic group 'client' in operation. However, given that all of the 'clients' had the same difficulty with unplanned pregnancy, a less favourable view might be that this 'need for approval' operating at an ethnic group level was in fact racism, or at least Eurocentrism, showing itself in the counter-transference process. This would support the arguments of Ridley (1989) and Vontress (1981) whose views on white counsellors and counter-transference were discussed in chapter 3. That is to say that Eurocentric attitudes, or negative counter-transference, do look likely to show themselves in the counselling 'encounter' and counsellors could neither claim to be objective or 'colour-blind'.

With all the results of the individual item analysis of the Vignette Rating Scale a cautious note must be sounded as there may have been counsellor gender differences in response which have not been identified through distinct analyses because of the relatively low numbers of men. The reader is reminded that this ratio of men to women was consistent with those numbers obtained in the postal questionnaire survey and as such appeared representative of the relative numbers of men and women in counselling.

The results of the Vignette Rating Scale suggested that there was difference in self identified counsellor emotional response to 'clients' on a number of items that was based not on the personal message of need from the 'clients', as all 'clients' had the same script, but based on 'client' ethnicity and assumed culture. These findings would support the view of Ridley (1989) in that there were specific dynamics in operation in the cross-cultural counselling 'encounter', e.g., cultural-counter-transference, and that counsellors could not claim to be offering a 'colour blind' response to the culturally different 'client'.

The outcomes of the statistical analysis of the Vignette Rating Scale were particularly revealing. It was found that there was a significant amount of bias in the difference of degree in perceived feelings between the different 'clients' and, since the personal messages for all 'clients' were the same, the difference in feelings between 'clients' was not seen as due to the 'clients' personal characteristics but due mainly to the 'client's' ethnicity. Counsellors would seem to ignore the individual needs of the client and concentrate on presumed cultural stereotypes.

8 The Research Findings Related to the Research Objectives

The aim of this chapter was to 'decontextualize and recontextualize' the findings from the previous chapter and relate these to the research objectives. No detailed theoretical debate will be entered into here as the findings have been previously discussed in their theoretical and practice implications context. The statistical analyses outcomes will be presented briefly under specific headings to inform the reader how they related to the research objectives. Transcribed quotations from the counsellors' interviews and written questionnaire comments section will be used to illustrate the subjectivities of thoughts and feelings of the counsellors to contribute to the meaning of the quantitative analyses. This can be, in a broad context, seen as a recognition that knowledge is situated (Maynard, 1994; Bhavnani, 1994; Mama, 1995) and some analysis of the counsellors' subjective experiences and knowledge should take place. This is to identify ideas about the interviewed counsellors' subjectivities rather than to test them and to bridge the divide between the individual and the social and the individual and the group (Henriques et al., 1984). Many of the research analysis findings will not be mutually exclusive and will show interconnections with other objectives. This to some extent reflects the nature of 'applied' as opposed to 'pure' research (Glaser and Strauss, 1967; Creswell, 1994).

As stated in chapter 1, the aims of the research were to discover and examine the existing attitudes and self reported specific practice orientations (as operationalized in chapter 6) of white therapists in their work with Black clients. A secondary aim was to identify what influenced the ability of counsellors to work appropriately with the culturally different. The specific objectives will be discussed in turn.

The First Objective

The first objective was to examine the existing views of counsellors on the significance of cultural and ethnic differences between counsellor and client in the counselling relationship (Nobles, 1976; Farrar and Sircar, 1986; d'Ardenne and Mahtani, 1989; Lago and Thompson, 1989; Littlewood and Lipsedge, 1989 Sue and Sue, 1990;).

Those variables which appeared to have an influence on the ability of counsellors to acknowledge the significance of cultural and ethnic differences between themselves and clients were measured by a number of statistically investigated questionnaire items which were:

Years of Counselling Experience

A statistically significant relationship was found between length of counselling experience and use of the clients' family networks to effect change in counselling, p<.01. With longer years of counselling experience came more use of the family network. This was seen as an appropriate acknowledgement of cultural difference translated into action. This may have been because of the possibility that with longer years of experience there was greater opportunity to make more use of the family network. However, this was, in the case of the majority of the counsellors in this sample, not strictly within the framework of either their theoretical orientation (see Table 21), their service delivery focus (see Table 26), or employment setting (see Table 27). The counsellors' use of the family network was, within the writings of Burke (1980), Farrar and Sircar (1986), Thomas and Althen (1989), Ho (1992), Ivey et al. (1993), a self reported 'behavioural acknowledgement' of cultural difference influencing client need.

The relationship between years of counselling experience and the self reported 'behavioural' acknowledgement of differing client need was not reflected in the cognitive component of the counsellors' attitudes as there was no significant statistical relationship between the belief in need for a different model and years of counselling experience for South Asian clients. However, there was a statistically significant relationship between the years of experience of counselling African-Caribbean clients and the belief in the benefit of a different model than that used with white clients, p<.01. One possible explanation for this difference between the African-Caribbean and South Asian ethnic groups was proposed in the context of Festinger's cognitive dissonance theory (1957). Here counsellors appeared to reduce dissonance between feelings and cognitions by suggesting that African-Caribbean clients may benefit from a different model. Exactly what the dissonant feelings may have been was uncertain. There was no significant relationship between the independent variable of years of experience and the Cultural Awareness Inventory as shown by the stepwise multiple regression analysis.

Direct Counselling Experience

There was no statistically significant relationship between the Cultural Awareness Inventory and the direct experience of counselling South Asian clients. However, there was a statistically significant relationship between the Cultural Awareness Inventory and the direct experience of counselling African-Caribbean clients. Those counsellors who had direct experience had a more favourable score on the Cultural Awareness Inventory than those counsellors who had no experience, p<.05.

One counsellor, a 28 year old woman, self assessed her feeling on this issue as being:

> I think if you ask most people in the street whether they're racist or not they'd probably say no, but I think most people are, and I think that is what I'm battling against, is that I know a lot of my feelings are, or have been, racist, and I'm battling with that as a counsellor ... I don't think it's overt racism, it's avoidance ... I suppose it's attitudes that may still be there and lingering there, from a lifetime of being surrounded by racism in white, middle class areas.

A 45 year old woman counsellor in training with little experience admitted the personal difficulties she felt she might encounter with Black clients:

> I don't know, I mean, you know there are issues that I still have to work out, and I think the lack of practical, you know, having clients that I can work with, that puts a block on it for me, really.

And another woman of 45 years of age, with a great deal of experience of counselling Black clients, contrasted the value of her experience to the reduced benefit of her training:

> It's hard to say no [the value of training] without seeming critical of my trainers. I went to college where the trainers were two white people, a man and a woman, and I would say that they made every effort that they could, but, by the time I went to do my diploma I was actually a great deal more experienced than they were in transcultural counselling, so, and that's mainly because of the setting I

work in and the volume of people, volume of clients that I see, so I actually didn't really learn very much from them.

As stated, there was no statistically significant relationship between the Cultural Awareness Inventory and the direct experience of counselling South Asian clients. This result, given the more favourable scores on the Cultural Awareness Inventory with direct experience of African-Caribbean clients, presented as a paradox until seen in the context of Festinger's cognitive dissonance theory (1957) and Batson et al.'s (1987) personal distress theory. It was suggested that the particular cultural distance difficulties that white counsellors may face with South Asian clients may mean that they experience greater interpersonal pressures with this group. This view was supported with the Vignette Rating Scale results. This greater cultural distance may have increased the personal distress of counsellors who may then have tended to 'blame' the individuals for their circumstances and lack of ability to bring about change. As one male counsellor, in the 60–64 age band, wrote on the postal questionnaire:

> I have observed a growing tendency in Britain for coloured people to blame the English for their problems. I feel that there has come a time for them to realize that all individuals are responsible for their own way in life and that many of the difficulties they face are due to the personal inadequacies of individuals and nothing to do with what is wrongly seen as a racist society. Personal choice needs to be owned!

A woman in the 55–59 age band wrote:

> Many of the Jamaican and Indian clients I have seen fail to take personal responsibility for the difficulties they face which they see purely as discrimination but which my view is one where they fail to fit in to expectations of the work place.

The Influence of Reading and Training

There was a significant statistical relationship between reading specific material on Black client need, $p < .01$, and the Cultural Awareness Inventory, with those who had read specific material on counselling need, having more favourable scores on the Cultural Awareness Inventory. It was acknowledged that there was a possibility that those who had read specific material may have been more favourably disposed initially. Personal motivation was likely to be a key factor. A 38 year old male interviewed counsellor made this point in saying:

> I think it was probably more down to me as an individual that made me better equipped because culture always interests me. People interest me. So I've always wanted to gain as much knowledge about other people, their culture, etc. as possible. So I set out to equip myself better. I don't think I was equipped for them through my training. We touched on things but reading, watching, talking to people and mixing with people from all sorts of cultures was better.

There was a significant relationship between having had training in the needs of Black clients, $p<.01$ and the Cultural Awareness Inventory. Those counsellors who had received training scored more favourably on the Cultural Awareness Inventory than those who had none. A 38 year old woman counsellor talking about her previous difficulties in exploring the area of cross-cultural counselling said:

> If you don't have the knowledge I think it's actually very difficult to check out your attitudes, it's certainly more than that but you have to have some knowledge to start with.

A 45 year old female counsellor spoke of how reading had influenced her views:

> I'm very aware of the area in loss and bereavement counselling that there are very much cultural and race differences, of how people handle loss and how they handle bereavement, and I've been trying to open this up to myself by reading, but then not actually having had the practical experience of having [Black] clients that I can, you know, link the reading to the practical side of things ... [and] follow up where I felt a lot of my work has been lacking. I haven't got a practical side to link that with a client who is bringing up issues, so I think my awareness is there, but I'm actually still very, very nervous of the whole area, because of lack of experience really.

From the statistical analyses results it would seem that training, particularly that with a cognitive or academic component and that with a specific relevance to the needs of Black clients (Katz, 1984; Pinderhughes, 1989), was most effective. One interviewed 45 year old woman counsellor recounted her class-room based learning experiences with regard to specific experiential training:

> I don't think there is an openness, and I think we're (counselling course members) all colluding in that avoidance, to a certain extent except ... perhaps one or two others who have worked very much and feel comfortable, but I do think for the majority on the course there is almost a collusion of it that it's quite safe not to address these issues and you know ... it's certainly something that I've battled

with and I know that when we have had sessions that have really helped ... one session where I remember going off into a smaller group and everybody sitting there and thinking, God, I'm finding this so difficult and I actually did voice that first. When I did, because you know I am prepared and wanting to take the risk, but I am frightened and when I actually did they were all saying God, I feel the same way. Why are we feeling all tense about this, you know, and we were actually able to sit down and talk about where the fear was coming from, was it our feeling of inadequacy and not feeling that we could, you know, were we not just not on the same wave length and thinking we haven't got skills that we can use? I think it's only now that I am beginning to realize, yes, I have got skills and I have got something, which if I can just lessen the fear, would be good.

Clearly experiential training represented an emotional difficulty for almost all of the interviewed counsellors. As the previous counsellor said:

I think it's taking the risk, I really do. If we're not prepared to take the risk and it is frightening, it's fearful to address what it really is and to actually admit it is racist attitudes in most of us, but how many of us will sit down and actually say that ... I'm frightened of making a racist remark, petrified so I shut up and this actually became evident in the personal development group working with (name of more experienced counsellor) and actually the times that she has said things back to me and I've thought oh God, ... why the hell have I said that ... and look what effect it's having.

Not all interviewed counsellors were convinced of the benefit of training as they had experienced it. One 38 year old woman said:

I think it's the most difficult thing for the person who's bringing up that topic ... so one would question whether they had the experience of being discriminated against or feeling powerless ... and I think it depends on the mix of people you're with as well, if you're all from a very similar kind of background then how much of a discussion, a stimulated discussion, are you going to have, and how much are you going to be challenged for the thoughts beliefs, prejudices.... I think the truth is you don't want to look at it.

This counsellor then went on to tell of an experience that a colleague of hers who was an experiential trainer in 'race' issues had experienced:

I know that a colleague of mine brought up this issue that we need some kind of awareness of the topic and he now does (experiential) training packages in that field, which I have heard that some people find it very disturbing, this is white people, and get very angry at it ... I'd see that as a good thing because if they're disturbed they're going to have to look at why they're being disturbed and what's going on inside them that they're getting so angry.

These quotations suggested that given the right impetus and support, classroom based learning, rather than simply being that of a didactic approach, could also integrate experiential group methods for specific training related to Black clients, as Pinderhughes (1989) advised.

There was a statistically significant association between counsellors' lengths of experience and having read specific material on the needs of both South Asian, p<.01 and African-Caribbean clients, p<.01.

The Influence of Gender

The independent variable of gender of counsellor showed no statistical relationship with the Cultural Awareness Inventory and it would seem from this finding that gender was not associated with predictive qualities of Eurocentrism. This was consistent with other research findings (Grantham, 1973; Geer and Hurst, 1976). However, the subject variable of gender was statistically significant in its relationship with the Vignette Rating Scale, p<.001, where women where shown to have less of an emotional response to the difficulty of unplanned pregnancy than men. Related to this was a significantly lesser degree of anxiety shown with the African-Caribbean 'client' than the white 'client' or South Asian 'client' suggesting a heightened degree of emotional withdrawal to cultural difference and unplanned pregnancy and an indication of 'cultural pigeonholing' rather than listening to the personal message of 'clients'.

The Influence of Age

There was a statistically significant negative relationship between increasing age and the Cultural Awareness Inventory. Counsellors with increasing age showed less favourable scores on the Cultural Awareness Inventory, p<.01.

The Influence of Certificated Qualifications

There was no statistically significant relationship between having an applied counselling qualification and the Cultural Awareness Inventory. There was a statistically significant relationship between academic qualifications and the Cultural Awareness Inventory, with those having an academic degree or academic postgraduate qualification scoring more favourably on the Cultural Awareness Inventory.

From these results it could be suggested that an academic based training that would exist in a first degree or postgraduate course looked more enabling of counsellors' attitudes in working with Black clients than did any form of applied general counselling training not specific to the needs of Black clients. Specific training in the needs of Black clients was statistically significant in its relationship with the Cultural Awareness Inventory, $p<.01$.

Summary of Variables Influencing Counsellors' Skills in Acknowledging the Significance of Ethnic Difference

The results of this study suggest that gender had no effect on the level of cultural awareness. Neither did a counsellor's years of counselling experience alone. However, longer years of experience did influence counsellors in their greater use of the family network, in that counsellors with longer experience used this facilitating mechanism more than counsellors with fewer years of experience. Years of counselling experience alone did not affect counsellors' views on the benefit of different counselling models than those used with white clients for South Asian clients. However, years of experience did show a statistically significant association with the belief in the benefit of a different counselling model for African-Caribbean clients. There was a significant statistical association between having direct experience of counselling African-Caribbean clients and the Cultural Awareness Inventory, with counsellors who had direct experience scoring more favourably. There was no relationship between having direct experience of counselling South Asian clients and the Cultural Awareness Inventory. The stepwise multiple regression analysis indicated the age of counsellor as a significant predictor of a counsellor's score on the Cultural Awareness Inventory with the older age groups of counsellors showing less favourable scores on the Cultural Awareness Inventory than the younger age groups. Counsellors with academic degrees scored more favourably on the Cultural Awareness Inventory than those counsellors with applied qualifications in counselling. Counsellors with specific training in the needs of Black clients scored more favourably than those without this training.

The Second Objective

The second objective was to investigate the influences on the ability of counsellors to empathize with the position of black clients in a social matrix

(Pinderhughes, 1989; Ridley, 1989; Littlewood and Lipsedge, 1989; Cochrane, 1979).

The questionnaire items which measured this objective were:

The Relationship of the Direct Experience of Counselling Black Clients and The Cultural Awareness Inventory

As was discussed in the previous section, there was a significant association between having had direct experience of counselling African-Caribbean clients with the Cultural Awareness Inventory which showed those counsellors who had direct experience scoring more favourably than those who had no direct experience. Direct experience presumably facilitated familiarity, knowledge and skills which combined to produce a favourable Cultural Awareness Inventory score. There was no statistically significant relationship between counselling South Asian clients and the counsellors' scores on the Cultural Awareness Inventory.

It was possible to speculate that the greater social and cultural distance from white counsellors may force the counsellor to reconsider the validity or adequacy of their counselling approach for South Asian ethnic groups and their cultural awareness skills. Counsellors may not always be willing or able to do this. As one indignant male counsellor in the 35–39 age band commented in the written response section of the questionnaire:

> The questionnaire overlooked the fact that counsellor-client dynamics are always unique, my workload is very mixed dealing with many issues and each new client will present a different perspective on their own situation. I am a little suspicious of counselling which identifies any one group as having special problems.

And another male counsellor in the 55–59 age band responded:

> Whatever their ethnic background, clients are first and foremost individuals and that is how I would approach them.

Again, another woman counsellor in the 50–54 age band, taking a more extreme view, commented:

> In my experience many Black people will accept that the reasons for their problems are just because they are an ethnic minority rather than searching for other reasons ... all problems should be dealt with individually.

The last quotation raised the question of whether counsellors might be 'blaming' the individual clients for their difficulties rather than considering the influence of social and economic forces? Sue (1978) made a case for this when he said that those who saw themselves as having a Rogerian or person-centred counselling orientation tended to believe that:

> success or failure is attributable to the individual's skills or person's inadequacies, and belief that there is a strong relationship between ability, effort and success in society (p. 113).

He argued against the myopic internalization of this belief in that, as social, economic and political forces in people's lives were so determining of life opportunities, success or failure tended to be highly dependent on the individual's social matrix, and 'not necessarily personal attributes'.

Not all counsellors will over individualize their clients and ignore the impact of socioeconomic forces. One counsellor female counsellor (in the 60–64 age band, living in a mainly white area) made the salient point that:

> Generally, I would like to consider the client as an individual first but one of the problems about bigotry, it seems to me, is that one lacks insight into bigoted, inherent attitudes and values. I also feel very torn between a strong belief that people have choice and an equally strong belief that people are socially and politically oppressed, often to the point that no real choice remains.

A male counsellor in the 35–39 age band commented:

> I think partly from a Black or Asian person's experience of life in this country is very different from a white person's and it is very easy to overlook that, at least to overlook the overt racism you can see, but I think other things like having less power in certain situations, being overlooked in certain situations, or just simply the assumption that everybody's white, which I believe what happens here because most of the population are white, I think you can very easily overlook that, and I think that makes empathy quite difficult, and also the background, cultural beliefs, you know, just where somebody else is coming from makes empathy difficult.

The importance of considering and being aware of the socioeconomic matrix of a client and its influence on counsellors' empathic responses was assessed by one 28 year old female counsellor as:

> Well, what I referred to earlier as a lack of cultural or political awareness on the counsellor's part can limit or can, yes, restrict empathic responses.

A white female counsellor, of 32 years of age, with a Black partner, said on the issue of developing personal awareness of the social forces on Black people:

> I think it's [social forces on life opportunities] significant. I wouldn't have said that seven years ago, but I believe that's true ... I would have to say the influence for that change of believing things comes through my partner who I've witnessed his oppression because it's very close and it's not just occasional, I mean it's everywhere ... it may be presumptuous but I imagine it's with them [Black people] all of the time, 24 hours a day, not that they're so acutely aware of it, that it's painful, but they have it all the time.

Another female counsellor of 44 years of age argued that:

> I think a lot of the issues that we see within counselling are about oppression and about oppression from within a particular society so I start from a position where most of the people I see are affected by one means or another by the structures and the society which is around them.

The issue of the relative influence of socioeconomic forces was best summarized by the words of one 36 year old male counsellor who said:

> People do come as individuals, but I think to accept people as individuals without having an awareness that they're operating in a (social) context is quite naive really.

Influences on Use of an Interpreter

There was no relationship between a counsellor's length of experience and their willingness to make use of an interpreter with African-Caribbean or South Asian clients. However, fewer counsellors were willing to make use of an interpreter with African-Caribbean clients than with South Asian clients.

There was no statistically significant relationship between length of experience and actual use of an interpreter. One counsellor in the 30–34 age band wrote the following response on the questionnaire about his use of interpreters:

> No, I would not use an interpreter in the ongoing one to one work with a client, but I would use an interpreter for an initial assessment.

It was not clear from this how a counselling service would be provided after the initial assessment. It was also not clear that if the counsellor intended to refer on to a bilingual counsellor, why this route was not chosen in the first place. Given the low number of bilingual counsellors who were likely to be available in any one geographical area to meet the needs of non-English speaking clients, the lack of openness to use of an interpreter may mean that no service could be provided. Furthermore, the issue went beyond the need of non-English speakers and was relevant to those who may speak a 'nonstandard' version of English such as Jamaican patois. This was recognized by a 28 year old female counsellor in saying:

> what overwhelmed me was that I just couldn't understand [the African-Caribbean women's language]. It seemed to me, and it felt to me, that we were both sitting in the same room and speaking the same language, we were both speaking English, and yet I really didn't feel that she was understanding me, and that I knew that there were times when I really didn't understand her, even though we were talking the same language. That was very difficult for me I think partly because you have to question yourself and how much you are able to relate to this person.

A 38 year old female counsellor said:

> I have felt a [language] separation. I have had a few occasions when there's something as simple as inflexion of speech or nuances that are familiar to the culture that they come from I know maybe I'm not picking up and I think this is especially true of people who are born in Jamaica and then come over here compared to [Black] people who are born in England.

A counsellor's orientation did significantly influence the willingness to use an interpreter with South Asian clients, $p<.05$, with those counsellors who saw themselves as eclectic more willing to use an interpreter than either Rogerian or psychodynamic counsellors. There was no relationship between a counsellor's orientation and willingness to use an interpreter with African-Caribbean clients. There was a significant relationship between counsellors' orientation and actual use of an interpreter, $p<.01$, with psychodynamic and eclectic counsellors more likely to have used interpreters than Rogerian counsellors.

Influences on Use of Family Network

There was no relationship between having received training in the needs of either South Asian or African-Caribbean clients and the use of the family network, p>.05. However, there was a statistically significant relationship between reading material on the needs of South Asian clients, p<.05, but not African-Caribbean clients, p>.05, and the use of the family network. Those who had read showed a greater tendency to make use of the family network for South Asian clients. One 38 year old female counsellor said about her openness to use of the family network:

> Well, I've always been open to that if the person themselves has suggested it. Again, I've found that it was quite a difficult issue for me when I worked with Asian clients, in as much as sometimes the families would 'phone up and want to be very involved, but the person themselves would be saying no, I don't want that, and from my perspective I would say well, that's fine, if you don't want it, we won't do it, but I think that's actually been very difficult for some of the families, not because they were being awkward or imposing, but just because it wasn't part of their family culture that somebody came and had something different.

This difference in use of family network for South Asian clients, but not African-Caribbean clients, may be due to a perception of African-Caribbean clients as having a culture more similar to white British people than the cultures of South Asian clients. Therefore, there may be a tendency to see African-Caribbeans as having an 'individualistic' counselling need as opposed to South Asian clients who may be perceived as more connected to a family network.

Use of the family network needs to be undertaken with knowledge and understanding of the effects it may cause and what is a culturally appropriate way of functioning. These points were made by a 32 year old counsellor working in a family counselling setting:

> I think one thing I felt, certainly from an Asian point of view and their cultural, … familial pressure, I think it's very hard for me or any other white counsellor to imagine the backlash we might actually start which never really ought to have happened, and I have been very aware of it because it clearly can be extremely dangerous. We tend to think of it in our own way we function, it is so rigid. From the Afro-Caribbean point of view, and [name of counsellor] was drawing on experience from case discussion groups, the one thing I was thinking about after that having seen quite a few Afro-Caribbean couples, and one thing that she felt was clear to her that was different, very different. Often it would be, say, the woman who almost assumed the role you expect men to assume in white couples in as much as they were the breadwinner and the husbands or partners were often there looking after the children being at home the women were quite powerful and in control, and that was something I thought quite interesting to look at.

*The Relationship Between the Cultural Awareness Inventory and Reading
and Training on Understanding the Social Matrix of the Black Client.*

The statistical analyses relating to this objective were previously discussed in
the section on reading and training under Objective 1 of the research, and will
only be summarized here although quotations will be used from the counsellor
interviews to illustrate views related to this particular research objective.

There was no statistically significant relationship between having had
training and length of counsellor experience, although there was a relationship
between length of counsellor experience and reading material, with those
counsellors with longer years of experience more likely to have read material
on both the needs of African-Caribbean and South Asian clients.

Reading on, the needs of Black clients appeared to reduce Eurocentric
attitudes as measured by the Cultural Awareness Inventory as did specific
training and 'combination' training. One 26 year old female counsellor said:

> You can be trained to an extent but there has to be a willingness to learn and that
> means being able to get in contact with your own feelings and experience as an
> individual and accept the contradictions.

This view was set in the context of searching out material outside of the
classroom both at a personal level of exploration and by additional reading.
In further considering how counsellors viewed the benefits of training, one
43 year old female interviewed counsellor said:

> I think training helps but it is not a panacea. It's part of a willingness to continue
> learning, being open to my own prejudices and fears in this area.

And as another 43 year old female counsellor said, relating the issue back to
the distinction Pinderhughes (1989) made between cognitive and affective
modes of training:

> Well I suppose there are two aspects to the training, one is, as I see it, the
> theoretical understanding and the understanding perhaps of the dynamics
> between yourself and another individual. The other thing is the emotional and
> what I call personal development aspect of it as a counsellor, and that side of
> things I'm not as confident about, there are certain attitudes which I know are
> betrayed at times in my behaviour and in my thinking and my feeling about
> things which, outside the counselling context I know are still there and that
> makes me unsure how realistic I am in the counselling setting.

Pinderhughes argued that, given the opportunity, most white counsellors would opt for training that only taught facts about cultural awareness and practices. This intellectual engagement was not seen as sufficient, as emotional conflicts could be avoided. This may be so of some individuals, as one fairly inexperienced 44 year old counsellor self assessed herself:

> That when I've been doing role play, for instance, that was a very good learning experience when I was actually counselling somebody who is Black, and I completely ignored it, completely, but to me they were sitting there and to me I was actually being very conscious of thinking I mustn't sort of, you know, even mention the word Blackness, or whatever, to do with any problem that she was talking about at the time, but in fact as the interview went on it got more and more difficult, she was turning away from me, I saw the actual despondency, and I acknowledged all this, I still didn't acknowledge that this might be something to do with being Black, and actually, we stopped the interview and at the end of it she said if only you had said to me that you know, it may be something to do with this, that the agency she was working in she was feeling very isolated and very alone, and you know, I was going round about and actually didn't pinpoint that she may be feeling isolated because of her Blackness. So she taught me something very valid in that session. I'm not saying that would be right for everybody, but somehow I chose to ignore it, but how can it be ignored?

However, for other counsellors the avoidance factor may be much less so. One very experienced 38 year old male counsellor in a management position said:

> I think I would be afraid of anything that hints of tokenism. To be quite honest I would rather have nothing. I think that if it's going to be done, and I really think it does need to be done, then it's got to be done thoroughly.

The question of whether the use of emotion raising techniques in counsellor training encourages counsellors to feel they are better able to empathize with clients can be raised by the previous results although no answer can be forthcoming in this investigation. An interviewed 44 year old counsellor took the view that:

> I have come to feel that anti-racist training is vital and that we need to be aware of cultural differences and the pressures of living in a multi-cultural society without imposing them on black clients.

A 44 year old male counsellor who claimed to take a Marxist perspective argued quite strongly that:

> It seems to me that the people, what's really required is for white people to be faced with their racism and, and this is, I don't want this to sound as if it's a white person placing the onus on Black people to educate white people because I think that is in a sense, I suppose that's racism, but I do think that if you're in a training course then it's all too easy for white people to stand up and say, what's good or bad practice in terms of working with Black people, and I don't think that really addresses the issue. I think that white workers need to be faced with their racism, their own personal racism, but also the racism within their working practice, so I think that Black people are best placed to actually formulate and put forward those sorts of training course, and not white people who have their own prejudices about it anyway.

Summary of the Variables Influencing Counsellors' Skills in Empathizing with the Position of Black Clients on a Social Matrix

The variables influencing counsellors' skills in empathizing with the position of Black clients in a social matrix were the direct experience of counselling African-Caribbean clients. Counsellors who had direct experience showed a more favourable score on the Cultural Awareness Inventory. Direct experience of counselling South Asian clients did not show a relationship with the Cultural Awareness Inventory at a statistically significant level. Fewer counsellors were willing to make use of an interpreter with an African-Caribbean client than a South Asian client.

Training did not influence the use of the family network for African-Caribbean or South Asian clients. Reading material did not influence the use of the family network for African-Caribbean clients, but did for South Asian clients; with those who had read material on the specific needs of South Asian clients more likely to make use of the family network.

Reading on the needs of Black clients indicated a more favourable outcome on the Cultural Awareness Inventory, as did specific awareness training.

There was no relationship between having had training and length of counsellor experience, although there was a relationship between length of counsellor experience and reading material, with those counsellors with longer years of experience more likely to have read material on both the needs of African-Caribbean and South Asian clients.

The Third Research Objective

The third research objective was to examine the influences on counsellors' awareness of the limitations of the use of Eurocentric counselling models with Black client groups (d'Ardenne and Mahtani, 1989; Sue and Sue, 1990; Banks, 1991; Locke, 1992; Ivey et al. 1993).

The variables which appeared to influence the counsellors' awareness of the limitations of the use of Eurocentric counselling models with Black clients were:

Reading Material and Training

The stepwise multiple regression analysis indicated that having specific training in the needs of Black clients was a significant predictor variable in its relationship with the Cultural Awareness Inventory, $p<.01$.

Having 'combination' training in the needs of South Asian clients and the belief in the benefit of a different model were significantly related, $p<.01$. There was also a significant relationship between belief in the benefit of a different model than that used with white clients for African-Caribbean clients and having received 'combination' training in the needs of African-Caribbean clients, $p<.01$.

One 44 year old male counsellor who had received specific training in the needs of both South Asian and African-Caribbean clients said:

> I'm not somebody who I think sticks to one theory or any theory in terms of counselling approach. I think it's about using the best bits of every theory and adapting them for whatever it is that you are able to do.

Reading material was a significant predictor variable in its relationship with the Cultural Awareness Inventory, $p<.01$. Reading material also showed an association with the belief of the benefit of a different model for both South Asian clients, $p<.01$ and African-Caribbean clients, $p<.05$. Again, however, as in previous comments about the influence of reading, a cautious note must be sounded as it may well be that specific material is read by those who have an existing openness to the recognition and acknowledgement of differing cultural need.

One 43 year old female counsellor who had recently been considering her learning through the use of both reading and training said:

> I think that with the Rogerian approach, some clients find it baffling and some

clients can actually get quite angry because some clients come wanting answers and so we actually have to step back a bit and have a look at what I understand counselling is, what the client is needing and wanting and whether the two match sufficiently for us to carry on working and certainly that was a hiccup, I remember that I did have, and have had on several occasions. I know it doesn't help everybody and one way it can be measured, one of the ways that I measure that is occasionally when I've made a follow-up appointment and the person doesn't come, or when that person has walked away, booked the appointment and my guess is they won't come back because they didn't find the session helpful.

A 38 year old female counsellor said:

I think there was some cultural difference [in client need]. For example, I found that Asian clients ask very much for advice and want well perhaps a more structured environment [compared] to white clients ...

Counsellor's Years of Experience

The independent variable of years of experience was not a significant predictor variable in the stepwise multiple regression analysis. However, there was a statistically significant relationship between length of counselling experience and use of the client's family network to effect change, $p<.01$. With longer years of experience came more use of the family network. There was a statistically significant relationship between years of counselling experience and having read material on the needs of African-Caribbean clients, $p<.01$, and South Asian clients, $p<.01$.

Variables with no Measured Influence on Counsellor's Awareness of Model Limitations

There was no relationship between years of counsellor experience and belief in a different model than used with white clients for either South Asian or African-Caribbean clients.

There was no relationship between counsellor orientation and having specific training in the needs of African-Caribbean or South Asian clients. There also was no relationship between counsellor orientation and having read specific material on the needs of African-Caribbean or South Asian client groups. There was no relationship between counsellors' years of experience and having had specific training in the needs of African-Caribbean or South

Asian clients. There was no significant relationship between participating in training and the belief of a different model for African-Caribbean or South Asian clients than that used with white clients. There was no significant relationship between counselling theoretical orientation and actual use of family network to effect the counselling process. There also was no significant relationship between counsellor orientation and the belief in a different model for African-Caribbean or South Asian clients than used with white clients. There was no significant relationship between the Cultural Awareness Inventory and the number of years of counsellor experience.

Summary of the Variables Influencing a Counsellor's Awareness of the Limitations of the Use of Eurocentric Models

From the research findings it would seem that the counsellors' cultural awareness, participation in specific training and specific reading influenced the counsellors' beliefs in the benefit of a different model for Black clients than that used with white clients. Years of counsellor experience was significantly related to use of the client's family network to effect change, and this was seen as a self reported behavioural manifestation of use of a different model. The next section considers the fourth and final research objective.

The Fourth Objective

The fourth objective was to explore the degree to which counsellors varied their usual attitude or strategic orientation towards practice with white clients when counselling black clients (Nobles, 1976; Atkinson and Schein, 1986; Casas, 1984; Lago and Thompson, 1989; d'Ardenne and Mahtani, 1989; Sue and Sue, 1990).

Use of a Different Model

Those in the survey sample, who had experience of counselling Black clients, tended not see the benefit of a different model for South Asian clients but did for African-Caribbean clients, p>.05. These findings suggested that counsellors might be more able to consider difference in need and vary their practice with African-Caribbean clients than with South Asian clients, and were tentatively interpreted in the context of cognitive dissonance theory (Festinger, 1957).

Tajfel's (1969, 1978) in-group/out-group model may also have some explanatory utility. Although the need for a different model for African-Caribbean clients, but not South Asian clients, was identified as statistically significant, not all the interviewed counsellors believed this to be so. One 38 year old woman said:

> I have not felt that [the need for a different model] so much with the Afro-Caribbeans, but with Asian groups I have in general. My perception has been that whichever counselling model is used, and I suppose I've largely tended to work with humanistic models, it seems as if the Asian group quite clearly tried out the resource available and it didn't seem as if it was appropriate to their needs or expectations. There was an expectation that things would be far more directed and far more interventionist.

Some of the interviewed counsellors took the viewpoint that it was important to vary their usual practice, as one 44 year old male counsellor said:

> I mean it's about taking good bits of ideas and then using them and adapting them to whatever way of thinking and working you feel that you can operate in
> ...

Some counsellors identified specific aspects of particular models that might not be appropriate with certain clients. One 44 year old female counsellor said:

> ... I think in a client-centred model it's very much a verbal model, somebody would have to in fact be very articulate I think and actually see sometimes that this might not be appropriate to use.

The same counsellor said of psychodynamic theories:

> I find those theories very rigid and in contrast to that it seems to me that Rogers is saying that we need to enter the client's world and I find that useful whether I'm working with a Black client or a white client ... and that being the main thrust of the model rather than ... the psychodynamic, which is kind of pigeonholing people ... and the Rogerian approach seems to look at the whole person rather than pigeonholing.

There was a trend in the interviews for counsellors with a Rogerian orientation to assert the 'value free' foundation of this model. For example, one 42 year old female counsellor said:

> I believe that a pure Rogerian model, where one can have a more open approach in terms of accepting the client's definition of the difficulties and their pace at which to work offers a good start for all ethnic and cultural groups.

And from a 34 year old female counsellor the view was:

> I think that because we live in a predominantly white culture it's inevitable that the theory that is most attractive to most people is Eurocentric. My most used model is Rogerian, I think that's the model that has the least dangers of being Eurocentric in its approach.

The results of the statistical analyses did not support these views, as in the main counsellors in the postal survey with an eclectic or psychodynamic approach appeared more in tune with Black client needs.

As stated before, no evidence was found to support the commonly held view of Rogerian counsellors that their model or practice was more appropriate for the needs of Black clients.

Use of Interpreters

There was no statistically significant relationship between actual use of interpreters and length of counsellor experience. Also, there was no statistical relationship between length of experience and use of an interpreter with Black clients.

Use of Family Network

There was a significant difference in the number of counsellors who had used the family network with Black clients and those who had not, $p<.001$, with fewer counsellors, 36 per cent, using the family network. There was a statistically significant relationship between the use of the family network and years of counsellor experience, $p<.01$. Not all counsellors were willing to involve the family at simply the request of the client. Other reasons for considering family 'participation' existed. One of the 38 year old female counsellors interviewed for this research gave a case which described the expectations of a client for the counsellor to intervene in his relationship with his wife:

> I can remember an Indian man came and he had been referred by his GP as he had a drinking problem. His expectation on arriving at our place was that things would be done to him, things would be basically on a prescriptive or medical

kind of orientation and when he realized that a lot of the difficulty was with him, he didn't want to continue. He also expected us to intervene with his wife whom he had a lot of concern about. He expected us to change the situation for him and there wasn't a recognition of how much the responsibility may have been his or his shared responsibility with his wife. I remember thinking it was due to the fact he was of Asian origin and he had clearly defined extreme expectations of us.

One male counsellor in the 35–39 year age band interpreted the meaning of the question on family use from a different perspective. He wrote on the questionnaire:

If you mean actually contacting other family members for direct counselling session involvement, the answer is no. If you mean the client talking to his/her family using genograms, involving extended family members for support then the answer is yes.

Vignette Rating Scale Results

The statistically significant Vignette Rating Scale results were seen as a measure of counsellors' variation of their usual attitudes towards practice with white clients when counselling Black clients. Although there was no significant difference between the full scale Vignette Rating Scale and the ethnicity of 'client', further investigation showed there to be statistically significant relationships between the ethnicity of 'client' and some of the individual Scale items. There were also some statistically significant relationships between the additional questionnaire items on the Scale proforma (those that did not form part of the Scale) which will be discussed.

The relationship between the ethnicity of client and 'anxiety', was significant at the $p<.001$ level. The degree of 'anxiety' was higher for the South Asian 'client' and much less for the white 'client' and the African-Caribbean 'client'. The 'sense of challenge' was significant, $p<.001$, with a higher degree of 'challenge' being experienced with the South Asian 'client' than with the white or African-Caribbean 'client'. In the interviews, one 38 year old female counsellor believed that a Black client's assessing them as unworkable with would lead them into self exploration:

Well I'd have some feelings of rejection if anybody met me and said that you're not the person I want to work with, I think it would challenge things for me, I'd probably expect that they'd see things in me which were, if not actually racist, were things I hadn't come to terms with, so I'd feel some rejection, and I'd feel some pressure on myself to check that out.

There was a significant degree of 'frustration', p<.05, more being felt with the South Asian 'client' than with the white or African-Caribbean 'client'. More 'hopelessness' was felt with the South Asian 'client' than with the African-Caribbean or white 'client' and less 'hopelessness' with the African-Caribbean 'client' than the white 'client'. Wanting to know about the family circumstances was significant at the p<.001 level with more counsellors wanting to know about the family circumstances of the South Asian 'client' than the other two ethnic group 'clients'. Counsellor competence was a significant variable, p<.001, with counsellors feeling more competent to support the white and African-Caribbean 'client' than the South Asian 'client'. Counsellors were more likely to refer the South Asian 'client' elsewhere for counselling than the other two ethnic group 'clients'. Counsellors saw the ethnic group of the South Asian 'client' as furthest away from their own with the African-Caribbean ethnic group 'client' closer to their own ethnic group. Finally, counsellors thought it more important that the white 'client' knew they were valued and liked more than the South Asian 'client' or the African-Caribbean 'client' at the p<.05 level of significance. There appeared to be a significant amount of what Ridley (1989) referred to as cultural-transference, as discussed in chapter 3, with service delivery to Black 'clients'. One 25 year old female counsellor acknowledged that some counsellors may be biased but hoped this would be explored in supervision:

> ... but surely the therapist would be aware of that and have time to look at why that is and explore those issues ... but I'd imagine there are counsellors with prejudice like that I suppose there's the hope that we would feel that that can't go on, that there are monitors and checks for all of us and that you have supervision in as much as the client is trying to be honest and open in that kind of therapeutic alliance that you could do the same thing and you'd perhaps have your own therapy, but I'm not sure it would help very much.

Summary of Variables Influencing Counsellor's Variation in Practice

The direct experience of counselling African-Caribbeans, but not South Asians, showed a statistically significant relationship with the belief in a different model, and this suggested that counsellors might be amenable to some variation in their usual strategic orientation towards practice.

There were several significant results with the Vignette Rating Scale suggesting various degrees of counter-transference with the different ethnic group 'clients' and therefore a suggestion that clients may be responded to differently according to their particular ethnic group. This indicates the possibility of a potential variation in practice according to client ethnicity. These differences in response included higher degrees of anxiety with the South Asian 'client' and less with the African-Caribbean 'client' than with the white 'client', less hopelessness with the African-Caribbean client than the other ethnic group 'clients', more frustration with the South Asian 'client' than the other ethnic group 'clients', feeling more competent to support the African-Caribbean 'client' than the other ethnic group 'clients', more likely to refer the South Asian 'client' elsewhere, feeling culturally further away from the South Asian 'client' and needing more to know that the white 'client' valued and liked them than the other ethnic group 'clients'.

This chapter has considered the findings related to the research objectives which were discussed under their various subheadings. The next chapter will discuss recommendations for the further training and supervision of counsellors stemming from the research results, as many of the findings have implications for the future development and delivery of counselling services.

9 Conclusions, Reflections and Recommendations

This final chapter will reflect on the overall outcomes of the research and make recommendations for improving the skills and knowledge of counsellors to work with Black client groups. In the final section the limitations of the research and implications for future research will be addressed.

There will be no discussion in this chapter of any particular theory to be adopted with Black clients, for this was not within the aims of the research. For this final chapter a number of conclusions can be drawn. Firstly, it can be said that specific training in the counselling needs of Black clients did appear to make a significant difference to how counsellors perceived Black clients' needs. Pinderhughes' (1989) and D'Andrea's (1990) claim that training which embodied a multi-approach model, utilizing both cognitive and experiential techniques, would have a greater effect on enhancing cultural awareness than use of a purely cognitive training strategy alone was not shown in this study but is worth testing in further research.

Contrary to frequent assertions, both in the reviewed literature and coming from the interviews of counsellors in this study, no evidence was found to suggest that Rogerian counsellors were less inclined towards Eurocentrism than those counsellors from other theoretical orientations. Indeed, there were some non-statistically significant trends for counsellors from the psychodynamic and eclectic models to show greater cultural awareness. However, it is accepted that this finding may relate to the relative numbers of the sample population for each counselling orientation.

Although there was no overall statistically significant association with emotional responses based on ethnicity of 'client' as assessed with the Vignette Rating Scale by ethnicity of 'client' in an ANOVA, there were particular emotions which were individually significant in their relationship with client ethnicity. This suggested that some emotions were more heightened in the cross-cultural encounter or sensitive to ethnic difference than other emotions. Thus the emotions aroused with counselling Black 'clients' of a particular gender, with a particular problem, would appear specific rather than a general

238

or global emotional arousal. The specific heightened emotional reactions from the individual item analyses of the Vignette Rating Scale results indicated that counsellors were showing different emotional responses to the video vignette case study 'clients' based on the client's ethnicity and perceived cultural difference. In the main, counsellors showed more of a heightened emotional response in the order of the South Asian 'client', the white 'client' and least emotional response towards the African-Caribbean 'client'.

This differing emotional response needed to be interpreted not as a generalized disposition, but seen in the context of single women discussing their difficulty in believing themselves to be pregnant and being concerned about their families' reactions. Also, there were statistically significant gender differences in the analysis of the Vignette Rating Scale by counsellor gender. This indicated that men had more of an emotional response overall than did women. This may have been related to the gender of the 'clients' and the perceived gender focus of the concern.

There were a number of recommendations that followed from the results of this research investigation into the attitudes and strategic practice orientations of white therapists with Black client groups. These will be discussed under the subheadings of 'Training' and 'Supervision' in turn.

The Training of Counsellors

The stepwise multiple regression analysis indicated reading and training to be significant predictor variables of the score on the Cultural Awareness Inventory.

The reader is reminded that the majority of counsellors in this research were found to have no specific training and not to have read about the particular counselling needs of Black client groups. Quality training should be seen as the cornerstone of good practice. Good counselling practice is most likely to hinge on the understanding and attitudes which the counsellor brings prior to the onset of counselling. For an appropriate delivery of service the counsellor should have an awareness of how racism informs and affects them as individuals and the society they live in, as well as its social and emotional impact on Black people. Thus, there was an identified need to have an understanding of the operation of racism in contemporary British society and the structural relationship between Black and white people and how this restricts and confines people's life opportunities in order to be able appropriately to conceive the particular needs of Black clients as distinct from white clients.

Ridley (1995) has identified that many counsellors assume that they are able to counsel clients regardless of the client's background. This arises, Ridley wrote, from the inherent philosophy of counselling theory that its techniques were appropriate for all people, regardless of their gender, race, ethnicity or culture. Ridley argued: 'Traditionally trained counsellors tend to believe they are competent enough to adapt to any differences among clients and serve their best interests' (p. 11). The assumption of universality of need and thus approach has, to a significant degree, been assumed without critical analysis. As most counsellors in this study had not undertaken specific training on the needs of Black groups, it would appear that counselling courses, if they are to meet the needs of all ethnic groups in society, will have to review their curriculum content. The curriculum of counselling courses would appear to require components which set out to address the particular sociopolitical history and group experiences of the Black communities in Britain. The reading of material specific to the counselling needs of Black clients did, at face value, appear to be effective in helping counsellors to better consider the needs of Black clients. It was suggested that this may have been because those who had read were more motivated to learn and therefore less inclined to Eurocentric thoughts than those who had not read. This may be so, as reading tends to be a voluntary and self directed activity. It may also be that reading allowed the individual to introspect and privately consider and order their thoughts, and therefore functioned as a multi-model technique more than simply a cognitive method. What this research did not assess is the exact nature of the reading material of which counsellors made use. Further research would be useful to address this and discover the relative value of particular material. Linked to establishing appropriate reading material related to cross-cultural counselling and setting guided reading tasks, there appeared an identified need arising from this research that the reading, in order to make an impact on counsellors' attitudes towards service delivery to Black client groups, needed to be wide ranging on a number of topics. These topics would include those of looking at the specific areas of power relations and power differences between different ethnic groups. This appeared, for some counsellors, in the present sample, to be an area of weakness as over-individualistic notions of an individual's position in society were identified without an adequate understanding of an individual's expectations and roles within a cultural context. Furthermore, for those counsellors who voluntarily seek out reading material, the process of 'change' is likely to be different from those who are 'involuntarily' directed to read. The point being made is that in many cases reading on its own, for those who are directed to read, may not be enough and may have to be supplemented by other forms of awareness raising.

There also appeared to be a lack of understanding about the particular position of specific ethnic groups within society. This has come to be seen as a 'traditional, historical evasion' and Pilgrim (1992, p. 225) has made this point when he argued that:

> In the case of psychodynamic therapies the problem resides in the limitations of interpretative systems which focus narrowly on intra-psychic events or group processes to the exclusion of their wider social context. In the case of humanistic therapies the problem mainly resides in over-valuing human agency and understanding material constraints on our ability to choose our destiny ... psychotherapy is condemned to psychological reductionism and political ignorance.

Pilgrim went on to say that the difficulties of 'alienated life', 'pain' and 'oppression' could not be reduced to problems of 'meeting and communication' which will 'simply melt away given the correct relationship' (p. 232). There are identifiable constraints on personal choice which are determined both by sociopolitical forces and cultural requirements which need to be recognized and addressed in helping clients to consider options. The South Asian ethnic groups were an example of how counsellors rated themselves as culturally distant in the Vignette Rating Scale but appeared to deny the impact of this in the need for considering different counselling models in the survey questionnaire. Furthermore, it appeared that direct experience of counselling South Asian clients did not have a predictable relationship with the Cultural Awareness Inventory although the experience of counselling African-Caribbean clients did. It was speculated that the result of direct counselling experience with South Asian ethnic groups' not having an awareness-enhancing influence may be related to a tendency in counsellors to 'blame' the individual for an inability to change their circumstances, rather than to consider the counsellor's own inadequate knowledge of cultural difference, and resulting inability to make an appropriate response to the South Asian client. Thus, it would seem that counsellors were showing an identified training need to be made aware of both the impinging political forces on ethnic minority group's cultural differences and the resulting effect on life opportunities. This identified need to acknowledge sociopolitical forces may also extend to the benefit of other oppressed groups in society such as women, and may need to take into account issues of social class, disability and sexuality to give counsellors a well rounded appreciation of client need when meeting those who are not white male, heterosexual, middle-class, Protestant, etc. Sue (1990, p. 171) went as far as to suggest that 'the culturally skilled counsellor is able to exercise institutional intervention skills on behalf of his/her client when appropriate'. This was seen as an innovative challenge to counsellor training which appeared in direct opposition to the traditional schools of thought, and indeed some may argue that this is more akin to the social worker's role.

Counselling training should prepare counsellors to have a critical awareness of the difficulties in setting goals and drawing conclusions about clients without regard to cultural issues. Counsellors' self awareness of personal attitudes towards the client's cultural group is also likely to be a training need. Furthermore, training should not be based on the narrow perspectives of one preferred counselling approach which has not taken cultural diversity into account and does not allow the counsellor to consider alternative perspectives of culturally influenced lifestyles. In establishing the counselling relationship, the counsellor should accept the client on a culturally equal basis, be aware of the effects of racism on the expectations both parties bring to the relationship, and of the relative effects of the client's inner emotional and outer social world, including the client's membership of a particular racial, cultural or religious group. Counsellors, in their professional capacity, should take responsibility for raising issues of race, culture and racism.

As well as specific reading, a further, identified activity which appeared to enable counsellors better to consider the position of other ethnic groups was specialized training. Disappointingly, Dryden and Feltham (1994), in a book entitled *Developing Counsellor Training*, devoted little space to the consideration of how to develop counsellor training course curriculum content for the culturally different. Even in the section which claimed to be concerned with 'specialist training and knowledge of specific interventions for certain client problems' (p. 79), little space was devoted. Suggestions that curriculum developers might use for cross-cultural development were not considered in enough depth or indeed with enough creativity to support the likely learning needs of course developers. Jewel (1994), in evaluating what he termed 'multi-cultural counselling research' indicated that a number of multi-cultural counselling courses had emerged over a 20 year period in the USA and that these had been evaluated by D'Andrea and Daniels (1991) who classified them into four groups which focused on a specific aspect of counselling:

1   the acquisition of communication skills (Pederson, 1977);

2   the need to become more aware of one's attitudes towards ethnic minorities (Hulnuck, 1971; Parker and McDavis, 1989);

3 the importance of increasing the counsellor's knowledge about ethnic minority populations (Banks, 1991; Mio, 1989); and

4 training formats encouraging counsellors to develop their awareness, knowledge, and skills in this area (Reynolds, 1995; D'Andrea, 1990).

Carter and Qureshi (1995) have suggested an excellent typology of assumptions in multi-cultural counselling training which outlines five types. These will be briefly summarized here, and the reader who wishes for further details should refer to their original paper.

Universal or Etic Approach

This suggests that all are basically the same with within group differences being greater than between group differences. Carter and Qureshi suggest that '[t]he universal approach does not deny the existence of culture as such; rather it calls for an intense focus on shared human experience while incorporating culture specific knowledge' (p. 245). They point out that some writers such as Lloyd (1987) have argued that training about specific cultures is of questionable value as this can have the effect of forcing clients into a cultural straitjacket without allowing them individual behaviour outside of cultural constraints. There arises in this view a danger that clients become exclusively culturally determined. Stereotyping may result, with the development of different standards for different groups. Carter and Qureshi point out that although he approach has some advantages a main disadvantage is that 'it downplays sociopolitical history and intergroup power dynamics by assuming that one group membership has no more meaning than any other' (p. 246).

Ubiquitous Approach

Carter and Qureshi suggest that, with this approach, the assumption is that any human difference can be considered to be a cultural difference. From this is would follow that essentially all counselling would be cross-cultural as an educated white middle class counsellor counselling an uneducated white working class client would constitute cultural difference. A broader definition of culture than is usual is therefore brought into play, which sees all differences between people as cultural. Some may consider this to be outside of the notions of culture discussed in chapter 2, in that culture appears to lose its specific and distinct meaning. However, the view taken with this approach (Margolis and Rungta, 1986; Fukuyama, 1990) is that it is difference that is the key to difficulties in human communication, and as such difference may cause the counsellor to function inadequately or at least ineffectively with the 'culturally different' client. The training focus is to encourage the counsellor to 'rise above' culture by making the counsellor comfortable with difference and able to acknowledge the differences that exist between them and client. The view is that an ethnocentric counsellor is less likely to facilitate change in the client. Training approaches focus on acknowledging and accepting difference in clients. Carter and Qureshi argue that an advantage of this approach is that it avoids pathologizing difference which, as with the universal approach, can lead to 'avoidance and denial of sociopolitical histories, intergroup power dynamics and the relative salience of various reference group memberships' (p. 247).

Traditional Approach

Carter and Qureshi note that, within this approach, culture is defined within the context of socialization and environment. Therefore one obtains cultural membership by birth, socialization and environment. Culture initiates and determines the range of possible experiences. Carter and Qureshi note that writers such as Lloyd (1987) have been critical of this approach as individual clients are made into 'cultural others' and primary differences are ascribed to them. As Carter and Qureshi indicate, it is as though 'one's cultural membership circumscribes the types of social and personality dynamics possible' (p. 249). Training approaches that take the traditional approach argue that some 'experience' or at least exposure of another culture is necessary. Carter and Qureshi note that this 'exposure' has typically taken place in a number of different ways. Cultural 'informants' may be used to develop cultural knowledge, courses may advocate counselling individual members of ethnic minority groups or having students watch video tapes of culturally different clients and/or role playing a counselling experience with a culturally different client. The view appears to be that any person can master the necessary aspects of another culture to be able effectively to counsel a culturally different client. There is also a cognitive component in the traditional approach as assessed by Carter and Qureshi, as they suggest that in this approach the key to counselling efficacy is through cultural knowledge and that prejudice arises due to 'erroneous individual beliefs'. Again as with the other approaches its weakness is the minimization of sociopolitical factors, intergroup dynamics and the influence of racism.

Race Based Training

Here, Carter and Qureshi argue, the approach assumes that the experience of belonging to a racial group defined essentially by colour, language and physical features defines and determines one's experience. Race becomes the salient factor determining how one is seen, interpreted and responded to. Sociopolitical aspects and intergroup power dynamics ignored in other approaches are to the forefront in this approach. Aspects of culture and group interaction vary according to racially grounded psychology and race becomes the defining feature of social exclusion, inclusion and social division. Racial groups are assigned behaviours and characteristics which are seen to determine their behaviour, and the group's social characteristics are seen as being fixed and unalterable. Whereas cultural behaviours are seen as changeable and fluid, racial characteristics are not. The responses of (white) powerful groups to less powerful (Black) groups affects the psychological development of the individuals within the less powerful groups. This is through a process of the individual's psychological response to the experience of racism. Ideas and philosophies about race feed into the development of racism, which fosters ideas, practices and social responses to those who are seen as different. In this approach, the racism of white people, intentional or not, is seen as the barrier to effective cross-cultural counselling. Training in order to produce able white cross-cultural counsellors should facilitate the process of passing through the necessary levels of white racial identity development (Helms, 1987 and 1990), as discussed in chapter 2. Carter and Qureshi point out that '[i]nasmuch as one's identity is defined by oneself and others, the relative "level" of racial identity of counsellor and client must necessarily affect the counselling situation' (p. 253). The race based approach takes the view that a counsellor cannot begin to empathize with a racially different client until the counsellor deals with their own racism and the relative position of their racial group. Carter and Qureshi quote Corvin and Wiggins (1989) as saying 'White racism is not the result of cultural differences, but the consequence of White ethnocentrism' (p. 253). This viewpoint, Carter and Qureshi maintain, 'shifts the focus from cultural knowledge to self knowledge, from an external emphasis to an internal emphasis, racism is not so much a function of misinformation about other peoples as a function of misinformation about the self that leads to distortions about others' (p. 254). Racism and racial identity development become the focus of training in this approach. Carter and Qureshi note that the advantage of this approach is that it recognizes sociopolitical and historical events and their effects on counselling delivery.

They suggest the disadvantage is one of counsellors needing to go through a painful journey of self discovery which may have the effect of stopping racial identity and awareness development. However, it may be that those who cannot make the journey are assessed as those who are not able to deliver effective cross-cultural counselling. The disadvantage Carter and Qureshi note may become an assessment and selection process that separates the potential competent cross-cultural counsellor from the potential non-competent cross-cultural counsellor.

Pan-national

The pan-national approach sees race as determining culture. This approach has been developed by Black people to explain and understand their sociopolitical position relative to white people. Carter and Qureshi suggest that the Africentric viewpoint which attempts to link all people of African origin to an African self consciousness stemming from African social theory. The experience of colonialism and slavery is seen as distorting the maintenance and development of an African self. Africentric notions attempt to return people of African origin to an African worldview with its African spiritual base. Writers in this tradition such as Bulhan (1985) focus on the imposition of European social theory on all non-European groups, which contributes to the oppression and psychological denigration experienced by African peoples. Thus African people, as with all oppressed groups, are seen as being alienated from their true selves and culture. The historical colonial relations between Black and white groups give Bulhan doubts about how effective cross-cultural counselling can be. He saw it as necessary to make explicit the power dynamics in the relationship to reach the goal of liberating the oppressed, and talked about the collective and active engagement of the oppressed. Carter and Qureshi state that 'a Pan-National training program would focus on thematizing and rejecting the anti-African (or Asian or Indian) power dynamics inherent in European psychology. It would attempt to enable trainees to understand and emancipate themselves from Eurocentric psychology as a requisite first step' (p. 256). Criticisms of the approach focus on its assumption that personality is 'biogenetically' determined regardless of sociopolitical forces and that it views racism as the single primary influence for communication difficulties between groups ignoring factors such as religion and social class.

The typology offered by Carter and Qureshi and the criticisms that followed from each approach would suggest that no one discrete approach should be used singularly. However, in this study it appeared that any type of focused training appeared to have a beneficial impact on counsellors. Although not shown to be statistically significant in the questionnaire survey, the interviewed counsellors suggested that training which had as its primary focus a factually informative or cognitive element was not challenging enough to enable counsellors to understand and acknowledge the differing and varying needs of the culturally different client. Another form of training which was identified by interviewed counsellors as effective was specific and varied in its approach in attempting to establish counsellors' insight into considering the culturally different reality and needs of clients. This was training which used a combination of strategies to enhance learning such as teaching cultural knowledge about different ethnic groups, teaching sociopolitical issues related to the position of different groups in society, and counsellor personal exploration, often in 'encounter group' form. In addition, the interviewed counsellors suggested that white counsellors' understandings of their own culture and ethnic group membership was a useful teaching component. These forms of counselling would appear more related to academic than applied counselling education, and this was shown by the multiple regression analysis to have a significant association with the Cultural Awareness Inventory. These findings lent support to the British Association for Counselling's criteria for counselling training programmes. These criteria require that courses include the separate components of cognitive/theoretical inputs, skills practice and work on self. The interviewed counsellors in this study tended to hold the view that these areas should be integrated where possible and that space for opportunities of structured self reflection on the personal meanings of the learning should happen within the counselling programme. McLeod (1993, p. 13) argued that '[i]n the field of counselling and psychotherapy ... the development of accurate, reflective self awareness is absolutely central to the aims of the curriculum'. One useful technique to allow counsellors to explore their personal experience and development of attitudes towards the culturally different may be the use of Helms' (1987) work, as discussed in chapter 2. Here, counsellors in training are asked to consider their personal developmental progress in line with her model of the development of white racial awareness and their ability and skills in transcending historical and current personal prejudices. The introduction of the notions of 'cultural-transference' and 'colour blindness' (Ridley, 1989) as discussed in chapter 3 would also be of use, as they directly interface and overlap with existing counselling concepts and therefore would seem to allow the trainer and student to extend the traditional concepts into work with the culturally different.

In addition to Helms' (1987) model of racial attitude development, various writers (Sue, 1990; Locke, 1992) have proposed models of curriculum development to aid both cultural and self understanding in counsellors. These models tended to emphasize the need for counsellors to consider sociopolitical factors, including institutional blocks to Black clients' gaining access to therapy, the cultural history of oppression (the counsellor's and the client's), the experience and understanding of prejudice and racism, the influence of second language and cultural/social class variants of language, religious practices, family roles and structures and personal attitudes and values towards the client's own and majority culture. The models tend to emphasize the need to be aware of and acknowledge the sociopolitical forces and the developmental and psychological meanings of ethnic and cultural differences. Clearly, the individuality of cultural members and differences within groups must be acknowledged so as not to stereotype and 'pigeonhole' members of a particular cultural group as seemed to happen in the Vignette Rating Scale video study.

As previously suggested, it would seem essential that information on training courses is not presented in isolated 'packages' of learning but in an integrated and systematic way in training delivery. What could be termed as a multi-cultural skills element to counselling courses should be considered to allow counsellors to become culturally skilled in relevant practical approaches. It may be necessary to evaluate the received benefit of these skills so as to 'avoid relying on humanistic rhetoric' (Dillard, 1987). Furthermore, it is important for counsellor trainers to make clear the bias and value based assumptions inherent in many western models of therapy, as discussed in chapter 4. From this, the appropriateness or lack of appropriateness of particular models should become apparent through the normal training process before attempting work with the culturally different client.

The direct experience of counselling African-Caribbean clients also appeared to lessen the measured Eurocentrism of counsellors. However, this did not appear to be so with South Asian clients. It was suggested in the discussion that this result may have been related more to the perceived cultural distance of the South Asian clients from white counsellors. This was explained within the theoretical context of Festinger's cognitive dissonance theory (1957), Batson et al.'s (1987) personal distress theory and Tajfel's (1979) in-group/out-group model. It was suggested that, because of the perceived cultural distance of the South Asian clients, there may have been a tendency to be less able to empathize appropriately with them. This was supported by the Vignette Rating Scale results. Also, perceived cultural distance may have had the effect of making counsellors feel powerless to help and hence reduce these feelings of powerlessness rather than to look at adequacy of their techniques for individuals within this group. Counsellors may have tended towards a blaming of the victim for an inability or perceived unwillingness on the client's part to change (Ridley, 1989; Pinderhughes, 1989; Sue, 1990).

As direct experience of counselling African-Caribbean clients had a measured cultural awareness enhancing effect, it would appear a useful addition to counsellor training if, as part of their practical experience, counsellors were required to gain direct experience with a client from an African-Caribbean background and for this to form part of a written assignment which was then produced and discussed in a group seminar for the purposes of receiving constructive feedback on counselling performance. This would also be beneficial with South Asian clients, as this may facilitate more effective learning with this group than direct experience alone. The learning benefit of this assignment may be enhanced for both South Asian and African-Caribbean clients if counsellors were instructed not to over-rely on theoretical notions of delivery but to explore their feelings about the client and how this effects the therapeutic alliance and service delivery. Where Black clients are not available to the counsellor because of geographical location, then the use of audio or videoed material should be considered. (This is available from sources such as the University of Birmingham Television and Video Department 'Counselling Black Client Groups' video series.) Furthermore, the value of role play, when attempts are made to enter into the reality of a client's circumstances, should not be underestimated. These suggestions follow in part from the results of the statistical analyses and also the interview comments of counsellors identifying what they found to be of particular use for their own learning. Certainly the self questioning that came from challenges about the counsellors' value laden assumptions or judgments appeared in the main to be welcomed in developing counsellor perspectives.

In developing counsellor awareness it may be that areas of particular difficulty are raised for the counsellor which show themselves as personal blockages. Counsellors may then need to identify personal learning objectives and strategies that go beyond those of the training course, and this may take place in supervision, which will be discussed next.

The Supervision of Counsellors

Counselling supervision is a requirement of the British Association for Counselling's Code of Practice. The results of this research however, indicated that only 61 per cent of counsellors received supervision. Boyd-Franklin (1989) described the key task of the supervisor as the empowerment of counsellors through the 'mobilisation of their feelings of confidence and competence in themselves and their work' (p. 244). However, the British Association for Counselling in their draft document on supervision (1987, p. 2) stated that supervision was not only for the awareness of the supervisor but also for the benefit of the client. They said that: 'The primary purpose of supervision is to protect the best interests of the client.' It can be argued that the role of the supervisor and training run parallel, i.e,. both should serve the aim of increasing quality service delivery to clients. The supervisory element in counselling can be seen as a process of checks and balances on counsellor interaction, with clients reviewing and exploring the counsellor's delivery of appropriate service. There may sometimes be difficulties which counsellors are unable to work through in large teaching or training groups that are best dealt with in supervision. Dryden and Feltham (1994) have quoted Reising and Daniels (1983) as saying: 'Beginning counsellors tend to be anxious, dependent, technique orientated and unready for confrontation' (p. 16). Typically, the issues that a counsellor brought to supervision were not those of a personal nature but were those related to counsellor practice with clients. Hawkins and Shohet (1993, p. 21) made the valid point that:

> we believe that supervision begins with self supervision; and this begins with appraising one's motives and facing parts of ourselves we would normally keep hidden (even from our own awareness) as honestly as possible. By doing this we can lessen the split that sometimes occurs in the helpers, whereby they believe they are problem-free and have no needs, and see their clients as only sick and needy.

Loganbill et al. (1982) have suggested a three stage model of supervision based on identifying supervisees functioning at various levels of development related to: stagnation, confusion and integration. 'Naive unawareness' or 'stuckedness' characterized the stagnant novice. Confusion indicated blocked growth which could be facilitated by the supervision until integration of ideas and feelings was achieved. Furthermore, the authors argued that each of the stages could be measured by issues of supervisees' skills, emotional awareness, autonomy, identity, respect for individual differences, purpose and direction, personal motivation and professional ethics. The supervision may use theoretical, practice, or personal challenge interventions as appropriate to the learning needs of the supervisee. This would fit in with the multi-model need perspective of Pinderhughes (1989). A supervisor may be expected to encourage and support the counsellor's work with a particular client if the counsellor believes themself to be experiencing difficulty with working through a client's difficulties. The Vignette Rating Scale video study discovered that there were likely to be significant counter-transference issues in operation in counsellors' direct work with Black 'clients'. Therefore, appropriate supervision to identify this difficulty and remedy the potential negative impact on the client was seen as a necessary step, in line with the British Association for Counselling Code of Practice requirements. This requirement does not appear founded on any empirical evidence to support the value of supervisors in enhancing counselling service or ability to correct and guide counsellors through the difficulties they face. Indeed, there was no evidence in the literature that supervisors rated counsellors who were more dogmatic, and by implication less sensitive to the cultural needs of others, as more ineffective with clients (Harrison, 1975). Therefore, the question may be asked: who supervises the supervisors? It was suggested in the literature that supervisors may be unaware of issues related to their own difficulties to do with ethnic difference. It would seem therefore, that the inclusion of sensitive issues related to cultural difference should be part of the accreditation of supervisors. Proctor (1988) has argued that it is an assumption of those in the helping services that they want to monitor their own practice, want to learn to develop their own competence and respond to support and encouragement. Where the services of a Black supervisor are not available, an alternative may be for supervisors or counsellors who are experiencing difficulties with sensitive issues around ethnicity to seek specialist consultation from an individual who has specialist knowledge in the required area. Steinberg (1992) has made suggestions of how consultation, in a cross-cultural counselling context, may take place, and these ranged from representatives of an ethnic minority group making themselves available for discussion on particular topics, to approaching community organizations, to searching out a specialist or knowledgeable professional in the area, such as a Black therapist. He argued that the value of consultation was that joint exploration could take place with individuals who were open to considering the limits of their own knowledge. In this way the responsibility, position and autonomy of the people who consult was not compromised, i.e., they were not placed in a threatening position. The benefit of consultation, it was argued, was that it allowed those involved 'to take action in the light of a broader perspective' (p. 63). It was seen as an active form of problem solving, drawing on the expertise of those experienced in the field. The use of a consultant is suggested as a positive step as, in doing so, the consultee has to acknowledge a difficulty. Once this is done then insight has been gained into how best to move forward in a positive way. This method of enhancing counsellor service delivery is suggested as a practical and beneficial mechanism for all those in the counselling exchange as it enables the learning of the supervisor or counsellor while at the same time helps to meet the counselling needs of the client.

Reflections

An important outcome of this research has been to suggest that white counsellors were not, on grounds of their particular cultures alone, unable to counsel Black clients, but were likely to be effective if they sought out information to build upon their cultural understanding of how cultural differences may affect the cross-cultural counselling encounter. It would seem that the acknowledgement of difference, the recognition that this can influence counselling process and outcome and a combination of attempts to gain information about cultural difference and experienced personal difficulties are likely to be a greater indicator of cross-cultural competence than the particular ethnic group of the counsellor alone. Those involved with counsellor training and supervision may need a 'conceptual hook' to hang their consideration of social/cultural differences upon. Rogers (1961) wrote that all clients should be understood from their unique frame of reference. This means that an empathic response is needed, and furthermore it may mean that, rather than simply having a purely emotional connection to the client's difficulties, the emotional connection must have an objective knowledge foundation to it. This should be based on the client's position as a single individual and also as an individual within a wider network of social linkages. This needs to take into consideration the individual's ethnic group membership and/or physical characteristics which may cause that individual to be responded to not as a unique individual but, as a negative stereotyped group member.

This section will end with a statement reflecting the view of Hawkins and Shohet (1993) which summarized what all counsellors should bear in mind in attempting to provide a quality service – a willingness to examine one's motives, 'good' or 'bad', pure or otherwise, is a fundamental prerequisite for being an effective helper. From this it is axiomatic that from this willingness to self examine a process of change is entered into when one's motives and skills are found to be wanting.

The Limitations of the Research

No presentation of a thesis would be complete without some discussion of the research limitations. This section will attempt to answer the question of how the researcher would have carried out the research with the benefit of hindsight.

The present writer considers it very fortunate that a good response rate was obtained. In hindsight it would have been useful to meet with the Research Committee of the British Association for Counselling to explain the pitfalls of poor response in surveys and ask for a more controlled system of identifying a cohort of counsellors to send initial and follow up requests for the return of questionnaires. This would have added significant administrative and material costs to a piece of self-funded research. In practice this proved not to be necessary, but was a line of action that would be pursued with any further research surveys undertaken.

There were a number of limitations with the postal questionnaire which became the Cultural Awareness Inventory. Most of these revolve around the way questions were structured, e.g., a distinction could have been made between Black clients born in Britain and those who were not as regards the questions which asked about the use and need of interpreters. The way that the counsellors were 'forced' into discrete orientation categories may have been more relevant to North American than British practice, and may have accounted to some degree for the high numbers in the 'other' category.

With hindsight, being a Black interviewer may have affected the response of interviewees who may have tended to give more 'politically correct' or guarded answers to the interview than they would with a white interviewer. Being interviewed by a Black interviewer may have also sensitized individuals to the nature of the research and made them think in terms of 'should do' rather than 'do do'. However, given the apparent honesty with which most of the interviewees appeared to have spoken, this did not appear to present as too much of a practical difficulty. It should be mentioned that the present researcher has a North American accent and to some extent this may have acted as a 'psychological separation' between him and the African-Caribbean and South Asian communities in the view of the interviewees, therefore allowing them to be much more 'off guard' than if the researcher had had a British accent. However, as any interviewer would not be free of 'ethnic group attachment' this effect would play a part, although with a different emphasis, with any interviewer.

A sample of Black counsellors would have been most interesting to compare against the responses of the white counsellors. As indicated early in chapter 6, the sample obtained from the postal survey questionnaire was much too small and too diverse to be used for comparative purposes. To overcome this a direct approach to the Association of Black Counsellors could have been made. The reader is reminded that the main aim of this research was to examine the attitudes and strategic practice orientations of white counsellors. Even so, data obtained from a sample of Black counsellors would have been most useful to look both at issues of similarity and difference.

The observation of counsellors in actual practice would have been interesting. In practice, given the confidential and personal nature of counselling, this would have been extremely difficult if not impossible. There are also ethical considerations which would have limited the possibility of this approach, in that an observer in the counselling scenario would have been intrusive and potentially affected the counselling process. The tape recording of sessions may have overcome this difficulty to some degree but would have also had its limitations owing to the absence of nonverbal communication indicators.

The investigation of the curriculum of counsellor training institutions to elicit the training objectives related to cross-cultural competencies of such institutions for counsellors in training could have formed an illuminating addition to the research. In any case, those institutions or trainers who wish to avail themselves of these research findings may benefit from the findings of the relative effectiveness of reading and different types of training. Another related issue to that of assessing the curriculum of training organizations would have been to interview counsellor trainers to obtain their views of and practices in the training of counsellors to meet Britain's multi-cultural population. The perceived priority of such training and how to best set about it may have been useful to capture and extend the findings of this research. Again related to training, it could have been useful to observe, actual training sessions of counsellors to see how issues related to Black clients were dealt with for the purposes of analysis. Did courses have distinct sessions of teaching, if any, or did they integrate the information and cross relate information about different groups and the relevance of theory and practice to diverse groups as the courses proceeded? How were counsellors assessed on their skills with diverse communities and were trainers from Black communities involved in the training and assessment of counsellors? These questions, given a different research emphasis, could have been addressed.

As well as counsellors and their trainers, the views of supervisors would have been useful to obtain. These form an important resource, as was suggested, for the further development of a counsellor's direct practice with all client groups. Furthermore, as was questioned, how do supervisors receive their training on the needs of diverse cultural groups? As well as extending the focus of the research, the actual research design may have been altered to allow for further data to evolve. For example, allowing for potential gender issues to be fully considered with an attempt to separate them from those of ethnicity. The video vignette client research could have contained male 'clients' with, obviously, a different difficulty than being pregnant. However, it could have been related to pregnancy in that their female partner could have been the pregnant individual to whom they were unsure how to respond or what steps to take. Thus, male and female counsellors and their emotional responses could have been compared. This, as the present writer considers the possibility and the implications of the extension of this design, had the feel of an additional thesis. Control groups consisting of Black female and male counsellors could have been used as well as beginning counsellors with less than two years of experience to see how relatively little experience, compared to 'medium' and 'significant' lengths of experience, influenced the results. The video vignette study could have also focused on the different reactions of counsellors as influenced by their theoretical orientation. This was not an oversight in the initial design, but was in fact a typing error where this category was not included on the typed instrument, not proof read, and inadvertently used with this specific omission. The present writer could have, to some extent, pursued more in depth questions in the postal survey asking respondents to illustrate certain issues by way of case material, e.g., showing a case example of why different counselling models were or were not seen as relevant for Black clients. In critically assessing the research instruments used, criticisms could be made of the length of the postal questionnaire which again, with hindsight, did appear excessively long. However, given the striking lack of information on the attitudes of white counsellors in Britain and with no existing research instruments to draw upon, the present questionnaire was an exploratory and pioneering instrument which future researchers may benefit from.

One may argue that the Cultural Awareness Inventory was measuring dimensions other than cultural awareness. It is possible to say that the Cultural Awareness Inventory was not measuring a single unitary dimension. However, given the sophisticated sample who would be alert to subtleties of semantic meaning, it was not surprising that one did not find a simplistic unitary measure. Some may argue for a more stringent validation of the Cultural Awareness Inventory. The reader is reminded that a standardized Likert scale was not within the objectives or means of this research. Given the Cronbach's alpha analysis it was clear that the Cultural Awareness Inventory 'hangs together' and was measuring 'something', and that this 'something' had a complex and meaningful interrelated structure. Furthermore, the validity of the research is to some degree a matter of the conclusions that follow from the data. It must be remembered that this research did not rely on a single research method and was one that employed three strands of evidence or a triangulated approach. The complexity of the counsellors' attitudes was further explored by both interviews and the video vignette study. In the interviews many counsellors gave examples of Eurocentrism or prejudice that they had either assessed in themselves or observed in others. In the video vignette study it could be argued that the responses were not ones of Eurocentrism or prejudice but different responses to different individuals and not to culture or ethnicity. However, given that the 'clients' had the same script, it is fairly clear that the 'clients' were presenting with the same difficulty and that the only major thing which differed was the ethnicity of 'client'. Therefore, the sample was responding to ethnicity on its own, which would suggest a robust measure of difference in reaction related to ethnicity of client. Furthermore, it should be remembered that the Cultural Awareness Inventory items were judged by four experienced therapists to be an accurate measure of bias in counsellors. The Vignette Rating Scale was further developed and statistically validated from another worker's research. The measurement of counter-transference, like its definition and display, will inevitably be problematic and open to debate but, given the results of this tool in two separate pieces of research, it seemed an acceptably valid instrument of measurement.

Implications for Future Research

Stemming from the limitations of the research there are a number of recommendations that can be made for future research, these being:

1   investigating the strategies that are used for teaching of counselling as it relates to the needs of cultural diversity and how these strategies relate to overall curriculum initiatives and coverage;

2   what difficulties in training are being encountered by counselling trainers;

3   what is the impact of training on counsellors and how is this assessed;

4   what is the impact of training on clients and how is this assessed;

5 what counselling models produce what counselling outcomes, with what clients, with what difficulties when used by which counsellors;

6 how are supervisors equipped and supported in their work with counsellors in addressing issues of cross-cultural counselling?

In fact, due to the paucity of information on white counsellors and their practices with Black clients in Britain, the list is almost endless as to what research would be of benefit. As this was the first piece of research of its kind with a solely British practice focus, the writer considers it to have been a worthwhile piece of pioneering activity which will contribute much to improving the understanding of white counsellors' attitudes and strategic practice orientations with Black clients in Britain.

References

Abdel-Gaid, S. (1984), *A Step by Step Procedure for Designing a Likert Attitude Scale*, unpublished doctoral dissertation, Pennsylvania State University.

Aboud, F. (1987), 'The Development of Ethnic Self-Identification and Attitudes' in J.S. Phinney and M.J. Rotheram (eds), *Childrens' Ethnic Socialisation: Pluralism and Development*, New York: Sage, pp. 188–215.

Aboud, F. (1988), *Children and Prejudice*, Oxford: Blackwell.

Abramowitz, S.T. and Murray, A.J. (1983), 'Race Effects in Psychotherapy' in J. Murray and Abramason (eds), *Bias in Psychotherapy*, Westport: Greenwood Press, pp. 235–56.

Acharyya, S. (1987), 'Research Findings: Part 2' in *Assessment and Treatment Across Cultures Nafsiyat*, London: Routledge and Kegan Paul.

Acosta, F.X., Yamamoto, J. and Evans, L.A. (1982), *Effective Psychotherapy for Low Income and Minority Patients*, New York: Plenum Press.

Adams, W. (1950), 'The Negro Patient in Psychiatric Treatment', *American Journal of Orthopsychiatry*, 20 (2), pp. 305–10.

Adorno, T.W., Frenkel-Brunswik, E., Levinson, D.J. and Sanford, R.N. (1950), *The Authoritarian Personality*, New York: Harper.

Ahmed, S., Cheetham, J. and Small, J. (1986), *Social Work with Black Children and Their Families*, London: B.T. Batsford.

Aiken, L.R. (1980), 'Attitude Measurement and Research' in D.A. Payne (ed.), *New Directions for Testing and Measurement*, No. 7, New York: Creswell Scientific, pp. 12–19.

Ajzen, I. and Fishbein, M. (1977), 'Attitude-Behaviour Relations: A Theoretical Analysis and Review of Empirical Research', *Psychological Bulletin*, 84, pp. 888–918.

Alexander, A.A., Workneh, F., Klein, M.H. and Miller, M H. (1976), 'Psychotherapy and the Foreign Student' in P. Pedersen, W.J. Lonner and J.G. Draguns (eds), *Counselling Across Cultures*, Honolulu: University Press of Hawaii, pp. 215–37.

Alexander, J. (1977), 'The Culture of Race in Middleclass Kingston, Jamaica', *American Ethologist*, 4, pp. 413–35.

Allen, G. and Skinner, C. (1991), *Handbook for Research Students in the Social Sciences*, London: Falmer Press.

Allen, S. (1971), *New Minorities, Old Conflicts: Asian and West Indian Migrants in Britain*, New York: Random House.

Allison, T., Cooper, C. and Reynolds, P. (1989), 'Stress Counselling and the Workplace – The Post Office Experience', *The Psychologist*, 2, pp. 9–12.

Allport, G.W. (1935), 'Attitudes' in C. Murshison (ed.), *A Handbook of Social Psychology*, Worcester, Massachusetts: Clarke University Press, pp. 798–844.

Allport, G.W. (1937), *Personality: A Psychological Interpretation*, New York: Holt.

Allport, G.W. (1954), *The Nature of Prejudice*, Reading, Massachusetts: Addison-Wesley.

American Psychological Association Committee (1954), 'Technical Recommendations for Psychological Tests and Diagnostic Techniques', *Psychological Bulletin Supplement*, 51 (2), pp. 1–38.

Anderson, L.R and Fishbein, M. (1965), 'Prediction of Attitude from Number Strength and Evaluative Aspect of Beliefs about the Attitude Object: A Comparison of Summation and Congruity Theories', *Journal of Personality and Social Psychology*, 2, pp. 437–43.

Anthony, W. and Carkhuff, R. (1977), 'The Functional Professional Therapeutic Agent' in A. Gurman and A. Razin (eds.), *Effective Psychotherapy: A Handbook of Research*, New York: Pergamon Press, pp. 145–66.

Anwar, M. (1979), *The Myth of Return*, London: Heinemann.

Ary, D., Jacobs, L.C.and Razavich, A. (1979), *Introduction to Research in Education*, 2nd edn, New York: Rinehart and Winston.

Ashmore, R.D. (1970), 'Prejudice: Causes and Cures', in B.E. Collins (ed.) *Social Psychology, Social Influence, Attitude Change, Group Processes and Prejudice*, Reading, Massachusetts: Addison-Wesley, pp. 245–339.

Atkin, L. (1979), 'Causal Modelling' in *DE304 Research Methods in Education and the Social Sciences*, Block 7, Milton Keynes: Open University.

Atkinson, D.R. (1983), 'Ethnic Similarity in Counselling Psychology: A Review of the Research', *The Counselling Psychologist*, 11 (3), pp. 79–92.

Atkinson, D.R. (1985), 'A Meta Review of Research in Cross-Cultural Counselling and Psychotherapy', *Journal of Multicultural Counselling and Development*, 13, pp. 138–53.

Atkinson, D.R. (1987), 'Research and Cross-Cultural Counselling and Psychotherapy: A Review and Update of Reviews' in P. Pederson (ed.), *Handbook of Cross-Cultural Counselling and Psychotherapy*, 2nd edn, Westport: Greenwood Press, pp. 191–9.

Atkinson, D.R. and Lowe, S.M. (1995), 'The Role of Ethnicity, Cultural Knowledge and Conventional Techniques in Counselling and Psychotherapy' in J.G. Ponterotto and J.M. Casqs, L.A. Suzuki, and C.M. Alexander (eds), *Handbook of Multicultural Counselling*, pp. 387–414.

Atkinson, D.R. and Schein, S. (1986), 'Similarity in Counselling', *The Counselling Psychologist*, 14, pp. 319–54.

Auerbach, A. and Johnson, M. (1977), 'Research on the Therapists Level of Experience' in A. Gurman and A. Razin (eds), *Effective Psychotherapy. A Handbook of Research*, New York: Pergamon Press, pp. 102–30.

Awatere, D. (1982), 'Maori Counselling' in F. Donnelly (ed.), *A Time to Talk, Counsellor and Counselled*, Australia: George Allen and Unwin, pp. 198–203.

Babbie, E. (1990), *Survey Research Methods*, 2nd edn, California: Wadsworth.

Bacchi, C.L. (1990), *Same Difference: Feminism and Sexual Difference*, Sydney: Allen and Unwin.

Baldwin, J. (1980), 'The Psychology of Oppression' in M.K. Asante and A.S. Vandi (eds), *Contemporary Black Thought: Alternative Analyses in Social and Behavioural Sciences*, Beverley Hills, California: Sage, pp. 95–110.

Bagley, C. and Young, L. (1983), *Multicultural Childhood*, Aldershot: Gower.

Bailey, F.G. (1963), 'Closed Stratification in India', *European Journal of Sociology*, 4, pp. 107–24.

Balarajan, R. and Raleigh, V.A. (1992), 'The Ethnic Populations of England and Wales: 1991 Census', *Health Trends*, Vol. 24, No. 4.

Ballard, C. (1979), 'Conflict Continuity and Change: Second Generation South Asians' in V.S. Khan (ed.), *Minority Families in Britain: Support and Stress*, London: Macmillan, pp. 106–29.

Ball-Rokeach, S. (1973), 'From Pervasive Ambiguity to a Definition of the Situation', *Sociometry*, 36, pp. 43–51.

Bamgose, O., Edwards, D. and Johnson, S. (1980), 'The Effects of Race and Social Class on Clinical Judgement, *Journal of Clinical Psychology*, 37, pp. 529–37.

Banks, N.J. (1990), *The Process of Building Positive Self-Esteem in Black Children*

Banks, N.J. (1991), 'Counselling Black Client Groups: Does Eurocentric Theory Apply?' *Counselling Psychology Review*, Vol. 6, No. 4, pp. 2–6, December

Banks, N.J. (1992a), 'Black Clients, White Counsellors. Working with Prejudice and Discrimination in the Workplace', *Employee Counselling Today*, Vol. 4, Issue 3, pp. 12–16.

Banks, N.J (1992b), 'Direct Identity Work With Black Children', *Adoption and Fostering*, Vol. 16, 3, Autumn, London: BAAF, pp. 19–25.

Banks, N.J. (1995), 'The Placement Needs of the Mixed Parentage Child', *Adoption and Fostering* Vol. 19, 2, June, London: BAAF, pp. 19–24.

Banks, W.C. (1976), 'White Preference in Blacks: A Paradigm in Search of a Phenomenon', *Psychological Bulletin*, 83 (6), pp. 1179–86.

Banks, W.M. (1980), 'The Social Context and Empirical Foundation of Research on Black Clients' in R.L. Jones (ed.), *Black Psychology*, New York: Harper and Row, pp. 283–93.

Banks, W.M. and Marten, K. (1973), 'Counselling: The Reactionary Profession', *Personnel and Guidance Journal*, 41, pp. 457–62.

Banton, M. (1988), *Racial Consciousness*, London: Longman.

Banton, M and Harwood, J. (1975), *The Race Concept*, Newton Abbott: David and Charles.

Basch, M.F. (1980), *Doing Psychotherapy*, New York: Basic Books.

Bateson, G., Jackson, Haley, J. and Weakland, J. (1956), 'Toward a Theory of Schizophrenia', *Behavioural Science*, 1, pp. 251–64.

Batson, C.D. and Coke, J.S. (1981), 'Empathy: A Source of Altruistic Motivation for Helping' in J.T. Rushton and R.M. Sorrentino (eds), *Altruism and Helping Behaviour: Social, Personality and Developmental Perspectives*, Hillsdale, New Jersey: Erlbaum, pp. 167–211.

Batson, C.D., Duncan, B.D., Ackerman, P., Buckey, T. and Birch, K. (1981), 'Is Empathic Emotion a Source of Altruistic Motivation?', *Journal of Personality and Social Psychology*, 40, pp. 290–302.

Batson, C.D., Fultz, J. and Schoenrade, P.A. (1987), 'Adults Emotional Reactions to the Distress of Others' in N. Eisenberg and J. Strayer (eds), *Empathy and its Development*, Cambridge: Cambridge University Press, pp. 163–5.

Batson, C.D., O'Quin, K., Fultz, J., Vanderplas, M. and Isen, A. (1983), 'Self Reported Distress and Empathy and Egoistic versus Altruistic Motivation for Helping', *Journal of Personality and Social Psychology*, 45, pp. 706–18.

Bavington, J. (1992), 'The Bradford Experience' in J. Kareem and R. Littlewood (eds), *Intercultural Therapy: Themes, Interpretations and Practice*, Oxford: Blackwell Scientific Publications, pp. 101–11.

Belkin, G.S. (1988), *Introduction to Counselling*, 3rd edn, W.M.C. Brown Publishers, College Division.

Bell, J. (1987), *Doing your Research Project*, Milton Keynes: Open University Press.

Bell, L. (1989), 'Is Psychotherapy More Empowering to the Therapist than the Client?', *Clinical Psychology Forum*, 23, October, pp. 12–15

Benedek, T. (1953), 'Dynamics of Countertransference', *Bulletin of the Menninger Clinic*, 17, pp. 201–8.

Benedict, R. (1940), 'Why Then Race Prejudice?' reprinted in R. Miller and P. Dolan (eds) (1971), *Race Awareness*, Oxford: Oxford University Press, pp. 243–53.

Bergin, A.E. and Lampert, M.J. (1978), 'The Evaluation of Therapeutic Outcomes' in S. Garfield and A. Bergin (eds), *Handbook of Psychotherapy and Behaviour Change*, New York: Wiley, pp. 108–23.

Berman, J. (1979a), 'Counselling Skills Used by Black and White Male and Female Counsellors', *Journal of Counselling Psychology*, 26, pp. 81–4.

Berman, J. (1979b), 'Individual versus Society Focus: Problem Diagnoses of Black and White Male and Female Counsellors', *Journal of Cross-Cultural Psychology*, 10, pp. 497–507.

Bernard, D., Beitman, B.D., Marvin, R., Goldfried, M.R. and Norcross, J.C (1989), 'The Movement Toward Integrating the Psychotherapies: An Overview', *American Journal of Psychiatry*, 146, 2, February, pp. 138–46.

Bernard, V. (1953), 'Psychoanalysis and Members of Minority Groups', *Journal of the American Psychoanalytic Association*, 1, pp. 256–67.

Berry, J.W. (1980), 'Social and Cultural Change' in H.C. Triandis and R.W. Brislin (eds), *Handbook of Cross-Cultural Psychology*, Vol. 5, Boston: Allyn and Bacon, pp. 211–80.

Berthoud, R. and Beishon, S. (1997), 'People, Families and Households in Ethnic Minorities' in T. Modood, R. Berthoud, J. Latey, J. Nazroo, P. Smith, S. Virdee and S. Beishon (eds), *Britain*, London: Policy Studies Institute, pp. 18–59.

Best, J.W (1981), *Research in Education*, 4th edn, New Jersey: Prentice Hall, Inc.

Beutler, L.E., Crago, M. and Arizmendi, T.G. (1986), 'Therapist Variables in Psychotherapy: Process and Outcome' in S.L. Garfield and A.E. Bergin (eds), *Handbook of Psychotherapy and Behaviour Change*, 3rd edn, New York: Wiley.

Bhavnani, K.K. (1994), 'Tracing the Contours: Feminist Research and Feminist Objectivity' in H. Afshar and M. Maynard (eds), *The Dynamics Of Race and Gender*, London: Taylor and Francis, pp. 26–40.

Bloch, P.M., Weitz, L.J. and Abramowitz, S.I. (1980), 'Racial Attribution Effects on Clinical Judgement: A Failure to Replicate Among White Clinicians', *American Journal of Community Psychology*, 8, pp. 485–93.

Block, C.B. (1981), 'Black Americans and the Cross-Cultural Counselling and Psychotherapy Experience' in A.J. Marsella and P.B. Pedersen (eds), *Cross-Cultural Counselling and Psychotherapy*, 2nd edn, New York: Pergamon Press, pp. 123–51.

Block, C.B. (1986), 'Black Americans and the Cross-Cultural Counselling and Psychotherapy Experience' in A.J. Marsella and P.B. Pedersen (eds), *Cross-Cultural Counselling and Psychotherapy*, 2nd edn, Elmsford, New York: Pergamon Press, pp. 177–94.

Bloom, L. (1971), *The Social Psychology of Race Relations*, Australia: George Allen and Unwin.

Bloombaum, M., Yamamoto, J. and Jones, Q. (1968), 'Cultural Stereotyping Among Psychotherapists', *Journal of Consulting and Clinical Psychology*, 32 (1), pp. 99–109.

Blum, H.P. (1986), 'Countertransference and the Theory of Technique: Discussion', *Journal of the American Psychoanalytic Association*, 34 (2), pp. 309–28.

Blum, L.A. (1980), *Friendship, Altruism, and Morality*, London: Routledge and Kegan Paul.

Blalock, H.M. (1971), *Causal Models in the Social Sciences*, London: Prentice Hall.

Boch, P. (1970), *Culture Shock: A Reader in Modern Anthropology*, New York: Knopf.

Bochner, S. (1980), 'Unobtrusive Methods in Cross-Cultural Experimentation' in H.C. Triandis and R.W. Berry (eds), *Handbook of Cross-Cultural Psychology: Methodology*, Vol. 2, Boston: Allyn and Bacon, pp. 319–88.

Bochner, S. (1982), *Cultures in Contact: Studies in Cross-Cultural Interaction*, Vol. 1, Oxford: Pergamon Press.

Bochner, S., Buker, E.A. and McLeod, B.M. (1975), 'Communication Patterns in an International Student Dormitory: A Modification of the Small World Method', *Journal of Applied Social Psychology*, 6, pp. 275–89.

Bogardus, E.S. (1925), 'Measuring Social Distance', *Journal of Applied Sociology*, 9, pp. 299–308.

Bohrnstedt, G.W. (1969), 'A Quick Method for Determining the Reliability and Validity of Multiple Item Scales', *American Sociological Review*, 34, pp. 542–8.

Bohrnstedt, G.W. (1970), 'Reliability and Validity Assessment in Attitude Measurement', in G.F. Summers (ed.), *Attitude Measurement*, Chicago: Rand McNally, pp. 154–92.

Bolton, R. (1979), *People Skills*, Spectrum.

Book, H.E. (1988), 'Empathy: Misconceptions and Misuses in Psychotherapy', *American Journal of Psychiatry*, 145, 4, April, pp. 420–4.

Bordin, E.S. (1979), 'The Generalisability of the Psychoanalytic Concept of the Working Alliance', *Psychotherapy: Theory, Research and Practice*, 16 (3), pp. 252–60.

Bose, G. (1926) 'The Genesis of Homosexuality', *Samiksa*, Vol. 4, No. 2, p. 74.

Boyd-Franklin, N. (1989), *Black Families in Therapy: A Multi Systems Approach*, New York: Guilford Press.

Brah, A. (1992), 'Difference, Diversity and Differentation' in J. Donald and A. Rattansi (eds), *Race, Culture and Difference*, London: Sage, pp. 126–48.

Brah, A. and Minhas, R. (1986), 'Structural Racism or Cultural Differences: Schooling for Asian Girls' in G. Weiner (ed.), *Just a Bunch of Girls*, Milton Keynes: Open University Press, pp. 14–25.

Brammer, L.M. (1969), 'Eclecticism Revisited', *Personnel Guidance Journal*, 48, pp. 192–7.

Brewer, M.B. and Campbell, D.T. (1976), *Ethnocentrism and Intergroup Attitudes*, New York: John Wiley.

Briggs, D. (1979), 'The Trainee and the Borderline Client: Countertransference Pitfalls', *Clinical Social Work Journal*, 7 (2), 136, 12, pp. 1578–80.

Brislin, R.W. (1976), 'Comparative Research Methodology: Cross-Cultural Studies', *International Journal of Psychology*, 11, pp. 215–29.

Brislin, R.W. (1981), *Cross-Cultural Encounters: Face to Face Interaction*, Elmsford, New York: Pergamon Press.

Brislin, R.W. (1990), 'Applied Cross-Cultural Psychology: An Introduction' in R.W. Brislin (ed.), *Applied Cross-Cultural Psychology*, Vol. 14, *Cultural Research and Methodology*, New York: Sage, pp. 9–33.

British Association for Counselling (1985a), *Information Sheet No. 4*, Rugby, England.

British Association for Counselling (1985b), *Values Leaflet* , Rugby, England.

British Social Attitudes Survey (1984), *British Social Attitudes: The 1984 Report*, eds Jowell, R., Witherspoon, S. and Brook, L., Aldershot: Gower Community Planning and Research.

Brody, E.M. (1990), *Effects of Therapist Experience and Patient Diagnosis on Counter Transference*, unpublished PhD Dissertation, AA9118531, Columbia University.

Brown, C. (1984), *Black and White Britain: The Third PSI Survey*, London: Gower.

Bryman, A. and Cramer, D.C. (1994), *Qualitative Data Analysis for Social Scientists*, London: Routledge.

Buffon, G. (1812), *Natural History*, translated by W. Smellie, London: Cadell and Davies.

Bullivant, B. (1989), 'Culture, its Nature and Meaning for Educators' in *Multicultural Education: Issues and Perspectives*, J. Banks and Banks (eds), Boston: Allyn and Bacon, pp. 12–22.

Burgess, L. (1984), *In the Field: An Introduction to Field Research*, London: Allen and Unwin.

Burke, A.W. (1980), 'Aetiological Aspects of Depression: A Community Survey, Transcultural Psychiatry Society Workshop, Edinburgh' cited in R. Littlewood and M. Lipsedge (1989), *Aliens and Alienists: Ethnic Minorities and Psychiatry*, London: Unwin and Hyman.

Burke, A.W. (1984), 'Racism and Psychological Disturbance Among West Indians in Britain', *Transcultural Psychiatry*, Vol. 30, 1 and 2, Spring, pp. 50–72.

Burke, A.W. (1986), 'Racism and Mental Illness' in J.L. Cox (ed.), *Transcultural Psychiatry*, London: Croom Helm, pp. 139–57.

Butler, R.O. (1975), 'Psychotherapy: Implications of a Black Consciousness Process Model', *Psychotherapy: Theory Research and Practice*, 12, pp. 407–11.

Byrnes, F. (1966), 'Role Shock – An Occupational Hazard of American Technical Assistants Abroad', *Annals of the American Academy of Political and Social Science*, 368, pp. 95–108.

Calder, B.J. and Ross, M. (1973), *Attitudes and Behaviour*, Morristown, New Jersey: General Learning Press.

Campbell , D.T. and LeVine, R. (1968), 'Ethnocentrism and Intergroup Relations' in R.A. Ableson et al. (eds), *Theories of Cognitive Consistency: A Sourcebook*, Chicago: Rand McNally, pp. 213–45.

Carkhuff, R.R. and Berenson, B.G. (1967), *Beyond Counselling and Therapy*, New York: Holt, Reinhart and Winston.

Casas, J.M. (1984), 'Policy Training and Research in Counselling Psychology: The Racial/ Ethnic Minority Perspective' in S. Brown and R. Lent (eds), *Handbook of Counselling Psychology*, New York: John Wiley, pp. 785–831.

Casas, J.M., Ponterotto, J.G. and Gutierrez, J.M. (1986), 'An Ethical Indictment of Counselling and Research and Training: The Cross-Cultural Perspective, *Journal of Counselling and Development*, 64, pp. 347–9.

Cattell, R.B. (1966), 'The Scree Test for the Number of Factors', *Multivariate Behavioural Research*, 1, pp. 245–76.

Chambers, M. (1993), lecturer in Urban and Regional Health, London Hospital Medical College Statistical Department, personal communication.

Chaplin, J. (1988), *Feminist Counselling in Action*, London: Sage.

Chaplin, J. (1989), 'Counselling and Gender' in *Handbook of Counselling in Britain*, London: Routledge, pp. 223–36.

Chapman, A. (1988), 'Male-Female Relations: How the Past Effects the Present' in H. McAdoo (ed.), *Black Families*, London: Sage, pp. 180–201.

Cheetham, J. (1972), *The Place of Ethnicity in Social Work: Introduction to the Issues in Social Work and Ethnicity*, National Institute Social Services Library, No. 43, Australia: George, Allen and Unwin.

Cherry, F. (1995), *The Stubborn Particulars of Social Psychology*, London: Routledge.

Clark, K. (1965), *Dark Ghetto*, London and New York: Gollancz.

Clark, K.B. and M.P. (1939), 'The Development of Self and the Emergence of Racial Identifications in Negro Pre-School Children', *Journal of Social Psychology*, 10, pp. 591–9.

Clark, K.B. and M.P. (1950), 'Emotional Factors in Racial Identification and Preference in Negro Children', *Journal of Negro Education*, 19, pp. 341–50.

Cobbs, P. (1972), 'Ethnotherapy in Groups' in L. Soloman and B. Berzon (eds), *New Perspectives in Encounter Groups*, San Francisco: Jossey-Bass, pp. 121–34.

Cochrane, R. (1977), 'Mental Illness in Immigrants to England and Wales: An Analysis of Mental Hospital Admissions', *Social Psychiatry*, 12, pp. 23–35.

Cochrane, R. (1979), 'Psychological and Behavioural Disturbance in West Indians, Indians and Pakistanis in Britain: A Comparison of Rates Among Children and Adults', *British Journal of Psychiatry*, 134, pp. 201–10.

Cohen, L. and Manion, L. (1985), *Research Methods in Education*, 2nd edn, London: Croom Helm.

Cohen, M.B. (1952), 'Countertransference and Anxiety', *Psychiatry*, 15, pp. 231–43.

Cole, J. and Pilisuk, M. (1976), 'Differences in the Provision of Mental Health Services by Race', *American Journal of Orthopsychiatry*, 46, pp. 510–25.

Comas-Diaz, L. and Jacobsen F.M. (1991), 'Ethnocultural Transference and Countertransference in the therapeutic dyad', *American Journal of Psychiatry*, 6 (3), pp. 392–402.

Comrey, A.L. (1973), *A First Course in Factor Analysis*, New York: Academic Press.

Comrey, A.L. (1998), 'Factor Analytic Methods of Scale Development in Personality and Clinical Psychology', *Journal of Consulting and Clinical Psychology*, 56, pp. 754–61.

Cook, S.W. and Selltiz, C.A. (1964), 'Multiple Indicator Approach to Attitude Measurement', *Psychological Bulletin*, 62, pp. 36–55.

Corsini, R.J. (1984), *Current Psychotherapies*, 3rd edn, Hasca, Illinois: F.F. Peacock Publishers.

Coten, A. (1969), *Customs and Politics in Urban Africa*, London: Routledge and Kegan Paul.

Cottone, R. (1991), 'Counsellor Roles According to Two World Views', *Journal of Counselling and Development*, 69, pp. 398–401.

Cox, J.L. (1986), *Transcultural Psychiatry*, London: Croom Helm.

Crano, W.D. and Brewer, M.B. (1973), *Principles of Research in Social Psychology*, New York: McGraw-Hill.

Creswell, J.W. (1994), *Research Design: Qualitative and Quantitative Approaches*, New York: Sage.

Cronbach, L.J. (1951), 'Coefficient Alpha and the Internal Structure of Tests', *Psychometrika*, 16, pp. 297–334.

Cronbach, L.J. and Meehl, P.E. (1955), 'Construct Validity in Psychological Tests', *Psychological Bulletin*, 52, pp. 281–302.

Cross, W.E. (1971), 'The Negro-to-Black Conversion Experience: Toward a Psychology of Black Liberation', *Black World*, 20 (9), pp. 13–27.

D'Andrea, M. (1990), *A Syllabus for Multicultural Counsellor Training*, Honolulu: University of Hawaii.

D'Andrea, M. and Daniels, J. (1991), 'Exploring the Different Levels of Multicultural Counsellor Training', *Education Journal of Counselling and Development*, 70, pp. 78–85.

d'Ardenne, P. and Mahtani, A. (1989), *Transcultural Counselling in Action*, London: Sage.

Dean, G., Walsh, D., Downing, H. and Shelley, E. (1981), 'First Admissions of Native Born Immigrants to Psychiatric Hospitals in South East England, 1976', *British Journal of Psychiatry*, 6, pp. 139–56.

de Shazer, S. (1991), *Putting Difference to Work*, New York: W.W. Norton and Company.

Deutsch, F. and Madle, R.A. (1975), 'Empathy: Historic and Current Conceptualisations, and a Cognitive Theoretical Perspective', *Human Development*, 18, pp. 267–87.

DeVellis, R.F. (1991), *Scale Development: Theory and Applications*, London: Sage.

Devine, D.A. and Fernald, P.S. (1973), 'Outcome Effects of Receiving a Preferred, Randomly Assigned or Non-Preferred Therapy', *Journal of Consulting and Clinical Psychology*, 41 (1), pp. 104–7.

Dillard, J.M. (1987), *Multicultural Counselling*, Chicago: Nelson-Hall.

Dominelli, L. (1988), *Anti-Racist Social Work*, London: Macmillan Education.

Donnelly, F. (1981), 'Counsellors and Their Techniques' in F. Donnelly (ed), *A Time to Talk: Counsellors and Counselled*, Australia: George Allen and Unwin, pp. 124–44.

Dovidio, J.F. and Gaertner, S.L. (1986), 'Prejudice Discrimination and Racism: Historical Trends and Contemporary Approaches' in J.F. Dovidio and S.L. Gaertner (eds), *Prejudice Discrimination and Racism*, New York: Academic Press, pp. 1–30.

Draguns, J.G. (1981), 'Cross-Cultural Counselling and Psycho-therapy History, Issues, Current Status' in A.J. Marsella and P. Pederson (eds), *Cross-Cultural Counselling and Psychotherapy Foundations: Evaluations and Ethnocultural Considerations*, New York: Pergamon Press, pp. 3–27.

Draper, N.R. and Smith, H. (1966), *Applied Regression Analysis*, New York: Wiley.

Dryden, W. (1989a), 'Issues in the Eclectic Practice of Individual Therapy' in W. Dryden (ed.), *Individual Therapy in Britain*, Milton Keynes: Open University Press, pp. 341–65.

Dryden, W. (1989b), 'Individual Therapies: Limitations' in W. Dryden (ed.), *Individual Therapy in Britain*, Milton Keynes: Open University Press, pp. 311–40.

Dryden, W. and Feltham, C. (1994), *Developing Counsellor Training*, London: Sage.

Dubois, W.E.B. (1903/1969), *The Souls of Black Folk*, New York: Signet Classic.

Dubois, W.E.B. (1903/1979), *Black Reconstruction in America 1860–1880*, New York: Antheneum.

Eaves, L.J., Eysenck, H.J. and Martin, N.G. (1989), *Genes, Culture and Personality – An Empirical Approach*, Academic Press: Harcourt, Brace, Jovanovich.

Edwards, A.L. (1957), *Techniques of Attitude Scale Construction*, New York: Appleton-Century-Crofts.

Edwards, A.W. (1982), 'The Consequences of Error in Selecting Treatment for Blacks', *Social Casework: The Journal of Contemporary Social Work*, 63 (7), pp. 429–33.

Ehrenhaus, P. (1983), 'Culture and the Attribution Process: Barriers to Effective Communication' in W. Gudykunst (ed.) *Intercultural communication Theory: Current Perspectives*, Newbury Park, California: Sage, pp. 86–99.

Eisenberg, N. and Strayer, J. (1987), *Empathy and its Development*, Cambridge: Cambridge University Press.

English, H.B. and English, A.C. (1958), *A Comprehensive Dictionary of Psychological and Psychoanalytic Terms*, New York: MacKay.

Erikson, E. (1950), *Childhood and Society*, New York: W.W. Norton.

Erikson, E. (1965), 'The Concept of Identity in Race Relations: Notes and Queries' in T. Parsons and K. Clark (eds), *The Negro American*, Boston: Houghton Mifflin, pp. 56–8.

Fanon, F. (1967), *The Wretched of the Earth*, London: Penguin.

Farrar, N. and Sircar, I. (1986), 'Social Work with Asian Families' in V. Coome and A. Little (eds), *A Psychiatric Setting in Race and Social Work: A Guide to Training*, London: Tavistock Publications, pp. 195–206.

Felman, A.C. (1974), 'Attitudes are Alive and Well and Gainfully Employed in the Sphere of Action', *American Psychologist*, 29, pp. 310–34.

Feltham, C. and Dryden, W. (1994), *Developing Counselling Supervision*, London: Sage.

Ferenzi, S. (1932), cited in Masson J. 1989, *Against Therapy*, London: Fontana

Fernando, S. (1989), *Race and Culture in Psychiatry*, London: Tavistock/Routledge.

Fernando, S. (1991), *Mental Health, Race and Culture*, London: Macmillan.

Feshbach, N.D. (1978), 'Studies of Empathic Behaviour in Children' in B.A. Maher (ed.), *Progress in Experimental Personality Research*, Vol. 8, New York: Academic Press, pp. 1–47.

Festinger, L. (1957), *A Theory of Cognitive Dissonance*, Stanford: Stanford University Press.

Fielder, F. (1950a), 'The Concept of an Ideal Therapeutic Relationship', *Journal of Consulting Psychology*, 14, pp. 235–45.

Fielder, F. (1950a), 'A Comparison of Therapeutic Relationships in Psychoanalytic, Non-Directive and Adlerian Therapeutic Relationships', *Journal of Consulting Psychology*, 14, pp. 436–45.

Fielder, F. (1951), 'Factor Analyses of Psychoanalytic, Non-Directive and Adlerian Therapeutic Relationships', *Journal of Consulting Psychology*, 51, pp. 32–8.

Fields, S. and Southgate, P. (1982), *Public Disorder*, London: HMSO.

Fishbein, M. (1967), *Readings in Attitude Theory and Measurement*, New York: John Wiley and Sons.

Fishbein, M. and Ajzen, I. (1975), *Belief, Attitude, Intention and Behaviour*, Reading, Massachusetts: Addison-Wesley.

Fishbein, M. and Ajzen, I. (1972), 'Attitudes and Opinions', *Annual Review of Psychology*, 23, pp. 487–544.

Flaskerud, J.H. (1986), 'The Effects of Culture Compatible Intervention on the Utilisation of Mental Health Services by Minority Clients', *Community Health Journal*, 22, pp. 127–41.

Fleming, D. (1967), 'Attitude: A History of a Concept', *Perspectives in American History*, 1, pp. 287–365.

Foddy, W. (1993), *Constructing Questions for Interviews and Questionnaires*, Cambridge: Cambridge University Press.

Fowler, F.J. (1993), *Survey Research Methods*, 2nd edn, New York: Sage.

Fox, D.J. (1969), *The Research Process in Education*, New York: Holt, Rhinehart and Winston.

Franklin, A.J. (1971), 'To be Young, Gifted and Black with Inappropriate Professional Training: A Critique of Counselling Programmes', *The Counselling Psychologist*, 2, pp. 107–12.

Freud, S. (1912/1965), *The Dynamics of Transference*, Standard Edition, New York: W.W. Norton and Company.

Freud, S. (1933/1965), *New Introductory Lectures on Psycho-analysis*, translated by J. Strachey, New York: W. W. Norton and Company.

Freud, S. (1949), *An Outline of Psychoanalysis*, London: Hogarth Press.

Freud, S. (1950), *Totem and Taboo*, translated by J. Strachey, New York: W.W. Norton and Company.

Fromm, E. (1973), cited in Vontress, E.E. (1981), 'Racial and Ethnic Barriers in Counselling' in P. Pedersen, J. Draguns, W. Lonner and J. Trimble (eds), *Counselling Across Cultures*, Honolulu: University of Hawaii Press, pp. 178–93.

Furnham, A. (1988), 'The Adjustment of Sojourners' in Y.Y. Kim and W.B. Gudykunst (eds), *Cross-Cultural Adaptation: Current Approaches*, London: Sage, pp. 42–62.

Fusion, and Tyssion (1972), *Fusion and Tension in A Minority Community in South India*, unpublished paper presented at the Annual General Meeting of the American Anthropological Association, November.

Gallup, G.H. (1972), *The Gallup Poll: Public Opinion 1935–1971*, New York: Random House.

Galton, M. (1988), 'Structured Observation Techniques' in J.P. Keeves (ed.), *Educational Research Methodology and Measurement: An International Handbook* Oxford: Pergamon Press, pp. 25–43.

Gardner, L.M. (1971), 'The Therapeutic Relationship Under Varying Conditions of Race', *Psychotherapy: Theory Research and Practice*, 3, pp. 78–87.

Gardner, P.L. (1975), 'Attitude Measurement: A Critique of Some Recent Research', *Educational Research*, 1975, 17, pp. 101–9.

Garfield, S.L. (1982), 'Eclecticism and Integrationism in Psychotherapy', *Behaviour Therapy*, 13, pp. 610–23.

Garfield, S.L. (1980), *Psychotherapy: An Eclectic Approach*, New York: John Wiley and Sons.

Garfield, S.L. and Kurtz, R. (1977), 'A Study of Eclectic Views', *Journal of Consulting and Clinical Psychology*, 45, 75, pp. 78–83.

Garfield, S.L (1971), 'Therapist Variables' in A. Bergin and S. Garfield (eds), *Handbook of Psychotherapy and Behaviour Change: An Empirical Analysis*, New York: Wiley, pp. 86–99.

Garfield, S.L. and Bergin, A. (1978), *Handbook of Psychology and Behaviour Change*, New York: Wiley.

Garfield, S.L. and Kurtz, R. (1974) 'A Survey of Clinical Psychologists: Characteristics, Activities and Orientations', *The Clinical Psychologist*, 28, pp. 7–10.

Gedo, J.E. (1981), *Advances in Clinical Psychoanalysis*, New York: International Universities Press.

Geer, C.A. (1976), 'Counsellor Subject Variables in Systematic Desensitization', *Journal of Counselling Psychology*, 23, pp. 276–301.

George, R.L. and Cristiani, T.S. (1990), *Counselling Theory and Practice*, 3rd edn, New Jersey: Prentice Hall.

Gibbs, J. Huang, L. and associates (1989), *Children of Colour: Psychological Interventions with Minority Youth*, San Francisco: Jossey Bass.

Gilligan, C. (1982), *In a Different Voice*, Cambridge, Massachusetts: Harvard University Press.

Giobacchini, P.L. (1972), 'Technical Difficulties in Treating Some Character Disorders: Counter-Transference Problems', *International Journal of Psychoanalytic Psychotherapy*, (1), pp. 112–28.

Glaser, B.G. and Strauss, A.L. (1967), *The Discovery of Grounded Theory: Strategies For Qualitative Research*, Chicago, Illinois: Aldine,

Goldstein, A.P. and Michaels, G.Y. (1985), *Empathy: Development, Training and Consequences*, Hillsdale, New Jersey: Erlbaun.

Goldstein, A.P. (1981), 'Evaluating Expectancy Effects in Cross-Cultural Counselling and Psychotherapy' in A.J. Marsella and P.B. Pedersen (eds), *Cross-Cultural Counselling and Psychotherapy*, Oxford: Pergamon Press, pp. 85–101.

Good, C.V. (1963), *Introduction to Educational Research*, 2nd edn, New York: Appleton-Century Crofts.

Gordon, M. and Grantham, R.J. (1979), 'Helper Preference in Disadvantaged Students, *Journal of Counselling Psychology*, 26, pp. 337–43.

Grantham, R.J. (1973), 'Effects of Counsellor Race, Sex and Language Style on Black Students in Initial Interviews', *Journal of Counselling Psychology*, 20, pp. 553–9.

Greene, B.A. (1986), 'When the Therapist is White and the Patient is Black: Considerations for Psychotherapy in the Feminist Heterosexual and Lesbian Communities', *Women and Therapy*, Vol. 5, pp. 23–36.

Greenson, R.R. (1974), 'Loving, Hating and Indifference Toward the Patient', *International Review of Psychoanalysis*, 1, pp. 259–66.

Griffith, M.S. (1977), 'The Influence of Race on the Psychotherapeutic Relationship', *Psychiatry*, 40, (1), pp. 27–40.

Gunnings, T.S. and Simpkins, G. (1972), 'A Systematic Approach to Counselling Disadvantaged Youth, , *Journal of Non-White Concerns in Personnel and Guidance*, 3, pp. 4–8.

Guthrie, G. (1975), 'A Behavioural Analysis of Cultural Learning' in R. Brislin, S. Bochner and W. Lonner (eds), *Cross-Culture Perspectives on Learning*, New York: Wiley, pp. 34–52.

Hahn, M.E. (1953), 'Conceptual Trends in Counselling', *Personnel and Guidance Journal*, 31, pp. 231–5.

Haley, J. (1976), *Problem Solving Therapy*, San Francisco: Jossey Bass.

Hansen, J., Steric, R. and Warner, R. (1977), *Counselling Theory and Process*, Boston: Allyn and Bacon.

Harding, J., Proshansky, H., Kutner, B. and Chein, I. (1969), cited in G. Lindsey and E. Aronson (eds), *The Handbook of Social Psychology*, 2nd edn, Reading, Massachusetts: Addison-Wesley, pp. 1–76.

Harper, R. (1989), 'Psychoanalysis and Psychotherapy' quoted in, J. Masson, *Against Therapy*, London: Fontana, p. 241.

Harrison, I.K. (1975), 'Race as a Counsellor Client Variable in Counselling and Psychotherapy: A Review of the Research', *The Counselling Psychologist*, 5 (1), pp. 124–33.

Hassan, A.M. (1982), *The Effects of a Persuasive Communication and Self-Esteem on Changing Attitudes of Preservice Elementary Teachers Towards the Teaching of Chemistry*, unpublished doctoral dissertation, Pennsylvania State University.

Hawkins, P. and Shohet, R. (1993), *Supervision in the Helping Professions*, Milton Keynes: Open University Press.

Hayes, W. (1972), 'Radical Black Behaviourism' in R.L. Jones (ed.), *Black Psychology*, New York: Harper and Row, pp. 212–34.

Heinmann, P. (1950), 'On Countertransference', *International Journal of Psychoanalysis*, 31, pp. 81–4.

Heller, D. (1985), *Power in Psycho-Therapeutic Practice*, New York: Human Services Press.

Helms, J. (1987), 'Cultural Identity in the Treatment Process' in P.B. Pedersen (ed.) *Handbook of Cross-Cultural Counselling and Psychotherapy*, Westport: Greenwood Press, pp. 239–46.

Helms, J. (1990), *Black and White Identity Theory*, Westport: Greenwood Press.

Henerson, N.E. and Morris, L.L. (1978), *How to Measure Attitudes*, Beverley Hills, California: Sage Publications.

Henley, A. (1986), 'The Asian Community in Britain' in V. Coombe and A. Little (eds), *Race and Social Work: A Guide to Training*, New York: Tavistock Publications, pp. 37–50.

Henriques, J., Holloway, W., Urwin, C. and Walkerdine, C. (1984), *Changing the Subject: Psychology, Social Regulation and Subjectivity*, London: Methuen.

Herder, J.G. (1808), *Thomas Churchill Outlines a Philosophy of the History of Man*, translated by C.T. Fitzgibbon, London: J. Johnson.

Hewstone, M. Strobebe, W., Codol, J. and Stephenson, G. (1988), *Introduction to Social Psychology*, Oxford: Basil Blackwell.

Higginbotham, N.N., West, S.G. and Forsyth, D.R. (1988), *Psychotherapy and Behaviour Change: Social, Cultural and Methodological Perspectives*, New York: Pergamon Press.

Hill, C.E. (1975), 'Sex of Client and Experience Level of Counsellor', *Journal of Counselling Psychology*, 22, pp. 6–11.

Hintikka, M.B. and J. (1986), *Investigating Wittgenstein*, London: Basil Blackwell.

Hitch, P. (1981), 'The Politics of Intervention in Asian Families', paper presented at the Transcultural Psychiatry Society Workshop, Leicester 1980, *Bulletin of The Transcultural Psychiatry Society*, UK, March.

Hitchcock, G. and Hughes, D. (1989), *Research and the Teacher*, London: Routledge.

Ho, M.K. (1992), *Minority Children and Adolescents in Therapy*, London: Sage.

Hodge, J.L. and Struckmann, D.K. (1975), 'Some Components of the Western Dualist Tradition' in J.L. Hodge, D.K. Struckmann and D.L.D. Trost (eds), *Cultural Basis of Racism and Group Oppression*, California: Two Riders Press, pp. 123–95,

Hoffman, M.L. (1984), 'Interaction of Affect and Cognition and Empathy' in C.E. Izard, J. Kagan and R. Bzajonc (eds), *Emotions, Cognition and Behaviour*, Cambridge: Cambridge University Press, pp. 103–31.

Hoinville, R., Jowell, R. and associates (1978), *Survey Research Practice*, London: Heinemann Educational Books.

Horney, K. (1937), *The Neurotic Personality of Our Time*, New York: Horton.

Horowitz, D. (1976), 'Ethnic Identity' in N. Glazer and D. Moynihan (eds), *Ethnicity: Theory and Experience*, Boston: Harvard University Press.

Hovland, C.I., Harvey, O.J. and Sherif, M. (1957) 'Assimilation and Contrast, Effects and Reactions to Communication and Attitude Change', *Journal of Abnormal and Social Psychology*, 55, pp. 244–52.

Howarth, K. (1989), 'The Evaluation of Outcome in Psychotherapy', *The Psychologist*, November, 8, pp. 6–9.

Hulnuck, T. (1971), 'Counsellor: Know Thyself', *Counsellor Education and Supervision*, 17, pp. 69–72.

Humboldt, A. (1849), *Cosmos: A Sketch of a Physical Description of the Universe*, Vol. III, translated by E.C. Otte, London: Bohn.

Hume, D. (1966), *Enquiries Concerning the Human Understanding and Concerning the Principles of Morals*, 2nd edn, Oxford: Clarendon Press (original work published 1777).

Husband, C. (1982a), *Race in Britain: Continuity and Change*, London: Hutchinson.

Husband, C. (1982b), 'White Media and Black Britain: A critical look at the role of the media' in *Race Relations Today*, London: Arrow Books.

Inkles, A. and Smith, D.H. (1974), *Becoming Modern*, Cambridge, Massachusetts: Harvard University Press.

Issacs, H. (1975), 'Basic Group Identity' in N. Glazer and D. Moynihan (eds), *Ethnicity: Theory and Experience*, Cambridge: Harvard University Press.

Ivey, A.E. (1986a), 'Counselling and Psychotherapy: Towards a New Perspective' in A.J. Marsella and P.B. Pedersen (eds), *Cross-Cultural Counselling and Psychotherapy*, Elmsford, New York: Pergamon Press, pp. 279–312.

Ivey, A.E. (1986b), *Developmental Therapy*, San Francisco: Jossey-Bass.

Ivey, E.A., Ivey, M. and Simek-Morgan, L. (1993), *Counselling and Psychotherapy: A Multicultural Perspective*, 3rd edn, Boston: Allyn and Bacon.

Jackson, A.M. (1973), 'Psychotherapy: Factors Associated with the Race of the Therapist', *Psychotherapy: Theory, Research and Practice*, 10, pp. 273–7.

Jackson, A.M. (1983), 'A Theoretical Model for the Practice of Psychotherapy with Black Populations', *Journal of Black Psychology*, August, 10, No. 1, pp. 19–27.

Jackson, G.G. (1980), 'The Emergence of a Black Perspective in Counselling' in R. Jones (ed.), *Black Psychology*, 2nd edn, New York: Harper and Row, pp. 294–313.

Jackson, G.G. (1986), 'Conceptualising Afrocentric and Eurocentric Mental Health Training', in H.P. Leffley and P.B. Pedersen (eds), *Cross-Cultural Training for Mental Health Professionals*, Springfield, Illinois: Charles Thomas, pp. 131–49.

Jackson, G.G. and Kirschner, S.A. (1973), 'Racial Self-Designation and Preference for a Counsellor', *Journal of Counselling Psychology*, 20, pp. 560–4.

Jackson, M.L. (1995), 'Multicultural Counselling: Historical Perspectives' in J.G. Ponterotto, J.M. Casas, L.A. Suzuki and C.M. Alexander (eds), *Handbook of Multicultural Counselling*, London: Sage, pp. 3–16.

Jacobs, M. (1988), *Psychodynamic Counselling in Action*, London: Sage.

Jacobs, M. (1989), 'Psychodynamic Therapy: The Freudian Approach' in W. Dryden (ed), *Individual Therapy in Britain*, Open University Press: Milton Keynes, pp. 23–46.

Jahoda, G., Thomson, S.S. and Bhatt, S. (1972), 'Ethnic Identity and Preferences Among Asian Immigrant Children in Glasgow: A Replicated Study', *European Journal of Social Psychology*, 2 (1), pp. 19–32.

James, A.G. (1974), *Sikh Children in Britain*, London: Oxford University Press.

Jewel, P. (1994), 'Multicultural Counselling Research: An Evaluation with Proposals for Future Research', *Counselling Psychology Review*, Vol. 9, No. 2, May, pp. 17–34.

Johnson, M. (1978), 'Influence of Counsellor Gender on Reactivity to Clients', *Journal of Counselling Psychology*, 25, pp. 359–65.

Jones, A. and Seagull, A.A. (1977), 'Dimensions of the Relationship Between the Black Client and the White Therapist: A Theoretical Overview', *American Psychologist*, 32, pp. 850–5.

Jones, A. and Seagull, A.A. (1983), 'Dimensions of the Relationship Between the Black Client and the White Therapist: A Theoretical Overview' in D.R. Atkinson, G. Morten and D.W. Sue (eds), *Counselling American Minorities: A Cross-Cultural Perspective*, 2nd edn, Duburque, Indiana: William C. Brown.

Jones, E.E. (1974), 'Social Class and Psychotherapy: A Critical Review of the Research', *Psychiatry*, 27, pp. 307–19.

Jones, E.E. (1984), 'Some Reflections on the Black Patient and Psychotherapist', *Clinical Psychologist*, 37 (2), pp. 58–62.

Jones, E.E. and Korchin, S.J. (1982), 'Minority Mental Health: Perspectives' in E.E. Jones and S.J. Korchin (eds), *Minority Mental Health*, New York: Praeger, pp. 3–36.

Jones, J.M. (1972), *Prejudice and Racism*, Reading, Massachusetts: Addison-Wesley.

Jones, J.M. (1986), 'Racism: A Cultural Analysis of the Problem' in J.F. Dovidio and S.L. Gaertner (eds), *Prejudice, Discrimination and Racism*, Orlando, Florida: Academic Press, pp. 279–311.

Jones, J.M (1988), 'Racism in Black and White: A Bicultural Model of Reaction and Evolution' in P.A. Katz and D.A. Taylor (eds), *Eliminating Racism: Profiles in Controversy*, New York: Plenum, pp. 117–35.

Jones, J.M. (1991), 'The Politics of Personality: Being Black in America' in R.L. Jones (eds), *Black Psychology*, Berkeley, California: Cobb and Henry, pp. 305–18.

Jowell, R., Witherspoon, S. and Brook, L. (1984) *British Social Attitudes: The 1984 Report*, Aldershot: Gower/Social and Community Planning Research.

Jowell, R., Witherspoon, S. and Brook, L. (1986), *British Social Attitudes: The 1986 Report*, Aldershot: Gower/Social and Community Planning Research.

Kakar, S. (1990), 'Stories from Indian Psychoanalysis: Context and Text' in *Cultural Psychology; Essays on Comparative Human Development*, New York: W.W. Norton and Co., pp. 427–45.

Kanzer, M. (1975), 'The Therapeutic and Working Alliances', *International Journal of Psychoanalytic Psychotherapy*, 4, pp. 48–73.

Kaplan, A.G. (1985), *Female or Male Psychotherapists for Women: New Formulations*, Stone Centre for Developmental Services and Studies, No. 83–03.

Kaplan, A.G. and Yasinski, L. (1980), 'Psycho-dynamic Perspectives' in A.M. Brodsky and R. Hare-Mustin (eds), *Women and Psychotherapy; An Assessment of Research and Practice*, New York: Guilford Press, pp. 191–216.

Kardiner, A. and Ovesey, L. (1951), *The Mark of Oppression*, New York: Norton.

Kareem, J. and Littlewood, R. (1992), *Intercultural Therapy: Themes, Interpretations and Practice*, Oxford: Blackwell Scientific Publications.

Katz, D. (1960), 'The Functional Approach to the Study of Attitudes', *Public Opinion Quarterly*, 24, pp. 163–204.

Katz, J.H. (1984), *White Awareness: Handbook for Racism Awareness Training*, Oklahoma: University of Oklahoma Press.

Katz, J.H. (1985), 'The Sociopolitical Nature of Counselling', *The Counselling Psychologist*, 13, pp. 613–24.

Katz, J.H. and Ivey, A.E. (1977), 'White Awareness: The Frontier of Racism Awareness Training', *Personnel and Guidance Journal*, 55 (8), pp. 485–8.

Keeves, J.P. (1988), *Educational Research, Methodology and Measurement: An International Handbook*, Oxford: Pergamon Press.

Kelly, J.G., Snowdon, L.R. and Munoz, R.F. (1977), 'Social and Community Interventions', *Annual Review of Psychology*, 28, pp. 323–62.

Kelvin, P. (1970), *The Basis of Social Behaviour, an Approach in Terms of Order and Value*, London: Holt, Rinehart and Winston.

Kerlinger, F. (1986), *Foundations of Behavioural Research*, 3rd edn, New York: Holt, Rinehart and Winston.

Kerlinger, F. and Kaya, E. (1959), 'The Construction and Factor Analytic Validation of Scales to Measure Attitudes Towards Education', *Journal of Educational and Psychological Measurement*, 19, pp. 13–29.

Khan, V.S. (1974), 'Pakistani Villagers in a British City', PhD thesis, University of Bradford, unpublished.

Khan, V.S. (1976), 'Purdah in the British Situation' in D.C. Barker and S. Allen (eds), *Dependence and Exploitation in Work and Marriage*, London: Longmans, pp. 45–68.

Khan, V.S. (1979), 'Migration and Social Class: Miripuris in Bradford' in V.S. Khan (ed.), *Minority Families in Britain: Support and Stress*, London: Macmillan, pp. 37–58.

Khan, V.S. (1987), 'The role of the Culture of Dominance in Structuring the Experience of Ethnic Minorities' in C. Husband (ed.), *Race in Britain: Continuity and Change*, 2nd edn, Hutchinson University Library, pp. 213–31.

Kiesler, C.A. and Munson, P.A. (1975), 'Attitudes and Opinions', *Annual Review of Psychology*, 26, pp. 415–56.

Kim, J. (1970), 'Factor Analysis' in *Statistical Package for the Social Sciences*, 2nd edn, New Hampshire: MacGraw-Hill Inc., pp. 468–508.

Kim, J. and Kohout, F. (1975), 'Multiple Regression Analysis: Subprogram Regression' in *Statistical Package for the Social Sciences*, 2nd edn, New Hampshire: MacGraw-Hill Inc., pp. 320–67.

Kim, J. and Mueller, C.W. (1978), *Factor Analysis, Statistical Methods and Practical Issues*, Sage University Papers on Quantitative Applications in the Social Sciences, Beverley Hills and London: Sage Publications.

King, P. (1980), 'The Life Cycle as Indicated by the Nature of the Transference in the Psychoanalysis of the Middle Aged and Elderly', *International Journal of Psychoanalysis*, 61, pp. 153–160.

Kirschenbaum, H. (1979), *On Becoming Carl Rogers*, New York: Delacorte.

Klagsbrun, S.C. (1967), 'In Search of Identity', *Archives of General Psychiatry*, 16, pp. 186–9.

Klein, J. (1980), *Jewish Identity and Self Esteem: Healing Wounds Through Ethnotherapy*, New York: Institute on Pluralism and Group Identity.

Kochman, S. (1981), *Black and White Styles in Conflict*, Chicago: University of Chicago Press.

Kovel, J. (1970), *White Racism: A Psycho-History*, London: Allen Lane.

Kraben, A.L. and Kluckhohn, C. (1952), *Culture: A Critical Review of Concepts and Definitions*, Vol. 47, No. 1, Cambridge, Massachusetts: Peabody Museum.

Krech, D., Crutchfield, R.S. and Ballachey, E.L. (1962), *Individual in Society*, New York: McGraw-Hill Inc.

Krumboltz, J.D. (1966), 'Promoting Adaptive Behaviour: New Answers to Familiar Questions' in J.D. Krumboltz (ed.), *Revolution in Counselling*, New York: Houghton Mifflin, pp. 3–26.

Labour Research (1989), 'Racial Equality at Work. Top Firms Fail the Test', *Labour Research Survey*, November, pp. 13–15.

Lago, C. and Thompson, J. (1989), 'Counselling and Race' in W. Dryden, D. Charles-Edwards, and R. Woolfe (eds), *Handbook of Counselling in Britiain*, London: Routledge, pp. 207–23.

Lamberts, M.J., Shapiro, D.A. and Bergin, A.E. (1986), 'The Effectiveness of Psychotherapy, in S.L. Garfield and A.E. Bergin (eds), *Handbook of Psychotherapy and Behaviour Change*, 3rd edn, New York: Wiley, pp. 183–95.

La Piere, R.T. (1934), 'Attitude Versus Actions', *Social Forces*, 13, pp. 230–7.

Lau, A. (1986), 'Family Therapy across Cultures' in J.L. Cox (ed.), *Transcultural Psychiatry*, London: Croom Helm.

Larson, P. (1982), 'Counselling Special Populations', *Professional Psychology*, 13 (6), pp. 843–58.

Laughlin, H.P. (1979), *The Ego and Its Defences*, 2nd edn, New York: Jason Aronson.

Laughlin, H.P. (1982), *Jungian Psychology*, Los Angeles: Pergamon Press.

Lazarus, A.A. (1969), commenting on Klien, M., Dittman, A.J., Parloff, M.B and Gill, M.M., 'Behaviour Therapy: Observations and Reflections', *Journal of Consulting Clinical Psychology*, Vol. 33, pp. 259–66.

Lazarus, A.A. (1981), *The Practice of Multimodal Therapy*, New York: MaGraw-Hill.

Lazarus, A.A. (1989), *The Practice of Multimodal Therapy*, 2nd edn, Baltimore: The Johns Hopkins University Press.

Leff, J. (1981), *Psychiatry Around the Globe*, New York: Dekker.

Levine, E.S. and Padilla, A.M. (1980), *Crossing Cultures in Therapy: Pluralistic Counselling for the Hispanic*, Monterrey: Brookes/Cole.

Levine, R. and Campbell, D. (1972), *Ethnocentrism: Theories of Conflict, Ethnic Attitudes and Group Behaviour*, New York: Wiley.

Likert, R. (1932), 'A Technique for the Measurement of Attitudes', *Archives of Psychology*, 140, pp. 44–53.

Lind, J.E. (1914), 'The Dream as a Simple Wish Fulfillment in the Negro', *Psychoanalytic Review*, 1, pp. 295–300.

Littlewood ,R. and Lipsedge, M. (1989), *Aliens and Alienists: Ethnic Minorities and Psychiatry*, 2nd edn, London: Unwin Hyman.

Littlewood, R. (1992), 'Towards an Intercultural Therapy' in J. Kareem and R. Littlewood (eds), *Intercultural Therapy: Themes, Interpretations and Practice*, Oxford: Blackwell Scientific Publications, pp. 3–13.

Lipsedge, M. and Littlewood, R. (1979), 'Transcultural Psychiatry' in G. Crossman (ed.), *Recent Advances in Clinical Psychiatry*, Illinois: Churchill Livingstone.

Liska, A.E. (1974), 'Emergent Issues in the Attitude Behaviour Consistency Controversy', *American Sociological Review*, 39, pp. 261–76.

Little, A., Day, M. and Marshland, D. (1978), *Black Kids, White Kids, What Hope?*, Leicester: Leicester National Youth Bureau.

Little, M. (1957), '"R" – The Analyst's Response to his Patient's Needs', *International Journal of Psychoanalysis*, 38, pp. 240–54.

Locke, D.C. (1992), *Increasing Multicultural Understanding: A Comprehensive Model*, London: Sage.

Loganbill, C. and Hardy, E. (1982), 'Supervision: a Conceptual Model', *The Counselling Psychologist*, 10 (1), pp. 3–42.

London, P. (1964), *Modes and Morals of Psychotherapy*, New York: Holt, Rinehart and Winston.

Lonner, W.J. (1979), 'Issues in Cross-Cultural Psychology' in A.J. Marsella, R. Tharp and T. Ciborowski (eds), *Perspectives on Cross-Cultural Counselling*, New York: Academic Press, pp. 125–43.

Lorenz, K. (1981), *The Foundations of Ethology*, New York: Springer Verlag.

Lorion, R.P. and Parron, D.L. (1987), 'Countering the Counter-Transference: A Strategy for Treating the Untreatable' in P. Pedersen (ed.), *Handbook of Cross-Cultural Counselling and Therapy*, Westport: Greenwood Press, pp. 79–86.

Lott, B. (1981), *Becoming a Woman: The Socialisation of Gender*, Springfield, Illinois Charles Thomas.

Lott, B. (1985), 'The Potential Enrichment of Social/Personality Psychology Through Feminist Research and Vice-Versa', *American Psychologist*, 40, pp. 155–64.

Lovell, K. and Lawson, K.S. (1970) *Understanding Research in Education*, London: University of London.

Luborsky, L., Singer, B. and Luborsky, L. (1975), 'Comparative Studies of Psychotherapies: Is It True That "Everybody Has One and All Must Have Prizes"?', *Archives of General Psychiatry*, 32, pp. 995–1008.

Lyon, M. (1972), 'Race and Ethnicity in Pluralistic Societies', *New Community*, Vol. 1, No. 4, Summer.

MacCarthy, B. (1988), 'Clinical Work with Ethnic Minorities' in F.N. Watts (ed.), *New Developments in Clinical Psychology*, Vol. 2, pp. 122–40.

Mackinnon, C. (1987), *Feminism Unmodified*, Boston: Harvard University Press.

Magnus, E.C. (1975), 'Measurement of Counsellor Bias (sex-role stereotyping) in Assessment of Marital Couples with Traditional and Non-Traditional Interaction Patterns', unpublished doctoral dissertation, University of Georgia, *Dissertations Abstracts International*, 36, 2635A.

Mahay, G. (1974), 'The Structure of the West Indian Family' in R. Prince and D. Barrier (eds), *Configurations*, Lexington: D.C. Heath, pp. 145–69.

Mahoney, M.J. (1980), 'Psychotherapy and the Structure of Personal Revolutions' in M.J. Mahoney (ed.), *Psychotherapy Process*, New York: Plenum.

Mama, A. (1992), 'Black Women and the British State: Race Class and Gender Analysis for the 1990s' in P. Braham, A. Rattansi and R. Skellington (eds), *Race and Anti-Racism*, Milton Keynes: Open University Press/Sage, pp. 79–104.

Mama, A. (1995), *Beyond the Mask: Race Gender and Subjectivity*, London: Routledge.

Mandelbauj (1972), 'Voluntary Associations and Problems of Diversity within the Creole of African Origin and Various Indian Ethnic groups', *Society in India II*, pp. 496–9.

Marcia, J. (1987), 'Empathy and Psychotherapy' in N. Eisenberg and J. Strayer (eds), *Empathy and its Development*, Cambridge: Cambridge University Press, pp. 81–103.

Marcos, L. (1979), 'Effects of Interpreters on the Evaluation of Psychopathology in non-English Speaking Persons', *American Journal of Psychiatry*, 136, pp. 171–4.

Maroda, K. (1991), *The Power of Countertransference: Innovations in Analytic Techniques*, New York: John Wiley and Sons.

Martin, J.G. and Westre, F.R. (1959), 'The Tolerant Personality', *American Sociological Review*, 24, pp. 52–8.

Marsella, A.J. and Pedersen, P.B. (1986), *Cross-Cultural Counselling and Psychotherapy*, 2nd edn, Elmsford, New York: Pergamon Press.

Masson, J. (1989), *Against Therapy*, London: Fontana.

Maultsby, M.C. (1982), 'A Historical View of Blacks' Distrust of Psychiatry' in S.M. Turner and R.T. Jones (eds), *Behaviour Modification in Black Populations: Psychosocial Issues and Empirical Findings*, New York: Plenum, pp. 39–55.

Maynard, M. (1994), 'Race, Gender and the Concept of Difference in Feminist Thought' in H. Afshar and M. Maynard (eds), *The Dynamics of Race and Gender*, London: Taylor and Francis.

Mayo, J.A. (1974), 'The Significance of Sociocultural Variables in Psychiatric Treatment of Black Outpatients', *Comprehensive Psychiatry*, 15 (6), pp. 471–82.

Mbiti, J.S. (1970), *African Religions and Philosophy*, New York: Anchor Books.

McClure, B.A. (1987), 'Measuring Counter Transference and Attitude in Therapeutic Relationships', *Psychotherapy*, 24 (3), pp. 325–35.

McCord, H. (1978), 'Psychotherapy Outcomes', cited in K. Howarth, 'The Evaluation of Outcome In Psychotherapy', *The Psychologist*, November, 1989, pp. 6–9.

McGrath, J.E. (1964), *Social Psychology: A Brief Introduction*, New York: Holt.

McGuire, W.J. (1969), 'The Nature of Attitudes and Attitude Change' in G. Lindzey and E. Aronson (eds), *The Handbook of Social Psychology*, Vol. 3, 2nd edn, Reading, Massachusetts: Addison-Wesley, pp. 136–314.

McGuire, W.J. (1985), 'Attitudes and Attitude Change' in G. Lindzey and A. Aronson (eds), *Handbook of Social Psychology*, Vol. 2, *Special Fields and Applications*, 3rd edn, New York: Random House, pp. 233–46.

McKennel, A. (1970), 'Attitude Measurement: Use of Coefficient Alpha with Cluster or Factor Analysis', *Sociology*, 4, pp. 227–45.

McLeod, J. (1993), 'Putting it altogether: Personal Learning on Counselling Training Courses', *Counselling Psychology Review*, Vol. 8 No. 4, November, pp. 12–16.

McNeil, P. (1985), *Research Methods*, London: Tavistock.

Mearns, D. and Thorne, B. (1988), *Person Centred Counselling in Action*, London: Sage.

Meichenbaum, D. and Gilmore, J.B. (1984), 'The Nature of Unconscious Processes: A Cognitive-Behavioural Perspective' in K.S. Bowers and D. Meichenbaum (eds), *The Unconscious Reconsidered*, New York: Wiley Interscience.

Meltzoff, J. and Kornreich, M. (1970), *Research in Psychotherapy*, New York: Atherton.

Menninger, K.A. and Holzman, P.S. (1973), *The Theory of Psychoanalytic Technique*, 2nd edn, New York: Basic Books.

Merluzzi, B.H. and Merluzzi, T.B. (1978), 'Influence of Client's Race on Counsellor's Assessment of Case Materials', *Journal of Counselling Psychology*, 25, pp. 399–404.

Merry, T. (1988), *A Guide to the Person-Centred Approach*, Association for Humanistic Psychology in Britain, Publication No. 2/88.

Meyer, M. and Freeman, T. (1976), *Explorations in Psychotherapy*, New York: Psychological Publications.

Miles, R. (1989), *Racism*, London: Routledge.

Miller, N. and Brewer, M. (1986), 'Categorisation Effects on Ingroup and Outgroup Behaviour' in J. Dovidio and S. Gaertner (eds), *Racism, Prejudice and Discrimination*, San Diego: Academic Press, pp. 209–29.

Miller, P.V. and Cannell, C.F. (1988), 'Interviews in Sample Surveys' in J.P. Keeves (ed.), *Educational Research Methodology and Measurement: An International Handbook*, Oxford: Pergamon Press.

Milliones, J. (1977), 'The Pittsburgh Project Part 2: Construction of a Black Consciousness Measure', paper presented at 3rd Conference on Empirical Research in Black Psychology, Cornell University, Ithaca, New York.

Milner, D. (1971), 'Prejudice and the Immigrant Child', *New Society*, 23 September, pp. 556–9.

Milner, D. (1975), *Children and Race*, Harmondsworth: Penguin.

Milner, D. (1983), *Children and Race Ten Years On*, London: Ward Lock Educational.

Mintz, J., O'Brien, C.P. and Luborsky, L. (1976), 'Predicting the Outcome of Psychotherapy for Schizophrenics', *Archives of General Psychiatry*, 33, pp. 1183–6.

Minuchin, S. (1974), *Families and Family Therapy*, Cambridge, Massachusetts: Harvard University Press.

Mio, J.S. (1989), 'Experiential Involvement as an Adjunct to Teaching Cultural Sensitivity', *Journal of Multicultural Counselling and Development*, pp. 23–31.

Modood, T. (1977), 'Employment in Ethnic Minorities in Britain' in T. Modood, R. Berthound, J. Nazroo, P. Smith, S. Virdee and S. Beisho (eds), *Ethnci Minorities in Britain*, Policy Studies Institute: London, pp. 83–149.

Mogul, K.M. (1982), 'Overview: The Set of the Therapist', *The American Journal of Psychiatry*, 139 (1), pp. 1–11.

Moinat, S.M., Raine, W.J., Burbeck, S.L. and Davison, K.K. (1972), 'Black Ghetto Residents as Rioters', *Journal of Social Issues*, 28, pp. 45–62.

Montague, A. (1964), *The Concept of Race*, New York: Free Press.

Montague, A. (1971), 'Race: The History of an Idea' in E.R. Miller and P. Dolan, (eds), *Race Awareness*, Oxford: Oxford University Press, pp. 175–200.

Morris, H.S. (1968), *Ethnic Groups in International Encyclopaedia of the Social Sciences* Vol. 5, London/New York: Macmillan/Free Press.

Moser, C.A. and Kalton, G. (1971), *Survey Methods in Social Investigation*, London: Heinemann Educational Books.

Muensterberger, W. (1969), *Man and His Culture: Psychoanalytical Anthropology After 'Totem and Taboo'*, London: Rapp and Whiting.

Mullard, C. (1973), *Black Britain*, London: Allen and Unwin.

Nachmias, C. and Nachmias, D. (1981), *Research Methods in the Social Sciences*, New York: St. Martins Press.

Nachmias, D. and C. (1976), *Research Methods in the Social Sciences*, London: Edward Arnold.

Nanton, P. (1992), 'Official Statistics and Problems of Inappropriate Ethnic Categorisation', *Policy and Politics*, Vol. 20, No. 4, pp. 277–85.

Nazroo, J. (1997), *Ethnicity and Mental Health Findings from a National Community Survey*, London: Policy Studies Institute.

Neff, J.A. and Husaini, B.A. (1980), 'Race Sociometric Status and Psychiatric Impairment: A Research Note', *Journal of Community Psychology*, 8, pp. 16–19.

Nelson-Jones, R. (1982), *The Theory and Practice of Counselling Psychology*, Cassell.

Neubauer, P.E. (1980), 'The Life Cycle as Indicated by the Nature of the Transference in the Psychoanalysis of Children', *International Journal of Psychoanalysis*, 61, pp. 137–44.

Newcomb, T.M., Turner, R.H. and Conberse, P.E. (1965), *Social Psychology. A Study of Human Interaction*, New York: Holt.

Nisbett, J.D. and Entwistle (1970), *Educational Research Methods*, London: University of London Press.

Nobles, W.W. (1976), 'Black People in White Insanity: An Issue for Black Community Mental Health', *The Journal of Afro-American Issues*, 4, pp. 21–7.

Nobles, W.W. (1972), 'African Philosophy: Foundations of Black Psychology' in R.L. Jones (ed.), *Black Psychology*, New York: Harper and Row.

Norcross, J.C. and Prochaska, J.O. (1982), 'A National Survey of Clinical Psychologists: Affiliations and Orientations', *Clinical Psychologist*, 35 (3), 1, pp. 4–6.

Norcross, J.C. and Wogan, M. (1983), 'American Psychotherapists of Diverse Persuasions: Characteristics, Theories, Practices and Clients', *Professional Psychology: Research and Practice*, pp. 529–39.

Nunnally, J.C. (1970), *Introduction to Psychological Measurement*, New York: McGraw-Hill.

Nunnally, J.C. (1978), *Psychometric Theory*, 2nd edn, New York: McGraw-Hill.

Oakes, P.J., Haslam, A. and Turner, J.C. (1994), *Stereotyping and Social Reality*, Oxford: Blackwell.

Oberg, K. (1960), 'Culture Shock: Adjustment to New Culture Environments', *Practical Anthropology*, 7, pp. 197–82.

Oppenheim, A.M. (1966), *Questionnaire Design and Attitude Measurement*, New York: Basic Books.

Oskamp, S. (1977), *Attitudes and Opinions*, New Jersey: Prentice Hall.

Paolino, T.J. (1981), *Psychoanalytic Psychotherapy: Theory, Technique, Therapeutic Relationship and Treatability*, New York: Brunner/Mazel.

Pardes, H., Papernik, D.D. and Winston, A. (1974), 'Field Differentiation in In-patient Psychotherapy', *Archives of General Psychiatry*, 31, pp. 311–5.

Parham, T.A. (1989), 'Cycles of Psychological Nigrescence', *The Counselling Psychologist*, 17, pp. 187–226.

Parham, T.A. and Helms, J.E. (1981), 'The Influence of Black Students Racial Identity Attitudes on Preferences for Counsellors Race', *Journal of Counselling Psychology*, 28, pp. 250–7.

Parker and McDavis (1989), cited in P. Jewel (1994), 'Multicultural Counselling Research: An Evaluation with Proposals for Further Research', *Counselling Psychology Review*, Vol. 9, No. 2, May 1994 (unreferenced citation), pp. 17–34.

Parkin, D. (1975), 'Context and Choice in Ethnic Allegiance, A Theoretical Framework and Caribbean Case Study' in N. Glazer and D. Moynihan (eds), *Ethnicity: Theory and Experience*, Cambridge: Harvard University Press, pp. 123–56.

Parloff, M.B., Waskow, I.E. and Wolfe, B.E. (1978), 'Research on Therapist Variables in Relation to Process and Outcome' in S. Garfield and A. Bergin (eds), *Handbook of Psychotherapy and Behaviour Change*, New York: Wiley Goldenholz.

Patterson, C. (1980), *Theories of Counselling and Psychotherapy*, 3rd edn, New York: Harper and Row.

Patterson, C. (1986), *Theories of Counselling and Psychotherapy*, 4th edn, New York: HarperCollins.

Paul, G.L. (1967), 'Strategy of Outcome Research in Psychotherapy', *Journal of Consulting Psychology*, Vol. 31, pp. 109–18.

Peabody, S.A. and Gelso, C.J. (1982), 'Counter-Transference and Empathy: The Complex Relationship Between Two Divergent Concepts in Counselling', *Journal of Counselling Psychology*, 29, pp. 240–5.

Pedersen, A. and P. (1985), 'The Cultural Grid: A Personal Cultural Orientation' in L. Samovar and R. Porter (eds), *Intercultural Communication : A Reader*, 4th edn, Belmont: Wadsworth.

Pedersen, P.B. (1977), 'The Triad Model and Cross-Cultural Counsellor Training', *The Personnel and Guidance Journal*, 56, pp. 410–8.

Pedersen, P.B. (1988), 'Orientation' in L. Samovar and R. Porter (eds), *Intercultural Communication : A Reader*, 4th edn, Belmont: Wadsworth.

Pedersen, P.B, Draguns, J.G, Lonner, W.J. and Trimble, J.E. (eds) (1981), *Counselling Across Cultures*, 2nd edn, Honolulu: University Press of Hawaii.

Pedersen, P.B., Lonner, W.J. and Draguns, J.G (1976), *Counselling Across Cultures*, Honolulu: University Press of Hawaii.

Peters, A. (1988), 'Parenting in Black Families with Young Children' in H. McAdoo (ed.), *Black Families*, London: Sage, pp. 226–8.

Phillips, D.C. (1987), *Philosophy, Science and Social Enquiry*, Oxford: Pergamon.

Phinney, J.S. and Rotheram, M.J. (1987), 'Childrens' Ethnic Socialisation: Themes and Implications' in J.S. Phinney and M.J. Rotheram (eds), *Childrens' Ethnic Socialisation: Pluralism and Development*, New York: Sage, pp. 186–215.

Pierce, C.M. (1969), 'Is Bigotry the Basis of Medical Problems in the Ghetto?' in J.C. Norman (ed.), *Medicine in the Ghetto*, New York: Appleton Century-Crofts, pp. 133–44.

Pietrofesa, J.J. Hoffman, H. and Splete, H.H. (1984), *Counselling: An Introduction*, 2nd edn, Boston: Houghton Mifflin.

Pike, K.L. (1954), 'Emic and Etic Standpoints for the Description of Behaviour' in K.L. Pike (ed.), *Language in Relation to a Unified Theory of the Structure of Human Behaviour*, The Hague: Houton, pp. 114–65.

Pike, K.L. (1966), *Language in Relation to a Unified Theory of the Structure of Human Behaviour*, The Hague: Houton.

Pilgrim, D. (1992), 'Psychopathology and Political Invasions' in W. Dryden (ed.), *Psychotherapy and its Discontents*, Milton Keynes: Open University Press, pp. 34–56.

Pinderhughes, C.A. (1973), 'Racism and Psychotherapy' in C. Willie, B. Kramer and B. Brown (eds), *Racism and Mental Health* Pittsburgh: University of Pittsburgh Press, pp. 61–121.

Pinderhughes, C.A. (1983), 'Empowerment for Our Clients and for Ourselves', *Social Casework*, 64 (6), pp. 331–8.

Pinderhughes, E. (1989), *Understanding Race, Ethnicity and Power: The Key to Efficacy in Clinical Practice*, New York: Free Press.

Ponterotto, J.G., Alexander, W.H. and Griesen, I.Z. (1986), 'Black Students' Attitudes toward Counselling as a Function of Racial Identity', *Journal of Multicultural Counselling and Development*, 14, pp. 51–9.

Ponterotto, J.G. and Pedersen, P.B. (1993), *Preventing Prejudice: A Guide for Counsellors and Educators*, Newbury Park, California: Sage.

Potter, J. and Wetherell, M. (1987), *Discourse and Social Psychology*, London: Sage.

Prochaska, J.O. and Norcross, J.C. (1983), 'Contemporary Psychotherapists: A National Survey of characteristics, practices, orientations and attitudes', *Psychotherapy, Theory, Research and Practice*, 20 (2), pp. 161–73.

Proctor, B. (1988), 'Supervision: A Co-operative Exercise in Accountability' in M. Marken, and M. Payne (eds), *Enabling and Ensuring*, Leicester National Youth Bureau and Council for Educational Training in Youth and Community Work.

Punetha, D., Giles, H. and Young, L. (1988), 'Interethnic Perceptions and Relative Deprivation: British Data' in Y.Y. Kim and W.B. Gudykunst (eds), *Cross-Cultural Adaptation: Current Approaches*, London: Sage, pp. 252–66.

Rack, P. (1982), *Race, Culture and Mental Disorder*, London: and New York: Tavistock.

Racker, H. (1968), *Transference and Counter-Transference*, New York: International Universities Press.

Reber, A.S. (1985), *Dictionary of Psychology*, Harmondsworth: Penguin.

Reed, K.L. (1988), 'The Relationship of Black Students Racial Identity to Counsellor Race Preference and Premature Termination from Counselling', unpublished doctoral dissertation, University of Wisconsin, Madison.

Reik, T. (1948), *Listening with the Third Ear, The Inner Experience of the Psychoanalyst*, New York: Grove.

Reiser, M. (1981), 'Latent Trait Modelling of Attitude Items' in G.W. Bohrnstedt and E.F. Borgatta (eds), *Social Measurement: Current Issues*, Beverley Hills: Sage, pp. 117–44.

Reising, G.N. and Daniels, M.H (1983), 'A Study of the Hogan Model of Counsellor Development and Supervision', *Journal of Counselling Psychology*, 30, pp. 235–44.

Reynolds, A.L. (1995), 'Challenges and Strategies for Teaching Multicultural Counselling Courses' in J. Ponterotto, J.M. Casas, L.A. Suzuki and C.M. Alexander (eds), *Handbook of Multicultural Counselling*, London: Sage, pp. 312–30.

Rex, J. (1970), *Race Relations in Sociological Theory*, London: Weidenfeld and Nicholson.

Rex, J. (1986), 'Introduction. Controversies and Continuities in Race and Ethnic Relations Theory' in J. Rex and D. Mason (eds), *Theories of Race and Ethnic Relations*, Cambridge: Cambridge University Press, pp. 1–19.

Richardson, J. and Lambert, J. (1986), *The Sociology of Race*, Causeway Books.

Ridley, C.R. (1984), 'Clinical Treatment of the Non-Disclosing Black Client: A Therapeutic Paradox,' *American Psychologist*, 39 (11), pp. 1234–44.

Ridley, C.R. (1985), 'Pseudo-Transference in Inter-Racial Psychotherapy: An Operant Paradigm', *Journal of Contemporary Psychotherapy*, 15 (1), pp. 29–36.

Ridley, C.R. (1989), 'Racism in Counselling as an Adversive Behavioural Process' in P.B. Pedersen, J.G. Draguns, W.J. Lonner and J.E. Trindle (eds), *Counselling Across Cultures* 3rd edn, Honolulu: University of Hawaii Press, pp. 55–79.

Ridley, C.R. (1995), *Overcoming Unintentional Racism in Counselling and Therapy: A Practitioners Guide to Intentional Intervention*, New York: Sage.

Ridley, C.R. and Tan, S.Y. (1986), 'Unintentional Paradoxes and Potential Pitfalls in Paradoxical Psychotherapy', *Counselling Psychologist*, 14 (2), pp. 303–8.

Robbins, R.S. and Jolkovski, (1987), 'Managing Counter Transference Feelings: an Interactional Model using Awareness of Feelings and Theoretical Framework', *Journal of Counselling Psychology*, 34 (3), pp. 276–82.

Rogers, C.R. (1942), *Counselling and Psychotherapy: New Concepts*, Boston: Houghton Mifflin.

Rogers, C.R. (1951), *Client-Centred Therapy*, Boston: Houghton Mifflin.

Rogers, C.R. (1956), 'Client-Centred Therapy: A Current View' in F. Fromm-Reichmann and J.L. Moreno (eds), *Progress in Psychotherapy*, New York: Grune Stratton, pp. 24–36.

Rogers, C.R. (1957), 'The Necessary and Sufficient Conditions of Therapeutic Personality Change', *Journal of Consulting Psychology*, (21), pp. 95–103.

Rogers, C.R. (1961), *A Therapist's View of Psychotherapy: On Becoming a Person*, London: Constable and Co. Ltd.

Rogers, C.R. (1962a), 'A Study of Psychotherapeutic Change in Schizophrenics and Normals; Design and Instrumentation', *Psychiatric Research Reports*, American Psychiatric Association (15) April, pp. 51–60.

Rogers, C.R. (1962b), 'Some Learnings from a Study of Psycho-therapy with Schizophrenics', *Pennsylvania Psychiatric Quarterly*, Summer, pp. 3–15.

Rogers, C.R. (1965), *Client-Centred Therapy*, Constable and Co. Ltd.

Rogers, C.R. (1980), *Ways of Being*, Boston: Houghton Mifflin.

Rothenberg, P. (1990), 'The Construction, Deconstruction and Reconstruction of Difference', *Hypatia*, Vol. 5, No. 1.

Rousseau, J.A. (1932), *Discourse on the Origin of In Equality and the Social Contract*, Everymans Library, translated by G.D.H. Cole, New York: E.P. Dutton, pp. 155–246.

Ruiz, P.P. (1983), 'Treatment Compliance Among Hispanics', *Journal of Operational Psychiatry*, 14, pp. 112–4.

Rummel, R.J. (1970), *Applied Factor Analysis*, Evanston: North Western University Press.

Runnymede Trust (1991), *Race and Immigration: Bulletin 247 and 248*, London: Runnymede Trust.

Russell, B. (1938), *Power: A New Social Analysis*, New York: Norton.

Rwgellera, G.G.C. (1970), 'Mental Illness in Africans and West Indians of African Origin Living in London', unpublished MPhil (Psychiatry) thesis, University of London.

Rwgellera, G.G.C. (1980), 'Differential Use of Psychiatric Services by West Indians, West Africans and English in London', *British Journal of Psychiatry*, 137, pp. 428–32.

Sager, C.J., Brayboy, T.L. and Waxenberg, B.R. (1972), 'Black Patient-White Therapist', *American Journal of Orthopsychiatry*, 42, pp. 415–23.

Sandler, I. and Holmen, M. (1978), 'Self versus Counsellor Perception of Inter-personal Characteristics of Female Welfare Schopper, A. Recipients: A Cross-Cultural Comparison', *Journal of Community Psychology*, 6, pp. 179–86.

Sarnoff, I. and Katz, D. (1954), 'The Motivational Basis of Attitude Change', *Journal of Abnormal and Social Psychology*, 49, pp. 115–24.

Sattle, J.M. (1977), 'The Effects of Therapist-Client Racial Similarity' in A.S. Gurman and A.M. Razin (eds), *Effective Psychotherapy: A Handbook of Research*, New York: Pergamon Press, pp. 252–90.

Scheffler, T. (1969), *Psychology and Change*, New Jersey: Ritter Books.

Schermerhorn, R. (1970), *Comparative Ethnic Relations*, New York: Random House.

Schneider, B.A., Schneider, E.I., Hardesty, A.S and Burdock, E. (1978), 'Interventions of Psychiatric Diagnosis: Psychological Profile and Ethnic Background', *Psychological Reports*, 43, pp. 55–61.

Schneider, L. and Bolljean, C. (1973), *The Idea of Culture in the Social Sciences*, Cambridge: Cambridge University Press.

Schweder, R.A. (1977) , 'Culture and Thought' in B.B. Wolman (ed.), *International Encyclopaedia of Psychiatry, Psychology, Psychoanalysis and Neurology*, Vol. 3, New York: Aesculapius, pp. 457–61.

Scott, C. (1961), 'Research on Mail Surveys', *Journal of Royal Statistical Society*, XXIV, A. 124, pp. 143–205.

Searless, H.F. (1987), 'The Analyst's Participant Observation as Influenced by the Patient's Transference', *Contemporary Psychoanalysis*, 13 (3), pp. 367–71.

Sedlacek, W.E. and Brookes, J.C. (1976), *Racism in American Education: A Model for Change*, Chicago: Nelson Hall.

Seeman, M. (1959), 'On the Meaning of Alienation', *American Sociological Review*, 24, pp. 783–91.

Segall, M.H. (1979), *Cross-cultural Psychology: Human Behaviour in Global Perspective*, Monterey, California: Brook-Cole.

Segall, M.H., Dasen, P.R., Berry, J.W. and Poortinga, Y.H. (1990), *Human Behaviour in Global Perspective: An Introduction to Cross-Cultural Psychology*, California: Pergamon Press.

Semaj, L.T. (1984), 'The Black Self: Identity and Models for a Psychology of Black liberation', *The Western Journal of Black Studies*, 5, pp. 158–71.

Serpell, R. (1976), *Culture's Influence on Behaviour*, London: Methuen.

Seward, G. (1956), *Psychotherapy and Cultural Conflict*, New York: Ronald Press.

Shaw, M.E. and Wright, J.L. (1967), *Scales for the Measurement of Attitudes*, New York: McGraw-Hill.

Sherif, C.W. (1976), *Orientation to Social Psychology*, New York: Harper and Row.

Sherif, M., Harvey, O.J., White, B.J., Hood, W.E. and Sherif, C.W. (1961), *Intergroup Conflict and Co-operation: The Robbers Cave Experiment*, Norman: University of Oklahoma Book Exchange.

Sherman, J.A. (1980), 'Therapist Attitudes and Sex Role Stereotyping' in A. Brodsky and R. Hare-Mustin (eds), *Women and Psychotherapy*, New York: Guilford Press.

Sherman, K. (1981), *The Flowering of Ireland: Scholars and Kings*, Boston: Little, Brown.

Shipman, M. (1973), *The Limitations of Social Research*, London: Routledge and Kegan Paul.

Shipman, M. (1985), 'Developments in Educational Research' in Shipman, M. (ed), *Educational Research: Principles, Policies and Practices*, Lewes: Falmer Press.

Shostrom, E. (1967), *Man, the Manipulator*, Nashville: Abingdon Press.

Shrigley, R.L. (1983a), 'The Attitude Concept and Science Teaching', *Science Education*, 67, pp. 425–42.

Shrigley, R.L. (1983b), *The Likert Scale Construction and its Implications for Attitude Measurement in Science Education*, mimeograph GAPH (a), Pennsylvania State University.

Silverman, I. (1964), 'In Defence of Dissonance Theory: Reply to Chapanis and Chapanis', *Psychological Bulletin*, 62, pp. 205–9.

Simkins, T. (1977), *Non-Formal Education and Development*, unpublished PhD thesis, University of Manchester.

Simpkins, G.A., Gunnings, T. and Kearny, A. (1973), 'The Black Six Hour Retarded Child', *Journal of Non-White Concerns*, 2, pp. 29–34.

Simpson, G.E. and Yinger, J.M. (1965), *Racial and Cultural Minorities*, New York: Harper and Row.

Singer, E. (1970), *Key Concepts in Psychotherapy*, 2nd edn, New York: Basic Books.

Sivanandan, A. (1985), 'RAT and the Degradation of Black Struggle', *Race and Class*, Vol. 26, No. 4, Spring, pp. 1–34.

Skellington, R. and Morris, P. (1992), *Race in Britain Today*, Milton Keynes: Open University Press.

Skodia, R. (1989), 'Counselling Immigrant Women: A Feminist Critique of Traditional Therapeutic Approaches and Re-evaluation of the Role of the Therapist', *Counselling Psychology Quarterly*, Vol. 2, No. 2 pp. 185–204.

Slavin, R.E. (1984), *Research Methods in Education: A Practical Guide*, New Jersey: Prentice Hall.

Smalley, W. (1963), 'Culture Shock, Language Shock and the Shock of Self Discovery', *Practical Anthropology*, 10, pp. 49–56.

Smith, D.J. (1977a), *Racial Disadvantage in Britain*, Harmondsworth: Penguin.

Smith, D.J. (1977b), *The Facts of Racial Disadvantage, Political and Economic Planning*, London: Penguin.

Smith, M.E. (1957), 'Progress in the Use of English After Twenty-Two Years by Children of Chinese Ancestry in Honolulu', *Journal of Genetic Psychology*, 90, pp. 255–8.

Smith, M.E. and Kasdon, L.M. (1961), 'Progress in the Use of English After Twenty-Two Years by Children of Fillipino and Japanese Ancestry in Hawaii', *Journal of Genetic Psychology*, 99, pp. 129–38.

Snygg, B. and Combs, A.W. (1949), *Individual Behaviour: A New Frame of Reference for Psychology*, New York: Harper and Row.

Speck, R. and Attneave, C. (1973), *Family Networks*, New York: Vintage.

Spitzer, R.L., Skodol, A.E., Gibbon, M. and Williams, J.B.W. (1983), *Psychopathology: A Casebook*, New York: McGraw-Hall.

Stallings, J.A. and Mohlman, G.G. (1988), 'Classroom Observation Techniques' in J.P. Keeves (ed.), *Educational Research Methodology and Measurement: An International Handbook*, Oxford: Pergamon Press.

Standal, S.W. and Corsini, R.J. (1959), *Critical Incidents in Psychotherapy*, Englewood Cliffs, New Jersey: Prentice Hall.

Steinberg, D. (1992) , 'Interprofessional Consultation: Creative Approaches in Therapeutic Work across Cultures' in J. Kareem and R. Littlewood (eds), *Intercultural Therapy: Themes, Interpretations and Practice*, Oxford: Blackwell Scientific Publications, pp. 59–74.

Sterba, R. (1947), 'Some Psychological Factors in Negro Race Hatred and in Anti-Negro Riots', *Psycho-analysis and the Social Science*, 1, pp. 411–27.

Stevens, G. (1981), 'Bias in the Attribution of Hyperkinetic Behaviour as a Function of Ethnic Identification and Socio-Economic Status', *Psychology in the Schools*, 18, pp. 99–106.

Stevens, S.S. (1946), 'On the Theory of Scales Measurement', *Science*, 103, pp. 677–80.

Still, R. (1961), 'Mental Health in Overseas Students', *Proceedings of the British Health Association*, working paper.

Stone, M. (1981), *The Education of the Black Child in Britain: The Myth of Multicultural Education*, London: Fontana.

Storr, A. (1980), *The Art of Psychotherapy*, New York: Methuen.

Strupp, H.H. (1958), 'The Performance of Psychologists and Psychiatrists in a Therapeutic Interview', *Journal of Clinical Psychology*, 14, pp. 218–26.

Strupp, H.H. (1960), 'The Performance of Psychoanalytic and Client-Centred Therapists in the Initial Interview', *Journal of Consulting and Clinical Psychology*, 22, pp. 265–74.

Sturtevant, W.C. (1964), 'Studies in Ethnoscience' in J.W. Berry and P.R. Dasen (eds), *Culture and Cognition: Readings in Cross-Cultural Psychology*, London: Methuen and Co. Ltd., pp. 126–39.

Sudman, S. and Bradburn, N.H. (1974), *Response Effects in Surveys*, Chicago: Aldine.

Sue, D.W. (1983), 'Ethnic Minority Issues in Counselling', *American Psychologist*, 38, pp. 581–8.

Sue, D.W. (1978a), 'World Views and Counselling', *The Personnel and Guidance Journal*, 56, pp. 458–62.

Sue, D.W. (1978b), 'Eliminating Cultural Oppression in Counselling: Towards a General Theory', *Journal of Counselling Psychology*, 25, pp. 419–28.

Sue, D.W. (1981a), 'Evaluating Process Variables in Cross-Cultural Counselling and Psychotherapy' in A.J. Marsella and P.B. Pedersen (eds), *Cross-Cultural Counselling and Psychotherapy*, Elmsford, New York: Pergamon Press, pp. 102–25.

Sue, D.W. (1981b), *Counselling the Culturally Different: Theory and Practice*, New York: John Wiley.

Sue, D. and D.W. (1977a), 'Barriers to Effective Cross-Cultural Counselling', *Journal of Counselling Psychology*, 24, pp. 420–9.

Sue, D. and D.W. (1977b), Ethnic Minorities: Failures and Responsibilities of the Social Sciences', *Journal of Non-White Concerns in Personnel and Guidance*, 5, pp. 99–106.

Sue, D.W. and D. (1990), *Counselling the Culturally Different: Theory and Practice*, 2nd edn, New York: John Wiley.

Sue, S., McKinney, H., Allen, D. and Hall, J. (1974), 'Delivery of Community Mental Health Services to Black and White Clients', *Journal of Consulting Psychology*, 42, pp. 794–801.

Sue, S. and Zane, N.S. (1987), 'The Role of Culture and Cultural Techniques in Psychotherapy: A Critique and Reformulation', *American Psychologist*, 42, pp. 37–45.

Suinn, R.M. (19), 'Research and Practice in Cross-Cultural Counselling', *Counselling Psychologist*, 13 (4), pp. 673–84.

Suinn, R.M. (1985), 'Research and Practice in Cross-Cultural Counselling', *The Counselling Psychologist*, 13, pp. 673–84.

Summers, G.F. (1970), *Attitude Measurement*, Chicago: Rand McNally.

Sumner, W.G. (1906) *Folkways*, Boston: Ginn.

Sundberg, N.D. (1981), 'Cross-Cultural Counselling and Psycho-therapy: A Research Overview' in A.J. Marsella and P.B. Pedersen (eds), *Cross-Cultural Counselling and Psychotherapy: Foundations, Evaluations and Cultural Considerations*, Elmsford, New York: Pergamon Press, pp. 28–63.

Sykes, D.K. (1987), 'An Approach to Working with Black Youth in Cross-Cultural Therapy', *Clinical Social Work Journal*, 15 (3), pp. 260–70.

Tajfel, H. (1969), 'Cognitive Aspects of Prejudice', *Journal of Social Issues*, 25, pp. 79–97.

Tajfel, H. (1978), 'Social Categorisation, Social Identity, and Social Comparison' in H. Tajfel (ed.), *Differentiation Between Social Groups: Studies in the Social Psychology of Inter-group Relations*, London: Academic Press.

Tajfel, H. (1987), 'The Social Psychology of Minorities' in C. Husband (ed.), *Race in Britain: Continuity and Change*, 2nd edn, Hutchinson University Library.

Taut, F. (1600), *Tresor de la langue Francaise*, Jean Nicot (ed.), Paris: P. Dovcer.

Terrell, F. and S.L. (1984), 'Race of Counsellor, Client Sex, Cultural Mistrust Level and Premature Termination from Counseling among Black Clients', *Journal of Counselling Psychology*, 31, pp. 371–75.

Terry, R.W. (1970), *For Whites Only*, Grand Rapids, Michigan: Eerrdmans.

Tesch, R. (1990), *Qualitative Research: Analysis Types and Software Tools*, New York: Falmer Press.

Theodorson, G. (1970), *A Modern Dictionary of Sociology*, London: Methuen.

Thomas, A. (1962), 'Pseudo-Transference Reactions Due to Cultural Stereotyping', *American Journal of Orthopsychiatry*, 32 (5), pp. 894–900.

Thomas, A., and Sillen, S. (1972), *Racism and Psychiatry*, Secaucus, New Jersey: Citadel Press.

Thomas, A.H. and Stewart, N.R. (1971), 'Counsellor Responses to Female Clients with Deviate and Conforming Career Goals', *Journal of Counselling Psychology*, 18, pp. 352–9.

Thomas, C. (1971), *Boys No More*, Beverley Hills: Glencoe Press.

Thomas, K. and Althen, G. (1989), 'Counselling Foreign Students in P. Pedersen, J. Draguns, W. Lonner and J. Trible (eds), *Counselling Across Cultures*, 3rd edn, Honolulu: University of Hawaii Press.

Thomas, P. (1967), *Down These Mean Streets*, New York: Knopf.

Thorne, B. (1989), 'Person-Centred Therapy' in W. Dryden, (ed), *Individual Therapy in Britain*, Milton Keynes: Open University, pp. 102–28.

Thorne, F.C. (1967), *Integrative Psychology*, Brandon: The Clinical Psychology Publishing Company.

Thurstone, L.L. (1928), Attitudes Can Be Measured', *The American Journal of Sociology*, 33, pp. 529–54.

Thurstone, L.L. (1931), 'The Measurement of Social Attitudes', *Journal of Abnormal and Social Psychology*, 26, pp. 249–69.

Thurstone, L.L. and Clarke, E.J. (1929), *The Measurement of Attitudes*, Chicago: University of Chicago Press.

Toi, M. and Batson, C.D. (1982), 'More Evidence that Empathy is a Source of Altruistic Motivation', *Journal of Personality and Social Psychology*, 43, pp. 281–92.

Torbiorn, I. (1988), 'Culture Barriers as a Social Psychological Construct: An Empirical Validation' in Y.Y. Kim and W.B. Gudykunst (eds), *Cross-Cultural Adaptation: Current Approaches*, New York: Sage, pp. 168–90.

Tracey, T.J., Hays, K.A., Malone, J. and Herman, B. (1988), 'Changes in Counsellor Response as a Function of Experience', *Journal of Counselling Psychology*, 35 (2), pp. 119–26.

Travers, R.M. (1994), *An Introduction to Educational Research*, 2nd edn, New York: Macmillan.

Triandis, H.C. (1971), *Attitude and Attitude Change*, New York: John Wiley.

Triandis, H.C. (1984), 'A Theoretical Framework for the most efficient construction of culture assimilators', *International Journal of Intercultural Relations*, 8, pp. 301–30.

Triandis, H.C. (1985), 'Some Major Dimensions of Cultural Variation in Client Populations' in P. Pedersen (ed.), *Handbook of Cross-Cultural Counselling and Therapy*, Wesport: Greenwood Press.

Triandis, H.C. (1990), 'Theoretical Concepts that are Applicable to the Analysis of Ethnocentrism' in R. Brislin (ed.), *Applied Cross-Cultural Psychology*, Vol. 14, *Cross-Cultural Research and Methodology*, New York: Sage, pp. 34–55.

Triandis, H.C. and Bontempo, R. (1986), 'The measurement of the ethnic aspects of individualism and collectivism across cultures, *Australian Journal of Psychology*, 38, pp. 257–67.

Triandis, H.C., Bontempo, R., Villareal, M.J., Asai, M. and Lucca, N. (1988), 'Individualism and Collectivism: Cross-Cultural Perspectives on Self Group Relationships', *Journal of Personality and Social Psychology*, 54, pp. 323–38.

Triandis, H.C., Leung, K., Villareal, M., and Clack, F.L. (1985), 'Allocentric vs ideocentric tendencies: convergent and discriminent validation, *Journal of Research in Personality*, 19, pp. 395–415.

Trimble, J. (1981), 'Value Differentials and Their Importance in Counselling American Indians' in P.B. Pedersen, J.G. Draguns, W.J. Loner and J.E. Trimble (eds), *Counselling Across Cultures*, Honolulu: University of Hawaii Press, pp. 171–204.

Trochaska, J.O. and Norcross, J.C. (1983), 'Contemporary Psychotherapists: A National Survey of Characteristics, Practices, Orientations and Attitudes', *Psychotherapy: Theory, Research and Practice*, 20 (2), pp. 161–73.

Trower, P. and Casey, A. (1988), *Cognitive Behavioural Counselling in Action*, London: Sage.

Troyna, B. and Hatcher, R. (1992), *Racism in Childrens Lives*, London: Routledge/National Children's Bureau.

Truax, C.D. and Carkhuff, R.R. (1967), *Toward Effective Counselling and Psycho-therapy*, Chicago: Aldine.

Truax, C.D. and Mitchell, K.M. (1971), 'Research on Certain Therapists Skills in Relation to Process and Outcome' in A.E. Bergin and S.L. Garfield (eds), *Handbook of Psychotherapy and Behaviour Change*, New York: Wiley, pp. 310–30.

Turney, B.L. and Robb, G.P. (1971), *Research in Education: An Introduction*, Hunsdale, Illinois: Dryden Press.

UNESCO (1967), *4th Statement on Race and Racial Prejudice*, Paris: UNESCO.

Van den Berghe, P.L. (1967), *Race and Racism: A Comparative Perspective*, New York: Wiley.

Verma, G.K. (1985), 'Intercultural Counselling: British Perspectives' in R.J. Samuda and A. Wolfgang (eds), *Intercultural Counselling and Assessment: Global Perspectives*, New York: C.J. Hogrete Inc., pp. 83–96.

Verma, G.K. and Bagley, C. (1982), *Self Concept, Achievement and Multi-cultural Education*, London: Macmillan Press.

Verma, G.K. and Beard, R.M. (1981), *What is Educational Research: Perspectives on Techniques of Research*, Aldershot: Gower.

Von Lue, T, (1975), 'Transubstantiation in The Study of African Reality', *African Affairs*, pp. 401–19.

Vontress, C.E. (1969), 'Cultural Barriers in the Counselling Relationship', *Personnel and Guidance Journal*, 48, pp. 11–7.

Vontress, C.E. (1971), 'Racial Differences: Impediments to Rapport', *Journal of Counselling Psychology*, 18, pp. 7–13.

Vontress, C.E. (1981), 'Racial and Ethnic Barriers to Counselling' in P.B. Pedersen, J.G. Draguns, W.J. Lonner and J.E. Trimble (eds), *Counselling Across Cultures*, Honolulu: University Press of Hawaii, pp. 87–107.

Wachtel, P.L. (1977), *Psychoanalysis and Behaviour Therapy: Towards an Integration*, New York: Basic Books.

Wachtel, P.L. (1983), 'Integration Misunderstood', *British Journal of Clinical Psychology*, 22, pp. 129–30.

Wade, P. and Bernstein, B. (1991), 'Culture Sensitivity Training and Counsellor's Role: Effects on Black Female Clients' Perceptions and Attrition', *Journal of Counselling Psychology*, 38, pp. 9–15.

Wallersteing, I. (1960), 'Ethnicity and National Integration', *Cahiers A Etudes Africaines*, 1, 3, July, p. 131.

Walker, M. (1990), *Women in Counselling and Therapy*, Milton Keynes: Open University.

Walton, D.E. (1978), 'An Explanatory Study: Personality Factors and Theoretical Orientations of Therapists', *Psychotherapy: Theory, Research and Practice*, 15, pp. 390–5.

Ward, C. (1995), *Attitudes Towards Rape: Feminist and Social Psychological Perspectives*, London: Sage.

Ware, V. (1992), *Beyond the Pale: White Women, Racism and History*, London: Verso.

Watkins, C.E. (1989a), 'Counter-Transference: Its Impact on the Counselling Situation' in W. Dryden (ed.), *Key Issues for Counselling in Action*, New York: Sage Publications, pp. 85–96.

Watkins, C.E. (1989b), 'Transference Phenomena in the Counselling Situation' in W. Dryden (ed.), *Key Issues for Counselling in Action*, New York: Sage Publications, pp. 73–84.

Watkins, B., Cowan, M. and Davis, W. (1975), 'Differential Diagnosis as a Race Related Phenomenon', *Journal of Clinical Psychology*, 31, pp. 267–8.

Watson, J.L. (1979), *Between Two Cultures: Migrants and Minorities in Britain*, Oxford: Blackwell.

Watson, J.L. (1984), *Between Two Cultures, Migrants and Minorities in Britain*, 2nd edn, Oxford: Basil Blackwell.

Webb, E.J, Campbell, D.T., Schwartz, R.D. and Sechrest, L. (1966), *Unobtrusive Measures: Non-reactive Research in the Social Sciences*, Chicago: Rank McNally.

Webb, T. and Salancik, O. (1970), *Psychology Observed*, New York: Vintage Books.

Weissbach, T. (1977), 'Racism And Prejudice' in S. Oskamp (ed.), *Attitudes and Opinions*, New Jersey: Prentice Hall, pp. 318–39.

Wetherell, M. and Potter, J. (1992), *Mapping the Language of Racism: Discourse and the Legitimation of Exploitation*, New York: Harvester Wheatsheaf.

White, J.L. (1972), 'Towards a Black Psychology' in R.C. Jones (ed.), *Black Psychology*, New York: Harper and Row.

White, J.L. (1984), *The Psychology of Blacks*, New Jersey: Prentice Hall.

White, L. and Dillingham, B. (1973), *The Concept of Culture*, Minneapolis: Burgess.

Wiersma, W. (1986), *Research Methods in Education: an Introduction*, 4th edn, Philadelphia: J.B. Lippingcott and Co.

Williams (1940), cited in Gardner, L.H. (1972), 'The Therapeutic Relationship Under Varying Conditions of Race' in J. Matarazzo, A. Bergin, J. Frank, P. Lang, I. Marks and H. Strupp (eds), *Psychotherapy 1971*, Chicago: Aldine Annual-Aldine-Atherton Publishers, pp. 162–71.

Willie, C.B., Kramer, B.M. and Brown, B.S. (1973), *Racism and Mental Health*, Pittsburgh: University of Pittsburgh Press.

Wilson, R. (1979), 'The Historical Concept of Pluralism and the Psychology of Black Behaviour' in W.D. Smith, K.H. Burlew, M.H. Mosely and W.M. Whitney (eds), *Reflections on Black Psychology*, London: University Press of America, pp. 41 6.

Wispé, L. (1986), 'The Distinction Between Sympathy and Empathy: To Call Forth a Concept, a Word is Needed', *Journal of Personality and Social Psychology*, 50, pp. 314–21.

Wolf, R.M. (1988) 'Questionnaires' in J.P. Keeves (ed.), *Educational Research Methodology and Measurement: An International Handbook*, Oxford: Pergamon Press.

Wrenn, G.C. (1987), 'Afterword: The Culturally Encapsulated Counsellor Revisited' in P. Pederson (ed.), *Handbook of Cross-Cultural Counselling and Therapy*, Westport: Greenwood Press, pp. 323–30.

Wrong, D. (1980), *Power: Its Forms, Bases and Uses*, New York: Harper and Row.

Wynne of Gwydir (1600), *History of the Gwydir Family* quoted in J. Richardson and J. Lambert (1976), *The Sociology of Race*, Causeway Books.

Yamamoto, J., James, B. and Bloombaum, M. (1968), 'Cultural Problems in Psychiatric Therapy', *Archives of General Psychiatry*, 19, pp. 45–9.

Yates, A.J. (1983), 'Behaviour Therapy and Psychodynamic Psychotherapy; Basic Conflict or Reconciliation and Integration?', *British Journal of Clinical Psychology*, 22, pp. 107–25

Yin, R.K. (1994), *Case Study Research: Design and Methods*, 2nd edn, New York: Sage.

Yinger, M. (1981), 'Towards a Theory of Assimilation and Dissimilation', *Ethnic and Racial Studies*, Vol. 4, No. 3.

Zanna, M.P. and Fazio, R.H. (1982), 'The Attitude-Behaviour Relation: Moving Towards a Third Generation of Research' in M.P. Zanna, E.T. Higgins and C.P. Hernman (eds), *Consistency in Social Behaviour: The Ontario Symposium*, Vol. 2, Hillsdale, New Jersey: Erlbaum.

Author Index

Abdel-Gaid, S. 131
Aboud, F. 42, 47
Abramowitz, S.I. 93
Abramowitz, S.T. 3, 9
Acharyya, S. 10
Acosta, F.X. et al. 38
Adams, W. 85
Adler, A. 119
Ahmed, S. et al. 2, 11, 13, 17, 24, 37
Ajzen, I. 75–8
Alexander, A.A. 68
Alexander, J. 102
Allen, S. 20
Allison, T. et al. 2
Allport, G.W. 41, 59, 74, 78, 81
Althen, G. 9, 197, 203, 215
Anthony, W. 58
Anwar, M. 24
Atkinson, D.R. 9, 19, 93, 232
Attneave, C. 204
Auerbach, A. 58, 170
Awatere, D. 6, 112

Babbie, E. 168
Bacchi, C.L. 15, 128
Bagley, C. 20, 47
Bailey, F.G. 37
Balarajan, R. 21
Baldwin, J. 123
Ballard, C. 4, 12, 30–1
Ball-Rokeach, S.J. 99
Bambose, O. 93
Banks, N.J. 3, 49, 50, 112, 152, 195–6, 230, 243
Banks, W.M. 8
Banton, M. 35
Basch, M.F. 66, 78
Bateson, G. et al. 204

Batson, C.D. 53, 62–5
Batson, C.D. et al. 62–3, 171–2, 182, 195, 211, 217, 248
Bavington, J. 197
Beishon, S. 24
Beitman, B.D. et al. 117
Belkin, G.S. 90, 118
Bell, J. 130
Bell, L. 125, 126
Benedek, T. 88
Berenson, B.G. 115
Bergin, A. 169
Bergin, A.E. 91, 170
Berman, J. 9, 141
Bernard, D. et al. 116, 117
Bernard, V. 84, 85
Berry, J.W. 29
Berthoud, R. 24
Beutler, L.E. et al. 55
Bhavnani, K.K. 81, 128, 152, 214
Blalock, H.M. 165
Bloch, P.M. 93
Block, C.B. 58, 84, 85
Bloombaum, M. et al. 82
Blum, L.A. 59, 61, 181, 207
Boch, P. 100–1
Bochner, S. 36, 77, 140
Bogardus, E.S. 79
Bolton, R. 64–5
Book, H.E. 55, 60, 121
Bordin, E.S. 57, 121
Bose, G. 104
Boyd-Franklin, N. 44, 185, 193, 249–50
Bradburn, N.H. 137
Brah, A. 47, 49
Brammer, L.M. 113, 115
Brewer, M. 172
Brewer, M.B. 42, 80

287

Briggs, D. 89
Brislin, R.W. 3, 26, 29, 31
Brody, E.M. 129, 142–3, 143
Brookes, J.C. 83
Brown, B.S. 45
Brown, C. 21
Bryman, A. 145–6
Bulhan, H.A. 246
Burbeck, S.L. 46
Burdock, E. 92
Burgess, L. 128
Burke, A.W. 3, 7, 10, 13, 45–6, 132; family
    networks 98, 201, 204, 215
Butler, R.O. 49
Byrnes, F. 99

Calder, B.J. 140
Campbell, D. 24, 29
Campbell, D.T. 42
Carkhuff, R.R. 16, 55–6, 58, 115
Carter, R.T. 243–6
Casas, J.M. 19, 93, 232
Casey, A. 55
Cattell, R.B. 138
Chambers, M. 21
Chaplin, J. 169, 206
Cheetham, J. 2, 3, 37
Cherry, F. 75, 77, 79–80
Clark, K.B. 45
Clark, Kenneth 45
Clark, M.P. 45
Cobbs, P. 38
Cochrane, R. 17–19, 100, 126, 222
Cohen, L. 128
Cohen, M.B. 181
Coke, J.S. 62
Cole, J. 93
Comas-Diaz, L. 92
Combs, A.W. 113
Comrey, A.L. 137
Cook, S.W. 76
Corsini, R.J. 5, 91, 120–1
Corvin, S.A. 245
Cottone, R. 204
Cowan, M. 92
Cox, J.L. 132
Cramer, D.C. 145–6
Crano, W.D. 80

Creswell, J.W. 137–8, 146, 168, 214
Cristiani 90
Cronbach, L.J. 138–40, 255
Cross, W.E. 45, 47, 48, 49–50, 68

D'Andrea, M. 238, 242, 243
Daniels, J. 242
Daniels, M.H. 250
d'Ardenne, P. 3, 4, 13, 19, 54, 187, 232;
    counselling relationship 71, 108, 122–5,
    151, 162, 215; Eurocentrism 43, 230;
    racism awareness 176; transference
    15–17
Davis, W. 92
Davison, K.K. 46
de Shazer, S. 188
Dean, G. et al. 17–18, 22
Deutsch, F. 59
DeVellis, R.F. 130–1, 137–8, 140
Devine, D.A. 121
Dillard, J.M. 13, 132, 248
Dillingham, B. 23
Dominelli, L. 13, 16, 187
Donnelly, F. 2
Draguns, J.G. 30, 39, 91
Draper, N.R. 165
Dryden, W. 55, 113, 115–18, 120–1, 163;
    training 242, 250
Du Bois, W.E.B. 47

Eaves, L.J. et al. 34
Edwards, D. 93
Ehrenhaus, P. 24, 29
Eisenberg, N. 58–9
English, A.C. 115
English, H.B. 115
Erikson, E. 45, 48
Evans, L.A. 38

Fanon, F. 6, 32, 47–8
Farrar, N. 6–7, 10, 11, 19, 98, 151, 201;
    counselling relationship 215
Fazio, R.H. 77
Feltham, C. 242, 250
Fernald, P.S. 121
Fernando, S. 3, 39, 93
Feshbach, N.D. 59
Festinger, L. 65, 171, 195, 215, 217, 232

Fielder, F. 55
Fields, S. 46
Fishbein, M. 75–8, 130, 140
Flaskerud, S.H. 9
Fleming, D. 79, 81
Fowler, F.J. 137, 140
Fox, D.J. 73
Freeman, T. 169
Freud, Sigmund 8, 55, 66, 95–8, 101, 103–4
Fromm, E. 105
Fukuyama, M.A. 244
Furnham, A. 99

Gardner, L.M. 3
Garfield, S.L. 39, 113–16, 117, 118, 120–1, 163, 169
Gedo, J.E. 61
Geer, C.A. 169, 220
Gelso, C.J. 71
George, R.L. 90
Gibbs, J. et al. 193
Gilligan, C. 169
Gilmore, J.B. 117
Giobacchini, P.L. 69
Glaser, B.G. 32, 214
Goldstein, A.P. 58, 59, 68
Gordon, M. 9
Grantham, R.J. 9, 169, 220
Greene, B.A. 72
Griffith, M.S. 69, 84, 85, 103
Gunnings, T.S. 9
Guthrie, G. 99

Hahn, M.E. 90
Haley, J. 204
Hansen, J 118–20
Hardesty, A.S. 92
Harding, J. et al. 41
Harrison, I.K. 45, 82, 196, 251
Hawkins, P. 250, 252
Hayes, W. 4
Heimann, P. 206
Heller, D. 124–5
Helms, J. 17, 37, 45, 48–50, 51–3; counselling relationship 62, 245, 247
Henley, A. 24
Henriques, J. et al. 75, 214
Hewstone, M. et al. 65

Higginbotham, N.N. et al. 28–9
Hill, C.E. 169, 181
Hintikka, J. 188
Hintikka, M.B. 188
Hitch, P. 18, 22
Hitchcock, G. 128
Ho, M.K. 193, 199, 201
Hodge, J.L. 103, 106
Hoffman, H. 95
Hoffman, M.L. 59
Hoinville, R. et al. 130
Holzman, P.S. 55
Horney, K. 38, 119
Hughes, D. 128
Hulnuck, T. 242
Hume, D. 59
Husband, C. 20, 22, 31

Ivey, A.E. 51–2, 58
Ivey, E.A. et al. 19, 151–2, 187, 204, 215; counselling models 192, 196–7, 230

Jackson, G.G. 3, 4, 39, 123
Jacobs, M. 15, 65–6, 69, 105–6
Jacobsen, F.M. 92–3
Jahoda, G. et al. 46
James, A.G. 30–1
Jewel, P. 5, 242
Johnson, M. 58, 141
Johnson, S. 93
Jolkovski, 172
Jones, A. 87
Jones, J.M. 30, 40, 41
Jowell, R. et al. 82

Kakar, S. 104–6
Kanzer, M. 55
Kaplan, A.G. 69, 108
Karasu, T. 91
Kardiner, A. 5–6
Kareem, J. 54, 60, 93, 123, 187
Kasdon, L.M. 188
Katz, J.H. 62, 51–2, 93, 99, 101, 124, 126, 176, 218
Keeves, J.P. 130
Kelly, J.G. et al. 82
Kelvin, P. 76
Khan, V.S. 20, 22, 24–5, 36–7, 93

Kiesler, C.A. 140
Kim, J 138, 144, 165
Klagsbrun, S.C. 181
Klein, J 38
Kluckhohn, C. 22
Kochman, S. 45
Kohout, F. 144, 165
Kornreich, M. 170
Kovel, J. 102
Kraben, A.L. 22
Kramer, B.M. 45
Krech, D. et al. 75
Krumboltz, J.D. 56
Kurtz, R. 113–16, 163

La Piere, R.T. 77
Lago, C. 19, 40, 44, 91, 151, 215, 232
Lambert, J. 33
Lampert, M.J. 91, 170
Larson, P. 43
Laughlin, H.P. 66
Lazarus, A.A. 55, 117
Leff, J. 11, 30
Levine, E.S. 58
Levine, R. 24, 29
LeVine, R.A. 42
Likert, R. 79–80
Lind, J.E. 104
Lipsedge, M. 3, 19, 60, 100–3, 126;
    counselling relationship 132, 151–2, 215,
    222
Liska, A.E. 140
Little, A. et al. 22
Little, M. 181
Littlewood, R. 43, 54, 93, 123, 187; with
    Lipsedge, M. 3, 19, 60, 100–3, 126, 132,
    151–2, 215, 222
Lloyd, A.P. 243–4
Locke, D.C. 3, 93, 230, 248
Loganbill, C. et al. 250
London, P. 5
Lonner, W.J. 28, 39
Lorenz, K. 34
Lorion, R.P. 69
Lott, B. 80
Lowe, S.M. 9
Luborsky, L. 91, 170
Lyon, M. 34

MacCarthy, B. 69
McCord, H. 9
McGuire, W.J. 13, 75
McKennel, A. 138
Mackinnon, C. 13, 20
McLeod, B.M. 247
Madle, R.A. 59
Magnus, E.C. 141
Mahay, G. 26
Mahoney, M.J. 117
Mahtani, A. 3, 4, 13, 19, 54, 187, 232;
    counselling relationship 71, 108, 122–5,
    151, 162, 215; Eurocentrism 43, 230;
    racism awareness 176; transference
    15–17
Mama, A. 2, 40–1, 43–4, 50, 80–1, 214;
    postmodernist feminism 92, 103, 128
Manion, L. 128
Marcia, J. 60, 61
Marcos, L. 188
Margolis, R.L. 243–4
Maroda, K. 95, 143, 150, 185
Marsella, A.J. 132
Marten, K. 8
Masson, J. 64–5, 110–11, 125, 184
Maultsby, M.C. 99
Maynard, M. 13, 20, 40, 44, 128, 214;
    discursive approaches 11, 75, 81;
    postmodernist feminism 152, 203–4
Mayo, J.A. 93
Mbiti, J.S. 93
Mearns, D. 55–8, 107
Meichenbaum, D. 117
Meltzoff, J. 170
Menninger, K.A. 55
Merluzzi, B.H. 82, 93
Merluzzi, T.B. 82, 93
Merry, T. 106, 107
Meyer, M. 169
Michaels, G.Y. 58, 59
Miles, R. 2, 17, 22, 32
Miller, N. 172
Milliones, J. 48
Milner, D. 45, 46–7
Minhas, R. 49
Mintz, J. et al. 169
Minuchin, S. 204
Mio, J.S. 243

Mitchell, K.M. 55–6, 58
Modood, T. 22
Mogul, K.M. 169
Moinat, S.M. 46
Montague, A. 31
Morris, H.S. 35
Muensterberger, W. 103
Mullard, C. 20
Munson, P.A. 140
Murray, A.J. 3, 9

Nanton, P. 187
Nazroo, J. 22, 100
Newcomb, T.M. et al. 78
Nobles, W. 19, 93–4, 98, 151, 215, 232
Norcross, J.C. 114–15, 116, 163
Nunnally, J.C. 137

Oakes, P.J. et al. 36
Oberg, K. 99
Oskamp, S. 13, 74–5, 77–8, 130
Ovesey, L. 5–6

Padilla, A.M. 58
Paolino, T.J. 66
Pardes, H. et al. 169
Parham, T.A. 4, 17
Parker and McDavis 242
Parloff, M.B. et al. 169
Parron, D.L. 69
Patterson, C.H. 5, 56–7, 90–1, 113, 115, 132
Paul, G.L. 56
Peabody, S.A. 71
Pearce, A. 141, 208
Pedersen, A. 31
Pedersen, P.B. 31, 93, 132, 242
Pederson, P.B. et al. 39, 193
Pierce, C.M. 40–2, 44
Pietrofesa, J.J. 95
Pike, K.L. 28, 29, 122
Pilgrim, D. 241
Pilisuk, M. 93
Pinderhughes, C.A. 87
Pinderhughes, E. 19, 53, 62–3, 101, 123–6, 151–2, 172, 175–6, 249; empathy 222; good practice 161–2, 185; training 218, 220, 227–8, 238, 250
Ponterotto, J.G. 93

Ponterotto, J.G. et al. 9
Potter, J. 42, 80
Prochaska, J.O. 114–15, 116, 163
Proctor, B. 251
Punetha, D. et al. 22, 30

Qureshi, A. 243–6

Rack, P. 3–4, 26, 33, 39, 69, 93, 132
Racker, H 71
Raine, W.J. 46
Raleigh, V.A. 21
Reber, A.S. 40, 140
Reik, T. 59–60
Reiser, M. 130
Reising, G.N. 250
Rex, J. 31, 33
Reynolds, A.L. 243
Richardson, J. 33
Ridley, C.R. 19, 43, 44, 54, 73, 249; counselling relationship 83–8, 151–2, 162, 208–9, 240; cultural transference 212–13, 236, 247; empathy 222
Robbins, R.S. 172, 205
Rogers, C.R. 12, 39, 56–7, 113–14, 123, 125, 252; client-centred therapy 106–12; transference 15, 67–9
Ross, M. 140
Rothenberg, P. 13
Ruiz, P. 193
Rungta, S.A. 243–4
Russell, B. 101

Sager, C.J. et al. 84, 92
Salancik, O. 127
Sandler, I. et al. 82
Schein, S. 93, 232
Schermerhorn, R. 33
Schneider, B.A. 92
Schneider, E.I. 92
Schweder, R.A. 23
Scott, C. 137
Seagull, A.A. 87
Searless, H.F. 181
Sedlacek, W.E. 83
Seeman, M. 100
Segall, M.H. et al. 23, 42
Selltiz, C.A. 76

Semaj, L.T. 50, 123
Serpell, R. 3
Shaw, M.E. 76, 82, 131
Sherif, C.W. 81–2
Sherif, M. et al. 172
Sherman, J.A. 141
Sherman, K. 141
Shohet, R. 250, 252
Shostrom, E. 93
Shrigley, R.L. 78
Sillen, S. 44, 84, 85, 87, 104
Simpkins, G. 9
Simpkins, G.A. 9
Singer, B. 91
Singer, E. 66
Sircar, I. 6–7, 10–11, 19, 98, 151, 201, 215
Skellington, R. et al. 1, 17, 22, 31, 82
Skodia, R. 123
Smalley, W. 99
Smith, D.J. 21, 22
Smith, H. 165
Smith, M.E. 188
Snygg, B. 113
Southgate, P. 46
Speck, R. 204
Spitzer, R.L. et al. 143
Splete, H.H. 95
Standal, S.W. 120–1
Steinberg, D. 251
Stevens, S.S. 93, 145
Stewart, N.R. 141
Still, R. 100
Stone, M. 47
Strauss, A.L. 32, 214
Strayer, J. 58–9
Struckmann, D.K. 103, 106
Strupp, H.H. 181, 206
Sturtevant, W.C. 29
Sudman, S. 134
Sue, D. 3, 4, 12, 19, 40, 43; counselling
    relationship 54, 68, 91, 151–2, 161, 172,
    215; Eurocentrism 131–2, 171, 230;
    language difficulties 188; racism 39, 51;
    racism awareness 176; self-disclosure 88;
    therapy theories 93, 187, 192, 232
Sue, D.W. 3, 4, 8, 9, 12, 19, 241–2, 249;
    counselling relationship 54, 68, 91, 151–
    2, 161, 170, 172, 215; Eurocentrism 43,

131–2, 171, 230; language difficulties
    188; racism 39, 40, 51; racism awareness
    176; self-disclosure 88; therapy theories
    93, 187, 193, 223, 232; training 248
Sue, S. et al. 17
Suinn, R.M. 99
Summers, G.F. 130
Sundberg, N.D. 81

Tajfel, H. 35–6, 45, 123, 171, 233, 248
Tan, S.Y. 88
Terrell, F. and Terrell, S.L. 9
Tesch, R. 129–30, 146–7
Thomas, A. 44, 84, 85, 87–8, 104, 141, 197,
    203
Thomas, C. 47, 38, 49–50, 215,
Thomas, P. 33
Thompson, J. 19, 40, 44, 91, 151, 215, 232
Thorne, B. 55–8, 107, 110, 121
Thorne, F.C. 115–16
Thurstone, L.L. 79–80
Toi, M. 63
Torbiorn, I. 23, 31
Tracey, T.J. et al. 181, 206
Triandis, H.C. 26, 28, 40, 43
Triandis, H.C. et al. 26–8
Trimbal, J.E. 39
Trimble, J. 193
Trower, P. 55
Troyna, B. 47
Truax, C.D. 16, 55–6, 58

Verma, G. 20, 47
Verma, G.K. 1, 2
Von Lue, T. 30
Vontress, C.E. 47, 87, 105, 212

Wachtel, P.L. 116–17
Walker, M. 169
Wallersteing, I. 35
Walton, D.E. 116
Ward, C. 78, 81
Watkins, B. 92
Watkins, C.E. 66, 69, 70–1, 143
Watson, J.L. 20, 33
Webb, E.J. et al. 128
Webb, T. 127–8
Wedding, D. 91

Weissbach, T. 83
Weitz, L.J. 93, 141
Wetherell, M. 42, 80
White, J.L. 4, 93–5, 97
White, L. 23
Wiersma, W. 130
Wiggins, F. 245
Williams 91
Willie, C.B. 45
Wilson, R. 19, 93
Wispé, L. 61–2
Wogan, M. 116

Wrenn, G.C. 39, 92
Wright, J.L. 76, 82
Wrong, D. 101, 125

Yamamoto, J. et al. 38, 93
Yasinski, L. 108
Yates, A.J. 116
Yinger, M. 33

Zane, N.S. 9
Zanna, M.P. 77

Subject Index

admission rates, psychiatric hospitals 17–18
affect, attitude 76–7, 238–9
affiliation, ethnic groups 37–8
African world view 94
African-Caribbean clients; counsellor experience 167–8, 194–7, 216–17, 221, 249; counsellor orientation 189–3; Cultural Awareness Inventory 171, 174–81, 241; family network 226; heterogeneity 25; language needs 186, 187, 225; single parenthood 26; therapeutic model needs 192–7, 215–16, 230–41
Africentrism 123–4, 246
age, of counsellor 181–2, 220–1
aggression, racial 42
aggressive dependency 67–9
American Psychological Association 10
anxiety 208–9, 235, 237
apathy, of counsellor 64–5
Association of Black Counsellors 10, 254
Association of Black Psychologists 10
attitudes (see also counsellors' attitudes study): affective nature of 76–7; change 13; components of 74–7; definition 74; development of 247; evaluation research methodology 127–50; measurement 79–81; transference link 73–89; white counsellors 1, 18–19, 92–3, 247
authority, hierarchical 25
autonomy, client 62
awareness: cultural 26, 170; training, racism 13–14, 176–9, 228–9, 239, 247

barriers: counsellor-client relationship 1; cultural 30–1
behavioural intentions 76–9
beliefs 76–9
bias: victim-blame 112, 217, 223, 248; white therapists 92–3

Black counsellors 9–10, 251, 253–4
Black ethnic groups, definition 2
Black identity, development of 47–51
British Association for Counselling 10, 12, 14, 136, 152; accreditation 157, 164; Code of Practice 163, 249–51; counselling definition 2; Race and Culture Committee 136–7; Research Committee 136–7, 253; training programme criteria 247
British Psychological Society, Race and Culture Special Group 10
British Social Attitudes Report (1986) 82–3
British Social Attitudes Survey (1984) 82

Canada, cross-cultural counselling 3
cannabis 60
Cartesian dualism 94–5
caste system, India 37
Census (1991) 20–1
change: social 83; strategies for 112; therapeutic 8, 107–10, 126, 215, 231–2; children: Black identity development 49; effects of racism on 45–6
choice: client 12–13; limitations of 241
client-centred counselling (see also client-centred therapy) 8
client rejection 62–5, 217, 248
client-centred therapy 91, 106–12
cognitive dissonance theory 65, 195–6, 215–17, 232, 248
collectivism-individualism 26–8, 38, 93–4, 98
collectivist cultures 26–8, 93–4
colonialism 106, 246
colour-blindness (ethnic), in counsellors 84, 247
colour-consciousness, in counsellors 84–5
combination eclecticism, therapies 116–17

communication, difficulties 3, 11
comparisons, African-European world views 94
competence, counsellors' self perception 210–11, 219, 237
conditions for change (*see also* Rogerian therapy) 107–8; limitations of 110–11; research findings 233–4; transference 67–9
confidentiality 7
conscience 96
control, counsellors 87
counselling
cross-cultural dyad dynamics (*see also* psychotherapies; therapies) 54–72, 222; definitions 2–3, 90–1; differing ethnic needs 191–7, 215–16, 230–41; outcomes 8–9
counsellor distress 62–5, 217, 248
counsellors' attitudes study (*see also* Vignette Rating Scale): counsellor orientation 148–9, 164, 183–93; counsellors' qualifications 147–8, 164–5; questionnaires 129–40, 152–61; research findings 214–37; research implications 256–7; research limitations 253–6; research methodology 127–50; research objectives 151–2, 214–37; statistical analyses 138–40, 146–50; video vignette case study 129, 140–6, 197, 238, 248
counter-transference 15–16, 24, 69–72, 88–9, 150, 172; cultural 86; Vignette Rating Scale 143, 205, 212, 236–7, 251
cultural awareness 26, 170
Cultural Awareness Inventory 140, 168, 170–83, 193–5, 216–22, 227–30; limitations of 253, 255–6; research findings 241, 247; training of counsellors 239; video vignette Rating Scale 143–4
cultural counter-transference 86
cultural difference 3–4, 211–12
cultural transference 85–6, 236, 247
culture shock 99–100
cultures: barriers 30–1; collectivist 26–8, 93–4; counselling significance 20–53; definition 23; emic/etic distinction 28–30; familiarity with 11; individual

differences 26–8; psychoanalytic theory 99; reactive identification 48–9; therapy 38–40; Third World 6
curriculum content, counsellor training 162, 240, 242, 247–8, 254

delusions 30
demography, ethnic minorities in Britain 20–2
developing countries (*see also* Third World): psychoanalysis 104–6, 105–6
development: Black identity 38, 47–51; White identity 51–3
dichotomies, Cartesian dualism 94–5
difference: acknowledgement of 252; collective-individualistic 25; counselling relationships 215–21; cultural 3–4, 211–12; over-focus on 20; racism 13
discrimination : employment 112; racial 22, 41–2
distress, of counsellor 62–5, 217, 248
dual consciousness, Black people 47
dynamics, client-counsellor relationship 54–72, 222

eclectic therapeutic practice 91, 112–21, 238; combination eclecticism 116–17; haphazard eclecticism 120–1; integrationism 118, 120; limitations of 113–14; technical eclecticism 117–18; theoretical eclecticism 116
ego 96–7, 101
ego ideal 96–7
empathy: continuum 64–5; of counsellor 55, 58–62, 108, 110; counsellors' attitudes study, research findings 221–9, 252; nature of 58–61; racism 16–18
employment, discrimination 112
encounter groups, multi-ethnic 110
equality, racial, therapy theories 92
ethnic background: clients 207–13; Vignette Rating Scale 235; respondent counsellors, attitudes study 153–4
ethnic groups: identification terms 1–2; political awareness 37–8; population statistics 20–2; psychoanalysis 103–6

ethnicity: of client 238–9; client-counsellor matching 9, 91; counselling significance 20–53; definitions 33–7; psychological criteria 35; therapy 38–40
ethnocentrism 5–6, 42–3, 245
ethology 34
Eurocentrism: client needs interpretation 26, 91; counselling techniques 3–6, 12–14, 38–40, 43–4; counsellors' attitudes study 151–2; research findings 230–2, 238, 248, 256; definition 43; empathy 58, 60, 91; psychotherapy 38–9, 93, 103–4; training 175
European world view, compared with African 94
evaluations, counselling 8–9, 91
expectations, of life 9
experience : counsellors' attitudes study 154–5, 165, 167, 173–4, 181–2; counsellor orientation 184–5; research findings 215–21, 231–2; Vignette Rating Scale 206–7; therapists' attitude 74

family 24–7, 210, 236
family centredness 6–7, 24–5
family network: use of 159–60, 200–5, 215, 231–2, 234; research findings 225–6, 234–5
family therapy 7
feminism 13, 69–70; postmodernism 44, 103, 128, 152
frustration 209, 236, 237

ganga (cannabis) psychosis 60
gender 69–70, 103; counsellors' attitudes study 153, 168–9, 181–2, 184, 220–1; racism 41; Vignette Rating Scale 206, 213, 239
genuineness, of counsellor 55, 108, 110
group therapy 7
groups 110, 245, 247

haphazard eclecticism, eclectic therapy 120–1
heterogeneity: African-Caribbean community 25; South Asians in Britain 24
hierarchy, of authority 25

holism, humanistic 93–4
hopelessness, client ethnicity 210
hospitality 11

id 96–7
identification: client-counsellor relationship 70–1; reactive 48–9; identity ; Black, development of 38, 47–51; cultural, negative 126; sense of, children 46–7; White, development of 51–3
immigration, postwar 20–2, 26
India, psychoanalysis 104–5
Indian Psychoanalytic Society 104
individual differences 18
individualism-collectivism 26–8, 38, 93–4, 98
individuality 94, 98, 105, 204
integrationism, eclectic therapeutic practice 118, 120
interpreters, use of 11, 160, 185–9, 198–200, 224–5, 234
interviews, counsellors' attitudes study 129–30

knowledge, socially situated 128

language, mis-communication 11
learning theory 113
life expectations, damage to 9
Likert scale 80, 127, 131, 138, 255
literature: cross-cultural counselling 4; racism 6, 40

marriages, South Asian 23, 25
mental health 3, 38; ethnic minorities 22, 41, 100; role of powerlessness 126
methodology, counsellors' attitudes study 127–50
migration, postwar 20–2, 26
models, of counselling, differing ethic needs 191–7, 215–16, 230–41
multi-cultural friendship networks 161
multi-cultural service delivery 161
multi-ethnic encounter groups 110

Nafsiyat 4, 10
National Front 40

need for approval 212
nondisclosure, client 88–9

Office of Population and Census Survey
(1991) 21
opinion polls 83
oppression 44, 47, 112, 223–4, 241; in
therapy 98
orientation, counsellors' theoretical 90–126,
148–9, 164, 183–93
outcomes, counselling 8–9
overcompensation, Black clients 82

paternalism, white counsellors 87
personality development, racism 44–7
personality theory, Freudian 95–8
political awareness, ethnic group affiliation
37–8
political oppression 223, 241
polls, racist attitudes 83
population, ethnic variety in Britain 20–2
postmodernism, feminist 44, 103, 128, 152
power: counselling relationship 87, 90, 124–
6; cross-cultural encounters 20, 101;
definitions 124–5; inter-group dynamics
245; white privilege 128; powerlessness
126; practice issues ; counsellors'
attitudes study 138–9, 149–50, 164;
research findings 197–205, 232–7, 236–7
pregnancy 11; video vignette case study 142,
212, 239
prejudice: racial 41–2, 77; of counsellors 71–
2, 81–3; counsellors' attitudes study 138–
9, 196
projection 102
Protestant work ethic 93–5
pseudo-transference 87–8
psychiatric hospitals, admission rates 17–18
psychoanalysis 61, 65, 91, 99–106; Freudian
personality theory 8, 95–8; learning
theory 114; racism 100–6; universality
failings 99, 104–6
psychodiagnosis, ethnocentric distortion 5–6
psychodynamic therapies (*see also*
psychoanalysis) 233, 238, 241
psychometrics, attitude measurement 79–81
psychosis 60

psychotherapy
Black-European values dichotomy (*see
also* counselling; therapies) 93–4; use of
term 90–1; qualifications, counsellors'
attitudes study 147–8, 156–7, 165–7,
170, 220–1; questionnaires, counsellors'
attitudes study 90, 129–40, 152–61

race: counselling significance 20–53; notions
of 31–33; training approach 245–6
Race Relations Acts (1968, 1976) 22, 40
racism 2, 54; awareness training 13–14, 176–
9, 228–9, 239, 247; colour-blindness
(ethnic) 84, 247; colour-consciousness
84–5; counsellor distress 62–3, 217, 248;
of counsellors 16–18, 71–2, 83, 92–3;
development of 245; difference 13;
effects on children 45–6; gender 41;
inter-group relationships 38;
psychoanalysis 100–6; psychological
effects 16, 44–7; surveys and polls 82–3;
therapeutic need 40–7; training *see*
awareness training; transference
situations 68–9; types of 40–1; violence
17–18, 22; white identity development
51–3; white privilege 128
racism awareness: counsellor training 13–14,
176–9, 228–9, 239, 247; counsellors'
attitudes study 138–9, 162
rapport, racism 16–18
reactive identification 48–9
reading 240; Black clients' needs ;
counsellors' attitudes study 173–6, 190–
1, 203
research findings 217–20, 227, 230–1, 240
referral elsewhere, client ethnicity 211,
237
relationships: client-counsellor 1–3, 12–
13, 54–72, 90, 222; ethnic matching 9,
91; identification 70–1; power 87, 124–6
rejection of client 62–5, 217, 248
repression 95, 103
research: counsellors' attitudes study 147–9,
164–5, 183–93; findings 214–37; future
study implications 256–7; limitations
253–6; methodology 127–50; objectives
151–2, 214–37; questionnaires 129–40,

152–61; video vignette (*see also* Vignette Rating Scale) 129, 140–6, 197, 238, 248; therapeutic relationships 55–6; white counsellors' attitudes 18–19

Rogerian therapy 9, 60, 65, 67–9
  learning theory 114
  research findings 234, 238
role play 249
Runnymede Trust 17, 83

sample size, attitude surveys 137–8
schizophrenia 18, 111
schools, of counselling 119
self: African 246; in oppression 112
self-disclosure, client's 88
self-esteem 9, 45–6, 49
set, transference 79
sexism, Freud, S. 106
single parenthood 26
slavery 25, 246
social change 83
social definition, ethnicity 35–6
social disadvantage 54
social matrices, Black clients 223–4, 227–9
social oppression 223–4, 241
Society for the Psychological Study of Ethnic Minority Issues 10
sociopolitical factors, ethnicity 112, 125
South Asian clients: counsellor experience 194–6, 209, 216–17, 221, 249; counsellor frustration 236; counsellor orientation 186, 189–93; Cultural Awareness Inventory 171–4, 177–82, 241; cultural barriers 30–1; cultural diversity 24; family network use 226; hospitality 11; therapeutic model needs 192–7, 215–16, 230–41
stage theories, Black identity development 47–51
statistical analysis: counsellors' attitudes study 138–40, 146–50, 164–8; video vignette case study 144–6
stereotyping 5–6, 54, 88, 213
students, foreign 100
superego 96–8, 101
supervision, of counsellors 163, 249–52, 254–5

sympathy, empathy relationship 61–4

technical eclecticism, eclectic therapeutic practice 117–18
theoretical eclecticism, eclectic therapeutic practice 116
theoretical orientation, counsellors 155, 163–4, 183–97, 231–4
theories, of counselling 5, 7–8, 10, 91–2, 119
therapeutic alliance 55–8
therapeutic change 8, 107–10, 126, 215, 231–2
therapeutic need: African-Caribbean clients 186–7, 192–7, 215–16, 225, 230–41; racism 40–7; South Asian clients 192–7, 215–16, 230–41
therapies (*see also* counselling; psychoanalysis; psychodynamic therapies; psychotherapy): Afri-centric model 123–4; client-centred (*see also* Rogerian therapies) 8, 91, 106–12; colour-blindness 84; colour-consciousness 84–5; counsellor orientation 90–126, 148–9, 164, 183–93; cross-cultural dyads 54–72; cultural transference 85–6; cultural-ambivalence 87; culturally connected approaches 121–4; eclectic 112–121; ethnicity and culture 38–40; group 7, 110; special needs of African Caribbean clients 186–7, 192–7, 215–16, 225, 230–41; special needs of South Asian clients 192–7, 215–16, 230–41; techniques of 91–2; variables 118
third person support, counselling dyad 10–11
Third World 6–7, 47
training: counsellors' attitudes study 151–2, 161–2, 165–7, 173–4, 182–3; cross cultural 177–81; racism awareness 176–9, 228–9, 239, 247; research findings 216–21, 227–32, 230–2, 238–49, 254; theoretic orientation 189–91; counter-transference 16; curriculum content 162, 240, 242, 247–8, 254; multicultural counselling; five approaches 243–9; research results 239–49; white therapists 13–15

transference 15–16, 65–72, 98; attitude link 73–89; client-centred therapy 67–9; cultural 85–6; pseudo- 87–8; set 79
transubstantiation 30

unconditioned positive regard 108, 110
unconscious, Freudian 95–8
unemployment 22, 126
United Nations Economic, Scientific and Cultural Organization (UNESCO) 32
United States of America (USA): cross-cultural counselling 3, 4; racial bias in therapists 92–3, 103; racial prejudice 77
urban conurbations, Black population concentrations 21
urban riots 46
USA *see* United States of America

validity, research 136, 137, 256
values 12–13, 38–9, 93–5
variables, therapeutic 118
video vignette case study 129, 140–6, 238–9, 248
Vignette Rating Scale 142–4, 150, 197, 205–13, 238–9; findings 235–9, 241, 248, 256
violence, racially-motivated 17–18, 22

Western imperialism, Freud, S. 106
White identity, development of 51–3
women (*see also* feminism; gender): Freud, S. 103; powerlessness 126
world view, African-European comparison 94

xenophobia 40